Management by Values

Towards Cultural Congruence

MANAGEMENT BY VALUES
Towards Cultural Congruence

S. K. CHAKRABORTY
Indian Institute of Management, Calcutta

with a Foreword by
PER GRØHOLT

OXFORD
UNIVERSITY PRESS

OXFORD

UNIVERSITY PRESS

YMCA Library Building, Jai Singh Road, New Delhi 110001

Oxford University Press is a department of the University of Oxford. It
furthers the University's objective of excellence in research, scholarship, and
education by publishing worldwide in

Oxford   New York

Athens   Auckland   Bangkok   Bogota   Buenos Aires   Cape Town
Chennai   Dar es Salaam   Delhi   Florence   Hong Kong   Istanbul   Karachi
Kolkata   Kuala Lumpur   Madrid   Melbourne   Mexico City   Mumbai   Nairobi
Paris   Sao Paulo   Shanghai   Singapore   Taipei   Tokyo   Toronto   Warsaw

with associated companies in   Berlin   Ibadan
Oxford is a registered trade mark of Oxford University Press
in the UK and in certain other countries

Published in India
By Oxford University Press, New Delhi

ISBN 019 563218 4

Printed at Sai Printo Pack Pvt. Ltd., New Delhi 110 020
Published by Manzar Khan, Oxford University Press
YMCA Library Building, Jai Singh Road, New Delhi 110 001

To

the golden quartet of the golden decade

RABINDRANATH TAGORE	(b. 1861)
SWAMI VIVEKANANDA	(b. 1863)
MAHATMA GANDHI	(b. 1869)
SRI AUROBINDO	(b. 1872)

who lived Indian thought for us and the world.

FOREWORD

During the 1980s I studied and wrote about management and leadership. Like others, my perspective was exclusively Western. In search of a different perspective, I travelled to India in 1988 where Professor Chakraborty and I became acquainted. The luxury of the Grand Oberoi Hotel where we met stood in sharp contrast to the Calcutta surroundings and to the humble and wise professor.

Professor Chakraborty has studied and written much about management and leadership from the Indian perspective. The professor identifies the Indian perspective, 'Indian Ethos', as being self/spirit oriented versus the Western paradigm of being ego/matter oriented.

In his books *Human Response in Organizations: Towards the Indian Ethos* (1985); *Managerial Effectiveness and Quality of Work-life: Indian Insight* (1987); and *Foundations of Managerial Work: Contribution from Indian Thoughts* (1989), Professor Chakraborty makes a strong case for Indian Ethos.

I had an opportunity of exploring the Indian Ethos at first hand in the autumn of 1989. Professor Chakraborty invited me to attend and to be a guest lecturer at a one week seminar,* 'Managerial Effectiveness' based on Indian Ethos, that he was conducting. The seminar was held at the Indian Institute of Management, Calcutta for executives from Indian companies.

The seminar was very different from European and American seminars I had attended. Professor Chakraborty had designed the seminar to allow each participant an opportunity to experience the Indian Ethos. He achieved this through integration of insightful lectures, selected readings, meditation and silence. Three times a day we meditated for 45 minutes. Mealtimes were times of silence. These experiences, although at first foreign to me, resulted in a deep inner learning far beyond that which any intellectual or rational experience could have provided. I became convinced that Professor Chakraborty had much insight to offer established Western thinking in the field of leadership.

In this book, *Management by Values: Towards Cultural Congruence*, Professor Chakraborty delivers his message of Indian Ethos even more profoundly than before. In a penetrating way he analyses the shortcomings of an ego/matter orientation and illuminates the 'reality' of the self/spirit orientation. He argues that 'It Is from the depth of inner silence that they [leaders] derive their power to vision, lead and build.'

A great contribution of this book is Professor Chakraborty's use of reason to help people open themselves to spiritual experiences that can result in a renaissance of true leadership in business and society.

Professor Chakraborty exposes the tragedy of India losing contact with her roots by importing Western ideas of management and leadership. It is ironic that as the West begins to discover what the East has always known, the East is in danger of changing and forgetting. It is possible that this book will be remembered even more for its importance in influencing Indian rather than Western leadership perspectives.

February 1990   PER GRØHOLT
Senter for Ledelsesutvikling AS
Drammensveien 37,
0271 Oslo 2
Norway

PREFACE

Management by Objectives was a book I wrote in 1976. Over succeeding years, through an extensive range of organizational studies, it struck me that despite the range of elegant, rational systematized, analytic approaches employed—MBO included— neither effective and concrete organizational results, nor a wholesome and humane quality of work-life had become manifest in India. It gradually began to dawn on me that the problem lay substantially in the weaknesses afflicting the sphere of human values. For instance, in MBO, setting the level of objectives, or evaluating performance against them, and all such activities inevitably get entangled in the human values implicit within the role-players. This book, therefore, bears the title *Management by Values*. It is offered as 'right brain' foundation for the 'left brain' *rational–analytic* approaches like MBO to yield their potential benefits in much greater measure than is evident now.

About the subtitle, 'Towards Cultural Congruence', there are at least two points to make. Why cultural congruence? Isn't humanity the same after all? Would we not, by aspiring for cultural congruence, undermine our openness to nourishment from other cultures? The premise of this book, as of its predecessors, is that it is a reality that cultures and civilizations *do* vary a lot at the empirical, manifest, *vyavaharika* level. World civilization appears to have evolved like an orchestra, with a great many instruments in the ensemble. Although the underlying notes struck on each may be identical, yet each instrument is necessarily played in its own *distinctive* style and technique for true response. This is the major reason for my concern with cultural congruence. Another is that when in the name of openness we merely imitate, it cannot promote a genuine and enduring development capable of earning respect and admiration for India in the world. This volume does not subscribe to the determinism that importing the latest technology also mandates the import of methods for handling the human side of organizations, except at a very superficial level. Moreover, our openness to other cultures does tend to be sham unless it is preceded by respectful openness to our own roots. Honest, sincere cultural 'chauvinism' (as many call cultural congruence) has a solid redeeming core in contrast to gullible aping of other cultures. Nor do I share the facile assumption that the modern mind is more enlightened in any real sense than the classical* mind. The second point about 'cultural congruence' is the widespread bewilderment affecting the Indian managerial mind—both academic and practising—about the very existence of a definable Indian culture. The surface strife and diversity in our Epics and society on so many scores confounds them and they surrender the task of delving deeper to discover the unity that lies beneath. It is sad therefore that our great modern thinkers—Tagore, Vivekananda, Gandhi, Aurobindo, for example—who have devoted their lives to the betterment of our society almost before the very eyes of this generation are often summarily dismissed in a scanty line or two as being irrelevant and much else. This seems to be one scourge that afflicts the contemporary Indian mind. Hence, in chapter 8 of this book, after a close, sustained and respectful scrutiny and assimilation of the thoughts of these modern *rishi*s of India, I offer readers the phrase 'sacro-secular symbiosis' to sum up Indian culture. As I understand it, it is India's mission to recreate this synthesis of the spiritual and material—the former showing the light to the latter— through each endeavour of hers. It seems to be a crucial failure of the modern mind not to comprehend the great truth about India, that her material affluence has always followed her spiritual efflorescence. To enact again and anew this unique script is our basic duty today. This is India's prime relevance to the world. The new-found, yet old-time, 'ecological awareness' syndrome of our days unmistakably points to the duty of expressing this symbiosis in all kinds of organizations. Of course, in the light of human values, ecology has to include both 'physical ecology' and 'mental ecology'. The call to India, therefore, is to foster and offer 'manager-*sadhak*s'; and similarly, we need teacher-*sadhak*s, politician-*sadhak*s and so on to cultivate genuine Indian values.

Another thing about culture in a highly pluralistic society like India's needs to be said. By culture we do not mean here just the sum total of external customs, i.e. *deshachara* (local customs) and

---

* It is more apt to use the adjective 'classical' for the mind which keeps intimate touch with the transcendent instead of 'traditional' or 'primitive'.

lokachara (folk customs), or manner of prayer and worship, or architecture and music, or dress and food, or poetry and painting... Culture viewed in this way has undoubtedly gained wonderful enrichment from the ceaseless currents flowing into India from various corners of the earth over millennia. Pluralism at this exterior level is therefore patent. But remaining content with our understanding of Indian culture at this level alone is akin to missing the wood for the trees. Nor is the 'historical–anthropological–sociological' interpretation of it adequate or integral. Tagore, in an essay entitled *The Centre of Indian Culture* (1919) said: 'The main river of Indian culture has flowed in four streams—the Vedic, the Puranic, the Buddhist, and the Jain. *It had its source in the heights of the Indian consciousness*' (emphasis added), and Tagore is recognized as the most universalized embodiment of the essence of Indian Culture which remains concentrated deep in the collective unconscious of its people. This assessment has been a major inspiration to me in my work.

Currently there is a legitimate and growing interest in discovering the 'Indianness' of Indian management. These efforts are based primarily on empirical studies of various categories of successful Indian enterprises, probably following the lead of many recent American books of this genre. The approach in this book is almost the reverse. Whatever Indians apparently do today—good or bad, successful or sloppy—is not intrinsic 'Indianness'. The empirical or the practical cannot determine the ideal or the normative. Rather, the empirical shall be judged as wholesome and worthwhile only if it represents the tireless striving to express the ideal. This is what 'management by values' should mean. Viewed thus, I doubt whether any Indian organization today reflects quite that ideal 'Indianness' which, as mentioned before, lies in 'sacro-secular symbiosis'.

All the chapters of the book have engaged themselves in the normative aspect of values. It is true that at the manifest plane each society and each time-span do present an endless array of differentiated values. But within each such space–time combination, variations inevitably revolve around 'right or improper'—whether it be of dress or food, pastime or social etiquette.... Thus, right through the so-called shifting course of relative values, concern for the *basic value* of what is normatively acceptable or not remains absolute, constant. There are many profound thinkers who today are inclined to consider, and even to suggest, that the future direction of movement could as well be going back to the classical, traditional systems of normative values. It is my view that the positivist–relativist approach to human values is both a result and a cause of decline in the strength and purity of human character. This posture seems to offer an intellectually respectable escape-route for self-indulgence.

Another aspect to note about the treatment of values in this book is its consistent emphasis on the values of 'individuals'. I believe that in the ultimate analysis 'organizational' values always derive from 'individual' values—especially those of the founding fathers and of the very top executives. Many of the declared organizational values often come to nought because individual values—revealed through the quality of interpersonal, inter-departmental, inter-divisional relationships—are in a mess. The common tendency to deal with organizational values, while skirting the complex domain of deeper normative values in our daily interpersonal dealings, tends therefore to border on irresponsibility. The individual is thereby implicitly invited to avoid looking within himself or herself—throwing the burden of such introspection on an abstraction called 'organization'.

Except in chapter 4 which provides and analyses some quantitative data, the rest of the volume relies on qualitative or anecdotal information. The realm of human values is subtle and subjective. This does not in any way diminish its comparative importance over the gross and objective. It has therefore seemed to me that forcing a second-order quantitative strait-jacket on a first-order qualitative domain would be hasty, unwise, even useless. To parody Shakespeare's Hamlet, it may be said that 'there are more things in human attitudes and behaviour 'management pundits' than are dreamt of in your quantitative assessment'. Do we not already know enough about the so-called reliability or objectivity of data handed out by accountants and economists who tread a much more concrete road than those concerned with human development?

Values-transformation is an experiential process. Sophisticated statistical writings often appear to evaporate this essence. To at least three kinds of scholarship Indian thought refuses to unlock its secret vault of treasures: the detached, the condescending and the arrogant. The chapters that follow therefore take pains to inform and invite readers to practise and experience the processes for themselves. Arms-length intellectual curiosity or academic knowledge-gathering is not intended to be their prime stimulus. The contents of chapter 4 might furnish the reader with the necessary confidence to make this distinction, and give priority to the former. It is indeed with this aim in mind, that a large number of personal, first person accounts have been included in this chapter. There may not be many striking differences amongst these personal testaments, but that itself is a positive aspect, in that experiences tend to converge through sincerity of practice. The processes used for the internalization of a culturally congruent (and yet universal) values-system would thus seem to be reliable across wide ethnic variations amongst the participants I have addressed. Besides, each chapter in the book has been fertilized by inputs from a continuous, cumulative process of discussion and dialogue on various concepts, principles and practices with a large number of managers, administrators and students. This effort was begun in 1983. It may be fair therefore to say that there is hardly any idea or assumption highlighted here which has not emerged from relentless probing and sceptical questioning by hard-headed practitioners and inquiring youth.

It might also be useful to share with the reader something on a personal note. As long ago as 1977, when I took my first hesitant steps towards integrating Indian thought with management, they were really a derivative of my earlier concern about some serious psychological difficulties afflicting a young, dearly cherished member of the family. I then began to explore spiritual psychology to find an answer to the existential problems facing this individual. The point I am trying to make is that my approach to Indian thought has not been that of a mere scholar handling the subject without personal involvement, aloof from the task of subjective self-transformation urged by such thought. I attempted the latter first for problem-solving. Subsequently, some systematic scholarship began to add itself to the main-line endeavour. This may account for the emphatic tone of much that appears below. The thoughts shared here emanate more from the heart than from the head. This, I believe, is a much-needed reverse movement to balance the overwhelming current of almost heartless management writing.

And finally to acknowledgements of indebtedness. The binding twine of this book is made up primarily of four strands—the

Tagorean, the Vivekanandian, the Gandhian and the Aurobindovian. I believe, to parody Wordsworth this time, that 'one impulse from the Tagores *et al.* can teach you more of India than all the scholars can'. We today skip, skate or study Indian thought, but who cares to live it humbly and deeply! And then I am grateful to hundreds of managers and scores of students for serving as the testing range for all that is contained in these pages. Those organizations which, since 1983, have been drawing upon my services, frequently on a sustained basis, to initiate and inculcate Indian concepts and processes for managerial effectiveness and quality of work-life, could claim to be pioneers in the history of the Indianizing process of Indian management in the true normative sense. It is the Centre for Management and Development Studies at the Indian Institute of Management, Calcutta which has supported the research underlying this work. The author is glad to repay a small measure of that debt through this book. Thanks are also due in no small measure to the small minority amongst fellow-academics and HRD professionals who have encouraged, and also to the large majority who have so far either denied or challenged or even ridiculed the line of thought I have adopted. The latter have, by maintaining the sceptic pressure, kept me ever on the alert and often forced me to dive deeper into the themes of this book. To Swapan Banik and Gopal Roy I owe abiding gratitude for graciously typing, retyping and doing the many other things that go into the preparation of a manuscript.

15 March 1991   S. K. Chakraborty
Indian Institute of Management
Calcutta

CONTENTS

1

VALUES FOR INDIAN MANAGERS
Roots in the Deep Structure

I. Values and Skills

Values can mean both 'end-state values', as well as 'values-as-means', e.g. to increase market share by falsely advertising a 'new and improved product', or to publish a paper by plagiarizing. In this chapter we are concerned chiefly with 'values-as-means'. End-state organizational values like productivity, profitability, market share, innovation, growth and the like are hardly liable to dispute. It is in the case of values-as-means that the normative stance can no longer be ignored. Our concern therefore here is not so much about what *is* valued, but rather about *how* one goes about achieving what is valued. Economic or political success cannot be the yardstick to measure normative 'values-as-means'. Rather, the former has to submit to the test of the latter for each person.

Values serve the process of 'becoming', in the sense of transformation of the level of consciousness to purer, higher levels. They help us to distinguish between the 'desired' and the 'desirable', between the 'delectable' and the 'electable', between the 'short-term' and the 'long-term', between the *preya* (the pleasant) and the *shreya* (the good).[1] Skills are concerned with the method of 'doing', in the sense of speed, dexterity, efficiency, etc. Values are, therefore, essentially subjective; skills essentially objective. While education is more germane to values, training relates more closely to skills. While human beings possess the potential to be educated for values, it is more natural for animals to be trained for skills (apologies to our sub-human cohabitants of this earth). We have said in an earlier book that the 'man' in the 'man-ager' comes first.[2] (Interestingly, a few years ago we were ridiculed by a Western management expert, well-known in India, through a long letter to the publishers of the book, for drawing attention to this split of syllables. Soon after, in July 1989, we were happy to learn that Watson, a founding father of IBM, used to talk to his managers with a flipchart showing as many as eight such splits—with 'man' preceding each!).³ Hence, values would seem to be a logical priority in the task of normative human *response* development. We are awaiting the day when subjects like leadership, negotiation, counselling, communication, public relations, team-building and so on will cease to be spoken of only in terms of 'positivistic skills', but at least as frequently in terms of 'normative values'. It needs grasping that unless healthy normative values are active within, positivistic skills will always run the risk of nefarious application, e.g. Shakuni's diabolical game of dice in the *Mahabharata*, for it is our thesis that *the subjective is the cause, the objective the effect*. The external milieu, with all its network and artifacts, is in truth a projection of man's internal milieu; individually and collectively.

To illustrate. You may visit a close friend one evening. You are shown into the interior of the house. One of the rooms, used as a study by the school-going son, which you observe to be spick and span, beautifully clean and well-ordered. The next room, occupied by the college-going daughter as her study, you notice to be in a great mess—as if a storm had just blown through it. The parents tell you that this is an everyday occurrence. What would you silently infer? The most plausible inference would be that while the son has an orderly, disciplined mind (i.e. 'subjective'), the daughter's is in a state of turbulence. Hence the striking contrast between the 'objective' conditions of the two rooms. This is the underlying truth in all human situations. It is, therefore, heartening to witness in recent years a prolific growth of literature in the field of values and culture-formation in organizations.

We surmise the cause of this recent academic efflorescence—in the West—to be rooted primarily in an anxious reaction to the sweeping success of Japanese industry. The spate of books on excellence, innovation and kindred goals seems to have a frenzied ring rooted in a fear of losing predominance in world markets. The underlying impulse seems to be: well, if we are tending to fall behind because of weak values and amorphous culture, then let us have a crack at it. The thrust may not thus be much more than utilitarian. Such a trend contains an incipient danger of trans-muting values also, eventually, to skills or slogans. Should this then also be the principal driving force for concern with values in India? If it were, would it be appropriate to call this a primarily humanistic inspiration?

It will be useful here to share some simple introductory information with our readers. Since 1983 we have been regularly offering in-house, as well as cross-company programmes on 'Managerial Effectiveness and Values System',* consisting of three modules for the same group of managers at quarterly intervals. In the initial half hour of the opening broad-spectrum module we induce the participants to air their views on values and skills. They invariably recognize and demonstrate two ideas: (a) values and skills are different (they explain this difference in their own ways of course); and, (b) values are as, if not more, necessary for effectiveness as skills. In the second stage we suggest to them the following four categories of organizational members:

(1) Values-weak, skills-weak,† or
(2) skills-strong, values-strong,† or
(3) skills-weak, values-strong,† or
(4) values-weak, skills-strong.†

We then seek a quick individual opinion poll on the question: 'In your assessment, looking at the organizational environments in India as a whole, which is the single largest majority group of employees—within the four categories suggested?' Amongst about 2000 managers—from Director-level downwards—we have invariably discovered that not less than seventy per cent of the participants say that it is the 'values-weak, skills-strong' group which constitutes the majority of organizational members. Thus, at the 30th Advanced Management Programme, held in June 1989 under the aegis of the All-India Management Association, of 38 participants, 32 (84 per cent) pointed out this category to be the dominant one.

In the third stage of this initial interaction we also ask: 'If you

---

* The particular style of opinion-polling mentioned below has been tried in about eighty programmes for companies like Tata Engineering and Locomotive, Bharat Electronics, Indian Petrochemicals, India Oil, Hindustan Paper Corporation, Hindustan Copper, Shri Ram Fibres, Godrej Boyce, ICRISAT, etc.

† Values-weak or values-strong in these pairs means weak or strong in the normative sense of good or bad, just or unjust, fair or unfair, from the point of view of broader, long-term interests.

have a free choice, which group of people would you prefer to work with or for: 'skills-strong, values-weak', or 'skills-weak, values-strong'? To this the response in favour of the latter group is even more overwhelming—never below eighty per cent.

And finally, we ask them which category of employees they would like to see as constituting the single largest majority set in the days to come. Here a hundred per cent response is for the 'values-strong, skills-strong' set.

What does this desirable transition, from 'skills-strong, values-weak' to 'skills-strong, values-strong' imply? Obviously, the gap in the level of value-orientation* is the key variable to tackle. How well are our human response development activities seized of this fundamental issue?

II. Values System: Japan and China v. America

In the widely read book on Japanese management by Pascale and Athos,[4] the following list of values in force in Matsushita Electric Co. is cited:

The Seven 'Spiritual' Values

    (A) (1) National Service through Industry,
        (2) fairness,
        (3) harmony and cooperation,
        (4) struggle for betterment,
        (5) courtesy and humility,
        (6) adjustment and assimilation,
        (7) gratitude.

In an equally well-known contemporary book on management in excellent American companies by Peters and Waterman,[5] the following crystallized list is furnished:

    (B) (1) A belief in being the 'best',
        (2) a belief in the importance of the details of execution...,
        (3) a belief in the importance of people as individuals,
        (4) a belief in superior quality and service,

* We have not tried in these forums to define values in the academic sense. Earlier, it may be mentioned, we attempted this, invariably ending up in sterile debate. In our experience all of us are instinctively aware of values of right and wrong in daily life. That is a good enough basis to start with.

(5) a belief that most members of the organization should be innovators ... ,

(6) a belief in the importance of informality to enhance communication,

(7) explicit belief in and recognition of the importance of economic growth and profits.

No picture of contrast, as revealed above in the two lists of seven values each, could have been more vivid. Thus, it can be nobody's case that Matsushita does not pursue growth and profits, and yet it is expressed through a superordinate frame, national service (B-7 v. A-1). Again, compare the tone of B-1 with that of A-4. Or, look again at B-3 in the light of A-3, -5 and -7. It is obvious that in American culture 'humility', 'gratitude', etc. are values too tender and soft. Not unexpected perhaps given the historical backdrop of the no-holds-barred conquest of the vast and wild west in the new world. Yet such tender, normative 'human' values have not prevented Matsushita from attaining the hard, positivistic 'organizational' goals: values of growth, quality, profits, etc.! Do the values of humility and gratitude deny or cancel respect for the individual? Do personal 'spiritual' values necessarily have to cancel out organizational 'material' values?

However, the truth of the matter is that neither American nor Japanese industrialists are seen to violate their respective fundamental ethos, which necessarily evolves slowly and organically within their respective socio-historical and geophysical conditions. Each list is authentic and has been useful from its own cultural perspective, yet the note of grass-root, close-to-heart, familial humanism is much more audible in the Matsushita list than in the American. We may choose to interpret this distinction as a mark of the instinctive oriental tendency to emphasize the subjective, even for eventual success in the objective realm.

The value 'loyalty' (which does not appear in lists A and B) in Japanese firms has been expressed by Pegels in these words:[6]

Because of [this] strong sense of loyalty, there is relatively little internal competitiveness in a Japanese firm.... Japanese employees ... endeavour to utilize all their talents and skills in the workplace ... not because they expect to receive praise individually ... [but] to increase the output and improve the quality of the products of their organization.... Cooperation is the key word ... The team approach in the Japanese organization is pervasive and requires that individualism must remain submerged.

A number of crucial points here are culture specific:

- Loyalty to the firm is an extension of the same emotion which binds a family. The family and the organization have not been sundered apart. It has been clearly grasped that loyalty is the very basis of human existence. It may centre on petty individual instincts, or on the family; it may revolve around God, or around the nation. Each focus of loyalty has it own consequences.

- Western thinking, by and large, prompts us to treat organizational loyalty as an anti-professional value. The truth is that today professionalism is almost a byword for loyalty towards personal mercenary aims. Yet no great achievement is ever possible without a focus of loyalty which transcends the individual self. Besides, in the long run, life itself loses meaning if every thought and action remains centred on the little self only.

- The need to foster the competitive spirit to get the best out of an individual is questionable. Why should the law of the jungle, of the survival of the fittest, be transplanted into human organizations? Surely human beings ought to depend on a higher principle for excellence—not merely for the group, but also for the individual. Vivekananda had long ago sounded America on this point, while expounding on Patanjali's theory of evolution:[7]

  Competitions are only momentary, unnecessary, extraneous effects, caused by ignorance. Even when all competition has ceased this perfect nature behind will make us go forward until everyone is perfect. Therefore there is no reason to believe that competition is necessary to progress.

- Mercer has time and again highlighted the strong belief in individualism and its virtues at IBM.[8] This he calls an element of 'advanced philosophy'. There can be no quarrel with that—in the USA. Yet the Matsushita list talks of 'harmony and cooperation' and, is still rated at par on all objective parameters with that of IBM and its equivalents in the West. Thus, one man's meat is another man's poison, as the old adage has it. What is a value in IBM could be the reverse in an Indian firm—to take the cue from Hiriyanna who makes this distinction at a general level in respect of *kama* or desire and says that it can easily degenerate from being a value to being the reverse.[9]

• Praise and recognition for the individual need not be the principal anchor for his or her commitment and dedication. Simply speaking, the Japanese adult has probably tamed his greed and petty ego from scraping and scrounging all the time for crumbs of recognition and the like. He has his consciousness pegged to a cause higher than himself. This seems to make the whole theory and practice of 'strokes' in human transactions rather suspect, at least in oriental settings. A stable sense of inner dignity may well overcome dependency on unreliable external 'strokes'. The Japanese is more secure and less vulnerable to this—one imagines.

In a paper written in 1967, Tannenbaum and Davis had foreseen the following abridged picture of transition of values in the domain of organizational development in the USA:[10]

(C) From	Towards
(1) Man as essentially bad.	(1) Man as essentially good.
(2) Negative evaluation of individuals.	(2) Confirming them as human beings.
(3) Individuals as fixed.	(3) Individuals being in process.
(4) Fearing individual differences.	(4) Accepting and utilizing them.
(5) The individual in terms of job description.	(5) Viewing him as a whole person.
(6) Walling off the expression of feelings.	(6) Appropriate expression and effective use of them.
(7) Maskmanship and game-playing.	(7) Authentic behaviour.
(8) Status used for power and personal prestige	(8) Status used for organizationally relevant purposes.
(9) Distrusting people.	(9) Trusting them.
(10) Avoiding facing others with relevant data.	(10) Appropriately confronting them.
(11) Avoidance of risk-taking.	(11) Willingness to take risk.
(12) Process work is unproductive effort.	(12) It is essential for task accomplishment.
(13) Primary emphasis on competition.	(13) Greater emphasis on collaboration.

Quite clearly, enumeration in the column on the right in list-C is more 'human' in orientation than that in list-B. Yet, the character of human values revealed in list-A is on the whole typically oriental in its tone compared even to that in list-C. Thus, 'gratitude' as a value is untraceable in the latter, yet we know that it is a great elixir for sound human interrelationships. It includes a major aspect of authenticity, trust and interdependence, but excludes sycophancy. Probably values like humility and gratitude are richer than being merely human so they appear under the caption 'spiritual' values. Similarly, whereas list-A mentions 'adjustment and assimilation', list-C talks of appropriate confrontation. Besides, unlike list-C which consciously attempts to project the impression of an improvement in value-orientation over time, list-A stays close to the pristine values in human effairs. The classical core value of 'duty' is the silent keynote of list-A, while that of 'rights' seems to be the implicit refrain in list-C.

In a 1988-study by Lee, covering the period 1965–86 for Sperry Rand, it is observed that, compared to 1965, only three out of fifteen value items showed a statistically significant shift in 1986— 'family obligations' (higher rank), 'respect for authority' (lower rank), 'hard work' (lower rank). The top three values retained their position throughout—1965, 1972, 1978 and 1986. These were: 'decision-making', 'developing new methods' and 'future planning'.* The author noticed that this very *slow change* matched better other studies about the American rate of cultural change, and asserted that 'Managers simply cannot change values or attitudes in a vacuum'. The need for a 'healthy level of doubt about the radical changes' was predicted in the realm of values.[11] These are sobering thoughts for those who show great concern for fast-changing values, new values and so on—especially in a culture like India's which is incomparably more ancient than America's.

At this stage we may do well to share with our readers some of the most sensitive yet accurate perceptions of Rabindranath Tagore about Japan and her people as long ago as 1916. We are obliged to do so through translations from Bengali, which have obvious limitations:[10]

---

* The other nine values are: belief in subordinates, sensitivity to feelings, capacity for loyalty, quantifiable variables, religious–ethical values, risk-taking, status differences, support of government, personal friendships.

(1) But, as I have mentioned before, in this Japanese ship the man is quite at home within the regulatory framework of work. Yet, repeatedly have I noticed that the regulation, the rule has never been quite overruled or pushed underground.

(2) One feature is clearly visible here in the outdoors: there is a crowd of people, but no noise at all. . . . I think this is the main source of Japan's strength. The Japanese does not dissipate his energy in shouting and quarrelling. Because there is no wastage of the vital energy, its supply is never wanting in times of need. This peace and tolerance in their body and mind is an integral part of their national upbringing.

(3) I had read in a book that the great medieval warriors of Japan used to learn the art of flower arrangement in their spare time. This, they thought, enhanced their skill and prowess on the battlefield. Thus we see that cultivating one's sensitivity to beauty is not treated by the Japanese as a mere luxury: they know such effort increases man's strength within his being, for tranquillity is [a source of] strength . . .

(4) In all aspects of life they blend power and skill with a feeling for beauty. Whenever I have praised them for this, many have replied: 'This is Buddhism's gift to us. Restraint on one side, and friendliness on the other—the pursuit of this blend through Buddhism has helped to conserve in us great strength based on frugality.

These penetrating observations made seventy-five years ago, and almost entirely corroborated by painstaking modern-day 're-search', suggest the following cues:

a) How is it that the Japanese ship on the high seas blended bureaucracy with humanity (in sharp contrast to the ships of the West in the poet's own testimony)?

b) Does restraint of impulsive anger and raw feelings make an individual inauthentic?

c) Is silence and economy of speech a true energizer?

d) Is cultivation of sensibility to beauty and quiet serenity opposed to toughness and dynamism in work?

In other words, Tagore appears to suggest going back once more to an earlier thesis of ours: the oriental temper seems clearly more subjective, inner-directed and right-lobe oriented. Remaining faithful to that, one can also attain matching excellence in the objective domain.

Now let us also turn to a few references to China. In a paper of remarkable insight on China, by Nevis (1983), we have noted some crucial cross-cultural comparisons which may be worth sharing[13]:

- This comparison [with Maslow's need hierarchy] shows that the concept of a hierarchy of needs is valid only in terms of a specific culture. It is a culturally relative concept, not a biological imperative...

- ... incentives and structure to further motivation can only succeed to the extent that they fit with basic values as reflected in culturally bound theory.

- In fact, it may be appropriate to give up this terminology [self-actualization] altogether, and call the highest Chinese order of need something like 'social confluence': the submersion of individual desires for superordinate goals, or working towards a truly collective consciousness.

Analysing his data in this vein, and corroborating the honouring of values like loyalty to the unit, sacrifice, ideology, age, avoidance of personal credit for an achievement, work as doing one's duty, Nevis reconstructs the five-level Maslovian need-hierarchy to a four-level one, along with changed ordering, to make it culturally consonant: at the base is 'belonging', next above 'physiology', then 'safety', and at the top 'self-actualization in the service of society'.[14] The much-touted 'self-esteem' need is gone! Relate this to the list- A value of 'humility'.

In another contemporary article analysing the interaction of American management teachers with China, while establishing an economic management institute at Beijing, Lindsay and Dempsey observe:[15]

- A fundamental difference clearly exists between the cultures and business management styles of the US and China ...

- Most American businesses in China have resisted integrating Chinese behavioural styles in their work-patterns, partially because they consider Chinese styles inefficient or ineffective. Americans who *do* take interpersonal and social variables into account, however, often analyse and account for them through an American cultural filter. This results in ineffective accommodation—a situation that becomes exacerbated when the original information about the Chinese culture gets distorted before it reaches the analysis filter.

The basic diagnosis of culture-specificity is identical in both the papers on China, and both treat this feature with respect. Hence the implied warnings voiced in them for those who tend to view some of the key aspects of a different culture as sub-standard and hence as aberrations. The other implication also seems to be that for improvement and success, even in the sphere of secular aims, the inherent strain of a culture should be identified and taken as the instrument for managing transitions. It seems that slowly this recognition is dawning upon management scholars, although a clear warning to this effect was sounded fifty years ago even by a non-management Western thinker, Guenon:[16]

The refusal to see things as they are and to admit certain differences ... involves complete failure to understand the eastern mentality ... So long as Western people imagine that there exists a single type of humanity, that there is only one type of 'civilization' at different stages of development, no mutual understanding will be possible.

That this strongly-worded caution has at last started percolating into some of the latest management writings is ably demonstrated in a very recent paper by Hofstede and Bond. While studying the value orientation of people in Singapore, Taiwan, South Korea, Hong Kong and Japan—which have the leading average annual sustained GNP growth rates over 1965–85—they had to incorporate a new dimension (relative to their earlier study on IBM in the West), namely, 'Confucian Dynamism'.[17] The component values of this composite dimension include the importance of persistence, relationships by status, thrift and a sense of shame; and the relative unimportance of personal steadiness and stability, saving face (dignity), respect for tradition and reciprocation of greetings, etc.* The authors discovered that the country scores on Confucian Dynamism were strongly correlated with their respective economic growth rates, and asserted that 'Culture in the form of certain dominant values is a necessary condition for economic growth ...'.[18]

Once more, like the Pegels and Pascale–Athos findings and Tagore's assessment of the Japanese, like the Nevis and Lindsay–Dempsey discoveries in China, the Hofstede–Bond research in east Asian countries too demonstrates that deep-seated cultural values in each society need not be regarded as faulty or aberrant. Difference (from Western values) should not be equated with inferiority. Besides, human values *precede* organizational (economic) values as well as role-centred skills. Guenon's diagnosis of the different western and eastern mentalities receives indirect acknowledgement from Hofstede–Bond when they suggest that

---

* It is not quite clear how the 'importance' of relationships based on status, sense of shame and personal steadiness can be reconciled with the 'unimportance' of respect for tradition, saving face and persistence respectively.

'Western thinking is analytical, while Eastern thinking is synthe-tic'[19]— a view which was clearly articulated for India too by Pangborn in a slightly diferent terms: 'the eastern mentality [is] the *believing* mind, and the western one the *critical* mind'.[20]

III. Values System: A Few Indian Examples

What is the situation in India today? Gradually more and more companies are emerging with formal statements of values or beliefs. We shall reproduce below three such lists, two from the private sector, another from the public, all highly successful by normal techno-financial yardsticks.

In the private sector firm, a household name in consumer goods, the Indian Chief Executive reprinted in 1988 a booklet on values evolved by its British parent company and circulated it, under his signature, in an in-house workshop on 'Commitment'. These beliefs are:

(D) (1) Competitive ability,
    (2) clear objectives,
    (3) taking advantage of change,
    (4) simple organization,
    (5) committed people,
    (6) openness,
    (7) responsibility,
    (8) quality.

Each of them has, of course, been elaborated and explained in the pamphlet. Like the American list, the British list too, by itself, is perfectly valid, but the contrast between list-C and list-A is at once revealing. The deeper, internalist, subjective focus on human values, so characteristic of list-A, is equally missing in both lists B and D. Which one is more natural to and germane for India today—A, or B and D? One wonders why there was no attempt by the Indian company and its top brass to do its own homework? Is this the way the IBM's or Matsushita's have gained the stature they now enjoy? The pamphlet rightly asserts, that 'openness and trust are the basis of good working relationships'. A rights–duties balance is required, in turn, for this achievement. Yet, the key issue of what kind of education one needs to develop this balance, and the resultant trust, has not been faced. Is it not essentially the 'honesty–unselfishness' value aspect of human character which underlies trust? What is the status of this value in Indian organizations today? Similarly, to develop committed people the plan is to demand high standards with appropriate rewards. Since we had been associated with this company for a few years as a trainer, we knew that 'appropriate rewards' had been a perennially elusive goal. The Indian theory of work argues that commitment in the true sense has to be inspired for a cause bigger and higher than the self. There will indeed be great difficulties in this because it must not be just a slogan: it must tingle in the blood yet the principle must be clear.

The public sector firm has the following list of values (slightly abridged) in current circulation:

(E) (1) Foremost is customer satisfaction,
    (2) employees being the most important resource, they will be treated with respect and dignity,
    (3) integrity, fairness and equity in business dealings,
    (4) positive encouragement to creativity and innovation,
    (5) a fanatic belief in quality excellence,
    (6) an ethos of discipline and commitment,
    (7) mutual loyalty and prosperity for vendors and suppliers,
    (8) contribution to a clean environment and the quality of life.

In contrast to list-D, no detailed elaboration accompanies these declarations—they all appear on a single page. However, this list too fails to echo any sentiment which can be clearly identified as being indigenous to the rhythm of Indian culture. The first two and the fifth values in this list, for instance, are only a marginally reworded and reordered replication of IBM's, now classic, basic belief-system.[21] Thus, is respect for the individual not also an Indian value? Yet what is the root of such respect which is unique to this culture? Was there no scope for hard and refined thinking about this? Unless values are articulated from the very depths of a highly developed and deeply ingrained culture, will they resonate authentically, and inspire the employees to maintain high levels of discipline and commitment in the face of increasingly disintegrating and normless tendencies afflicting Indian organizations?

In another successful private sector company, belonging to a well-known large industrial house, we recently saw the following articulated list of values:

(F) (1) Ensure customer satisfaction,
    (2) seek excellence in all we do,

   (3)   set high standards of ethics,
   (4)   foster creativity and innovation,
   (5)   avoid all discrimination,
   (6)   contribute to the benefit of society,
   (7)   respect the dignity of each individual.

Items 6, 5, and 2 in this list echo broadly the same value-themes found in items 1, 2 and 4 in list-A. So far as items 1, 4 and 7 in list-F are concerned, they closely resemble the typical western (e.g. IBM) values. The inclusion of 'ethics' in list-F, we guess, is due to the halo-effect of the departed legendary founder of the group who was a man of high character first, and only then an industrialist. It is, of course, an entirely different matter how the present management actually attempts to *live* up to it, for inclusion in the list may not necessarily mean implementation. Once again, another remarkable feature of list-F is the absence of list-A values like harmony, humility, gratitude, and adjustment. For instance, have the authors of list-F worked through the implications of the value: 'respect the dignity of the individual' which, if not thoroughly impregnated with values like humility or adjustment and the like, may give the message that members have the right and claim to be accorded respect and dignity—with no matching obligation to *earn* it? This question applies to item 2 in list-E too. We are afraid of the danger that such lists, devoid of the power of eliciting concentrated introspection and creating resolute will, may fail to inspire organizational members to strive for higher levels of consciousness which is the purpose of human values.

   Ten years ago Singh published a valuable work[22] on the occupational values of Indian managers (and hardly any subsequent work of this nature has come to our notice). The ranks of values amongst 280 sample members were:

		Rank
(G)	● Freedom from supervision/subordination	1
	● Adventurous experiences/challenges	2
	● Use of special ability/talents	3
	● Creativity/originality	4
	● Social status and prestige	5
	● Opportunities to work with people	6
	● Exercise control over others	7
	● Earn a good deal of money	8
	● Stable and secure future	9

Singh included these value items in his study because he suspected, as he tells us in the Preface, that the prevailing notions about what values Indian managers generally held did not accurately reflect 'existing realities'.[23] However, a decade later, we may now like to reflect on these G-list values, taking a view of the reality-behind-the-veil, as it were:

- If autonomy is ranked number 1, what about the value of self-discipline? What is its status in India today? What has been the more crucial variable behind the growth and development of an economy like Singapore or South Korea or Japan? Does self-discipline prepare the ground for giving autonomy, or vice-versa? What has been the Indian experience as a whole over the last four decades? Do we have to draw the specious distinction between manager and worker at this point?

- What percentage of jobs/roles in any organization *can* offer challenging/adventurous work? How is challenge to be defined? Is it not true that quite often the mental approach of the job-holder does more than anything else to turn a given task into a challenge from being mere drudgery? May not innovativeness be either tapped or sealed by this very process?

- To control others is apparently a dis-value, but if we strip the word of its pejorative connotation, then is not all leadership and influence basically a control process? To seek autonomy (or self-indulgence?) and not to enjoy controlling others are, of course, mutually consistent. Is this to be regarded as acceptable? Is it not true that a person who cannot exercise self-control/self-discipline, is also unable to control or discipline others? Should we abandon our concern for this devitalizing process in Indian organizations?

- Earning a lot of money stands as low as eighth in the list of nine values, yet does it *really* reflect the existing reality? We do not think it does. Several organizational studies by us through interviews (not questionnaires) throughout the hierarchy have revealed quite the contrary picture, and even worse. The mercenary disposition of most managers, both in public and private sector enterprises, no matter how pampered they may be with ever-increasing perquisites and fringe benefits, indicates an utter lack of idealism amongst a key component of the upper ten per cent income bracket of a poor country like ours. The fact is that earning a lot of money and the like is indeed *the* top value. Managers (and all of us for that matter) may like to project, through replies to questionnaires that they (we) are inspired by a sort of transmaterial zeal, but the reality *is* otherwise. Thus, if this value were indeed so low, how many examples of managers can we offer who, given the chance, would opt for a job with lower earnings if so-called creativity etc. were expected to be given better scope? Negligible indeed! This may be an explanation for the problem of the pervasive and increasing corruption at all levels.

Thus, the burden of our argument is first that such empirical studies as Singh's normally use value-items employed in similar work in the West, without thoughtful adaptation to our cultural context. Let us recall the earlier reference to Nevis's re-structuring of the Maslovian need-hierarchy for organic resonance with Chinese culture. He has gone to the extent of saying that the super-ordinate goal internalized by the Chinese is 'my country needs me to do the best', and that this *moral* imperative contrasts sharply with the *narcissistic* quality of self-actualization in America. He concludes the argument in these words:[24] '... each culture will have its own definition of the meaning and means of satisfaction of ... need level. The very concepts of belonging and safety are culture-bound and will reflect differences in basic assumptions and values.'

A very important issue for Indian management to then ponder upon is that Americans have come to India too, and worked with us over a much longer period than in China. Yet, how is it that they have never thought fit to modify the need-hierarchy model for the Indian context? Nor have we Indians ever thought of challenging its wholesale transmission to our students and managers. Could it be that post-independence Indian culture has been so character-less, and our intellectual spinelessness so shameful, that the well-intentioned Americans have never really faced a solid and genuine challenge to review the intellectual wares they have brought over to do us good?

An even more serious problem with such studies is that, in the absence of a firm normative framework for guidance, whatever prevailing reactions are elicited begin to be treated as respectable because they are real. It must however be understood that even if a certain mood or opinion is dominant at any given time, it does not automatically confer legitimacy on it. Sooner or later a society comes to realize this error of elevating prevailing moods to the status of an ideal, but by then it may be too late to make amends. Just one example. In a recent survey of British social attitudes, it was discovered that whereas in 1983 62 per cent of the public believed homosexual relationships to be always or mostly wrong, in 1987 this figure had risen to 74 per cent. Thus, the researchers noted that there had been a marked increase in the disapproval of extra-marital sexual relationahips.[25] Ideals and values are only so because they stand above passing social fads. If everything is changing, mutable, fluctuating, then there is no permanent guide. Is it such normless drifting—in the name of autonomy, modernization, etc.—towards which we may be heading?

To conclude this section, a brief reference to a recent article by a Japanese author, Fukuda, on the application of Japanese-style management in south-east Asia is pertinent.[26] The author prefaces his empirical survey in Hong Kong and Singapore by quoting a report which discovered, in 1985, that few of the Japanese manufacturing subsidiaries in Europe tried to export Japanese management practices wholesale, but chose to adapt to local conditions.[27] Thereafter, analysing his own findings about Japanese companies operating in Hong Kong and Singapore, which have geographical proximity to and cultural similarity with Japan, Fukuda concludes:[28]

... the findings from our study indicate that Japanese companies in these two Southeast Asian countries are not very different from those operating in the West in their views on the export of Japanese management practices. Whether operating in Hong Kong or Singapore, they are cautious about the wholesale employment of their own practices.

Looking at India, once more we notice that the current mood is not at all one of caution regarding the adoption of Japanese management rituals. Some public and private enterprises alike are uncritically jumping into the fray of Japanese-style management as a ready escalator to the golden pot at the end of the rainbow. Board papers, as well as the accounts of HRD experts who have paid flying visits to Japan, echo the same sentiment. This naïvette is aggravated further by the convenient and comforting assumption that Indian culture is much closer to the Japanese than the American. Once more the same reluctance of the contemporary Indian mind to work hard independently, and to try to lift itself up by its own boot-straps, as it were, is in sad evidence. Besides, in this second-phase imitation spree too—to our eternal shame—it is our American friends who have shown us the way. Is not this, for India, imitation raised to the power of two?

IV. VALUES FROM THE 'DEEP STRUCTURE'*

For all the present-day high-priests of Japanese management in India, it may be chastening to be reminded that it was Vivekananda who had, ninety-five years ago, drawn our attention to the need to learn from Japan:[29]

All I want is that large numbers of our young men should pay a visit to Japan and China every year. Especially to the Japanese, India is still the dreamland of everything high and good. And you, what are you ... talking twaddle all your lives, vain talkers, what are you? Come, see these people, and then go and hide your faces in shame.

A few years later, in an interview with *The Hindu*, he remarked that while the Japanese sacrified everything for their country and were sincere to the backbone, his Indian brethren sacrificed everything only for their own families and possessions.[30] (Where is there a shred of evidence in support of this value, 'sacrifice', in Indian organizations today?) Significantly, when the reporter asked whether India should become like Japan, Vivekananda thundered back:[31]

Decidedly not. India should continue to be what she is. How could India ever become like Japan, or any nation for the matter of that? *In each nation, as in music, there is a main note, a central theme*, upon which all others turn. Each nation has a theme:** everything else is secondary' [Emphasis ours].

Interestingly, sometime in 1904, Tagore too had been voicing this very view at public meetings:

* This significant phrase has been borrowed from linguistics, and is attributed to Noam Chomsky who distinguistes 'deep structure' from 'surface structure'. We first found its use in a paper 'Kataragama: A Study in Deep Structure' (mimeo) by Patrick Harrigan of the University of California, Berkeley.
** To summarize, the millennia-long super-ordinate theme for the Indian is: to manifest the divinity already potential in man.

The mainspring of different civilizations lies imbedded in different bases....
In England if the state-power weakens, the whole nation gets dilapidated.
Hence the great role of politics there. In our country if the society (*samaj*)
becomes decrepit, the country faces crisis. That is why we have never so far
staked our lives for political independence, but have always preserved social
independence.... The English survive if their state survives, we live if we
preserve our *dharma vyavastha* [social contract?].[32]

Inspired with such a thesis, we now offer for consideration the
following enumeration of a values-system which could be organically more valid and resonant for the Indian psyche in the Indian
management context. We have distilled these items on the basis of
our limited study of Buddhist, Vedantic and Yogic psychology, as
well as derivative epic and Pauranic literature, which by and large
still silently nourish Indian society and culture outside the organized, urbanized, university-stamped and rootless upper crust of
our population. These are the values rooted in the deep-structure
of Indian culture and society.

(1) *The Individual Must Be Respected*: not because of his or her
individuality but because of the transcendent, the divine enshrined in him or
her, whether good or bad, older or younger, rich or poor.

(2) *Cooperation and Trust*: because the divine inner being of all individuals is a Unity—deception or deprivation of others is deception or
deprivation of oneself; besides such inner disposition also helps the digestion,
believe it or not.

(3) *Jealousy Is Harmful For Mental Health*: just as cigarette smoking is
harmful for physical health.

(4) *'Chitta-shuddhi' or Purification of the Mind*: with the noble
thoughts of compassion, friendliness, humility, gratitude, etc.—these *bhavana*s lead to a refined and accurate perception of human relationships,
contributing to sounder decisions.

(5) *Top-quality Product/Service*: which is primarily a function of the
quality of the mind or consciousness of the doer, and only secondarily of
quality circles or statistical quality control.

(6) *Work-is-Worship*: because the best way to approach the divine
through secular life is to offer each piece of work—mentally—in as complete,
perfect, humble, and pure in form and spirit as one offers a flower or a fruit or
a sweet to Him—this can stimulate work-ethic in the healthiest way.

(7) *Containment of Greed*: whether of tangibles, e.g. money, or intangi-
bles, e.g. praise, because it causes stress and robs the individual of wisdom.

(8) *Ethico-moral Soundness*: because every action or *karma* is a cause for a subsequent effect—wholesome as well as unwholesome; and also because ethico-moral soundness gives peace of mind and promotes mental health.

(9) *Self-discipline and Self-restraint*: because they conserve energy, strengthen will-power, create trust, and confer dignity.

(10) *Customer Satisfaction*: because he is the divine come upon us in human garb.

(11) *Creativity*: because human creativity is an integral component and extension of cosmic creativity; but this link has to be experientially cultivated through mind-stilling.

(12) *The Inspiration to Give*: as opposed to the motivation to need, grab, etc. because giving is more fulfilling, it adds more meaning to work and life; also, the individual lives in society with 'debts' to supra-human, human and sub-human beings. Besides, giving with humility is more dignified than petty needing.

(13) *Renunciation and Detachment*: not of or from duties and responsibilities, but of/from selfish results/rewards and egotistic demands in the workplace; of/from the lower, unregenerate ego and its vanities.

Such then is a very compact profile of human values, anchored in the transcendent aspect of human existence, which Indian management should immediately begin to understand, explore and implement. Such implementation has, of course, to be conceived and executed with the 'first person, singular' as the focus, i.e. 'I'—not you or they, or boss or subordinate or society and so on. The false clamour for 'new' must also die. It is these basic values which must be re-lived by each generation, and this is no child's play. It is worth again reiterating that all the end-result organizational values essentially derive from these causal human or personal values. As the sage Vyasa so pitifully cried out at the conclusion of the Mahabharata: 'Here with up-raised arms I have been beseeching that *artha* and *kama* can both be attained through *dharma* [values for righteous conduct]. But alas! who listens.' The contemporary doyen of industry in India, JRD Tata, struck a similar note in 1990: 'It is possible to do business legally—except you probably won't enjoy as much profit.'[33]

We shall return once more to Lee's longitudinal study on values cited earlier. It is interesting to note that he mentions his list of fifteen values as intending to furnish the profile of 'the ideal manager' through rank-ordering. Now, we wonder whether the three top-ranked values (decision-making, future planning, developing new methods) quite reflect the normative aspect of an ideal man-ager. Besides, the item 'religious–ethical values' in his list was ranked 10th in 1965, 1972 and 1978, and went up to only 8th in 1986. For decision-making the description states accuracy and timeliness.[34] But what about fairness, freedom from bias or prejudice? Be that as it may, it could well be that the deep structure of American culture produces the kind of profile-list of an 'ideal manager' that Lee has offered. It is our hypothesis that, in terms of India's own deep structure, it is the list just outlined which would conform closely to the culturally-relevant norms of an 'ideal man-ager'. In any case, it is doubtful whether we would have an 'ideal manager' anywhere without a base of vibrant 'idealism'.

Besides, we feel that Indian management has precious little to hope for in terms of any practical guidance from learned academic social scientists of the present generation. For instance, it is quite symptomatic that in a recent edited volume of papers on formulating a cultural policy for India by some of the luminaries in the social sciences, the lengthy index does not contain a single entry on 'values'. Equally significant is the absence of any entry for 'spirituality', and along with that the omission of Aurobindo and Vivekananda.[35] In our opinion, the four great Indians spanning the ninety years from 1860 to 1950—Tagore, Vivekananda, Gandhi and Aurobindo—are far more reliable and authentic guides to the true nature of Indian society and ethos. This is so simply because they have *lived* Indian thought in their marrow for the cause of the country. We academics can scarcely have the faintest glimmer of the unerring clarity and profundity that such *sadhana* can foster for diagnosing the strengths and weaknesses of our culture.

It is prejudicial to the real interest of Indian management not to know or to choose to ignore the two fundamentally different streams of human temperament in the world: the western (especially since the Renaissance) masculine, logical, rational aggressiveness, and the Eastern feminine, intuitive, receptive realization. While Griffiths argues rightly for a balance between the two[36]—clearly this balance has today to be sought more in terms of a revival of the latter. It is in this respect that India has inherent advantages which her human development efforts continue to unwisely sidetrack. Authentic success in Indian organizations will remain an elusive purple patch if superficial emulation of techniques springing from the Western temper remains their mainstay. They will tend to be swept away by dominantly left-brained techniques. An apt instance of this blind process is the continuing teaching of T-group exercises to students and exposure of managers to them in India. Look at this in the light of Lessem's assessment in one of the latest and most comprehensive management textbooks: 'Sensitivity training, with its emphasis on the uninhibited expression of feelings, *was never received as well in Europe* as in America'"—(emphasis added). So, into a territory where even Europe has feared to tread, India has merrily been romping about—naïvely oblivious of her cultural backdrop. When shall our 'dynamic' intellectuals, engaged in 'knowledge production', be able to shed their cultural unconsciousness?

It may be noted that although most of the values capsuled above have connotations similar to those of the Japanese or Chinese values-systems, yet a fundamental difference is concealed behind such apparent similarity. Both the Japanese and Chinese values-systems are predominantly set within the framework of temporal ideologies—hypernationalism and state communism respectively. (The Western value-systems are of course set against the temporal ideology of capitalism.) In contrast, the Indian values-system outlined is clearly set within the frame of a transcendent ideology—the cutting edge of India's deep structure. Because it is transcendent it is also therefore more certain and reliable in the long-run, irrespective of the shifts which temporal ideologies might undergo. We are becoming increasingly convinced of this assessment in the light of the undercurrent of events recently occurring in America, Russia, China and even Japan—not to speak of the open explosions in East European countries.

Recently we saw a paper by an eminent Indian management adviser advocating the case for using Indian insights for human development. In the process he adapted the sequence '*dharma–artha–kama–moksha*' (the four-goals system for managing human life) to that of '*artha–kama–dharmā–moksha*' to suit Indian entrepreneurs and businessmen. That this very sequence is already the prevalent one, causing steep degradation in business ethics, was apparently forgotten. When we pointed out the error and danger in such modifications, he could not see the point. For, the traditional sequence had in fact been formulated for the householder, the man-in-the-world himself, not for the monk. Such then is the threat inherent in the surficial attempts, without a clear grasp of the deep structure, to adapt classical insights for modern times. Since this tendency might grow in the near future, we must be very cautious. Gandhiji had very rightly said long ago (1921) about the relationship between Indians and Indian culture:[38]

We have not known it, we have been made even to deprecate its study and depreciate its value. We have almost ceased to live it. An *academic grasp without practice behind it is like an embalmed corpse*, perhaps lovely to look at but nothing to inspire or ennoble. [Emphasis added.]

Lastly, while we agree with Bond, from the scholastic viewpoint, that 'cross-cultural psychology is in dire need of more theory-driven, multicultural studies', yet we cannot equally concur with his hope of universalizing psychology.[39] Universalization is possible only at the metaphysical, trans-empirical, trans-social level. For, all is unity only on this plane, yet this is above and beyond empirical psychology. At the psychological level social and empirical differentiation is (and perhaps should be) a permanent reality. So, just as playing the *same* musical notes on a violin or a sitar or a clarionet require *different* practical tools and methods, so are the requirements to make each culture yield its best at the empirical level. Universal metaphysics is all right, but not perhaps universal psychology. We should aim at a healthy coexistence of universal metaphysics with culture-specific psychology.

V. CONCLUSION: CLOSING OF THE INDIAN MIND

At the end of an in-house values-system programme in November 1989, a senior manager gave us one xeroxed page from the reading materials offered to him at another recent management development course. It was conducted by a management consultant who happened to be a senior post-graduate from one of the premier Indian Institutes of Management. We reproduce below the following Table from that page:

Comparative Values Profiles

US Culture	Indian Culture	Japanese Culture
(1) Individuals can influence future.	(1) Life is pre-planned, human action is pre-determined.	(1) Groupism.

US Culture	Indian Culture	Japanese Culture
(2) I can change work to achieve objective commitment to organizations.	(2) I need to adjust, human action is predetermined.	(2) Homogeneity.
(3) Data-based decisions, and they are healthy.	(3) Decisions flow from the experience and wisdom of authorities.	(3) Confucian ethics.
(4) I can disagree without being disagreeable.	(4) Deference to age and seniority, suppression of negative feelings.	(4) High educational levels.
(5) Protestant ethic.	(5) Joint family and authoritarian values.	
(6) Authentic collaboration.	(6) Self-realization.	

To attempt a point-by-point critique of the Table is unnecessary. What is crucial to grasp is the negative, depressing view it presents about the Indian ethos compared to that of the American and Japanese. Obviously, it echoes what the energetic consultant had learned during his Institute days. This is a typically representative case of the mental conditioning management students of independent India are still imbibing at our prestigious institutions. The message they absorb and transmit goes something like this: Whatever an affluent or technologically advanced society might say or do must be right and good; whatever might have been enshrined and institutionalized in an old but living culture, if it is economically poor or technologically backward, must be wrong and bad; therefore the path to the lost paradise lies in imitating the former and disowning the latter. The sample of values presented by us above, culled from the deep structure of Indian culture, seems to be mere primitive prattle, 'intellectual inertia' to them. Our young students and adult managers are systematically tutored to associate Indian tradition chiefly with the evils of casteism, joint family, sati, ritualism, feudalism, child marriage, widowhood and so on. They are equally carefully trained not to link Western modernity with colonialism **and apart**heid, world wars and nuclear weapons, Berlin

Walls and Prague Springs, North and South Koreas, North and South Vietnams, ozone layer piercing and greenhouse effects, no-parent or single-parent children and AIDS, and much else. Shall we forever stop ourselves from asking then: what has done more harm to the world, Indian casteism, for example, or western colonialism for instance? Such then is the great curse of the closed Indian mind of today.

We shall therefore examine in greater detail the ways and means of prying open this closed mind in the following chapters. We are not very sure, however, whether much heed will be paid, for did not in 1902 Sister Nivedita, that noble Irish lover of India, passionately knock at the door of the Indian mind in these words:[40]

For, you have devised a scheme of life which leaves the refinement of the individual intact, though all wealth be taken from him. Under all other forms known to me, good breeding diminishes with loss of means.... Here these things are not so. And why not so? Because before Europe was born, India had grasped the essential fact that the end of civilization lies in the making of men not wealth, not power, not organization.

Did we then open our mind's door and respond to her rousing appreciation of India's deep structure? Do we, after forty-five years of political independence, feel and think any differently—that we have a deep moral responsibility to prove her and others like her correct? Should we introspect, even as we jump into the bandwagon of an economic theory that skilled, professional human capital is the most important source of wealth, as to why India today—despite vaunting the third largest pool of skilled scientific and technological manpower in the world—is held in low esteem everywhere both in terms of human qualities and economic success? Could we tell ourselves: 'If skills are lost, little is lost; if values are lost, everything is lost'? To return to the two examples in the opening paragraph of this chapter, the absolute value of honesty or truthfulness stands eroded in them. For a restoration of this universal values-as-means, Indian management has to pursue processes which conform to the underlying grain of the Indian temper. Tagore gives voice to this grain, in respect of honesty, in these words[41]:

'... upon this wealth of goodness—where honesty is not valued for being the best policy, but because it can afford to go against all policies—man's ethics are founded'.

REFERENCES

1. Swami Gambhirananda, *Katha Upanishad* (Calcutta: Advaita Ashrama, 1980), verses I. ii 1–2, pp. 34–6.
2. S.K. Chakraborty, *Managerial Effectiveness and Quality of Work-life: Indian Insights* (New Delhi: Tata McGraw Hill, 1987), pp. 2–3.
3. D. Mercer, *IBM: How the World's Most Successful Corporation is Managed* (London: Kogan Page, 1987), p. 31.
4. R.T. Pascale, and A.G. Athos, *The Art of Japanese Management* (Harmondsworth: Penguin, 1982), p. 51.
5. T.J. Peters, and R.H. Waterman, jr., *In Search of Excellence* (New York: Harper and Row, 1982), p. 285.
6. C.C. Pegels, *Japan vs. The West* (Boston: Kluwer Nijhoff, 1984), p. 16.
7. Swami Vivekananda, 'Rajyoga' in *Collected Works* (Calcutta: Advaita Ashrama, 1962), vol.I, p. 293.
8. Mercer, op. cit., pp. 231–3.
9. M. Hiriyanna, 'Philosophy of Values' in *The Cultural Heritage of India* (Calcutta: Ramakrishna Mission Institute of Culture, 1983), vol.III, p. 648.
10. R. Tannenbaum, and S.A. Davis, 'Values, Man, and Organizations', in *Organizational Development*, eds. N. Margulies and A.P. Raia (New Delhi: Tata McGraw Hill, 1975), pp. 12–25.
11. J.A. Lee, 'Changes In Managerial Values', *Business Horizons*, July–August, 1988, p. 32.
12. Rabindranath Tagore, *Japanyatri* (Calcutta: Vishwabharati, 1976), in Collected Works, vol. 29, pp. 330, 340–1, 347.
13. E.C. Nevis, 'Using an American Perspective in Understanding Another Culture: Towards a Hierarchy of Need for the People's Republic of China', *The Journal of Applied Behavioural Science*, vol. 19, no. 3, 1983, pp. 250, 255.
14. Ibid., p. 256.
15. C.P. Lindsay and B.L. Dempsey, 'Ten Painfully Learned Lessons About Working in China: The Insights of Two American Behavioural Scientists', *The Journal of Applied Behavioural Science*, vol. 19, no. 3(1983), p. 266.
16. R. Guenon, *East and West* (London: Luzac & Co., 1941), p. 10
17. G. Hofstede, and M.H. Bond, 'The Confucius Connection: From Cultural Roots to Economic Growth', *Organizational Dynamics*, Spring, 1988, p. 17.
18. Ibid., p. 18.   19. Ibid., p. 20.
20. C.R. Pangborn, 'India's Need and The Ramakrishna Movement' in *A Bridge To Eternity—An Anthology* (Calcutta: Advaita Ashrama, 1986), p. 523.

21. D. Mercer, op. cit., p. 204.
22. P. Singh, *Occupational Values and Styles of Indian Managers* (New Delhi: Wiley Eastern, 1979), p. 14.
23. Ibid., p. v.   24. Nevis, op. cit., pp. 261–2.
25. *The Statesman*, Calcutta, 19 Nov. 1988—magazine section.
26. K.S. Fukuda, 'The Practice of Japanese-style Management in South East Asia', *Journal of General Management*, vol.13, no. 1, 1987.
27. Ibid., p. 71.   28. Ibid., p. 81.
29. Swami Vivekananda, *Collected Works* (Calcutta: Advaita Ashrama, 1989), vol. v, p.10.
30. Ibid., p. 210.   31. Ibid., p. 210.
32. Rabindranath Tagore, translated from *Atmashakti*, Collected Works in Bengali (Calcutta: Vishwabharati, 1975), vol.3, pp. 528–9.
33. *The Statesman*, 2 August 1990.
34. J.A. Lee, op. cit., pp. 30–1.
35. *Towards a Cultural Policy*, ed. S. Saberwal (New Delhi: Vikas Publishing House, 1985).
36. B. Griffiths, *The Marriage of East and West* (London: Collins, 1985), pp. 151–3.
37. R. Lessem, *Global Principles of Management* (London: Prentice Hall, 1989), p. 322.
38. M.K. Gandhi, *India of My Dreams* (Ahmedabad: Navajivan, 1959), p. 183.
39. M.H. Bond, 'Finding Universal Dimensions of Individual Variations in Multicultural Studies of Values', *Journal of Personality and Social Psychology*, vol. 55, no. 6, 1988, pp. 1014–15.
40. Sister Nivedita, *Complete Works* (Calcutta: Ramakrishna Sarada Mission, 1972), p. 451.
41. Rabindranath Tagore, *Lectures and Addresses* (New Delhi: Macmillan, 1988), p. 81.

2
ANATOMY OF ETHICO-MORAL MANAGEMENT

I. The Ferment

It would appear that the citadel of rational, positivist management thinking has by now received a number of cracking knocks. Along with the concern for excellence, literature on shared culture and values has also been growing rapidly. One among the latest manifestations of this growth is the courage shown by a few practitioners and academics alike in speaking openly about ethics and allied issues in the context of business enterprises. We do not know whether ethics in politics is also receiving similar attention. If not yet, it is almost certain to occur soon. It is high time it does. Essential!

However, this new enthusiasm for ethics in business management (rather than, as hitherto, brushing it aside as an idle moralizing posture) is, as usual, an American phenomenon. In India there are no signs yet of such a movement—except a single work by Monappa long ago in 1977.[1] We ourselves had dealt with this aspect in a book published in 1985.[2] The well-publicized, full-page speeches delivered by private sector company Chairmen at the annual general meetings almost invariably devote some space to human resource development and other issues. But nowhere are business or management or employee ethics and morals mentioned. These addresses are probably no more than effective public relations exercises. Neither do our management academics feel the need to be frank about it. It is not realized that pursuit of HRD in a state of growing ethico-moral bankruptcy is chimerical. Why is this so? Perhaps a few illustrations about how seriously this concern is growing in the USA could spur Indian management into greater sincerity and introspection.

(A) Here are a few emphatic statements from J.F. Akers, the Chairman of the Board of IBM:

- We do face ethical and competitive problems, to be sure.[3]

- ... common moral sense ... does not come out of nowhere or perpetuate itself automatically. Every generation must keep it alive and flourishing.[4]

- I wholeheartedly favour ethical instruction—in a business school or anywhere else in the university ...[5]

- Our ethical standards come out of the past—out of our inheritance as a people ... And the more we know of that past, the more surefootedly we can inculcate ethical conduct in the future.[6]

(B) Two academics, Victor and Cullen, conclude a research study by pointing out:[7]

It is our belief that organization theory needs to attend more explicitly to the ethical content in organizational processes. Ethical issues in organizations increasingly preoccupy theoreticians and practitioners. Firms are attempting to control the ethical decision-making of individuals, and society is attempting to influence directly the ethical decision making of firms.

(C) Blanchard (management consultant) and Peale (moral consultant?) voice their concern about the theme of this chapter with disarming frankness:[8]

Everywhere we turn to-day there are signs of ethical deterioration. In business, bright young people have made immoral millions by using insider trading information. In government, hardly a day goes by without some public official being involved in an ethical dilemma in Capitol Hill. In education, cheating scandals among students and under-the-table payments to college athletes by alumni have become commonplace.

(D) Murphy, yet another academic, after surveying methods and systems to foster and maintain ethical standards in several companies, says:[9]

In conclusion let me add that managers in firms with active ethics structures ... are genuinely enthusiastic about them. They believe that ethics pays off. Their conviction should provide others with an encouraging example.

Thus, economic activity and competition are no longer considered to be bedfellows altogether incompatible with ethics and morals. This is correct because man is always much more than mere commerce and competition. He has the ineffable domain of ethics and morals also to manage—whether in business or politics.

(E)   Andrews, a former editor of the *Harvard Business Review*, after batting straight to drive home the point that the 'Darwinian implications of conventional economic theory are essentially immoral', observes that while increasingly US business schools [are] reintroducing ethics courses as electives, yet most education in business ethics has to occur within organizations. He also speaks of the need for 'instinctive' ethical decisions by decision-makers,[10] but hints at no means to fulfil this need.

(F)   From a nation-wide survey, Longenecker *et al.* have furnished a disquieting pointer towards an important social dimension of ethico-moral behaviour, the 'generation gap'. Sixteen incidents of ethico-moral transgression in business were to be scored on a 7-point scale of 'never acceptable' (1) and 'always acceptable' (7). The results showed that the 21–40 age-group respondents nursed significantly (in the statistical sense) tolerant and permissive views on 10 out of the 16 incidents of ethical deviation, compared to those held by the 51–70 age group.[11]

II. Glimpses of the Indian Backstage

It does not need a high-fidelity camera to catch glimpses of the following kind in the world of Indian business:

(1)   A young manager scolds a worker for gross dereliction of duty; the latter stealthily puts a new spare part in the dicky of the former's car; the manager is caught by the security men, charge-sheeted and finally dismissed with Board approval.

(2)   A top executive starts a small enterprise in his wife's name, and arranges for it a lucrative, long-term contract for its substandard output with his own company.

(3)   An existing business house, with long-standing monopoly for an industrial product, goes to any length in trying to stall the government (the bureaucracy) from awarding another licence to a new business house.

(4)   The purchase manager of a large enterprise systematically exploiting small scale entrepreneurs, by obliging them to bid one against the other for personal gifts, before a purchase order is issued.

(5) The Vice-President of a company is nominated by the Chairman to attend a residential course on value-based management; the cheque has been sent and a seat booked. One fine morning the V-P comes and tells the Chairman about a dream he had the night before requiring him to visit the Vaishno-Devi temple; the religiously-inclined Chairman does not insist on his going to the programme the following day. A couple of months later the V-P is caught trying to swindle the company by arranging a deal with a shipowner for a second-hand oil drilling rig at an exorbitant price.

(6) A well-known firm had advertised on an all-India basis for a senior marketing executive. A candidate from a particular state was adjudged the best. He was asked to wait for some more time. Then the Director, Personnel came out and told him: 'Look, the interview panel is unanimous that you are the best person for the post—in all respects. Unfortunately, we have a standing internal policy not to recruit any person from your state. The most we may do is to offer you a job at the next lower level and not the one you were interviewed for.'

(7) Young executives, belonging to the same bank, reaching out for the same prospective client for deposit mobilization, and offering competing schemes to win the business to gain promotion at the end of the year by out-scoring their colleagues.

(8) Annual managerial performance appraisal formats, in the name of objective or result-oriented criteria, gradually eliminating 'subjective' criteria like honesty, integrity, sincerity which all relate to ethical behaviour.

(9) A business house had established two modern textile plants at a distance of about 100 kilometres of each other. There was some degree of dependence of the bigger plant on the smaller one for processing and finishing. The original purpose was to make the two units engage in healthy market competition, contributing to their own excellence as well as to that of the business house. After a few years the Chairman would often lament his decision, and confess that the two plants were mostly at loggerheads, and that the two unit chiefs were no longer even on speaking terms.

(10) The Executive Director of a large and modern plant of a

highly profitable public sector company recently retired. He was a man of property having inherited more than a dozen buildings at different places in his home state. It came to light, after he had left, that out of the half-a-dozen new room air-conditioners bought for the management development centre, he had managed to appropriate, through his network of cronies, two units for his personal use.

(11)   Exasperated with the poor work-ethic and weak discipline of unionized office staff, the headquarters management of an industrial house has begun inducting such people through 'dealers' in unemployed youth. These 'dealers' recruit the hapless unemployeds and become their employers. Such individuals are then 'leased out', so to say, to the bigger organizations who can in this way avoid their becoming regular employees. The 'dealer' charges a fee, say, Rs 1500 per month for an attendant from the industrial house, while paying barely 50 per cent of that sum to the person concerned. This happens even for overtime earnings.

(12)   A public utility company depends heavily on field staff— both unionized and officer categories. Servicing the installations of the client citizens is one of their major responsibilities. However, over the last several years the entire chain of such field-employees has been increasingly involved in claiming unofficial and clandestine payments in response to client calls. The flimsiest excuse is good enough to extort some payment from the citizen—whether corporate or individual—exploiting its or his total dependency. The goodwill and trustworthiness of the utility company, built over decades, are now in jeopardy. Its training wing is at its wits end as to how this scourge is to be combatted.

(13)   The government alters the tax laws and tax rates in its annual budget. Therefore, certain intelligent academics, along with the majority of captains of industry and accountants nowadays argue: What is so sacrosanct about such rules and rates; after all they are *relative* and changing, so how can there be an *absolute* standard of honesty? It is conveniently forgotten that ethical conduct demands that abiding by whatever be the ruling in force at a given point in time, enacted by a democratically elected parliament, is an absolute value for the citizen, not meek submission to bureaucratic caprice.

(14)   The Chairman of a very-well known public enterprise had

briefed the press at the year-end that, among many management innovations in his firm, one that was to come into being immediately was the conversion of its huge R & D outfit into a profit centre. We wrote several letters to the Chairman and the Chief of Finance, but no reply came. After a year we met a senior R & D executive of that company at a management development programme, and inquired about the R & D profit centre. He said the scheme had merely been aired casually at a few meetings; nothing had actually happened or was likely to happen. Just a few months ago the General Manager of a plant of another large public sector firm, which received bulk input supplies from the previous firm, remarked that the said Chairman was a perfect public relations man: he had a penchant for making similar more crucial pronouncements each year just before the commencement of the Parliament session on budgets.

(15) A very large, profitable company had just concluded a long-term settlement (three years) with its workers. We had gone for a management programme to one of its plants. One evening the Executive Director, during an informal get-together, informed those present that each worker had received a total cash inflow of between Rs 30,000 and Rs 90,000 so they thought that now they could get down to real work for some time in an atmosphere of contentment and peace. But alas! the big union leaders had already started organizing protests, go-slows and even *gheraos* on the grounds that subsidized food in the canteen should be replaced by cash payments!

Each episode mentioned above is true, and is based on the author's direct knowledge; and of course they are happening all the time in countless ways—sometimes crudely executed, often brilliantly. Yet we often seek shelter behind the sly argument that after all values are *relative*. Still, we continue to wish to talk of shared values, organizational health, quality of work-life and so on. Can such end-states be attained in the absence of ethico-moral rectitude? The crux of the problem in our view lies in the absence of a clearly understood theory of ethico-moral conduct and the will to internalize and implement it. However, before we reach out to this fundamental task, it would be useful to examine the relationship between science and technology on the one hand, and ethics and morals on the other.

III. Science and Technology vs. Ethics and Morals

Vivekananda once said: 'Man's development lies in rising above both external nature and internal nature.' Science and technology are concerned solely with man's victories over external nature, the material world. They have nothing to offer for man's internal progress. Ethics and morals relate to this internal domain. Yet the majority of academics and intellectuals claim the superiority of the assumed scientific–modern mind over the alleged superstitious–traditional mind. Probably this assumption is itself a great prevailing superstition. Let us see why.

(1) One of the biggest and most pervasive fall-outs of scientific–technological development for the common citizen has been the fuelling of his propensities for greed and acquisitiveness. This has been unequivocally admitted by Toynbee and Ikeda. As Toynbee asserts:[12]

The average level of moral behaviour has not improved. There is no evidence that so-called civilized societies are morally superior to so-called primitive societies ... The progress that we call civilization is an improvement in technology, science, and the impersonal manipulation of power; it is *not an improvement in morals*—that is, in ethics. [Emphasis added.]

No wonder the *Koran* declares: 'Greed robs a learned man of his wisdom'; and the *Gita* warns: 'Desire, anger and greed [*kama, krodha* and *lobha*] are the gateways to hell.'

(2) Science and technology emphasize accuracy and excellence in our external, objective endeavours. By itself this is not wrong. However, an inevitable consequence of this temper—perhaps not for the few scientists and technologists, but for the rest of the population which is a passive recipient, is rampant exteriorization of the psyche. Such unremitting externalization is caused by products like television, VCRs and a hundred other artifacts. So, complex, externalized living takes over from simple, interiorized living, and without the latter as a balancing factor, ethical values cannot sprout and grow. Thus, Einstein was obliged to declare:[13] 'Everything is dominated by the cult of efficiency and of success, and not by the value of things and men in relation to the moral ends of human society. To that must be added the *moral deterioration* resulting from a ruthless economic struggle.' [Emphasis added.]

(3) It appears that large-scale, highly expensive, organized science has been blinded by its own momentum. 'Politicized economism', if we may suggest this phrase, has become the master of this powerful yet blind horse. Consequently, the present-day researcher acquires a constricted and pedestrian view of his role. As the computer scientist Weizenbaum of MIT observes:[14]

I am sad to say that if at all we look for an aspect of human nature that comes most into play in modern science, *it is greed*—the need to be funded, the need for promotions and so on.... publishing papers has turned into an *enormous bureaucracy*, including the bureaucracy to keep track of *all this junk ... distorting the whole evaluation mechanism* by which science and scientists are judged. [Emphasis added.]

All this is entirely true for the bulk of research activities pursued in our own management institutes. The social sciences seem to demonstrate, by comparison with physical sciences, a greater reluctance or inability to look at the dark side of the moon, as it were. Perhaps this is so because the social sciences(?) are much younger and therefore lack the mature self-confidence to question their own basic premises.

(4) Modern science and technology have drawn inspiration from the Baconian dream of complete domination of man over Nature. Their primary consequence, if not purpose, has been to derive utility—in ever-increasing doses—by subjugating the environment. It is this process that has been the chief vehicle on which 'knowledge is power' has been taking its merry ride. What then could the Upanishadic prayer to the Sun at early dawn: '*Om! javākusum shankāsham kashyapeyam mahādyutim dhāntārim sarva pāpaghnau pranathosmi divākaram*'* mean to the scientist? Instead, he 'enlightens' the young boy of today by 'informing' him about the sun's gaseous composition, temperature, distance, orbits, eclipses and much else. Yet, with such enlightened knowledge in lieu of primitive superstition, a Nobel laureate neuro-scientist like John Eccles laments the overwhelming feeling of frustration and tragedy—at least for those who have sensitivity and imagination. So he confesses with touching sincerity:[15]

In short, the public was led to believe that science could and would ... solve

* *Om*, the crimson china-rose-like Sun of brilliant effulgence—cleanse me Thou of all impurity and vice.

all the problems of mankind ... The marvels of scientific technology provided assurance for this faith in the promised scientific utopia.... *We scientists should have been more modest in our claims.* [Emphasis added.]

(5)   Disowning the normative, the should, the ought, is a chief mark of the scientific temper. Yet, at every turn of daily life we are normative. We come out of a lecture and say, 'Oh! how excellent it was.' We watch a film and cry out, 'Oh! what a torture!' We reflect on a colleague's behaviour and think, 'Oh! how I wish he were less petty-minded.' At the end of the day we tell our wives: 'Oh! what a frustrating day. I was deceived and cheated thrice, and now you are so peevish!' Thus it is for us all each day. Maurice Wilkins, a Nobel laureate bio-physicist, says about this issue,[16] 'The whole question of moral, spiritual and other dimensions is pushed out of science normally. So it is something to do with the *nature of science that leads people towards destruction*! [Emphasis added.]

A little later Wilkins reinforces this opinion of his by arguing that science has fostered an undesirable mentality by focusing so much on material needs, and by offering technical responses to human problems.[17]

(6)   Our journals, newspapers and television screens frequently exhort us to cultivate the scientific temper. The majority of contemporary Indian opinion-builders feel so genuinely ashamed of their 'dark, superstitions tradition', that P.N. Haksar once roused his audience, saying: 'Courage [of] irreverence towards old scriptures is the necessary precondition of our survival.'[18] Slogans such as this might appear absolutely childish if, for instance, we listen to what Bertrand Russell had said much before the illustrious Indian civil servant:[19] 'Men in the past were often parochial in space, but the dominant men of our age are parochial in time. They feel for the past a contempt that it does not deserve, and *for the present a respect that it deserves still less.*' [Emphasis added.] Adding, 'Not all wisdom is new, nor is all folly out of date.'

(7)   Another eminent British thinker, Joad, had sometime ago embarked on the task of providing us with a 'guide to modern wickedness'! As we hear him presently we come once more face-to-face with the stark contrast between the intellectual courage, honesty and detachment shown by the very people who gave birth to modern science and technology, and the ostrich-like mentality of our own élite. Joad says on science and man:[20]

While mankind has advanced increasingly in respect of its power, it has remained stationery in respect of its wisdom. The begetter of power is science. Science has given us powers fit for the Gods, and to their use we bring the *mentality of school boys and savages....* The contrast between the marvel of our scientific achievements and the *ignominy of our social childishness* meets us at every turn. [Emphasis added.]

True enough. Thus, a VCR can be used to watch blue films to excite us at home, or it can be used to learn ethico-moral lessons from great lives to purify our mind. A tape-recorder can be used to play deafening and crazy rock 'n'-roll, or to listen to elevating hymns sung to God. A car can be used to visit a strip-tease joint or to drive to the serenity of an *ashram*.

(8)   One of the major offensives launched hitherto by science and technology has been on the Transcendent. Science has so long been making it a point to scoff at the supra-sensory dimension of human life, dubbing it lock-stock-and-barrel as obscurantist, notwithstanding vast evidence to the contrary. This has led to the perfection of *sthula* knowledge, rather information, at the expense of *sukshma* wisdom. About this, Bede Griffiths says:[21]

Modern science and technology are the fruit of the tree of the knowledge of good and evil. They are not evil in themselves, but they become evil when, as usually happens, they are separated from wisdom. Science is *the lowest form of knowledge*—the knowledge of the material world through the discursive reason.

In contrast to the above excerpts from the views of eminent western scientists and thinkers we may refer to two recent articulations by Indian authorities (besides Haksar mentioned earlier). Murthy, a systems engineer, admires the Western attempts to unravel the secrets of nature to raise our standard of living, and castigates the stultification of the process of social adaptation and use of the intuitive, experiential insights of Indian heritage. Perhaps he is right, but he also says later that,[22] 'Being an open society, India is not receiving the impact of this great scientific, industrial, and technological revolution. The achievement of harmony of the two great movements—the spiritual and the material scientific—is now in the offing all the world over ...' Murthy's language seems to place the material and spiritual on the same plane, and speaks of their harmonization as equals. This is contrary to the message communicated by the previous extracts

from Toynbee, Russell, Wilkins, Joad and others. The order of
priority is clear: the spiritual, ethical and moral must guide the
pursuit of the material. This has always been the grain of the Indian
ethos: *dharma* and *moksha* to regulate *artha* and *kama*. It is not true
that the common man in India today has not been affected by
science and technology. In fact, he has largely received it
prematurely as well as unnecessarily, adding to his woes and
miseries—especially in the urban and industrial centres. It is
therefore our own spiritual base that has to be seriously revitalized
before the material sciences can be used sensibly. Yet, this is
precisely what we are undermining. Weizenbaum is worth quoting
here once more,[23] 'I only hope that our present predicaments will
lend us the desperation and inspiration to look at this *first and last
source of knowledge—ancient knowledge* and pay serious attention
to it.' [Emphasis added.] Does India deserve the folly of traversing
the full western cycle once more to re-learn this truth?

A reputed Indian sociologist, Madan, after alluding to a point
from Radhakrishnan's exposition of Hinduism, has recently assailed his assessment:[22]

One would have thought that events since the above was written, more than
half a century ago, had decisively disproved the everlasting viability of
traditional Hinduism; but the apologists survive and are confident that
western science and technology do not pose any threat to their faith ... This
confidence is, in fact, only naïvety, when it is not a posture, for modern science
as philosophy and as technology, is fundamentally opposed to all religion.

Alas, for the Griffiths and Weizenbaums and Eccles'! Our own
Madans are going to be the last bastions of assumed scientific–
technological infallibility.

If we now relate the contents of sections I and III, it is possible
to suggest a quite reasonable hypothesis: *the lack of concern for
ethico-moral processes while managing business entities and individual selves has been positively correlated with growing insensitivity
about the subjective consequences of the scientific–technological
movement*. The examples in section II also indicate that the
devaluation of ethico-moral behaviour in India has occurred at a
remarkable pace since the adoption of planned economic development and technological modernization. Consumerism and oppor-
tunism, nourished by the systematic exploitation of human greed,
is evident everywhere. Without making any value-judgements, a
positivist might say: so what; after all this is leading to greater

industrialization, production and GNP. This view rests on a quantitative notion of 'standard of living'. As we had argued earlier, this is a misnomer. It would be truer to call this 'standard of consumption',[25] and then we can throw ethics and morals out of the window. But 'standard of living' must mean ethico-moral living. Let the raising of 'standard of consumption' be pursued, but we must avoid equating it with 'standard of living'. If this view is acceptable, then the Toynbees and Einsteins would not have spoken in vain about the fall-out of science and technology.

It would be interesting to share some data regarding this. A very large and growing private enterprise had been recruiting large numbers of engineering, management and science graduates during the last five or six years. Each year's batch on joining was given a questionnaire to answer by an external research agency with a view to obtaining a picture of their overall personality profile. Ten items were covered, e.g. emotional maturity, stress management, intellectual ability, values, etc. 'Values' covered order and discipline, work-commitment, concern for colleagues, readiness to help/develop others *vis-à-vis* competitive selfishness which led to unethical behaviour, and sincerity. The inter-correlation matrix with the scores obtained from the trainees showed not only no correlation—for the sample as a whole—between 'intellectual ability' and 'values'; but also, in a large number of individual responses they were discovered to be negatively correlated. This seems to corroborate a general feeling that although across the time span of recent generations the IQ levels have rapidly increased, this has not been matched by similar rise in the levels of values-oriented behaviour.

For a correct insight into this dilemma of *rising consumption standards accompanied by falling living standards*, we must return to Vivekananda with whom this section opened. Science and technology have helped man to progress merely by controlling 'external nature'. The more basic task of controlling his 'inner nature' and rising above it has been relegated to an invisible back seat. We are, therefore, now ready to explore the 'practical theory' of ethico-moral conduct, and bring back man's inner nature to the front seat. Otherwise scientific–technological fundamentalism itself could become more than a match for religious fundamentalism. Science and technology should heed the aphorism: 'Physics is bounded on both sides by metaphysics' propounded by Vivekananda a century ago.[26] Religious fundamentalism at least accepts something above and greater than oneself, but the hubris of scientific–technological fundamentalism is leading to ozone layer depletion, green-house effects, AIDS and much else.

IV. ETHICS AND MORALS: INTELLECT OR EMOTION?

Let us recount four tales briefly.

(A) One day prince Siddhartha, before becoming the Buddha, was sitting in calm contemplation beneath a tree in the palace garden. Suddenly the prince was startled by a white swan with an arrow stuck deep in its bosom, falling into his lap and began to nurse the wounded swan with deep compassion. Presently Devdatta, his cousin, comes and asks the prince to hand over the swan to him. Why? Devdatta's logic was: 'I hit the swan with my arrow, and the rules of the game say that it is mine to take.' The prince refused. His logic was: 'the right of a person who gives life back to a dying creature is more inalienable than that of one who tries to take its life away'.

(B) At one stage in the *Mahabharata*, due to a certain dramatic turn of events, both Yudhisthira and Duryodhana became crown princes. After agonizing deliberation Bhishma ruled that the kingdom should be divided between the two cousins. Its implementation was left to the blind, but ambitious and greedy king Dhritarashtra. So he told his nephew Yudhisthira: 'You know, I am blind and also ageing. It will not be possible for me to leave Hastinapur, and you are aware also how deeply attached Duryodhana, my eldest son, is to me. He too cannot leave me alone and go elsewhere. Therefore, while I award Khandavprastha to you, let Hastinapur remain with Duryodhana.' Khandavprastha was a barren desert-like territory!

When Arjuna and others angrily challenged Yudhisthira for meekly foregoing the legitimate rights of the Pandavas, the eldest of them replied: 'Look, all you say is justified, but I had to choose between two alternatives: to disagree with our uncle's verdict and face a fraternal battle which would really mean immediate destruction of life and property merely to defend our territorial rights, or to forego such an ambition to protect the integrity of the land and the people's welfare. I have opted for the latter.'

(C)   After Siddhartha had blossomed into the Buddha, he formed the Sangha, and his son Rahula was also admitted to it. Gradually the Buddha began to hear a lot of complaints about Rahula's conduct, so one day he summoned his son to the open sitting of the Sangha, and asked him to fetch a large pitcher of water. He then bade Rahula to wash his feet in it. Afterwards he asked him: 'Is this water of any use now?' 'No.' 'So throw it away, and bring the pitcher back.' The Buddha then stood up holding the empty pitcher in his hands, lifted it over his head, whirled it around a few times, and then pausing for a moment asked: 'Rahula, if I now throw it to the ground, what will happen?' 'It will be smashed.' 'Will that mean any loss to anyone?' 'No.' 'So, now listen carefully: you are a lying and corrupt member of the Sangha. You are contaminated, hence useless like this pitcher. So I order you out of this Sangha. When I am sure you have reformed yourself, you may be readmitted.'

(D)   In the Mahabharata, when Duryodhana and his cohorts were committing the great sacrilege of disrobing, abusing and making the vilest suggestions to Draupadi, Dhritarashtra, the father and king, maintained an eerie silence. At no stage did he utter a single word, or make a single gesture showing revulsion towards his son Duryodhana's behaviour.

These four examples show how intellect can be and is used by man to take perverse, ethically questionable decisions, e.g. Devdatta and Dhritarashtra. At the same time, by contrast, it is intellect again which was used by Siddhartha and Yudhisthira to put forward their morally sound arguments. Therefore, intellect alone does not seem to guarantee sound ethico-moral decisions—for all of us. What makes for this variation in the application of intellect by individuals? Here is the answer.

We see that in the case of the Buddha, his emotions being exalted and purified, the intellect behaved as was expected of it—expulsion of Rahula. On the other hand, the senior but blind Dhritarashtra's thwarted ambition of becoming the first king of Hastinapur, instead of Pandu, never ceased to haunt him. This emotion he had been projecting through Duryodhana, and was evidently enjoying when in the dice contest Yudhisthira was losing every round. His emotions being thus degraded and vicious, the intellect never functioned as it was expected to.

Vivekananda, while addressing a London audience on 'Practical Vedanta', had sharply distinguished the role of the intellect from that of the heart for the correct assimilation of the spirit of *vedanta*. It is best to hear him in his own idiom:[27]

The intellect is only the *street cleaner*, cleansing the path for us, a *secondary worker*, the *policeman*; but the policeman is not a positive necessity....

Intellect is necessary, for without it we fall into crude errors.... Intellect checks these; but beyond that do not try to build anything upon it. It is an inactive secondary help; the real help is *feeling, love*. Do you feel for others? If you do, you are growing in *oneness*.

[Emphasis added.]

Such an appraisal of the intellect must come as a surprise, if not a shock, to readers. Yet, is it not clear that while Siddhartha and Yudhisthira had the heart to feel and love, broadly and humanely, Devdatta and Dhritarashtra had constricted feelings which clouded their intellect to argue the way they did? Reason, contrary to what we believe, is not perfect so it cannot evaluate truth from untruth. Reason or intellect can do its job well provided the true facts, the right materials are presented to it.

Thus, elsewhere Vivekananda explains:[28] 'The intellect has to build the house; but it cannot do so without bricks, and it *cannot make bricks*'. [Emphasis added.]

While formulating his thoughts for a system of national education in India, Aurobindo made nearly the same point as Vivekananda:[29] 'These sensations and impressions (received by the mind or *manas*) are the material of thought, not thought itself; but it is exceedingly important that thought should work on *sufficient and perfect material*.' [Emphasis added.] Thought is used by Aurobindo in the sense of intellect or *buddhi*. The intellect is one layer, a higher layer, in the structure of *antahkarana* or the 'inner organ' of Indian psychology. Its function is to order, arrange, classify, accept, reject inputs stored by the *chitta* or memory and acquired by the *manas* or mind. Unless the earlier layers of *chitta* and *manas* are trained and tuned to receive and store the wholesome, the beneficial, the intellect or *buddhi* cannot help but tends to work itself out in perverse ways, i.e. in ethico-morally degrading ways. That is why Aurobindo is so categorical,[30] 'In the economy of man the mental nature rests upon the moral, and the education of the intellect divorced from the *perfection of the moral and emotional nature* is injurious to human progress.' He also gives clear direction about how to proceed in the task of emotional perfection, which inheres in the *manas* and *chitta*, and not *buddhi*.[31] 'The only way for him to train himself *morally is to habituate himself to the right emotions*, the noblest associations, the best mental, emotional and physical habits . . .' [Emphasis added.]

The import of this will become vivid if, for instance, one recalls the emotional atmosphere repeatedly generated by the combination of Shakuni, Duryodhana, Dhritarashtra—and to a lesser extent of Karna—in the *Mahabharata*, which starkly contrasts with that of Krishna–Kunti–Yudhisthira. The former combination time and again brushes aside the ethically sound Bhisma–Vidura pair, of course within a proper literary scheme of the impending dramatic climax. The tragedy of Dhritarashtra's character is that of a man who is sensitive of heart, yet not pure and strong enough, so that his intellect serves only his endless perversities and frailties. It is because of this universal tension within man that Vivekananda was so critical about intellectual education alone at the expense of the heart (or mind or emotions):[32]

'It [intellectual education] only makes man *ten times more selfish* . . . The intellect can never become inspired. Only the heart, when it is enlightened, becomes *inspired*. . . . When it [the heart] is desirous of doing good to others, your brain may tell you that it is not politic to do so, but follow your heart and you will find that you make fewer mistakes than by following your intellect. The *pure heart is the best mirror* for the reflection of truth. . . . [Emphasis added.]

In fact, with a pure heart, intellect and reason are more effective. As Satprakashananda aptly says:[33] 'Without moral purity intellect does not brighten, right understanding does not develop, insight does not grow.' Moral purity is of the heart, the emotions.

To use a couple of Sanskrit phrases, efforts for the perfection of *buddhi-vritti* (intellectual abilities) alone, to the neglect of *hridaya-vritti* (emotional faculties), are the quintessence of educational philosophy nurtured by science and technology. It is simply not true that our *hridaya-vritti*s need no planned cultivation. To have forgotten this principle has contributed to the widening gap between rising consumption standards and declining living standards. Gandhiji's work of a lifetime for the political emancipation of India has been a classic example of high living standards with low consumption standards. Like Vivekananda, his aim in life too was *moksha*, and he also proceeded towards it by satisfying both his reason *and* his heart.[34]

At this stage a possible confusion ought to be faced and resolved. In one of the major Upanishads it is said:[35]

> *Atmānam rathinam viddhi, shariram rathameva tu;*
> *Buddhim tu sārathi viddhi, manah pragrahameva cha.*

This means:

> Know the [individual] Self as the master of the chariot, and the body as the chariot; Know the intellect as the charioteer, and the mind as verily the bridle.

Here the imagery of the intellect, as the charioteer suggests for it, is the role of a guide for the individual *vyavaharika* (empirical) self along the right path. The intellect does so by using the mind as the bridle for the horses of our senses. The intellect is therefore always perfect, right, pure—such an inference is often drawn. In fact, a little later in verse I. iii. 10 this Upanishad goes on to state that the intellect is higher than the mind. To stretch the imagery a little further, it is easy to visualize that even with well-trained horses and the reins held tight, a charioteer may lead one to either a brothel or a temple. In other words, in real life we see perverse intellects as well as exalted ones. If intellect were by definition, and in practice, superior to the mind, then why all this concern with ethico-moral deterioration in our lives? We think that it is in verses I. iii. 5 and I. iii. 7 of the same work that the real clue to this apparent confusion lies. They say that being associated with an uncontrolled, impure mind, the intellect becomes devoid of discrimination or becomes non-discriminating, so intellect is after all not fully autonomous. Thus, the hierarchical superiority of intellect (*buddhi*) in our *antah-karana* loses its power and meaning if the mind is uncontrolled and impure. That is where the *real dynamics* springs forth from the fountain of emotions and feelings, its direction depending on whether they are ethico-morally sound. Purity and control of the mind and its emotions are what ethico-moral conduct fosters.

Buddhist thought too, like Vedanta, is quite clear about the role of reason (or intellect).[36] Although reason initially did create and bring order and civility, yet it also added fuel to the fire of hatred and passions. Being the helpmate of the lower self, reason expanded the scope of lust, envy and sin. Right application of reason is not automatic for it does not make room for truth. Rationality being a *two-edged sword*, it *serves* the purpose equally of love and hatred. Truth rests in righteousness, love, justice and goodwill— emotions of the heart, rather than the intellect of the brain.

The above analysis is borne out well by the following observations of Satprakashananda:[37]

... there are factors in man's psychophysical constitution, such as old habits, wrong tendencies, sense-desires, passions and prejudices, that often vitiate his judgment and retard his power of action. *Undesirable emotions prevail against the remonstrance of reason and the resistance of will.* [Emphasis added.]

This indeed has been the story of the Devdattas and Dhritarashtras, and their equivalents in our times. Hence the great emphasis in Indian psychology on *bhava-shuddhi* or *chittashuddhi*, e.g. *yama* and *niyama* practices of Patanjali.[38] Before intellect and reason can render a proper account of their office, methodical ethico-moral education and culture is essential. What are the main constitutents of such a programme in both its positive and negative aspects? To follow Satprakashananda again,[39] on the positive or *virtue* side the elements are:

- truthfulness
- sincerity
- honesty
- obedience
- humility
- purity
- endurance
- consideration for fellow-beings etc;

and on the negative or *vice* side the ingredients are:

- falsehood
- anger
- hatred
- jealousy
- vanity
- covetousness
- deceitfulenss, etc.

Thus, we are back to classical, traditional, eternal values. They must be cultured and internalized again and again by every generation. It is plain self-deception to brush them aside by invoking the sinister argument that all values are relative to time and space. Quite often our sharp intellect poses exceptions, and tends to question the virtues listed above, e.g. is the endurance of a thief commendable? or if my boss asks me to hatch a plot to get a competitor murdered, is obedience then a virtue? or, is enduring a difficult colleague the right approach? and so on. Similarly, regarding the vices, it is common to hear: is there no case for anger when a subordinate is repeatedly telling lies? or should one abandon ambition in the name of eschewing covetousness? and so on. All such questions usually indicate a tendency to avoid looking deeply within oneself. It is self-defeating to cite exceptions at the outset and to use them to stall one's own efforts for transformation in a wide range of daily events. Such dilemmas do indeed occur. Experience tells us that as one undertakes a serious job of internalizing these virtues, and neutralizing the vices, the mind gains greater strength and power by the day. Then an instinctive capacity develops to make fine judgments in specific situations as to which virtue is inappropriate or vice suitable, if at all—as a temporary reversal—for a cause greater than one's self-interest. The mind itself then becomes one's guru—as the seers say.

We ought to draw a vital distinction between 'emotions' and 'emotionalism'. What Dhritarashtra had been doing for his son Duryodhana is plain emotionalism. When a mother plies her young boy with chocolates and cakes and sweets just for the asking, apparently out of love, in fact she is merely being emotionally indulgent—a false impulse of love for the child. The same mother may, if the poor child of a beggar happens to ask for one sweet from the large box she is carrying home, frown and briskly walk past. The emotion of love is not expansive in her, nor does her intellect come to her aid. Clearly, the task here is to purify and expand the emotion of love and consideration—not to sharpen the intellect.

The word 'emotion' tends to be commonly used in a pejorative, negative sense. 'That person is emotional' is a way of stigmatizing him or her. Hence the proclaimed emphasis on intellect or reason. We should however also ponder over the fact that both emotions and intellect can be positive or negative. When an emotion has a virtuous basis, e.g., compassion or *maitri* for the unhappy, it can inspire the intellect to act usefully, but when an emotion is vicious, e.g. envy, it can drive the intellect to act destructively. Emotion is indeed the motive power behind intellect. This is what must have prompted: (a) Einstein to declare: 'And certainly we should take care *not* to make intellect our God. . . . The intellect has a sharp eye for methods and tools, but is *blind to ends and values.*'[40] (b) Aurobindo to assert: 'The spirit that manifests itself in man . . . is great and *profounder than his intellect* . . .'[41] (c) Russell to warn: 'Science is *no* substitute for virtue . . . If men were rational in their conduct . . . intelligence would be enough to make the world a paradise. . . . But men are actuated by passions which distort their view . . . That is why the *heart is as important* as the head. . . . Where they [kindly impulses of the heart] are absent, science only makes man *more cleverly diabolic.*'[42] (d) Vivekananda to affirm: 'But the professor is bound by his intellect, and he can be a devil and an intellectual at the same time; but the man of *heart* can never be a devil; *no man with emotion was a devil.*'[43] (e) Toynbee to detect that 'The effect emotion exerts on human actions is as strong as—perhaps stronger than—that of reason. Consequently, emotion can get the upper hand and suppress theoretical knowledge, which is dependent on reason.'[44] [Emphasis added.]

The unanimity amongst some of the best contemporary eastern and western minds about the heart or emotion not itself being the arch villain, and about the intellect or reason not by itself being the supreme hero is remarkable. Unless our emotions, our hearts are adequately cultured, intellect tends to play havoc. How far-sighted therefore has been the emphasis in Indian psychology on *chitta-shuddhi*, i.e. purification or *hridaya-vritti* as the more important and prior requirement in human development. The edifice or *buddhi-vritti* can be safely mounted only on such a base.

V. Ethics and Morals: Differentiation or Unity, Cause or Effect, Grabbing or Giving?

(a) A major cause of ethico-moral deterioration is fear and insecurity arising out of the conditioned identity of our separateness. Greed, envy, jealousy, anger all spring from this congenital fear, associated with inner emptiness. Another foundation for ethics, still more profoundly logical than that explored in section IV, resides thus in our understanding of the self. The principle is beautifully expressed in the following verse:[45]

Ishwaranugraha-eva pumsam advaita vasana,
Mahadbhaya-paritranat vipranam upjayate.

48 *Management by Values*

i.e., 'Through the grace of God alone, the *desire for non-duality arises in wise men to save them from great fear*' [Emphasis added]. It is this *vedantic* keynote of non-duality or *advaita*, i.e. unity which is proposed as the final objective of realization at the level of feeling in our heart. Science indeed is proving this at the level of matter and energy, but this is mere intellectual knowledge. Unless we strive to *feel* this oneness, gradually recognize this alone as the ultimate goal, in one's inmost self things will not really improve. Let us turn once more to Vivekananda:[46]

The infinite oneness of the Soul is the eternal sanction of all morality, that you and I are not only brothers... but that *you and I are really one*. This is the dictate of Indian philosophy. *This oneness is the rationale of all ethics and all spirituality*. Europe wants it today as much as our downtrodden masses do.... [Emphasis added.]

Through various imageries like the lump of clay and the many things made of it, or the many pitchers full of water floating in an ocean and so on, *vedanta* attempts to convey relevant hints to this conception of essential *unity* through apparent differentiation. There must of course be simpler and more practical approaches towards achieving vibrant morality on the basis of this principle. Let us turn again to Vivekananda for such guidelines:

(1) That is the *pravritti*, the natural tendency of every human being; taking everything from everywhere and heaping it around one centre, that centre being man's own individual self. When this tendency begins to break, when it is *nivritti* or going away from, then begin *morality* and religion.... This *nivritti* is the *fundamental* basis of all morality...'[47]

(2) The only definition that can be given to morality is this: *That which is selfish is immoral, and that which is unselfish is moral*.[48]

(3) ... We find that, as knowledge comes, man grows, morality is evolved, and the idea of *non-separateness* begins. Whether men understand it or not, they are impelled by that power behind to *become unselfish*. That is the *foundation of all morality*. It is the *quintessence of all ethics*. 'Be thou unselfish', 'Not "I" but "thou" '—that is the background of all ethical codes.[49]

(4) ... the highest ideal of morality and unselfishness goes hand in hand with the highest metaphysical conception, and that *you need not lower your conception to get ethics and morality*; but on the other hand, to reach a real basis of morality and ethics you must have the highest philosophical and scientific conceptions.[50]

(5) Why should a man be moral and pure? Because this *strengthens his will*.

Everything that *strengthens the will, by revealing the real nature is moral.* Everything that does the reverse is immoral ...'[51]

(6) This world is neither good nor evil.... It is beyond both good and evil, perfect in itself.... It is a *great gymnasium* [moral] in which you and I, and millions of souls must *come and get exercises,* and make ourselves strong and perfect.[52]

(7) *Renounce the lower* so that you may get the higher. What is the foundation of society? Morality, ethics, laws. Renounce. *Renounce all temptation* to take your neighbour's property, to put hands upon your neighbour, all the pleasure of tyrannising over the weak, all the pleasure of cheating others by telling lies. Is not *morality the foundation of society.* What is marriage but the *renunciation of unchastity.* The savage does not marry. Man marries because he renounces.... Renounce! Sacrifice! Give up! Not for zero.... But to *get the higher.*'[53]

[Emphasis added.]

The above statements lead to the following scheme of ideas:

• The foundation of a healthy society is sound morals and ethics.

• For the individual's own peace of mind and strength of will morality and ethics are essential.

• The world is not good or evil, but man's selfishness is the chief source of evil, of diminished morals and ethics.

• Selfishness springs from the non-cultivation and non-realization of the feeling of oneness with all.

• The feeling of separateness fuels itself on *pravritti.* Selfish, unethical actions are stimulated by the dominance of *pravritti* in man's mental make-up. A very large proportion of the results of science and technology is serving the insatiable *pravritti* of the common citizen.

• *Nivritti* means renouncing bit by bit the impulses and doings of the lower, selfish self. It helps the process of realizing unity in the midst of differentiation, and unity-feeling (*ekatmanubhuti*) is the basis of ethico-moral dealings.

• We should not lie or cheat or hurt, or perform similar unethical acts to others because 'we' and 'they' essentially constitute a unity. Hurting or hating others means hurting or hating ourselves—whether we realize it or not (in our present state of imperfect awareness).

Now, the whole structure of Enlightenment thinking, of which modern society and its temper is a sequel, rests on four major pillars:

(a) The separation, by Francis Bacon and others, of man from Nature, for the latter to be exploited and vanquished by the former, thus imparting to science and technology the overall character it now has.

(b) Adam Smith's infallible 'invisible hand' of human selfishness on which rests the whole economic edifice of most nations.

(c) Charles Darwin's 'survival of the fittest' which has given almost a license to man to interpret fitness in the way that best suits his self-interest.

(d) Karl Marx's 'dialectical materialism', forecasting the doom of the system born of (b) and (c), but leaving (a) untouched.

Hence, unless these basic ingredients of the ruling paradigm are thoroughly reviewed against an alternative paradigm, like that just distilled from Vivekananda's works, India may not be striking the log along the true grain for, as Warsh has quite recently commented:[54]

Emotions such as love, loyalty, and outrage, like a sense of fairness, have little or no place in today's utility functions; a *narrow selfishness* is pervasive; [and then again—]

Efforts to produce a theory of *cooperation* or of *altruism* suggests that much of the certitude about the nature of man that economists have advanced these last 100 years may have been misleading. There may be a *good and logical foundation for doctrines of loyalty* and *sympathetic understanding after* all.[55]

[Emphasis added.]

Similarly, Bloom is also blunt in saying that contemporary society has unleashed selfish human desires from the taming or perfecting influence of virtue. By allowing desire to be the only consultant of our behaviour, modern psychology has only corroborated the Machiavellian view that selfishness is somehow good.[56] It is indeed our hope, therefore, that for Warsh and Bloom and their ilk, with whom we agree, enough of a clear and consistent model or doctrine of healthy and sound human emotions has been furnished above.

Of all the positive, healthy emotions what might be the convergent apex? It appears to us to be *ānanda* or Bliss. Whether man knows it or not, he is constitutionally prone to seeking infinite, stable, independent *ānanda* within himself. Love, in the purest sense, or Truth–Goodness–Beauty (*satyam-shivam-sundaram*) may also be considered to be the very last stepping stone to the one apex value (in the sense of a desired state of realization or feeling or awareness) of *ānanda*. *Pravritti* hitches us to an endless convoy of finite objects. Infinite *ānanda* cannot however spring from the mere accumulation, however large it may be, of finites. This is a truth which each one of us experiences—though does not recognize. Because of this unrecognized fallacy, false emotions and misdirected intellect or reason grow unchecked, driven by *pravritti*. In effect, we lose our *freedom* to *pravritti*. The result is erosion of the level of our ethico-moral conduct. For attainment of *ānanda*, 'freedom' is indispensable. Indeed, 'freedom' is the foundation of Love, Truth, Goodness and also of Beauty. Indian thought therefore distinguishes between 'freedom of' and 'freedom from'. Whenever self-restraint from giving indulgence to an impulse like anger or hatred or greed is applied, one changes track—from 'freedom of' to 'freedom from'. This is because the impulse of hatred or of greed, for instance, normally strongly sways our mind and propels it to one kind of expression or another. This process is characterized by 'freedom of', but in reality it constitutes our subjection, our bondage to a lower state of consciousness. *Pravritti* ties us down to this level. Therefore the reverse movement of *nivritti*, inspired by the principle that infinite *ānanda* is *within*, implies an effort to gain 'freedom from' the externalizing, hypnotizing spell of *pravritti*. This enables us to slowly regain our original lost paradise of 'freedom'; fear, anxiety,insecurity, jealousy, and allied feelings begin to wane. The slumbering ethico-moral impulses then begin to wake up.

As Roubiczek suggests, either we opt for 'freedom of choice', or for 'choice of freedom'.[57] He is right. A *pravritti*-conditioned mind will tend to zealously seek and protect 'freedom of choice', which is commonly the same as the 'freedom of' going about satisfying whatever we desire by adopting any means that may be expedient without any testing against the inner standard: does it bind or free us? However, once *nivritti* begins to be cultivated as a countervailing disposition, increasingly does 'freedom' in itself tend to become 'the choice'—unconditioned, independent, secure and permanent *ānanda*. (This is why the vast majority of monks in India have names ending with 'ananda'.) Consequently, the feeling of unity, *ekatmanubhuti*, begins to ripen faster. As Roubiczek says:[58]

'To make freedom real, we must therefore not only choose, but choose those values which give the right content to freedom, by enabling us to give the fullest expression which can possibly contribute to our ethical self.'

These words echo the *vedantic* concept of freedom, through a modern western mind, to resound within our social existence. In this light, we shall continue to play the accepted roles and committed works in our respective stations, but from progressively higher levels of consciousness based on greater ethico-moral sensitivity. This is precisely the lesson the greats of human history have repeatedly imparted to us.

(b)   *Karmavada* or the theory of *karma* is the social counterpart of the universal, cosmic law of cause-and-effect. We should remind ourselves that all classical wisdom, especially Indian, has *seen* the sub-human, human, terrestrial, transcendental and universal in an unbroken continuum. The generalized theory of *karma* in human existence is therefore a product of the highest and most acute level of objective observation and verification of events occurring in the lives of individuals, groups, communities, etc. It tells us that an ethically wrong *karma* (e.g. inventing or suppressing figures to prove one supplier of costly equipment to be better than another in order to receive personal underhand gains from the former) being a wrong *cause*, it cannot but invite a corresponding adverse effect(s)—at some time, in one way or another. Those who have the mind and the patience to examine the network of successive events developing around individuals, organizations, nations, cannot but fail to discover the truth of this theory. So, this internal deterrent consciousness within the decision-maker must be awakened. It is idle to pretend that in contemporary society such built-in fear has no role. To keep alive a healthy conscience, genuine internalization of the theory of *karma* is essential. Whenever one is tempted to commit ethico-moral infractions, this principle can sound a strong warning from within so that, even if the net of the internal auditor or the clutches of the CBI or the indictment of the Supreme Court can be eluded, never can there be any escape from the effect(s) of the *cause(s)*. We believe that an adequate comprehension of the theory of *karma*, in the sense of the law of cause-and-effect, is both urgent and important. It will speedily help us keep our emotions and impulses on the right track in the first place, and then prevent our intellect and reason from derailment.

The experience of unity or oneness needs longer-term *sadhana*.

(c)   The third aspect is that of the grabbing consciousness versus the giving consciousness. The greed-inspired, high-standard-of-consumption ethos is evidently manifesting itself as an unbridled grabbing consciousness amongst the haves. Sophisticated marketing techniques continue to stoke its fires. We thus see the gradual breaking away of restraint, patience, dignity in everyday behaviour. All this results in ethico-moral compromises and violations of varying degrees.

Now, this trend can be reversed if only we try to convince ourselves of the classical principle that the true growth and flowering of human personality lies in learning to cherish and possess the joy of 'giving'. In Nature the flower and the tree are the best examples of the 'giving' principle. If we can learn 'grabbing' by studying animal consciousness, is it not at least equally relevant to learn 'giving' by delving into floral consciousness? The grabber may not know, but is forever insecure, vulnerable, fragile and poor. This alone explains Alexander's lamentation, 'Aren't there anymore lands to conquer?' This crisis is, however, a gratuitously invited one because of faulty conditioning. The grabber is an abjectly dependent individual. The 'giver', on the other hand, is rich within and can say, after Tagore, 'The more hast thou received from me, the more hast my debt to thee grown.' Giving does not mean merely money and goods and similar gross objects. They have their place, but it is the spirit which is most important—the spirit of humility—in discharging one's debt and obligation to the several segments of the existential matrix which make every moment of an individual's existence a practical possibility. Thus, to work hard and with dedication is imperative not because an individual needs quick promotions, but because he is already indebted for what he or she now is and this obligation must be discharged before leaving this world.

Some people do not like the idea of 'debt' underlying the giving consciousness. They are willing to go only so far as to acknowledge the 'gifts' they receive from various quarters. This too is a good idea, but we suspect it does not go far enough. When we receive a 'gift', we may or may not return it. The sense of obligation does not therefore underlie this act. 'Debt' implies mandatory obligation. It is this feeling deep within amongst the upper echelons of our society which is essential to neutralize the rights-oriented, grabbing consciousness. This is another way of preventing the deterioration in our ethico-moral conduct.

VI. On to The Pilgrim-Path

The starting point on the road to the recovery of ethico-moral standards probably cannot be anything other than these two convictions:

(a) that business and commerce can and need to succeed—even in competitive environments—with higher degrees of ethico-moral rectitude;

(b) that each individual is as much a 'cause' as an 'effect' of the quality of society and environment where he or she functions.

We agree with the advisor's observations in Blanchard and Peale's book that there is a strong case to restore our faith in the long-range consequences of rectitude, to appreciate a more universal timing, to believe in something greater than ourselves—call it God or spirituality or a higher power. Then things begin to work out properly.[59] This indeed was Vyasa's clarion call in the *Mahabharata*: *artha* and *kama* can very well be attained on the foundation of *dharma*.[60] Is the twenty-first century AD going to be a return to the twenty-first century BC?

Next, it is necessary to recognize the following matrix of the ethico-moral interface between organizations and organizational members:

Organization's Ethics / Member's Ethics	High	Low
High	(1) Most desirable (Congruent)	(2) Problematic (Incongruent)
Low	(3) Problematic (Incongruent)	(4) Least desirable (Congruent)

Cell 2 would seem to be most agonizing for the individual, and such examples are quite frequent, e.g. when a young graduate takes up his first job in the marketing or taxation department of an enterprise which is adept in shady deals and practices. Cell 3, however, seems to have an equal chance of either slowly reforming the deviant individual, or the latter eventually quitting the organization for a better environment. In both these cases there is an organizational ethico-moral culture which pre-exists the entry of a new member. To trace this culture back to the starting point, one needs to reach its founding fathers. Through their vision of rectitude and sound values, and by constantly modelling and living upto them, the existing culture has blossomed, e.g. the house of Tatas and J.R.D. Tata. Without naming them, we know there are many more business houses of the opposite character. About the former, we have this recognition from the critical Chairman of another Indian industrial house, that the lure of under-the-table money is not a means of recruiting or motivating competent executives. This is nevertheless a widespread practice in the majority of Indian industrial houses, including that of the Chairman just mentioned. This also goes with summary dismissal at the pleasure of the owner.

So, Gellerman rightly warns that unusually high rewards and unusually severe punishments—for good performance or toeing the line, and for poor performance or trying to stand up—are both inducements to ethico-moral deterioration.[61] In fact, a fabulous amount of energy wastage occurs in such organizations through the incessant play of what Zaleznik very aptly terms 'psycho-politics'.[62] Cells(1) and (4), of course, are alliances—one is holy, the other unholy. They are nevertheless congruent, so psycho-politics may be relatively less furious within organizations approximating these two cells.

And now we arrive at the more important task of the individual's self-transformation. As has been amply demonstrated through references to both western and eastern thinkers, the critical breakthrough has to occur in the sphere of the emotional or feeling's purification. Conceptual clarity or cognitive awareness does not suffice here. According to Tomkins:[63] 'An affect revolution is now required to emancipate this radical new development from an overly imperialistic cognitive theory.' So, amongst the most practical and potent methods of lifting the heavy lid of merely cognitive or intellectual understanding (fostered by the modern scientific–technological *élan*) is to meditate on what is called the *ishtam* within one's heart. The *ishtam* is one's chosen embodiment of all the purest emotions, e.g. a Buddha, a Christ, a Nanak, a Ramakrishna, a Shiva, a Krishna ... While concentrating on a living luminous visualization of this chosen *ishtam*, all the vital and mental forces are soaked and saturated in its radiance of utter selflessness, holiness, freedom and *ānanda*. Regular practice of this process, with sincerity and devotion, is one of the quickest and surest ways for the achievement of *bhavashuddhi* or *chittashuddhi*. Simultaneously, some daily reading of their biographies, and other authentic legends invariably growing around them, is of immense help in reconditioning our emotions. *Nivritti* then becomes a natural, spontaneous process—without having to wage a frontal attack on the ruling *pravritti*. The 'giving consciousness' now also starts slowly to displace the 'grabbing consciousness'.

The practice of such concentration is possible, and necessary, even when not sitting formally for a mind-stilling exercise. For instance, while waiting at the bank counter to encash a cheque, or waiting for delayed flights at airports one may think such ideas. The eyes need not be closed, but the mind may be frozen, as it were, for a few moments with held breath, and a dip taken into the serene, smiling, glowing aura of the *ishtam*. It is like a freeze shot in a film. This technique is sometimes called 'stepping back'. It can be practised even during office work, reading, writing, walking, bathing—almost anytime anywhere. A slow walking, talking and breathing pace is a useful package of habits to inculcate to support ethico-moral sensitivity.

Finally, the feeling or emotion of *ekatmanubhuti*, not merely an intellectual acceptance of the fact of essential unity (not uniformity) underlying differentiation or diversity, can be cultivated by extending the previous practice. The method consists of attempting to visualize one's own *ishtam* as residing in the heart of everyone else—the man in the street, the colleague, the friend, the detractor, the student, the worker, the bad, the good, the poor, the rich and so on. As this feeling slowly emerges by determined practice, the emotion of unitive relationship with others grows. It is good to tell the mind, in the early morning at least, by means of a firm *sankalpa* or resolve that this mood *will* last throughout the day. Of course, this *sankalpa* has to be repeated for several months before it enters into the subconscious and then instinctively influences conscious attitudes towards others. It is by means such as these that the hope of people like Andrews (quoted in section I) for instinctive ethical decisions can be fulfilled in the course of time. Once such a deep unitive feeling takes hold of the mind, the standard of ethico-moral behaviour in interpersonal and intergroup relationships is bound to improve. This is because, for example, the thought then arises spontaneously: 'How could I give false information to deceive him? Am I not then hurting my own *ishtam* which is as much his essence as mine?' Towards our beloved son or mother or wife such an inner check is automatic. Towards all the rest in our work-environment this process has to be systematically cultivated—with patience.

VII. CONCLUSION: TRUE COUNSEL

As we draw to a close of this chapter it is useful to draw a few more inspiring insights from Aurobindo, Vivekananda, Gandhiji and Tagore:

Perceive always and act in the light of thy *increasing perceptions* but not those of the reasoning brain only. God speaks to the heart when *the brain cannot understand Him.*[64]

If the horses* are very strong and do not obey the rein;* if the charioteer, the *intellect, does not know how to control* the horses then the chariot will come to grief.[65]

... I know that ultimately one is guided not by the intellect but by the heart. The heart accepts a conclusion for which the intellect subsequently finds reasoning. Argument follows conviction. *Man often finds reason in support of whatever he does or wants to do.*[66]

... all attempts to radically moralize the race within the limits of his egoistic nature ... end in general failure ... since *reason has also to start from the senses which are consistent falsifiers of values*, rational knowledge is ... pursued by vast dimnesses and uncertainties.[67]

He [man] can amply afford to say that goodness is for the sake of goodness. And upon this wealth of goodness—where *honesty is not valued for being the best policy, but because it can afford to go against policies*—man's ethics are founded.[68]

[Emphasis added.]

---

* Horses—senses, rein—mind. If the emotions or the mind are pure, senses become tamed, and then only can the intellect do its job well in terms of ethical values.

Amartya Sen has correctly detected the manifest symptom of ethical impoverishment in economics caused, in his view, by the dominance of the 'engineering approach' and 'the self-interest view of rationality'. He explains this by saying:[69] 'If one examines the balance of emphasis in the publications in modern economics, it is hard not to notice the eschewal of deep normative analysis, and the neglect of the influence of ethical considerations in the characterization of actual human behaviour.' We suppose the hypnotic spell of mathematical and statistical modelling in the field of economics is one reason for this negligence. However, with an open confession from Sen about this impoverishment in the domain of economics it becomes easier to appreciate why ethical issues within organizations are even more down-to-earth and crucial. The remedies implied in Sen's diagnosis have to be sought from the ideas of Tagore and others just quoted.

In this context we feel somewhat apprehensive about the over-simplification in Maslow's view that 'what passes for morals, ethics, and values may be the *gratuitous epiphenomena* of the pervasive psycho-pathology of the average'.[70] [Emphasis added.] Even Maslow's self-actualizer (unless he has attained his spiritual Higher SELF, as discussed later in this book), cannot afford to adopt such a cavalier stance towards ethics and morals. There is enough recent writing to show that the assumed self-actualizers are mostly self-aggrandizers. In any case, 99 per cent of us are just average human beings (even though great experts in our fields). Ethics and values must, therefore, remain at the centre of our concern for human response development.

In sum, the prevailing excessive cultivation of left-brained, intellect-sharpening human development processes must be moderated by careful attention to right-brained, mind-purifying efforts. While the search for international or global management principles at the level of the intellect may be correct, it would be unrealistic to deny culture-specificity when it comes to attempts at transforming the quality of emotions and feelings towards greater expansiveness and ethical purity. In this phase the need to explore and utilize culturally authentic symbols, myths, rites and rituals, with careful adaptations or innovations when necessary, cannot be escaped. The theory of meditation on the *ishtam* described above is one such culture-specific process for the great majority of Indians.

REFERENCES

1. A. Monappa, *Ethical Attitudes of Indian Managers* (New Delhi: All India Management Association, 1977).
2. S.K. Chakraborty, *Managerial Effectiveness and Quality of Work-life—Indian Insights* (New Delhi: Tata McGraw Hill, 1987), pp. 76–112.
3. J.F. Akers, 'Ethics and Competitiveness—Putting First Thing First', *Sloan Management Review*, Winter 1989, p. 69.
4. Ibid., p. 69.   5. Ibid., p. 70.   6. Ibid., p. 70.
7. B. Victor, and J.B. Cullen, 'The Organizational Bases of Ethical Work Climates', *Administrative Science Quarterly*, vol. 33, 1988, p. 123.
8. K. Blanchard and N.V. Peale, *The Power of Ethical Management* (New York: William Morrow, 1988), p. 6.
9. P.E. Murphy, 'Creating Ethical Corporate Structures', *Sloan Management Review*, Winter 1989, p. 87.
10. K.R. Andrews, 'Ethics In Practice', *Harvard Business Review*, September–October, 1989, p.100.
11. J.G. Longenecker, J.A. McKinney and C.W. Moore, 'The Generation Gap in Business Ethics', *Business Horizons*, September–October, 1989, p.11.
12. A. Toynbee and D. Ikeda, *Choose Life* (Delhi: Oxford University Press, 1987), pp. 306–7.
13. A. Einstein, *Out of My Later Years* (London: Thames & Hudson, 1950), p. 24.
14. *Interviews With Nobel Laureates and Other Eminent Scholars* (Bombay: The Bhaktivedanta Institute, 1986), p. 83.
15. *The Search For Absolute Values: Harmony Among The Sciences* (New York: The International Cultural Foundation Press, 1977), vol. I, p. 14.
16. *Interviews With Nobel Laureates and Other Scholars* (Bombay: The Bhaktivedanta Institute, 1986), p. 37.
17. Ibid., p. 44.
18. P.N.Haksar, *Reflections on Our Times* (Delhi: Lancers, 1982), p. 111.
19. B. Russell, *The Scientific Outlook* (London: George Allen & Unwin, 1931), pp. 277, 279.
20. C.E.M. Joad, *Guide To Modern Wickedness* (London: Faber & Faber, 1947), pp. 261, 262.
21. B. Griffiths, *Return to The Centre* (London: Collins Fount Paperbacks, 1987), p. 18.
22. P.N. Murthy, 'Management of Change—A Philosophical Perspective', *Bulletin*, Feb. 1986, p. 5.
23. *Interviews With Nobel Laureates and Other Scholars*, p. 88.
24. T.N. Madan, *Non-Renunciation* (Delhi: Oxford University Press, 1987), p. 165.

25. S.K. Chakraborty, *Human Response in Organizations—Towards the Indian Ethos* (Calcutta: Vivekananda Nidhi, 1985), pp. 115–16.
26. Swami Vivekananda, *Collected Works* (Calcutta: Advaita Ashrama, 1989), vol. VIII.
27. *Idem, Collected Works* (Calcutta: Advaita Ashrama, 1956), vol. II, pp. 306, 307.
28. *Idem,* vol. VI, p. 42.
29. Sri Aurobindo, *A System of National Education* (Pondicherry: Sri Aurobindo Ashrama, 1970), p. 4.
30. Ibid., p. 7.   31. Ibid., p. 8.
32. Swami Vivekananda, op. cit., vol. I, pp. 412–14.
33. Swami Satprakashananda, *The Goal and The Way* (Madras: Ramakrishna Math, 1981), p. 43.
34. M.K. Gandhi, *The Story of My Experiments With Truth* (Ahmedabad: Navjivan Publishing House, 1972), p. x.
35. Swami Gambhirananda, *Katha Upanishad* (Calcutta: Advaita Ashrama, 1980), verse I. iii. 3, pp. 64–5.
36. P. Carus, *The Gospel of Buddha* (Madras: Samata Books, 1987), pp. 228–30.
37. Satprakashananda, op. cit., p. 83.
38. Swami Vivekananda, *Collected Works*, vol. I, *Rajyoga*, verses II. 29–32, pp. 260–1.
39. Satprakashananda, op. cit., pp. 90–1.
40. A. Einstein, *Out of My Later Years*, p. 260.
41. Sri Aurobindo, *Social and Political Thought* (Pondicherry: Sri Aurobindo Ashram, 1972), vol. 15, p. 105.
42. B. Russell, *The Future of Science* (London: Kegan Paul, Trench Trubner, 1927), pp. 58–9.
43. Swami Vivekananda, *Complete Works,* vol. I, p. 413.
44. A. Toynbee, and D. Ikeda, *Choose Life*, p. 305.
45. *Avadhuta Gita*, trans. by Swami Ashokananda (Madras: Sri Ramakrishna Math, 1981), I–1, p. 1.
46. Swami Vivekananda, *Collected Works*, vol. III, p. 189.
47. Ibid., vol. I, p. 86.   48. Ibid., p. 110.
49. Ibid., vol. VI, p. 5.   50. Ibid., vol. II, p. 355.
51. Ibid., vol. VIII, p. 223.   52. Ibid., vol. IV, p. 207.
53. Ibid., vol. IV, p. 243.
54. D. Warsh, 'How Selfish Are People Really?', *Harvard Business Review*, May–June 1989, p. 27.
55. Ibid., p. 30.
56. A. Bloom, *The Closing of the American Mind* (New York: Simon & Schuster, 1987), pp. 175–8.
57. P. Roubiczek, *Ethical Values in The Age of Science* (Cambridge University Press, 1969), p. 238.

58. Ibid., p. 239.
59. K. Blanchard and N. Peale, V, pp. 59–60.
60. P.H. Prabhu, *Hindu Social Organization* (Bombay: Popular Prakashan, 1963) p. 358.
61. S.W. Gellerman, 'Managing Ethics From Top Down', *Sloan Management Review*, Winter 1989, p. 74.
62. A. Zaleznik, 'Real Work', *Harvard Business Review*, Jan.–Feb. 1989, pp. 57–8, 60.
63. S. Tomkins, quoted by R.I. Levy in 'Emotion, Knowing and Culture', *Culture Theory*, eds. R.D. Shweder and R.A. Levine (Cambridge University Press, 1984), p. 215.
64. Sri Aurobindo, and The Mother, *On Science* (Pondicherry: Sri Aurobindo Society, 1972), p. 28.
65. Swami Vivekananda, *Rajyoga, Collected Works*, vol. I, p. 235.
66. M.K. Gandhi, *The Teaching of The Gita* (Bombay: Bharatiya Vidya Bhawan, 1962), p. 11.
67. Sri Aurobindo, *The Hour of God* (Pondicherry: Sri Aurobindo Ashram, 1982), p. 47.
68. Rabindranath Tagore, *Lectures and Addresses* (Delhi: Macmillan, 1988), p. 81.
69. A.K. Sen, *On Ethics and Economics* (London: Basil Blackwell, 1990), p. 7.
70. A.H. Maslow, *Motivation and Personality* (New York: Harper and Row, 1954), p. 231.

3

FROM SELF TO SELF
The Ascent From Pettiness to Dignity

I. THE SETTING

Our Workshops and Courses on 'Values-System'—both for students and in-house audiences of managers—are based on the model shown below:*

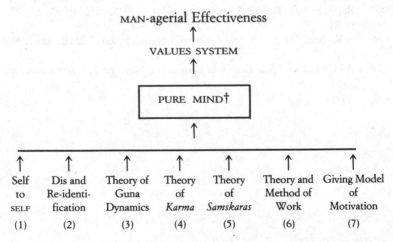

Progressive attainment of 'pure mind' being the superordinate yet operative basis for sensitivity to and sustenance of wholesome values (we shall explain this presently), several complementary theories and processes are available from Indian psycho-philo-

---

* This presentation is an adaptation of chart 1.2, p.8, in the author's book: *Managerial Effectiveness and Quality of Work-life—Indian Insights* (New Delhi: Tata McGraw Hill, 1987).

† This is the same as the pure subjective, or pure heart, or pure emotions/feelings.

sophy to work towards it. The most vital and critical of them is the boxed item 'self to SELF'. This is the theme of this chapter. The sum-total of transformational psychology is contained in the elevation, not mere transition, implied by 'self to SELF'.* The theory behind this rests primarily on the *vedantic* concept of man, and in addition with partial support from Sankhya psychology. The theory and practice of SELF is also the foundation of the list of deep-structure values presented in section IV of Chapter 1.

Besides, we shall offer below the findings from questionnaire data on self v. SELF, collected from nearly 500 managers and others, to indicate the present state of the managerial mind on this vital perception.

II. VALUES AND PURITY MIND

In chapter 2 we have already clarified that brilliance of intellect has little to do with upholding universally healthy values. It is the quality of the emotions and feelings which, independently of the intellect, so to say, determines the level of purity of mind or heart in man. In the realm of daily choices and decision-making, therefore, it is the quality of the subjective of the agent of choice or decision which ultimately determines its degree of objectivity (or fairness or equity). To repeat, the principle is: '*The subjective is the cause, the objective the effect.*'

Now, this crucial 'subjective' in the human agent has been squarely dealt with in all branches of Indian psycho-philosophy —instead of wishing it away, or labouring under the folly that more and more external systems, models, tools, techniques can do the trick in favour of objectivity, i.e. value-consonant choices and decisions. Thus, in one of the major Buddhist texts, *Majjhima Nikaya*, the following 'defilements of the mind' are listed:[1]

greed, covetousness, malevolence, anger, malice, hypocrisy, spite, envy, stinginess, deceit, treachery, obstinacy, impetuosity, arrogance, pride, conceit, indolence.

True of course that all major revealed texts like the Bible and the Koran also keep warning us about these mental contaminations. It is, however, Indian psychology alone, it appears, which offers first

---

* It is correct to say that, in the ultimate sense, from 'self to SELF' is the goal, and 'pure mind' is the means or instrument. But unless the latter itself is treated as the goal for a long time, SELF-hood cannot be practically realized by any of us.

theories to examine intellectually, rationally the roots of these defilements; and then supplies practical methods to work on them through systematic discipline at the level of feeling and emotion. Let us explore this claim.

It is a consistent observation of ours, also corroborated by the views solicited from managers in our programmes on 'Values System', that the two simple words—*pettiness* and *dignity*—sum up the daily range of all experiences in the domain of human relationships—whether interpersonal, inter-departmental, inter-organizational, inter-governmental, inter-party, inter-union and so on. Managers are also almost unanimous that the proportion of experiences reflecting 'pettiness' is overwhelming compared to those revealing 'dignity'. It is in these frequent pettinesses that behavioural dilutions take place, and it is in the rare event of a dignified response that value concentration takes place. Thus, when one spreads rumours about the recent promotion of a colleague, inspired by grudge and envy, pettiness is at work; or when someone bills his or your organization for expenses in excess of actuals or allowed limits, supported by 'intelligent' arguments; or, when the boss praises another member in an individual's presence, and the latter uses this as the subject of innuendoes in his inter-personal conversations, they again are pettiness. On the other hand, when one feels it is too low to stoop to submit an inflated bill for a little more money, then dignity is evident—and positive values are reinforced. This problem of petty, low-value human behaviour has been clearly expressed by Sri Aurobindo:[2]

For there is in front in men a heart of vital emotion similar to the animal's . . . its emotions are governed by egoistic passion, blind instinctive affections . . . heart besieged and given over to the lust, desires, wraths, . . . little greeds and *mean pettinesses* of an obscure and false life-force and debased by its slavery to any and every impulse.

Hammarskjöld, a former UN Secretary-General, has also lamented and eloquently warned about the scourge of pettiness:[3]

It is not sufficient to place yourself daily under God. What really matters is to be *only* under God: the slightest division of allegiance opens the door to daydreaming, *petty* conversation, *petty* boasting, *petty* malice—all the *petty* satellites of the death instinct.

Thus, the crucial, honest admission about pettiness as a governing reality is made by both, on behalf of us all. The reason why a clear or sharp intellect cannot remedy this scourge is because, unsupported by a purified mind (i.e., emotions), the intellect itself tends to be dominated by raw impulses. Man then tends to become more dangerous than in his natural condition due to the lost innocence of the latter state.[4]

The theoretical response to this dilemma is this:

(a) The human personality has two layers as it were—the empirical, lower, surface self, or *vyavaharika vyaktitwa*; and the trans-empirical, higher, deeper SELF, or *parmarthika vyaktitwa*;*

(b) The empirical self or *vyavaharika vyaktitwa* is constitutionally 'deficit-driven', conditioned, dependent, apprehensive, insecure and hence prone to 'pettiness';

(c) the trans-empirical SELF or *paramarthika vyaktitwa* is constitutionally 'surplus-inspired', *poorna*, unconditioned, independent, fearless, ever-secure and hence prone to 'dignity'.

(d) Our workings, so long as they remain tied up exclusively with the lower-self base, promise little hope for moving away from petty, low-value behaviour—since the mind-function of this lower self is inherently polluted, i.e., subject to *vikara* or *vikriti*.

(e) The breakthrough towards dignified, high-value behaviour, choice, etc. can occur provided we can awaken the now-dormant higher SELF in us, for here the mind-function can begin to feel its inherent *poornatwa* (wholeness) and *vishuddhi* (purity).

(f) The *vyavaharika-vyaktitwa* is the same as the secular or material self, and *paramarthika vyaktitwa* the same as the spiritual SELF or *atman*.

(g) Finally, the basic *avidya* or ignorance lies in thinking that it is the body-mind frame, this empirical self, which possesses consciousness, soul, spirit, *atman*. True understanding consists in realizing that it is consciousness, *atman*, which possesses a body, a mind, etc.

The primal alienation of man lies in this severance within his being from the higher, *poorna* SELF.[5] Every other alienation is an offshoot from here. The so-called value-erosion or pettiness stems from this

* See Chapter 10.

root alienation. Let us give here two examples to show how, in the absence of awareness of or *sthiti* in this higher SELF, individuals may slide down the slope of mental pollution:

(a)   Recently an OD Consultant shared the entire process, from getting a management programme assigned to a private institution, to its planning and then to a large proportion of its teaching load. On the day of valediction, four chairs were placed on the lecture platform. It was shared by three Directors from the sponsoring firm and the founder of the training institution. The Consultant was quietly left out and took a seat with the participants. As the proceedings went on, he rankled at what he thought was an insult and a show of ingratitude. His loyalty to the institution and respect for its founder suffered heavily in consequence. Over the next few days he, however, slowly began to realize that it was his own petty ego, little self which was causing all the turmoil in his mind, unmasking to him his own fragile psychological make-up. (He had some understanding of the self v. SELF syndrome.)

(b)   An author once opened a packet of publicity brochures about recent books from a well-known publisher. In one he saw many good reviews of a certain book reproduced. Suddenly the author recalled that in an earlier similar packet, the brochure about his own book published by them had not only not contained any such extracts, but had not even mentioned a national award which his book had won. Enviousness of the other author and anger at the behaviour of the publishers upset him. He continued to suffer from this mental debilitation for several days.

Thus, the mind, caught in the lower-self matrix, continues to suffer from deficit-feelings, and ninety per cent of the time they spring from such comparisons. Each time such feelings occur, the level of consciousness plummets—no matter how intellectually brilliant an individual might be. Then mean letters are written, petty words are exchanged, and human relationships are distorted or crumble. Surely such instances in other organizational settings—bureaucracy, industry and what have you—are galore. Pettiness or meanness from one side is usually matched by an equal, if not higher, dose of the same from the other. The mischief of the downward spiral in thought, word or deed is thus set in motion. Rarely do we witness an upward spiralling process in such situations.

III. TOWARDS A FEEL OR AN *Anubhuti* of the Self

The SELF is a supremely subjective Reality felt deep within one's being. Hence symbolism and imagery-laden language abounds in the work of Indian seers to convey hints about Its nature. Thus, in the *Avadhuta Gita* the image of the infinite, indivisible blue sky is abundantly employed to suggest the feel of the SELF,[6] e.g.

nishkalo gaganopaham (1.6),
akasha kalpam (1.58),
vishalam gaganopaham (1.67),
gaganophamo'si (1.68),
shantam chaitanyam gaganopaham (2.4),
jnanamritam, samarasam gaganopaham (3.3) . . .

By contrast in the *Kathopanishad* the SELF is symbolized as *angus-thamatrah purusho*, i.e. *purusha* (not of Sankhya) of the size of the thumb, lodging in the centre of our being like light without smoke.[7] Reflection and meditation on these images of extension or concentration is one way of building the alternative platform of SELF in our consciousness, for meditation is nothing but a willed soaking in of the mental fabric in a qualitatively pure and exalted object or medium.

Similarly, in Shankaracharya's famous song on self-identity, *Nirvan Shatakam* or *Atma Shatakam*,* the same willed mental training is being advised for lifting the mind from its association with the *upadhi*s (attributes)—conditioned empirical self to that of mergence in the *nirupadhic* (attributeless), unconditioned, transempirical SELF. Thus, the first stanza is:

Om! mano-buddhi-ahankara chittani naham,
Na va shrotra jivhe, na cha ghran netre,
Na cha vyom-bhumir, na tejo na vayu,
Chidananda rupah, Shivoham, Shivoham; i.e.,

I am neither the mind, nor intellect, nor ego, nor memory;
Neither the ears, nor tongue, nor the nose nor eyes;
Neither ether nor earth, nor fire nor air;
I am Existence–Knowledge–Bliss—like Shiva.

The rest of the stanzas amplify this very theme from other diverse empirical points of view, yet each time converging on the same

* A free English rendering of this composition by Vivekananda has been included as an Appendix to chapter 10.

trans-empirical affirmation of the Shiva-like SELF. That is to say, the mythological-God Shiva is a symbolic representation of SELF with which the mind can intensely associate itself by meditation and achieve gradual inner growth and transformation. Sister Nivedita offers us a poetic word-picture about the Nature-bound basis of the Shiva imagery which is equally elevating:[8]

Those snowy heights* became the central object of their love. Look at them. Lifted above the world in silence, terrible in their cold and distance, yet beautiful beyond all words, what are they like? Why, they are like—a great monk, clothed in ashes, lost in meditation, silent and alone! They are like—like—the Great God Himself, Siva, Mahadev!

This process of internalizing within our heart a vivid, luminous, effulgent, pure form representing our very own personally cherished, emotionally consonant idea of the SELF is what is called *ishta dhyanam*.

In one of the *Upanishads* the seer paints the following picture:[9]

> *Dwa suparna sayuja sakhaya*
> *samanam nriksham parishaswajate,*
> *Tayorantya pippalam swadwatya*
> *ansanam anayao abhichakshiti.*

The verse means: two birds (self and SELF) of the same origin cling to the same tree (body); of this one bird (self) eats the fruits of diverse tastes (varied experiences), while the other (SELF) which is free, pure, eternal remains a witness without eating. Similarly, Shankaracharya teaches us elsewhere to distinguish the self from SELF by realizing how the seer of the jar is distinct in all respects from the jar,[10] and Vidyaranya asks us to know that the SELF is the invariable while the body etc. are the variables.[11]

While the range of choice is thus very wide, the principle is always the same. *Ishta dhyanam* is amongst the most practical methods for inner re-conditioning, transformation and elevation. It fulfils a basic psychological law: you become what you think. Transpersonal psychologists in the West are now testifying the validity of this method. Ken Wilber calls the *ishtam* the 'high Archetypal Form' which mediates the ascension of consciousness to an identity with that Form.[12] Let us recall the refrain: *'Chidananda rupah, Shivoham, Shivoham'*—I am Shiva, I am Shiva. Yes,

---

* The Himalayas.

initially while meditating on one's *ishtam*, the duality of a devotee, a *bhakta*, is more natural. After sufficient practice the aim is to let one's separate self merge and dissolve in the *ishta*-SELF, to identify oneself with It. This is a practical method of obtaining the feel, the *anubhuti* of SELF—free, indivisible, dignified—and much more. Even a faint feeling, for a few moments, on a few occasions, is worth all the while from the standpoint of the needs being addressed here. Similarly, deep contemplation of the imagery of the SELF-bird, separate and serene from the excited self-bird within the heart, is a practical way to prepare for the eventual standing ground of our *poornatwa*.

This discussion leads us to a brief reference to the second theme in the diagram given above—dis-identification and re-identification. Our present exclusive and tremendous identification with the deficit-driven, secular self makes us a slave to its blind impulses—although we mistake our urge to gratify them at any cost as the manifestation of freedom. This is the name of the game called *maya*. The real job in seeking transformation to higher order values, from pettiness to dignity, is to refuse to remain identified entirely with the lower self, and to boldly assert our identification within with the SELF. Shankaracharya's *Atmashatakam* can be summarized as follows:

I have a body, but I am not the body;
I have the senses, but I am not the senses;
I have a mind, but I am not the mind;
I have an intellect, but I am not the intellect;
I AM THE SELF-LUMINOUS PURE CONSCIOUSNESS WHICH IS POORNA (LIKE SHIVA).

Deliberate and emphatic, slow and sincere assertions of this set of statements within a quiet mind—after deep rhythmic breathing—will recondition our consciousness to the higher SELF. Later on this mood can remain with us even during work. As Vivekananda points out forcefully from the depths of his own realization:[13]

When the hands work, the mind should repeat, 'I am It.
I am It'. Think of it, dream of it, until it becomes
the bone of your bones, and flesh of your flesh . . .

These statements open the road to self-mastery, to real freedom from the thraldom of pettinesses stemming from the mind, the senses and the rest. The body, mind, etc. are merely the instruments, merely the *upadhi*s. Man has lost his sense of ownership of them. Instead, they rule and dictate to him. This illusion needs to be confronted by reviving the lost awareness of the Shiva-SELF, the real master, the proprietor. The lower self, symbolized by the Duryodhana–Shakuni–Dhritarashtra axis has usurped the throne of the SELF symbolized by the Pandavas.[14] Hence, the need for an inner Mahabharata for each one of us.

Besides this 'dis-identification–re-identification' exercise, the remaining five props of the model constitute an essential systems-approach to awaken the SELF that one *really* is, but this is not the place to dwell on them.

IV. What Next?—From 'Outsight' to 'Insight'

Let us now deal with some of the issues raised by the participants in 'Values System' programmes after being presented with the preceding thoughts:

(a) 'The interpretation of the individual in terms of defilements, impurity, slavery and all that projects him or her in a very negative, pessimistic light. This is a feature of Indian thought.'

This view, aired by some participants, has its academic proponents too. It may, however, be said that viewing the individual so is neither pessimistic nor negative. It is a statement of *fact*. We may not enjoy looking at our ugly face in the mirror, yet it *is* there. Introspection being a big casualty of the exteriorized, high-speed, gadget-choked modern life-style, this ostrich-like mentality is understandable, though not pardonable.

But does the theory described above stop at this picture of the individual? What about *Shivoham* then? What about the Gita's testimony about SELF:[15]

> *Nainam chhindanti shastrani, nainam dahati pavakah,*
> *Na chainam kledantya-apoh, na shoshayati marutah;*

that is, weapons cannot cleave it, nor the fire burn, nor do waters drench it, nor the wind dry?

Here is the clue: while being totally objective and ruthless towards the empirical self or *vyavaharika vyaktitwa* as it is, man is simultaneously offered the most powerful and grand conception about his true Being, his Essence, his Reality, his Truth—the *poorna* SELF. If the word optimistic is at all permissible in this context, can any other view of human personality surpass this in optimism?

(2)   A related question is often asked: 'if the SELF is our true personality, how is it that we do not perceive it? It must be a figment of the imagination'.

Let us relate here a brief *pauranic* tale. Once, when the earth abounded with tremendous evil forces personified by the demon Hiranyaksha, the Gods urged Lord Vishnu to incarnate himself into an earthly being and annihilate the demon. The Lord agreed and assumed the form of a *varaha* (boar), descended to earth, and completed his task. But lo! He did not return to Heaven. The Gods were perplexed and approached Shiva for help. He understood, and in turn descended to earth. There he discovered that the Lord had married, and was moving around in muck with a litter of pigs. Sometimes the *varaha* would allow the pigs to fondly trample on his body, at other times he would be found sniffing around, snorting and grovelling in the muck with his mate. The dazed Shiva asked the boar: 'What's all this Lord! Have you forgotten that you must return to Heaven? Your job here is done. Let's go.' The boar gave a grunt and continued with his pleasures accompanied by his mate and litter, and would not do Shiva's bidding. Shiva, in desperation hurled his trident hard into the body of the boar. In a flash the Lord emerged from the smashed body, smiling and effulgent, and repaired to Heaven.

What psychological message does this convey? Even Lord Vishnu can forget his true identity, his real SELF, and suffer the *maya* or illusion of earthly, empirical, sullied satisfactions. What then of the ordinary mortal? Why should this net of illusion then be cast on humanity? The Vedantist would reply: just as a trainer in athletics would put up hurdles or benchmarks before his trainee to enable him to aim higher and better and thus excel himself, so does the Supreme Creative Consciousness or Intelligence interpose this *maya* merely as a hurdle before human consciousness as a challenge to pierce and cross over. Of course this explanation presupposes that one is ready to discard the mechanical, purposeless theory of creation, and to adopt the view that the entire Universe is a play of purposive, goal-directed network of Consciousness symbols. Just as the trainer wishes his trainee well while being tough with him, so does the Supreme Godhead in relation to man—because of all creation, it is man who is endowed with organized, reflective consciousness and intelligence, unlike the instinctive intelligence of a tiger or the undeveloped mental system of a tree.[16]

This story also conveys that in each of us two selves exist: the lowly *varaha* self and the exalted Vishnu SELF. The latter is the true being, but remains shut and encased within the former. The purpose of human life is to unveil this Vishnu SELF.

(3) The next question which often follows is: 'If this be the nature of the superordinate goal of SELF, what happens to ambition, progress, social change and economic development? The world will stop and die.'

This question suffers from two infirmities: it jumps the gun too soon and turns the focus away to the externals when the question of values must start with unfailing attention to the internal. The sad truth, the glaring fact is that it is the contemporary notions of progress, social change and the like which are driving humanity towards destroying this earth. It is the technologically-fuelled greed of man which is causing all kinds of lethal distortions in our eco-system. It is the purely materially-inspired motto of development which is driving the educated élite towards a schizophrenic existence. It is ambition which is rearing its ugly head through unhealthy competition in all spheres of life. Yet we still rationalize this kind of ambition as the route to excellence. It is the pseudo-equalizing (because it is downward) aspect of social change which is causing anarchy in all kinds of institutions. All this is squarely due to the conditioned, empirical, *vyavaharika*, secular, insecure personality of man romping on the world-stage. The Kaurava-self is in, the Pandava-SELF out. So, the worry voiced in this question is baseless. With the SELF slowly returning to the front stage, everything will fall into place correctly, harmoniously. Besides, this return journey of the SELF is a long one, a quiet one. Toynbee (1976) is worth listening to at this stage:[17]

- What I mean by self-mastery is the conquest of desire pertaining to man's lesser self in the course of integrating the lesser self with universal life.
- The individual self is alienated from the universal self by greed. This greed is a desire to exploit the universe for the individual self's purposes; the converse of greed is compassion.

And Tagore (1913) is pure inspiration when he warns us:[18]

... man's individuality is not his highest truth; there is that in him which is universal; ...

When the individual man in us chafes against the lawful rule of the universal man we become morally small, and we must suffer.

(4) Another difficulty posed by participants is: 'All this talk about SELF could be very good for individual salvation. What will this do, however, to team-work, cooperation, trust and the like within organizations? One may become more self-centred in pursuit of SELF and thus harm the organization.'

This doubt apparently has much merit but springs from an inadequate comprehension of the SELF, and hence is untenable. It is now time to clearly grasp yet another fundamental principle: differentiation and separation pertain only to our empirical, *vyavaharika* selves; the trans-empirical, *parmarthika* SELVES constitute unity. It is this one SELF which Toynbee has spoken of as the universal self. Since, as mentioned earlier, it is undifferentiated Consciousness or SELF or Intelligence or Energy which differentiates itself into all forms and shapes—from the amoeba to the human—the intrinsic, inviolate *fact* of original unity is always there in the background. Just as a potter lifts successive lumps of clay from the *same* mass, and turns out a whole *variety* of items on his wheel, so is the truth with this manifest Universe and all it contains. So, the task of realizing SELF-hood implies undoing the present conditioning based on differentiated, and hence adversarially-related, selves within us. This is the vital theoretical implication for organizational values like team-work and the like.

In this context we may reflect on the word 'individual'. The correct sense derives from the idea of an entity which cannot be divided, i.e. in-dividual. However, when modern personality development theory speaks of individuation, personal growth and so on, it is 'dividuation' which receives the boost—commonly implying even stronger entrenchment in our lesser selves. This obviously erodes team spirit, cooperation ... because this self has to justify itself primarily on limitations and boundaries: an infinite, boundless, all-encompassing self-perception is its antithesis. Yet in the growing awareness of the latter lies the long-term and true answer to trust, sharing, etc. Of this Vivekananda says:[19]

We are not individuals yet. We are struggling towards individuality, and that is the Infinite, that is the real nature of man.... When he can say, 'I am in everything, in everybody, I am in all lives, I am the Universe', then alone comes the state of fearlessness.... No Infinity can be divided ... It is the same one undivided unity for ever, and this is the individual man, the Real Man.

(Obviously Vivekananda has used the phrases 'apparent man' and 'Real Man' in exactly the same sense implied by the empirical, lower, *vyavaharika*, secular self and trans-empirical, higher, *paramarthika*, spiritual SELF.) It is, therefore, encouraging to hear a modern physicist like David Bohm and Renée Weber, a scholar of philosophy, talk about the problems of prevailing individuality in terms of 'rampant ego-centredness', 'ego-centredness centres on the self-image which is an illusion', 'impossible to have true individuality except when grounded in the whole', and the like,[20] echoing after several decades the views of Vivekananda and Tagore.

From this vantage point we may also re-assess the two popular 'needs' in the theory of motivation: 'self-esteem' and 'self-actualization'. If it is the 'apparent self' of Vivekananda, or the 'lesser self' of Toynbee, or the 'boar-self' of mythology which demands esteem and actualization opportunities, then this pursuit will almost invariably end up in the blind alleys of lower-order values or dis-values—no matter what modern motivation theory may try to propagate. The superior spiritual or farther heights of man are attempted to be understood in terms of his biological roots. This is theoretically false and destined to fail—the higher cannot be explained by the lower. Thus, long ago William James, the father of American Psychology, had devised a convenient formula:[21]

$$\text{Self-Esteem} = \frac{\text{Success}}{\text{Pretensions}}$$

Given a certain level of pretensions, higher success should increase self-esteem. How do we, in such a case, cope with the 'rampant ego-centredness' most likely to occur, as just cited in the Weber–Bohm dialogue? Of course, given a certain success rate, reduction of pretensions can also increase self-esteem. Could this be a better option than the first—by the criterion of egotism? Unfortunately it is too deceptively simplistic a formulation to reveal much practical wisdom in self-management. In any case, all self-esteem based on external feedback, signals, recognition— which is generally the case—is quite vulnerable and insecure, and ego-centredness becomes the automatic internal defence against such vulnerability springing from dependency. Thus, reporting recently on the crisis of social values in the USA, Bremner informs us that many school educators are arguing for breaking with the prevailing doctrine which makes teachers believe that their main task is to foster 'self-esteem' amongst the students and ensure that they have no negative feelings about themselves.[22] Here once again is proof against the academic stance of motivation theorists, challenging the justification of stoking egocentricity in the name of satisfying the needs of self-esteem—so long as it is the lower, empirical self which is the object of esteem. Humility is essential for an individual to acknowledge his many and frequent short-comings, and also to prevent himself from becoming swollen-headed when there is some recognition or success. These processes are more vital than those of lightly glossing over lapses and getting over-greedy about praise, etc. SELF-esteem has to be instilled, as also SELF-actualization (strictly speaking SELF-realization). It is only the SELF which is worth holding in esteem, by slowly renouncing the self, seeking liberation from the self. Team-work, dignity, sharing, cooperation, harmony, trust and the like are grounded in the SELF, not in the self.

To nurse and cherish self-respect by being honest in word and deed, by giving one's due share of effort, by being upright in means towards ends, by being contented and charitable is, however, an altogether different kind of self-esteem. The greater danger today is of harbouring false pride in the name of self-esteem. It is a moot question, as is suggested by Blanchard and Peale, whether it is self-esteem which leads to ethical life.[23] Ethics, at the base, is a strong spiritual feeling, flourishing essentially on unselfishness and ab-sence of greed. The self is always fragile by such criteria. So, often a mask of integrity is assumed, supported by crafty intelligence. We could therefore agree more with Blanchard and Peale only if SELF-esteem is substituted for self-esteem. Then we have a universally valid principle to sustain ethical behaviour. For the self a sense of guilt is as necessary, if not more so, than pride.

(5) Yet another frequent question on the theme of 'self v. SELF' is: 'Will not the feeling of *poornatwa*, which is suggested as the defining characteristic of SELF, aggravate arrogance and egotism, and thus mar the quality of work-life?'

This doubt clearly needs to be dispelled. In practice, the

internalization of *poornatwa* is meant to prevent or reduce suc-
cumbing to temptations of various kinds, provocations from varied
quarters, denials from different sources. A very large proportion of
our low order value responses occur because we lack the inner
strength and capacity to absorb and sublimate these negative
experiences. Let us offer a list of situations, as examples only, to
show where the feeling of *poornatwa* within can help us from
falling a prey to mental impurities:

- A colleague Mr Y has spoken ill about Mr X behind his back,
  to the common boss. X wants to hit back with equal might.

- A large proportion of cash advance can be easily appropriated
  by Mr A on the strength of a fictitious voucher.

- Mr B knows of a particular vulnerability in Mr Y's dealings,
  and is inclined to use this secret to put Y's career in jeopardy
  through jealousy.

- Mr M has got a certain facility which Mr N also covets but has
  been denied so far. N now whips up the employee association
  to bring a charge of discrimination against M's boss.

- A boss suppresses the original idea of a subordinate and
  appropriates the credit to himself.

- A departmental head is assumed to be manipulating faster
  promotions for his own subordinates. Another departmental
  head begins to retaliate by concocting a strong case for his own
  subordinate colleagues.

- The expected promotion has not come Mr P's way. He is
  downcast and work has lost all meaning for him.

- The superior has praised Mr Q's work in the presence of
  several people. Mr Q is very puffed up.

It is in such situations that the awareness of inner *poornatwa* can
prevent the lowering of one's consciousness, and hence of mental
purity. Proper perspective can be restored and dignity returned to
the work-situation. Often the feeling of *poornatwa* even within one
person in the game may halt the downward spiral. Otherwise,
deficit-driven exchanges by both the parties aggravate the process
of deterioration in values-orientation. Thus, *poornatwa* has to be

internalized and invoked as the antidote to deficit-driven prompt-ings in our behaviour. Without cultivating this true inner working, calling oneself *aham brahmasmi* is arrant nonsense. To be petty, greedy and mean within at every turn, and yet utter *aham brahmasmi* is blasphemy, and is warned against by all the great masters.

On the positive side, a feeling-level conviction about the *poor-natwa* of SELF within will always enable a leader to take a stand, announce a decision, and execute it without the kinds of fear or favour to which the externally dependent self is always prone. The process of living up to a high principle is a joy in itself—even though external sacrifices and deprivation may follow.

Collins has repeatedly urged on the leader the cultivation of a *broader* and *enlarged* self-concept, *freedom* from his personal past, grounding in *objective* reality and a *strong* and *consistent* sense of self.[24] All this is quite correct, although significantly enough she does not speak of a heightened or deepened consciousness of self. But Collins' writing seems to offer no theory to support the understanding and cultivation of these essential attributes of leadership. The theory of self v. SELF described above, however, provides all the vital clues to this task of transformation. Thus, it is only when one can burst open the shell of the clouded, insecure, deficit-driven self-concept (the *varaha* self), and stand on the illumined, surplus-inspired, secure SELF-concept (the Vishnu SELF), that the pure mind can begin to see reality as it is. One can then be free from one's hang-ups and conditioning, and be sure of a consistent self-concept which refuses to be at the mercy of the see-saw of empirical experiences. Moreover, there is no hint about any practical experiential process to attain this consistent, enlarged self-concept anywhere in her exposition. This is symptomatic of all leadership and motivational writings. We may therefore once more suggest that Indian psychology is indeed *practical* transformational psychology because it rests on a perfect *theoretical* framework.

Brouwer has discussed the issue of transitional conflicts in self-concept, e.g. father v. businessman; heading a small enterprise v. running a fast-growing outfit; a sales manager v. a marketing director and so on. He rightly urges self-appraising introspection, self-examination, etc. to lay the groundwork for insight in order to handle such transitions competently, maturely. For obtaining such insights or new perceptions he mentions the avenues of reading, observing, studying, attending conferences and meetings, and membership of clubs.[25] We are, however, concerned here not so much with the secondary subject of role transitions, as with the primary one of performing the role that one already has at a given point in time. Thus, by beginning at the beginning, it appears that Brouwer and his ilk do not appreciate that to gain 'insights' one must be able to go 'inside' one's self. The recipe for insights offered by Brouwer is a purely exteriorizing package, inducing more cerebral overload. One remains stuck with the muddied empirical self which by nature is incapable of detachment (*nirliptatā*). Without detachment there can be no insights or wisdom. The *practical* psychological processes of deep rhythmic breathing, emptying and stilling the mind by slow degrees and such other steps are indispensable for standing above or reaching below the messy empirical self. Only then can it be seen in its totality. The progressively filterless, silent and authentic mind can then transmit its own cues and feedback, with little need for conferences, meetings, etc. But even these can be of better use if the *prior* task of mind-stilling is carried out faithfully as a daily discipline. The next chapter will produce some evidence from managers about this.

Moreover, with a growing feel of the higher SELF and its conscious invocation during mind-stilling sessions (via *ishtam* and other means), it begins to penetrate our normal consciousness. With its light the lower or empirical self then starts to work its way with greater balance and maturity than before, through both present roles and role transitions.

V. The Indian Manager on self v. Self

A simple questionnaire (see appendix-II to this chapter) used to be given to each participant in a wide variety of management development programmes—both on our campus and within organizations. If the programmes were on 'Values-System'—partly or wholly—then the instrument was handed over before uttering a word on the subject and responses collected immediately. The profile of the sample of 460 responses is included in appendix-III below.

The first item required the participant to write five short sentences about himself or herself, each beginning with 'I am ...'.

Three typical modes of self-description emerged:
  (a) *Non-Evaluative*: Thus one respondent writes—

> I am an engineer,
> I am a manager,
> I am a father,
> I am an Indian,
> I am married.

This example is representative of this category. The total number in this category was 91.
  (b) *Critically Evaluative*: Here is a set of rather strongly critical (except one) self-appraisal statements from one person—

> I am short-tempered,
> I am honest,
> I am a miser at heart,
> I don't try to improve myself.

This set of responses from one person is also fairly typical of this class which usually combine some critical statements with a few positive ones. Taking even one self-critical statement to constitute a response in this category, the frequency was 36.
  (c) *Positively Evaluative*: Here is the set of such statements from one participant—

> I am sincere,
> I am hardworking,
> I am not selfish,
> I am helpful,
> I am honest.

The total number of responses in this category was 317. This figure includes those responses also which were of (a)-type, i.e. non-evaluative for as many as four statements, but had at least one positive statement about the individual. There were 16 non-responses to item 1.

The first broad indication from this frequency-distribution is that less than 10 per cent of our sample thought critically or negatively—even marginally—about themselves. By contrast, 317/444, i.e. 71 per cent of those who responded to item 1 thought positively about themselves. In fact, one sub-group of responses in this majority category produced a set of statements of the following exalted kind (just one instance):

> I am pure consciousness,
> I am potentially divine,
> I am inseparable from nature,
> I am a tool in the hands of the Creator,
> I am engrossed in Maya but at one with the Creator.

Now, the big question that stares us in the face is: if such a large proportion of our sample members think so positively about themselves, then how are we to explain an equal proportion of managers replying to another question in the same setting that the proportion of 'values-weak: skills-strong' people constitute the single largest majority group of employees (see chapter 1)? Two hypotheses may be suggested:

(a)   We all are constitutionally prone to highlighting the defects of others while making short work of their strengths. Exactly the reverse happens when we assess ourselves. So, what worth introspection, self-appraisal and so on?

(b)   Through the positively-evaluating self-statements people are merely projecting their idealized selves, neither knowing the gap between their real selves and the ideal, nor appreciating the *sadhana* required to bridge the gap.

The next aspect is one of deeper theoretical interest. It may be evident to some readers that the question was phrased with only two words 'I am', and left at that in order to elicit data to demonstrate the key fact that each one of us sees oneself as an agglomeration of multiple characteristics and attributes, e.g. an engineer, a father, sincere, God-fearing, happy, frustrated and so on. This kind of self-concept—positive or negative or merely descriptive—is what Indian psychology calls the *upadhic* self, or the apparent man. What is this 'I' to which is attributed all these *upadhis*—good, bad, neutral—of our empirical self? Logically, it must be separate from the *upadhis* which cling to it, e.g. air by itself does not smell, yet appears to be foul- or sweet-smelling because of some *upadhic* association. If the air loses its original perception of odourless identity, and regards itself as malodorous or fragrant, it is a wrong self-concept—*maya*. The *upadhis* make us panicky and fragile from within. Yet we chase after them. That again is *maya*.

Item 2 in the questionnaire sought to obtain a little more insight into this dilemma of self-concept. Excluding the 11 non-responses,

225 people favoured the idea that 'I am because I think', while 224 opted for 'I think because I am'. This pattern clearly reflects that our sample is quite confused on this dimension of self-concept (though not to be blamed). In truth, 'thinking' is an *effect* of the *cause* that is 'I'. So, to interpret the cause in terms of effect is an imperfection fraught with grave implications. It is because 'I' is self-existent in the first place that, among many human functions, thinking also is possible—this indeed is the theory.

Question 3 had jumbled up the set of five dis-identification and re-identification statements shown in section III above, and re-framed them to suit the forced-choice technique adopted in the instrument. There is a correct combination of responses chosen: namely $(a_1, b_2, c_1, d_1, e_1)$. From our sample 56 individuals, i.e. nearly 13 per cent, responded correctly. It is not possible to say whether they arrived at the right choice-set through prior know-ledge or intuitively. The first possibility is likely to be negligible. The single largest frequency choice-set, in other words the most common view held, was yielded by the combination $(a_1, b_2, c_1, d_2, e_1)$ with 211 individuals.

For items 3a to 3e, the separate responses were:

	Frequency		Frequency
a_1	360	d_1	131
a_2	82	d_2	313
NR	18	NR	16
b_1	49	e_1	340
b_2	398	e_2	106
NR	13	NR	14
c_1	343		
c_2	101	[*NB* : NR	= no response]
NR	16		

This implies that the self-concept is far too frequently held in terms of 'I have ...'. If there is an answer which chooses 'I am', even then it is as much in terms of the instruments as in terms of 'pure-consciousness'. At times more than one item has been scored for 'I am', including item (d). What is this 'I' then which 'have' the attributes and instrumentalities like body, senses and so on? If an academic were to say 'I am Ph.D.', or a new house-owner were to assert 'I am the house', surely we would laugh at such statements. In both cases 'I' is distinct from the items it 'owns'—the Ph.D. and the house. The 'self to SELF' journey implies a gradual inner awakening to this vital distinction—the *owner* and the *owned*—within a more comprehensive self-concept.

Why is this awareness useful and essential? Simply because when, through practice, an individual is able to *feel* that he or she '*has* a mind', but '*is* not the mind' the person is on the road to self-mastery. He or she can then dictate to the mind, and not be dictated by it. The SELF is the autonomous, luminous anchor which will keep the drifting, chaotic mind in place. The mind we now use is but one *upadhi* which is prone to inanities and pettinesses. So is the relationship of the SELF with the other instrumentalities/*upadhi*s. That is why Shankaracharya has sung in one of the stanzas of *Atmashatakam*—that quintessential song of Vedantic psychology—

> *Na me dwesha ragau, na me lobha mohau;*
> *Mado naive me, naiva matsarya bhavah;*
> *Na dharma na cha-artho, na kamo na mokshah;*
> *Chidananda rupah Shivoham, shivoham.*

That is, one's attachments and aversions, greeds and infatuations, pride and jealousy, one's aspirations for the *chaturvarga*s (four goals of human life)—all these are truly separate from, really do not belong to, the SELF which is already, in fact, *poorna* like Shiva. With even a little resonance of this mood, our inner being could experience the thrill of joy, hope, freedom and purity, and this transformation is the key to sensitivity to and sustenance of *shreya* values.

Mrs Rhys Davids has been amongst the earliest (1914) Western scholars to have clearly grasped the Indian distinction between self and SELF:

(a)   We [westerners] cannot rid ourselves of muddle in our idiom: 'my self, my soul, my spirit'. Everywhere this *darkens our vision*. We do not see that self*, soul*, spirit* is not 'of me', 'mine', but is just I.* We do not see that the self, soul, spirit is the *one and only reality*.'[26] [Emphasis added.]

(b)   If there be a question of property at all, it is the visible live man: the beminded body, *which is the property of the self,* the atman,* the purusa,* and not the other way round, no less than is any tool or apparatus the property of its owner, the user'.[27]

---

* She uses these words in the sense of SELF.

It is not unlikely that she might have read Vivekananda's 1896 lectures on *Jnanyoga* in London! And again, as recently as 1976, yet another British scholar–savant—Bede Griffiths (mentioned earlier)—speaks on the same theme, with more direct insight than academic finesse:[28]

It is only in modern man that the problem of suffering has become acute. He has cut himself off from the Self, with its awareness of transcendent Reality, and concentrated his powers of reflective consciousness on his ego and its environment, and so is exposed to all the terrors of a self-centred consciousness...

As for the remedy, Griffiths offers the hope to modern man that, if he were to choose, this very sharp reflective consciousness can be made to trace its journey back to the Self, and thus save himself and others from agony and pain.

Returning to the questionnaire, all the remaining items are of an applied, day-to-day experience-related kind—through all of which the self-concept permeates. The response pattern to item 4 is, however, contradictory to that observed for item 3. Option 4(b), i.e. 'When man dies, it is the soul which leaves the body' has been chosen as the correct statement by 419 sample members, as against only 32 for option (a), no response being 9. We believe it is the traditional lore prevalent in India that the *atman* never dies which has prompted the overwhelmingly correct choice made here. The terminology and phrasing of item 3 must have struck nearly all the respondents as being unfamiliar. Hence the mix-up in responses to that item. However, there is no need to assume that the correct choice in item 4 implies any depth of 'feeling' in the matter, and corresponding reflection of it in value-oriented behaviour.

Similarly, the correct choice (b and c) in item 5 has also been overwhelming—454. Our comment for item 4 applies to this too.

But confusion returns once more in the response patterns to items 6 (sickness), 7 (distress), and 9 (personal beauty). The responses are divided almost 50:50 between the underlying issues of 'I have' v. 'I am', body, mind and senses raised in the three items respectively.

The response to item 8 is, however, more unequivocal: 313 have chosen as correct the statement 'I want success in life', whereas only 136 have opted for 'My mind wants success in life'. Now, this wanting success in life is called ambition, but all ambitions in the empirical realm are indeed deficit-driven. It is an unpalatable insight, yet it is true. It is only one ambition—that of realizing the transcendent Reality, the SELF—which is a sure neutralizer of the decline in value-oriented behaviour. In fact, theoretically, it is the mind of the lower self, *vyavaharika vyaktitwa*, which hungers for success in the physical world, and fights and bleeds in the process. The only non-competitive route to success, ambition and fulfilment is the search for inner *poornatwa*. While this search progresses, the empirical self begins to function in ways which we all generally wish to see in the behaviour of others towards us. People may retort: this *poorna* SELF is abstract, unseen, hence useless. But so are mathematics, quantum physics, and much else. Are they useless? 'Concrete' space launches or nuclear weapons, for instance, are founded on these 'abstracts'. This is equally true of man's inner life and its growth. The ability to live and sustain more by the subtle and the unseen than by the gross and the seen should be beneficial to the individual and the society. (We mean here people of the kind who might be reading this book, and not those who are hungry and utterly deprived.)

Responses to the last item on 'sleep', however, like those to items 4 and 5, fall preponderantly along the correct choice: 323 say that it is the body, senses, etc. which fall 'asleep' during sleep. Once again this apparent rectitude does not appear to make much real sense in terms of the actual feeling-level self-concept.

In sum then, the data presented in this section show that our managers and administrators, as much as anybody else, are pretty confused in their self-concepts at the base level. Beneath the changing, superimposed roles in their careers they harbour conflicting internalizations. Hardly any education exists regarding SELF. Hence the fruitless toil of Sisyphus in striving to cultivate higher, positive values within the soil of the self itself. The breakthrough from pettiness to dignity, via pure mind, needs dedicated attention to the SELF.

VI. CONCLUSION: THE TRYST WITH SELF FOR TEAMWORK

As already mentioned in section IV, amongst the most cherished, yet wanting, 'organizational' values in India today is team-work. The real answer to this gap is to develop the inner conviction and feel about one's true identity to be the SELF, and not self. Work from the plane of SELF-perception shall lead us to see unity in diversity. For, this SELF in all, the *swarupah* of all is one; only the self, the *rupah* is differentiated in each. As Tagore says, the self is prone to exercising 'negative freedom',[29] and that is the graveyard of cooperation, sharing, trust, etc. Tagore's own answers to this predicament are:

(a) The *finite aspect* of the self is conscious of its separateness, and there it is ruthless in its attempt to have more distinction than all others. But in its *infinite aspect* its wish is to gain that harmony which leads to its perfection and not its mere aggrandizement.[30]

(b) ... consciousness of personality *begins* with the feeling of separateness from all, and has its *culmination* in the *feeling of unity* with all.[31]

[Emphasis added.]

He, therefore, prays that we proceed to cultivate the pulsating feel of the universal, the infinite, which is seeking consummation through each of us—whose uniqueness is but one pole of the whole.[32] The former is the SELF, the latter self. SELF is unity (not uniformity), self is diversity. This kind of extended psychic positioning seems to be indispensable to combat pettiness. It is this growing *anubhuti*, in ever-extending circles, which should become the real firm basis of team-work and the like. Besides, we are assured by Tagore, as much as by our seers of the past, that man is born with this urge for the SELF, or universal, or infinite (or shall we say divine?) built into him. Only the seal has to be removed, so to say, to let it flower. This process requires first, profounder intellectual clarity about the self-concept by getting acquainted with the thoughts of Tagores, Aurobindos and their ilk; and second, the practical experiential *sadhana* of the kind suggested earlier.

Frances Vaughn* has recently made the point with good effect that the 'trans-personal self' is an embodiment of 'values which transcend egocentric concerns.[33] The 'trans-personal self' is the SELF written about here.

We appreciate and rejoice in this 'reinvention of the wheel' sort of phenomenon in the West, seen against the backdrop of what even our modern seers have been telling the world since the 1890s. However, we wish to add that the expression 'trans-empirical self'

---

* She is an exponent of what is now called 'fourth-force' psychology or 'trans-personal psychology' in America, formally dated from 1969.

appears to convey the intended sense more accurately than 'trans-personal self'. The state of awareness, *anubhuti* of the SELF, etc. is very personal, yet transcends the egocentric, petty empirical personality.

It ought to be acknowledged too that there have been profound western thinkers, much ahead of the fourth-force psychologists, who had drawn our attention to the psychology of SELF in India. Thus, Max Müller had written with full approval in his preface to the *Sacred Books of The East* about the existence of the *Atman* or Self beyond the *Aham* or Ego.[34] Similarly, Keyserling had also spoken about the continuous transformation of the Ego into the Self—the latter being man's intrinsic personality.[35]

Mention by Tagore of 'negative freedom', and by Vaughn of 'ego-centric concerns', prompts us to put a practical aspect of oriental (and Indian) psychology in the right perspective. There are too many 'don'ts' and 'nays' in Indian scriptures complain many learned commentators on India—in management as well as other disciplines. This is one source of their conclusion that Indian thought adopts a conformist[36] or passive[37] view of man. Now, this is quite a superficial inference, mainly because such empirically-oriented writers abstain from correctly perceiving the 'other' view of man which abounds in Indian thought—that he is born free, *poorna*. Only the veil—a veil which is no doubt thick and heavy—has to be rent. Secondly, while love, freedom, compassion, charity, and so on are highly positive values, yet they are, at this moment, only ideals for each of us. On the other hand, the here-and-now reality is that envy, anger, selfishness, crookedness and the like grip us within their iron-embrace. Is it not therefore honest, practical and essential that the process of transformation first begins with loosening the grip of these 'negative freedoms'? The mirror has to be cleaned before it can reflect the bright moon within our room. Disciplining the lower self for the higher SELF is not conformity. Neither is frank appraisal of the inanities of the empirical self pessimism. After all, the *poorna* SELF has in it all the optimism of the world.

In a recent new year's eve goodwill address, the Resident Director of a highly successful and large private enterprise in Eastern India spoke frankly to his employees about the growing 'small-mindedness' in all aspects of organizational life and re-peatedly exhorted them to become 'good men', 'big-hearted', 'big-minded' and so on. He ended by declaring: 'To my mind the target of developing "Big Men", "Better Men", and therefore, Better Managers is the most important of all.' In this chapter we have held up the truth before such managers that their SELF is indeed Big and Better. Also, some hints on practical processes to regain the lost awareness of one's constitutional SELF-hood have been offered to them here (and in other chapters). For the Resident Director's fervent pleas for Big-ness the best response seems to lie in such concepts and processes.

To conclude, we might in passing recall Jung's concept of 'individuation'. He described individuation as a process of differentiation with the objective of the development of the individual.[38] This is in sharp contrast to what Tagore has said. Although Jung predicts that individuation should ultimately lead to broader and more intense collective relationships,[39] this in reality rarely occurs. Probably what happens more commonly is that it is those persons who somehow possess an inborn sense of expansive, universal other-relatedness, also tend to 'individuate' in willed and disciplined isolation with concrete inner growth objectives. Our Tagores and Gandhijis and others seem to testify to this. We are not however denying entirely the individuation–unity sequence. Yet we think that the Jungian concept is perhaps theoretically flawed because its starting point is not the feel of metaphysical unity—the harmony in the Infinite. The individuation/differentiation idea has to be understood in the light of the truth that the empirical human is an entity in temporary transition—from unity, through differentiation, back to unity. Jacobs has pointed out clearly the difference between 'individuation' and the Indian idea of ultimate healthy growth of the individual. He even goes on to say that sensitive minds—both in the East and West—hold individuation to be imprisonment.[40] We therefore think that the Indian view of SELF-centred *ekatmanubuti* is a safer avenue for our journey towards teamwork.

A FEW THINGS ABOUT YOURSELF

1) Write five different short sentences about what you are, each starting with 'I am ...'

2) Which of the two statements seems to be correct? (Tick one box.):
   a) I am because I think ☐
      or
   b) I think because I am ☐

3) Which option in the following pairs do you prefer? (Tick the preferred box.)
   a_1) I have a body ☐, or
   a_2) I am the body ☐
   b_1) I am the senses ☐, or
   b_2) I have the senses ☐
   c_1) I have a mind ☐, or
   c_2) I am the mind ☐
   d_1) I am pure consciousness ☐, or
   d_2) I have pure consciousness ☐
   e_1) I have an intellect ☐, or
   e_2) I am the intellect ☐

4) Which statement seems to be correct? (Tick one box.):
   a) When man dies, the body releases the soul ☐
   b) When man dies, the soul leaves the body ☐

5) When someone falls down and breaks a leg, for instance, how does he or she usually express the event? (Cross one box.)
   a) I am broken ☐
      or
   b) My leg is broken ☐

6) Which seems to be the correct statement? (Cross one box.):
   a) I am sick ☐
      or
   b) My body is sick ☐

7) Which seems to be the correct statement? (Cross one box.):
   a) My mind is distressed ☐
   b) I am distressed ☐
8) Which seems to be the correct statement? (Cross one box.):
   a) I want success in life ☐
   b) My mind wants success in life ☐
9) Which seems to be the correct statement? (Cross one box.):
   a) My senses are capativated by that beautiful person ☐
   b) I am captivated by that beautiful person ☐
10) Which of the following statements seems to be correct? (Cross one box.):
    a) During sleep I fall asleep ☐
    b) During sleep my body and senses fall asleep ☐
11) Any other comments you would like to make?
12) *Some Personal Data Please*:
    a) Age   b) Sex
    c) Qualifications   d) Mother Tongue
    e) Religion

APPENDIX–II
Total Sample Size — 460

1. *Age-wise frequency*

Upto 35	70
36 – 45	153
46 – 55	212
56 and above	25

2. *Language-wise frequency*

Bengali	90
Hindi	117
Gujarati	46
Tamil	54
Telugu	25
Malayalam	13

Punjabi	22
Kannada	41
Marathi	14
English	3
Others*	35

* (Oriya, Rajasthani, Maithili, Bhojpuri, Kashmiri, Kodava, Assamese, Sindhi, Manipuri, etc.)

3. *Profession-wise frequency*

a) Graduate (254)
   - Engineering 190
   - Science 35 } = 225
   - Commerce 3
   - Arts 26
   - MBA/CA 36

   = 291

b) Post Graduate (183)
   - Engineering 26
   - Science 40 } = 66
   - Arts 25
   - Commerce 14
   - Others (IAS/LLB/Doctor etc.) 42

c) Ph.D.   23

4. *Sex-wise frequency*

Female	8
Male	452

5. *Religion-wise frequency*

Muslim	8
Jain	3
Christian	12
Sikh	6
Hindu	431

REFERENCES

1. E. Conze, *Buddhist Texts Through The Ages* (Oxford: Bruno Cassirer, 1954), p. 52.
2. Sri Aurobindo and The Mother, *On Self-Perfection*, part I (Pondicherry: Sri Aurobindo Society, 1973), p. 20.
3. D. Hammarskjöld, *Markings* (London: Faber & Faber, 1964), p. 99.
4. Sri Aurobindo, *The Ideal of The Karmayogin* (Pondicherry: Sri Aurobindo Ashram, 1974), pp. 79–80.
5. B. Griffiths, *Return To The Centre* (London: Collins, 1987), pp. 49–50.
6. Swami Ashokananda, *Avadhuta Gita* (Madras: Sri Ramakrishna Math, 1981).
7. Swami Gambhirananda, *Katha Upanishad* (Calcutta: Advaita Ashrama, 1980), II.i. 12–3, pp. 92–3.
8. Sister Nivedita, *Siva and Buddha* (Calcutta: Udbodhan, 1981), p. 8.
9. Swami Gambhirananda, *Svetaswatara Upanishad* (Calcutta: Advaita Ashrama, 1986), verse 4.6, pp. 145–6.
10. Swami Jagadananda, *Vakyavritti of Shankaracharya* (Madras: Ramakrishna Math, 1979), pp. 10–12.
11. Swami Swahaananda, *Panchadasi of Vidyaranya Swami* (Madras: Ramakrishna Math, 1980), pp. 18–19.
12. K. Wilber, *The Atman Project* (Wheaton: Theosophical Publishing House, 1985), p. 70.
13. Swami Vivekananda, 'The Open Secret' in *Complete Works* (Calcutta: Advaita Ashrama, 1958), vol.II, p. 405.
14. B. Griffiths, *Cosmic Revelation* (London: Collins, 1983), p. 91.
15. Sri Aurobindo, *The Message of The Gita* (Pondicherry: Sri Aurobindo Ashram, 1977), verse 2.23, p. 20.
16. *Idem, The Hour of God* (Pondicherry: Sri Aurobindo Ashram, 1982), pp. 58–8.
17. A.J. Toynbee, and D. Ikeda, *Choose Life* (Delhi: Oxford University Press, 1987), pp. 316, 317.
18. Rabindranath Tagore, *Sadhana* (Delhi: Macmillan, 1988), pp. 50, 51.
19. Swami Vivekananda, 'The Real Nature of Man' in *Complete Works* (Calcutta: Advaita Ashrama, 1958), vol.II, pp. 80–1.
20. R. Weber (ed.), *Dialogues With Scientists and Sages* (London: Routledge and Kegan Paul, 1986), pp. 30–1.
21. W. James, '*The Self*' in *The Self in Social Interaction*, ed. by C. Gordon and K.J. Gergen (New York: John Wiley, 1968), vol.I, p. 45.
22. C. Bremner, 'USA Facing Crisis of Social Values', *The Statesman* (Calcutta), 3 July 1989.
23. K. Blanchard, and N.V. Peale, *The Power of Ethical Management* (New York: William Morrow & Co., 1988), p. 48.

24. E.G.C. Collins (ed.), *Executive Success: Making It in Management* (New York: John Wiley, 1983), pp. 4–11.
25. P.J.Brouwer, 'The Power to See Ourselves' in Collins, op. cit., pp. 18–25.
26. R. Davids, *The Birth of Indian Psychology and Its Development in Buddhism* (Delhi: Oriental Books Reprint Corporation, 1978), p. 26.
27. Ibid., p. 28.
28. Griffiths, *Return to The Centre*, p. 48.
29. Rabindranath Tagore, op. cit., p. 69.   30. Ibid., pp. 68–9.
31. *Idem, Personality* (Delhi: Macmillan, 1985), p. 97.
32. *Idem, Sadhana*, p. 58.
33. F. Vaughn, *The Inward Arc* (Boston: New Science Library, 1986), pp. 43–5.
34. M. Müller, *Sacred Books of the East* (Delhi: Motilal Banarasidass, 1975), p. xxx.
35. H. Keyserling, *From Suffering to Fulfilment* (London: Selwyn Blount, 1938), pp. 307–8.
36. H.J. Leavitt, 'Educating our MBA's', *California Management Review*, Spring 1989, p. 48.
37. E.H.R. Schein, 'Coming to a New Awareness of Organizational Cultures', *Sloan Management Review*, Winter 1984, p. 5.
38. C. Jung, quoted in *International Encyclopaedia of Psychiatry, Psychology, Psychoanalysis and Neurology* (New York: Van Nostrand, 1977), vol.10, p. 121.
39. Ibid., p. 122.
40. H. Jacobs, *Western Psychotherapy and Hindu Sadhana* (London: George Allen & Unwin, 1961), pp. 118–19, p. 159.

4

MANAGEMENT-BY-VALUES PROGRAMMES
A Qualitative Appraisal

We now offer a simple, matter-of-fact account of our endeavours to carry the message of management-by-values, grounded in the Indian ethos (evolved and perfected roughly between 1500 BC and AD 500), into contemporary Indian organizations. This chapter presents a review of our efforts to launch the deep-structure values of chapter 1, the ethico-moral paradigm of chapter 2, and the pettiness-to-dignity ascent of chapter 3 into mainstream management practices. No startling revelations of dramatic transformations should be expected, nor a parade of statistical artistry and other artillery of rigorous academic research. It is a straightforward running commentary, mostly letting the participants do the speaking, on events as they have occurred so far. We have chosen to respond to the more urgent need of applying to good use the ideas and methods which have stood the test of human development efforts for centuries, rather than await corroboration anew by modern management and sociological research, much of which seems to be form without content, losing precious time in consequence.

I. The Panorama

While research at IIM-C on values within the Indian ethos had begun around 1977–78, the process of exposing these concepts and principles to both industry and our students (as a second year option) commenced in mid-1983. Since then till about the end of 1990, over a hundred in-house programmes have been conducted, covering almost 2000 participants ranging from the Chief Executive down to managers two or three levels below. Here is a list of the organizations which have so far opened their doors to these progammes:

- Bhilwara Group of Industries (Delhi).
- Hindustan Copper Ltd. (Malanjkhand).
- Indian Petrochemicals Corporation Ltd. (Baroda).
- Bharat Electronics Ltd. (Bangalore and Chandigarh).
- TELCO (Jamshedpur).
- Indian Oil Corporation Ltd. (Delhi and Plants–Refineries Division).
- Indian Oil Corporation Ltd. (Pipelines Division).
- Shri Ram Fibres Ltd. (Madras).
- Godrej & Boyce Ltd. (Bombay).
- International Crops Research Institute (Hyderabad).
- TISCO (Jamshedpur).
- Bharat Heavy Plates and Vessels Ltd. (Vizag.).
- Oil India Ltd. (Duliajan).
- Hindustan Paper Corporation Ltd. (Calcutta).
- Reserve Bank of India (Bombay).
- Bharat Heavy Electricals Ltd.

Of these seventeen organizations, the first eleven have or had engaged themselves in fairly long-term (two years or more), widespread educational programmes on values. Several batches of managers have been put through a package of multiple modules (to be described below) over a stretch of six to nine months. Within the next six, one to three programmes only have been conducted. In eight of the seventeen organizations, the value-orientation programmes were launched at the initiative of the Chief Executive, or the next immediate person in command. In the rest the initiative sprang from the Heads of HRD or Training or Personnel.

II.   THE THREE MODULES: CONCEPTS AND PRACTICE

(A)   The first module is a broad-spectrum one, exploring the basic, universal roots of 'performance effectiveness', held for three successive forenoons (9 am—1.30 pm). The framework of this module has been shown on page 1 of chapter 3. The nucleus of this module is PURE MIND. It is 'pure mind' which is the basis of values-based effectiveness. The participants are repeatedly made conscious that all the ideas and principles of transformation discussed in this and the following modules have to be focused on oneself. 'First person singular'—not we, you, they, he or she and so on—has to remain the basis of internalization. Mind-purification (*chittashuddhi*) is understood and explained in terms of seven major notes of Indian thought:

- From lower self to Higher SELF
- Dis-identification and re-identification
- The Theory of *Guna* Dynamics (or Psychological 'substances')
- The Theory of *Karma* (or Cause and Effect)
- The Theory of *Samskaras* (or Residual Impressions)
- The Theory and Method of Work
- The Giving Model of Motivation.

Since all these igredients of module one have been presented elaborately in one of the earlier books by the author,[1] and is to some extent covered in various parts of this volume too, they are not being repeated here.

Each day of the module takes the participants through two practice sessions. By the end of the third day they learn, through six rounds of practice, an experiential process for *internalizing* the critical idea of each major theme listed above. By the time the first module culminates in the *mind-stilling* exercise, as we call it, the following steps* have been taken and introduced gradually over the three days:

i) Slow, deep and full breathing through alternate nostrils, in and out over 10–15 cycles, without holding the breath;

ii learning to breathe in a *sattwa guna* which is pure and is to be sought, and to breathe out a *rajo* or *tamo guna* which pollutes and hinders the mind;

iii) breathing normally, but the mind continuing to closely observe the gentle rhythmic breathing process; a very enjoyable, harmonious feeling results;

iv) trying to experience a feeling of serene void in the brain-space (clear blue-sky imagery helps); a deep sense of release and freedom results;

---

* The lights in the room are switched off, and fans or airconditioners are also stopped to provide greater silence. The steps are announced by us at a measured pace.

v) trying to open up the body-bottle, as it were, at the top of the head, and aspiring for the Universal Energy/Intelligence/ Consciousness to descend into one's physical and nervous frame (blooming lotus, morning sun imagery); this also helps to expand one's caged-in awareness into the Infinite, and thus to gradually overcome mental constrictions and pettiness;

vi) shifting the awareness down inside the psychic heart-centre (the inner space corresponding to the small cavity at the centre of the chest), and then silently reflecting upon and assimilating clearly the set of four dis-identification and one re-identification statements (p. 69), relating respectively to the *variables* and the *constant* in our being, in that space;

vii) concentrating on a luminous core or sphere (or one's *ishtam*) comprising a pure, serene and radiant light—that is the true, higher SELF, one's purest, indestructible essence, and trying to wholly identify with it.

To perform this entire exercise with real feel and meaning, a minimum of thirty to forty minutes are required. Rushing through them is not of much use.

During tea and lunch-breaks silence is prescribed for all participants, including the author. For, silence, interiorization, introspection and value-sensitivity/sustenance are intimately correlated.

Pertinent books, reading materials are also provided by the organization. Each exercise session is preceded by playing the recorded Sanskrit song on Self-identity (*Nirvan Shatakam* or *Atma Shatakam*)* composed by Shankaracharya twelve centuries ago. Besides creating a serene and heightened mood for the exercise, this song serves as a skein of thread passing through the web of ideas presented in the module.

(B) The second module, for the same group of participants, is offered after three or four months. During this interval they are advised to meet once a fortnight to collectively perform the exercise outlined above. Each session is led by one of the participants by rotation. Before leaving, they are each expected to write a personal letter to the author describing their efforts and

---

* See appendix I to this chapter.

experiences in applying the concepts in their daily lives—at home and the work-place. Each one of them is advised also to perform the exercise individually in their home.

The second module is held for two successive forenoons, and is organized around the following model on 'Leadership and Teamwork'—a specific theme of managerial effectiveness:

Process Constituents	LOVE	DISCIPLINE
LEADER	• Impersonal Love	• Self-Restraint
	• Higher SELF	• Self-Control
	• *Sattwa Guna*	• Renunciation
	• *Dharma-Moksha*	• Charisma
	- - - -	- - - -
TEAM-MEMBERS	• *Maitri*	• Hierarchism
	• *Karuna*	• Obedience
	• *Mudita*	• Rituals, rites, symbols
	• *Upeksha*	• *Dandaniti*
	- - - -	- - - -
BOTH	• De-egoization	• Mind-stilling
	• Surrender	• Meditation

The basic ideas incorporated in this model have been elaborated in chapter 13 of another book by us.[2] Here we shall only summarize its salient features.

The 'love' dimension for the leader revolves around the basic desideratum of true impartiality and non-exclusivity. Impersonality is not cold apathy or aloofness, but a wider all-embracing movement of the mind which transcends petty loyalties and affections, as well as mean antagonisms and aversions. The 'higher SELF—*sattwa guna—dharma/moksha*' process of self-culture slowly ripens into this kind of impersonal love.

The 'love' dimension for team-members relates to lateral relationships, constituting the foundation for trust, cooperation, openness, sharing and so on. *Maitri* implies the culturing of friendliness with the happy and fortunate *karuna* of compassion for the unhappy and afflicted, *mudita* of joy towards the good and virtuous, and *upeksha* of indifference to the wicked (though not in the context of work). The cultivation of these positive dispositions creates a peaceful and calm state of mind which serves well to smoothen the many small frictions that are apt to creep into team functioning.

The 'love' dimension common to both the leader and his team-members is spelt out as de-egoization and surrender—not to any temporal authority, but to the Universal Intelligence or Supreme Consciousness (or God), which is both the sub-stratum and the substance of human intelligence or consciousness. The latter habitually runs into all sorts of difficulties because it has cut itself loose from this Supreme anchor—due to *avidya* or primal igno-rance. Inner humility before the Supreme impels response from It. This also helps conflict resolution in the team-setting because humility before the Supreme also enables gradual de-egoization in interpersonal relationships.

The 'discipline' dimension for the leader is founded on self-restraint, self-control and selflessness. History shows that true leaders have always inspired people to great endeavours and results by demonstrating exemplary self-command and selflessness. Real charisma is grounded in such self-transcendent leadership.

The 'discipline' dimension for team-members, following 'love' and 'discipline' in the leader, is grounded in the constructive bonding quality of hierarchism, obedience and rituals, etc. The true import of these processes is neither feudal–authoritarian, nor mechanical–subversive. *Dandaniti*, the availability of chastizement as a mode of ensuring discipline if need be, also cannot be denied its place in a practical scheme of things. Credibility of *dandaniti* has of course to be first restored through 'love' and 'discipline' in the leader.

The 'discipline' dimension common to both the leader and his team-members has ultimately to be supported by the regular practice of systematic mind-stilling, leading eventually—at least for some—to real meditation. Enough has already been said earlier about this process.

As detailed discussion on these ideas proceeds during the two-day module, the following steps are added on to the seven-step module exercise already learnt:

i) By concentrating on the luminous core or *ishtam* within one's psychic heart centre one is able to gather and feel the glow of radiant peace, serene harmony, pure bliss. Each member is then invited to share this acquisition with *all*, without exception. The participant is thus led to contemplate that he is radiating and sending out thought-waves of goodwill, peace, love, health and joy to everyone—friend and foe, supporter and detractor alike. This process progressively converts the scheme of *maitri bhavana* and the rest into an emotional reality which gradually becomes instinctive and reliable.

ii) After this phase of conscious radiation is over, the awareness is localized once more for a few moments on the luminous core in the centre of the heart. Then it is to be imagined that the luminous core from within the individual is gently moving out towards the centre of the room. Each luminous core, the true SELF or essence of each empirical personality, is gradually travelling and converging at the centre with those of the rest. They are slowly merging into one another. Finally, a single, large, unified whole core of radiant luminosity is visible in the centre of the room. That is the Unity, the real relationship, amongst all the members. Effort is made to *feel* this wholeness, this Unity. After a while they again visualize the individual luminous cores re-emerging from the core of unity and slowly returning to the respective body-mansions.

(C) The third module works on 'Managing Stress, Communication and Counselling'. Usually it follows the second module after three months or so, and is again conducted over two successive forenoons. The conceptual design underlying the third module is illustrated below:

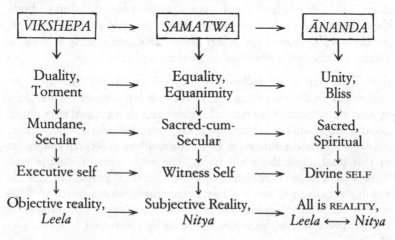

We found it difficult to identify a Sanskrit word to convey exactly the sense of the word 'stress'. A good approximation for us seemed to be *vikshepa*. For the rest, readers must have already become familiar with the terminology which has been used earlier in this volume. Only the last two terms *leela* and *nitya* call for some elucidation. *Leela* is the ever-changing flux of empirical phenomena which are real to our sense-related existence. *Nitya* is the unchanging causal foundation, the original 'stuff' from which the web of *leela* is spun endlessly. This is REAL, although at the time we are unaware of it. Progress in self-transformation demands in the long initial phase a conscious prioritization of the *nitya* and over the *leela*, to overcome the blinding, confusing spell of the latter. But when consummation is approached, *nitya* and *leela* both assume equivalent REALITY—there is then no negation, all is affirmation.

Most of the ingredients of this model too have been dealt with by the author elsewhere.[3] Here we shall only mention two additional steps in the exercise bearing specifically on stress management (although it should be remembered that the entire exercise sequence developed upto the end of module two is actively stress-reducing). It involves contemplation and concentration on any one of the two imageries or both, to be undertaken when *acute* stress is felt in domestic or work life:

(a) After the normal exercise upto step seven is over, one should try to visualize within the psychic centre of the heart the two layers of the sea: the roaring, turbulent, ever-changing surface; and the deep, calm, steady bed. As the simultaneous visualization of both these layers becomes increasingly vivid, one should identify with the deep, calm seabed and assert quietly that one's being is like this serene steadiness, untouched by surface upheavals.

(b) This step could follow (a). It goes something like this: the individual clearly visualizes and hears that into one of his/her ears is pouring a stream of praise, adulation, recognition and everything good about him/her from somebody; into the other is flowing in abuse, insult and villification from someone else. Yet, in the midst of this dual input the inner being, the SELF, remains serene and unmoved. The SELF neither gulps the nectar of praise nor does it vomit the poison of insult. They both simply do not touch it. This is how the state of *nirdwandwic* inner poise—the trans-empirical counterpoint to empirical stress—may be cultivated.

At the end of each module we recapitulate for the participants the key objectives underlying these integrated, individual psychological exercises, as follows:

- To purify and de-clog the nerve channels;
- To strengthen will-power.
- To increase the power of penetrating insight.
- To develop a holistic, synthesizing and expansive capability.
- To acquire and feel a perfectly tranquil inner world.
- To enable the mind to give its own authentic feedback.
- To pursue ethico-moral fitness.
- To capture the unitive awareness.

The main ideas on *counselling* will appear in Chapter 12. As for *communication*, the key points are derived from the works of Sri Aurobindo and the Mother.⁴ A sample of useful principles is given below:

[1] Never utter a word when you are angry.⁵

[2] Don't allow the impulse of speech to assert itself too much or say anything without reflection—speak always with conscious control....⁶

[3] If there is gossip about others and harsh criticism, don't join in—they only lower the consciousness from the higher level.⁷

[4] Cultivate the habit not to throw yourself out constantly into spoken words.⁸

[5] The less one speaks of others—even in praise—the better it is. Already it is difficult to know exactly what happens in oneslf, how to know then with certainty what is happening in others.⁹

[6] You must criticize nothing unless you have at the same time a conscious power and an active will in you to dissolve or transform the movements you criticise.¹⁰

[7] To discourage is wrong. But false or wrong encouragement is not right.... Very often if an inner communication has been established, a silent pressure is more effective than anything else.¹¹

[8] What is needed for success in the outward field.... is the power to transmit calmly a Force that can change men's attitude and the circumstances, and make any outward action at once the right thing to do and effective.¹²

[9] Outburst of anger or temper means the tongue is projecting bad vibrations into the atmosphere.... nothing is more contagious than the vibration of sound.¹³

[10]   One must state only what one wishes to see realized.[14]

III. (TOWARDS AN) ASSESSMENT OF RESULTS FROM THE MODULES

Three kinds of data will be used, all derived from the participants of the modules, for this section:

a)   Written notes during the modules at the end of exercise sessions at various stages. They include notes from several foreigners and Indian Christians, Muslims and others who have participated in our modules.

b)   Written letters, as a sequel to their own individual/collective follow-up during the intervals between modules.

c)   A brief questionnaire response obtained personally from the participants before commencing the second and third modules (see appendix I to this chapter for the questionnaire).

(A)   *Participants' Notes During the Programmes*

We shall refrain from making any comments, but only present a sample of direct extracts from these notes which we preserve as a data-bank. Each extract will represent one individual, and it will appear in his/her own language. It is left to the reader to form his or her opinion after examining the quoted views.

(1)   *End of 1st Module, In-House*: Several times of inhaling the *sattwa* guna of 'patience' and exhaling the *rajo guna* of 'anger' gave me a feeling of ease and calmness. I could concentrate better on the luminous spot in the corner of my mind and felt relaxed—devoid of all disturbances and stray thoughts. By repeating the five sentences (of dis- and re-identification) several times I felt I had rejected to some extent my *ahankar* (vanity) and was able to control myself. I concentrated fairly well on these sentences in the core of my heart.

(2)   *End of 1st Module, In-House*: Able to follow the song well. Better breath control than yesterday. Since I concentrated on only one *guna* at a time it was easy for me to do the exercise. I still have difficulty in emptying the brain. Other thoughts come in, but was able to do it better than yesterday. Was able to concentrate on the heart cavity. Uttered the five sentences. Good experience, but difficult to stay on for long.

(3)   *End of 1st Module, In-House*: With greater ease I was able to direct

my attention to breathing in and out. By expelling one of the *rajas* traits and imbibing one of the *sattwic* ones I felt that gradually in course of time I could increase the *sattwic* content. By chanting the five sentences I was able to realize that though a physical possessor of the body, senses, mind and intellect, in reality I was something more—especially when I feel the self-luminous pure consciousness which is *poorna*. Concentration on the thoracic centre, the psychic heart centre or the core makes it realizable easily.

(4) *Composite Module—National Management Programme*: The whole process seems to be taking place without effort now. I could inhale the selected *sattwa guna* and exhale the *rajo guna* with synchronized mind. I do feel that I am slowly getting rid of the selected *rajo guna*. Draining the space inside the head was easy and began as soon as I put my attention there. The inflow of the all-pervading, supreme creative Intelligence was without hindrance, giving me a feeling of enrichment within. Concentration within my heart was possible with a distinct feeling for it, and I uttered the five sentences four times, meaning them sincerely. While I was uttering these sentences with my mind in my heart, I did not hear any instructions but had a feeling that something beyond uttering the sentences with sincerity was to be done. However, after completing the course of sentences, I continued concentrating on my luminous inner core which seemed glowing, and then came the instructions of awareness.

(5) *Composite Module, Advanced Management Programme*: Inhaling *sattwa guna* or exhaling *rajo guna* during the breathing exercise gave some feeling towards the ultimate desire to shed the *rajo guna* and adopt the *sattwa guna*. I feel that continuous practice may help reach the desired goal. I found it still difficult to shift the mind from the head to the luminous core in the heart. But I am sure that in course of time a feeling will develop for it as I can see faint signs of it while slowly reciting the five sentences.

(6) *End of 1st Module, In-House*: Creation of a serene void in the brain space in order to accept the existence of the ultimate Supreme is not easy, and to me is not relevant because my conviction is deep-rooted. But it helps in transcending. I think I was benefited today more than by the methodical practice of TM, which I once did and have left.

(7) *Towards the End of 1st Module, In-House*:* Got into stride with the rhythm of synchronizing the breath and mind more easily and smoothly. Cleansing of the mind was a good base to receive the Supreme Consciousness. You could feel the bliss (not associated with the repetition of the sentences) creeping into and pervading your mind and body. You feel light, leaving the make-believe world behind. The external world goes on mechanically. But you have discovered a new life within which gives you a tinge of happiness. The

* A Christian.

light within seems to glow. I like it to grow and spread.

(8) *End of 1st Module, In-House*:* Deep breathing gave me a feeling that I was forgetting my existence. I selected 'poise' as *sattwa guna* for inhaling and 'fluctuating moods' as *rajo guna* for exhaling. The opening of the 'body-bottle' at the top gave me a very relaxing feeling as if all stress and strain were let off. Inviting the Supreme to come in was a very unique experience. Taking the Supreme Intelligence to the heart cavity and concentrating all thoughts there was also very good experience. I, however, have some difficulty in sitting straight. I hope to make further improvement in repeat exercises.

(9) *Composite Module, Advanced Management Programme*:** Emptying mind of thoughts was easy. The best feeling was when I opened the mind to permit the Divine power to enter the body and found my concentration to be far better. Most important: I could prevent stray thoughts from entering into my mind very easily. Regarding repeating the sentences, I did as advised, felt better, but did not really understand why we did it. Regarding the lamp in the centre of the heart, I could do that easily and felt better. The best feeling I got was when I slowly opened up my eyes after all the steps—a feeling of *purity* which I cannot really describe.

(10) *End of 1st Module, In-House*:*** During the course of inhaling and exhaling the sequences of *sattwa guna* and *rajo guna* respectively was followed strictly by the mind, except for a few moments when an incident of morning office talk came in. During the course of uttering the five sentences, the mind was full with these words and was automatically repeating the same sequence—except that during some moments the mind went out to the day-to-day job.

(11) *End of 1st Module, In-House*:† The breathing exercise has become more effective, more consciously done, more mindful. Using my selected words, I believe with practice it will help me to become aware of that which I lack and would like to inculcate (patience), and that which I would like to diminish in my personality (anger). Yes, it is easier for me to be conscious of the 'heart centre' into which power flows. With the breathing exercise and a conscious effort I was able, slightly, to perceive its presence.

(12) *End of 1st Module, In-House*:†† The music (*Atmashatakam*) is soothing and relaxes me. My concentration settled on two words—rejection of anger and bringing in patience. In step two I persisted with slow, normal breathing. The next step was a little difficult in that I had to try to switch from two words—anger and patience—to completely opening up to allow free inflow of the radiance. I finally settled down to a dreamy feeling. The last step was very intensive and required more concentration. But it was heartening and a feeling of easiness and joy came. Have a feeling that I can tolerate a few things more than I used to.

---

* A Muslim.   ** A Parsi.   *** A Sikh.   † A Nigerian.   †† A Zambian.

(13) *End of 1st Module, In-House:** I tried breathing with both nostrils open. My *guna* for taking in was 'forgiveness' and out was 'anger'. But they got mixed up and I could not get into proper rhythm. Yet I tried. The second step was easy, I could concentrate in a relaxed way. I next felt very early the space inside my head—a real opening on the top and emptying out. Fewer thoughts passed through my mind. Also felt that I was receiving [the Supreme] from outside. I felt, not so clearly, the concentration in the heart centre.

(14) *End of 1st Module, In-House:*** The music was not very helpful. Concentrating on breathing in *sattwa guna* and breathing out *rajo guna* was difficult. I could much better concentrate when just breathing. After sometime I could concentrate better on these *guna*s. Concentration on my heart centre gave me a feeling of detachment, which was disturbed by the utterance of the five lines. Concentration on the luminous core in the heart centre was not easy. It felt like it was present, not inside but outside my body.

(15) *End of 1st Module, In-House:*† The addition of the *sattwa* and *rajo guna* requires additional concentration which will hopefully improve with practice. I think the technique is useful. It was easier to concentrate on the *guna*s during slow, normal breathing. The mind felt uncluttered, and the external disturbances were nearly totally blocked off by the end of the third step. The reach for the infinite seemed heightened today at the end of the fourth step. I have a little trouble distinguishing my physical and psychic heart as being separate. This impaired my concentration. However I was able to feel a hint of warm (glow) once in a while.

(16) *End of 1st Module, In-House:*†† It became easy to breathe through one nostril. It was also easy to exhale one element of *tamas* and *rajas*, but not possible to inhale *sattwa*. During normal breathing my mind was much more flat—a kind of calmness. When I located my mind in the top of my head, I felt a sort of warmth there, although this was very momentary. I could not shift my mind to the centre of the body. I felt that the centre of the body was empty.

(17) *End of 2nd Module, In-House:* Both the steps, i.e. emitting from the luminous core in the psychic heart-centre peace, tranquillity and happiness for all, including those not liked, is a good idea for reaching the higher Self. The other step shall definitely help in team-work for solving organizational problems. The results have to be seen, but the steps and theory are very correct. The 'thought power' talked of in our scriptures shall be on trial/test in these steps.

(18) *End of 2nd Module, In-House:* The experience of the exercise was

---

* A Syrian Muslim.   ** An Englishman.
† An American.   †† A Singaporean.

particularly excellent when for the first time I transmitted the waves of goodwill to all, including my friends and enemies. I felt so relieved, and further felt as if I had removed some kind of burden from my mind. Regarding the second step I felt that all those who are sitting in the room are one, and have a common cause for which all are working.

(19) *End of 2nd Module, In-House*: The various steps, whatever impact they may have on my behaviour (I wonder whether any impact will be there), I feel peaceful, relaxed and calm. Tensions go away. I am very receptive to ideas. I feel this peaceful state of mind for at least four or five hours. I have not yet realized any impact of all this on my colleagues. I am not sure if they notice any change in me. But whatever impact these may have on me, when my colleagues do not change, will it benefit me?

(20) *End of 2nd Module, In-House*: The luminous core within me is glowing bright and radiant. There is warmth within me. There is serenity and calmness. A slowing down of bodily activity. I am now imagining the body to melt away with the warmth, and slowly the luminous core is being uncovered which shines even brighter now. I reach out to the luminous cores around me, almost all of them shining with the same brightness. Now we all begin to move these cores to the centre table. There is a large radiance now—a coming together, Unity and Total One-ness. We keep it this way and feel the merging of all the core—*ekatmanubhuti*.

(21) *Composite Module, National Management Programme*:* I was listening to the heart beats after the initial sense of voidness. I could feel the all-pervading energy and comfort in my heart. I could 'feel' the presence of a being beyond my being. But the 'elevation' part of my spirit was brief indeed. I could 'feel' the all-comforting soothing experience taking possession of me. A different life altogether inside.

(22) *Composite 5-day MDP, IIM-C*:** My experiences of steps one to four were similar to those before. But this time perhaps a little more intense—especially the emptying of the brain in step 3. In stage five I got a strong feeling of the mind and SELF integrated for the first time in my life. I was able to feel the SELF in the psychic heart centre.

(23) *Composite 5-day MDP, IIM-C*:† Opted to focus on the 'luminous core'. This was much easier than previously. I found that as I internalized my focus, I was able to 'objectify' my body. It was as if my body was that of another, or rather my consciousness was detached from the body. Very refreshing stuff. The images of two luminous cores—one in my heart centre, the other in the centre of the room—were more easily visualized than previously. The idea of a core inside myself identical to an external larger core was very helpful in fathoming oneness with the Supreme Intelligence. This is, I

* A Muslim.   ** A Norwegian.   † An American.

realize, only an image—a teaching aid—but it is nonetheless an effective one that will hopefully assist further endeavours.

(24) *Composite 5-Day MDP, IIM-C*:* Breathing was again easy as were all the steps to the concentration on the heart centre. I still haven't quite got the sentences though. Concentrating on the heart centre I could visualize a spherical ball, no larger than the fire-ball of yesterday, but tinged with blue. Like the sun rising in the morning it was providing warmth but not stifling heat. When I projected the consciousness externally, I found I could focus the rays. I wanted to focus them on particular people—those I liked, those I didn't. At one point I wanted to break out of the experience—to prove my personal strength. I didn't. I kept in and was wiser for the experience.

(25) *End of 3rd Module, In-House*: The first step of the song conditions and tunes the mind. The next step produces calmness and relaxation of mind. It gives a filtering effect towards pure mind. The added steps in the exercise produce further conditioning and take one to a state where the apparent effects of outward things do not change or affect the mind. They produce a state of undisturbed calmness. Going deeper into the psychic heart centre gives the feeling that we can secure this calmness even in a turbulent or crisis situation. A great relief mentally.

(26) *End of 3rd Module, In-House*:** Yesterday's exercise of listening to heavy praises through the right ear and abuses through the left, with a view to narrowing the gap between the two. As a matter of fact it is our daily routine to hear such remarks. We get praise from some of our patients, and equally curses from some others. The reaction to all this from us is minimal. Concentrating on an entity whom I love and respect is a pleasant experience, and much more practical. Today the step involving going deep into the soul is soothing. Might improve further when I practise more of it, and then I might get real results.

(27) *End of 3rd Module, In-House*:† The placement of *ishtam* in the luminous core of the heart centre could be done. I was doing this practice regularly in earlier days, and also during the last two months or so. Perfect calm, a fully composed mind could be experienced. I do not know how to express the state of mind in words. In the Christian teachings too, in which I believe, there is the state of attainment of the holy spirit. This is something related to the attainment of wisdom. Meditation shall lead me to attain this wisdom some day. Probing into the deepest corner of darkness and finding the light—it was a good experience. I have decided to continue this exercise in the future—to probe the light which is hidden in the darkness of all my foolishness, absurdities and all bad habits.

(28) *Composite 5-day MDP, IIM-C*:* A good method of identification

* An Englishman.   ** A Muslim.   †A Christian.

with the Almighty, irrespective of faith and belief. Since this is a spiritual exercise, it is well-rooted in our ethos. Experienced trance and intense emotional serenity and bliss at the final stage.

(29) *End of 3rd Module, In-House*: I did not feel sleepy today. I could concentrate more. I thought that radiating goodwill etc. are simple things which can be easily shared. At the same time I also felt that before radiating these good things, I should have them within myself. I chose ... as my *Ishtam*. I realized that I must be peaceful myself before I can radiate peace. The experience of the sea imagery was very good. It gave the feeling of a bigger heart and more depth.

(30) *End of 3rd Module, In-House*: While receiving the rays (concentrating on Ishtam) I actually felt receiving the rays. I felt a luminous source in my heart. I think I was so involved at that stage that I am unable to recall whether I transmitted my rays of goodwill or even heard your voice. Next, on hearing bad and good words I remained calm and they had practically no effect on me. In the last step I could hold my breath and could see the waves as well as the calmness of the sea. After this step I was finding myself fresh and feeling total calmness within myself.

(31) *End of 3rd Module, In-House*: There is good improvement in concentration and coordination compared to the second module. Listening to good words [praise] and bad words [criticisms] simultaneously by recalling past instances was a good experience. Effort has to be made to keep the mind still to both of these. Experiencing the waves and roars of the sea was almost real as I imagined myself to be standing on the beach. Going deeper and deeper into the sea to experience the calm and stillness of the seabed requires more imagination. Perhaps a little more knowledge of this will enrich the experience.

(B) *Letters Received During the Interval Between Two Modules*

As a step towards the institutionalization of values-based functioning, it is suggested to participants in each location that they meet on a fixed date and time, once a fortnight, for collective performance of the exercises learnt and also for specific discussions on a chosen topic or chapter of a relevant book. The group chooses a leader for each meeting who is responsible for reading and thinking about the topic, and for conducting the exercise and discussions. Thus, the teacher's role is assumed in turn by each member of the group. Before they leave the collective forum, each is advised to write an informal letter to the author about his

* A Muslim.

experiences and efforts in relating to values during the fortnight. Each of them gets a reply from the author. It is urged that this collective reinforcement process be carried out at least for six months after the first module. It is now from these letters that we offer some extracts:

(1) *From the Executive Director of a Large Plant, After 1st Module*: I gathered from my colleagues that they are conducting the Group Meetings, and I also could attend the one which took place on ... From the interaction which I had with them I got the impression that the majority of them are practising the exercise. There is a visible change in their managerial approach. The lectures given by you ... and subsequent continuation of the exercises by the individuals seems to be one of the reasons.

As far as I am concerned, I am able to carry out the exercise with the cassette song only in the morning hours. Often this is also missed whenever I am on tour.

I strongly believe that the teachings described in our scriptures, which have been lucidly brought out and shown their applicability in our day-to-day jobs by your efforts, is the right way of managing both the personal and professional life in the present competitive atmosphere.

Your advice of giving personal inspiration to the group members shall be complied with.

(2) *A Group Leader, After 1st Module*: After the breathing exercises etc., the experiences of the different members were discussed. All present mentioned that after attending this course it has become easier to cope with adverse situations. Regarding the daily exercises, the members are finding it difficult to maintain the fixed schedule, but all of them promised to make it more regular. The group was worried about the poor attendance at this meeting. One of the reasons, it was felt, might be due to heavy pressure of work which we normally experience during the last quarter of the year. To improve participation the Management Training Centre has been requested to remind all the members regularly about this meeting. At the end all the members expressed the desire to bring in some values in their respective lives. The leader for the next group meeting will be ...

(3) *A Group Member, After 1st Module*: Thanks for your reply to my first letter. I was not able to sustain the practice of breathing exercises due to a lot of work-pressure. My plant duty is from 8 a.m to 9/10 p.m, almost daily with no Sunday or rest. This group meeting is the only time I have an opportunity of doing the exercise in a group.

Regarding adopting *sattwa guna* and rejecting *rajo guna*, I am facing bitter criticism from my family members when they see our neighbours and friends enjoying themselves at the employer's expense. However, I am holding on till now and resisting.

However, as a result of the above two factors, I have no family life and am full of tension. Please guide me on the way out.

(4) *A Group Member, After 1st Module*: I have been feeling more soothed/pleased in carrying out the breathing exercise. My imagination about replacing the *rajo guna* of 'ceaseless activity' with the *sattwa guna* of 'patience' gives me a feeling of much practical achievement. Concentration of mind, as well as mind–breath synchronization, has been felt strongly. It is becoming easier day by day. With my new assignment, I feel I am supposed to be wiser than earlier—have developed more patience than earlier. However, I feel I need to practise more and more to have more patience and tolerance.

(5) *A Group Member, After 1st Module*: I thank you for your letter. It reminded me of a new direction in life. Though I am quite active and trying to be peaceful, yet whenever I am alone and free I observe two things:

(i) I am still disturbed with a problem as alternatives available are not working. The organization, even at Directors' level, has one answer: rules, no exception under any circumstances.

(ii) Quite often I tell my problems to others who are not directly involved and they sympathize. I am now thinking: why do I go on telling them? should I tell them again or not? Sometimes I do get some consolation, a warm word and brotherly behaviour. I do read your letter and make efforts to strengthen my mind. I believe God shall help me.

(6) *A Group Member, After 1st Module*: After you left, I tried to practise breath control, and then thought of the *rajo guna* of 'egotism' out, while the *sattwa guna* of 'straightforwardness' in. But I could not make this daily. Even on the days I could afford the time, I was not able to exceed 10 minutes. It is extremely difficult to control the thinking process and to acquire detachment—because lots of pressing problems start haunting me during that period. Perhaps I am myself to blame for not being able to practise.

Regarding work-life, I think I am going towards a broader perspective—a little of *sattwa guna*. At least two incidents I distinctly remember where I have helped people which, perhaps, I would not have done in my previous frame of mind. I am happy to note this change in my attitude. We assembled on . . . at . . . and practised the exercises which were a pleasant experience.

(7) *A Group Member, After 1st Module*: (i) There is an acute technical problem in the unit. My mind is almost totally involved in this. My seniors fired me on a number of occasions which only told me of their ignorance about the problem. Only on one occasion did I lose my temper and told them that I was losing regard for them. Later on I felt bad about my behaviour. I am continuously on the job, and I am sure that the problem will be sorted out soon.

(ii) The respect of my subordinate officers and staff towards me has shot up.

All of them are fully cooperating with me forgetting about restrictive practices.

(iii) I am engaged in tremendous activity but inside I am very calm—although the problem is not yet solved.

(iv) I feel more for the poor now more than ever before, and whatever help I can render I am giving. I feel for them.

(v) I am much more involved with my family members, though there are severe problems in office.

(vi) I have more courage and strength—I am not worried or under tension as I used to be.

(8) *The Head of Training Department, After 1st Module*: Out of 17 participants for the programme 14 attended the group practice session. I am pleased to inform you that the response of the participants in carrying out the practice is very positive. During the practice session one non-participant also joined. I am getting requests from some more people to allow them to attend the session. I think with a little briefing about the exercises it would be desirable to allow the willing officers to participate in the practice session. The discussion during the session was quite lively with good participation from everyone present.

(9) *A Group Member, After 1st Module*:* As scheduled we met today at 5 p.m. in our factory. The breathing exercise was much easier. Brain-stilling and emptying gave me a floating feeling—just like when you are on a swing, or while driving fast suddenly you go down a slope. Apart from this exercise, I am having an inner feeling that I should change. I must remember my indebtedness before talking or acting. I have attended about 20 to 25 seminars/courses during the past nine years, but this is the only course I am able to remember in a systematic way and discuss with others even after about two weeks. Hope I will change for the better in future.

(10) *Executive Director—Group Leader, After 1st Module*: Making an allowance for lack of experience in guiding such a practice, the session went off fairly well. We should get into the groove with time and practice. The discussions on wisdom v. knowledge, and the need for rooting our values in Indian culture were actively participated in and will be productive of some results. Further, for myself I have had to integrate my personal *pranayama* and *shavasana* practice with yours. While I have largely adhered to my previous practice, yet I have introduced needed changes as suggested by you at appropriate points.

(11) *A Group Leader, After 2nd Module*: Today I have conducted the practice of breathing exercise etc. Before the exercise was started I read out a

* A Christian.

hand-out compiled from your book on the theory of *guna*s.

I copied your instructions on breathing exercise on a piece of paper and gave instructions accordingly. While doing so I felt that my mind was becoming calm. I was coming nearer to the Supreme Consciousness. I had no worldly feeling at that time except that of holy happiness.

It is a real experience which I would not have realized if I were not given the opportunity of conducting the practice session.

(12) *A Group Member, After 2nd Module*: Namaskar. We are now doing breathing exercises once a week in our club. As regards myself, I find that patience in me is increasing day by day, and I am able to keep myself cool even in provocative conditions. In this connecton an incident happened when one of my subordinates informed me that one of the senior officers had said something insulting about me. I kept my cool, and after a few minutes I found that the same senior officer himself came to me and did more of a favour to us (in the same context).

(13) *The Head of a Unit, After 2nd Module*: With God's grace the exercises are continuing. I am able to attend whenever I am in town on the scheduled day. It definitely gives peace of mind and helps in concentrating when needed. In our morning sessions which, of late, are done almost every Saturday, the attendance ranges between 50 to 60 per cent. Briefs on what you had taught are practically over. They were covered by many participants, part by part.

(14) *The Head of Training Department, After 2nd Module*: We are eagerly awaiting the 3rd Module on 'Values System'. We have started:

(i) practising the exercise for 10–12 minutes before and after each Local Management Committee meeting;
(ii) assembling and exchanging our views on subjects covered by you once a fortnight;
(iii) experimenting with some of your ideas in other training programmes, e.g. conflict resolution, productivity, team-building etc.;
(iv) within my own department we have started doing these sessions twice a week with other officers and staff.

(15) *The Head of a Plant, After 2nd Module*: As per practice, we arranged a review programme with our members on . . . , along with invitees from other sections. During our practice session we felt that if we continue the practice regularly, we may be able to put to test the *Gita*'s psychological principle. We are in receipt of your letter dated . . . and indeed happy to read the contents of the same. We have also circulated copies of your letter to our participants. While going through our practice we remember the spirit of *nishkam karma*, i.e. to work without anxiety for the results. . . . In the review session we are also reading a few pages from the Rajyoga and the *Gita* as desired by you.

(16) *A Group Member, After 2nd Module*: I was unable to attend my own group's regular session, but was accommodated later in the group session of another plant. As I had mentioned to you earlier, I have been receiving positive response from several members of the department who have not attended the programme. I am personally explaining and discussing the philosophy. Very soon, once genuine interest is established, it would be possible to induct more persons. Personally, the second module on 'love and discipline' has benefited me immensely.

(17) *A Group Member, After 2nd Module*: I owe you an apology for not having written to you earlier … I am at least happy to be able to keep up the adage: 'better late than never'. Well, after having the pleasure of attending your second module, I have started doing the exercise. Though at present I am not very regular in this, I am confident that I will be able to make it a regular habit in the days to come. As you have rightly pointed out, this exercise does have a soothing effect on one's attitude and behaviour towards others, and the continued practice of this exercise will go a long way in improving one's image. I was also able to discuss this with some of my colleagues who could not attend your lectures, and tried to impress upon them the necessity of doing this exercise. The response from them was favourable. In fact, I was able to convince one of my subordinate officers who is a Christian.

In Appendix III to this Chapter we reproduce a long but rich account of the experience of the Head (a Muslim) of a Management Development Centre in one of the largest and best-known industrial enterprises in India.

Since by the time the second module is over, nearly four to five months have elapsed, and the group follow-up would have more or less stabilized, no correspondence on this process after the third module has been pursued.

Considering the preceding forty-eight participant responses together it is clear that after all classical concepts like Higher SELF, *guna*s, sacro-secular symbiosis, breath control, mind-stilling and so on still hold good for the practical men of the world. They also prove that intellectual misgivings about these concepts being of a religious and Hindu origin, and so likely to invite the resistance and ire of non-Hindus, are speculative. Responses from a number of foreigners and also from non-Hindu Indians show that if the deep-structure is properly assimilated and personally experienced before communicating with the audience, there are few problems. On the contrary, the participants are grateful. A purely scholastic approach lacks the certitude of inner experience. It is possible that the intellectual's defensive denial of these fundamentals reflects also his or her own unexamined reluctance to embark on self-change.

(C) *Questionnaire Survey Prior to the Start of Second or Third Modules*

It may be recalled that usually an interval of three to four months is allowed to elapse between each successive module. This interval is meant to be used by the participants for individual and group follow-up on the ideas and processes of the respective modules. It is also supposed to provide an opportunity to test the values-oriented principles in the work-situation. When they assemble again for the second or third module, they begin by filling up a simple questionnaire (included as Appendix II to this Chapter). The items in it represent a few *key end-result variables* for improved quality of work-life and performance in organizations. A summary of data so collected from a little more than four hundred participants in various organizations is presented below.

It may be useful to examine the 'no change' column first. The data here are probably a mixture of two types of responses: (a) one which may indicate the ineffectiveness of the module(s) to produce a desired positive change, (b) and the other which may indicate that the existing state of the particular end-result variable is already very positive and the module has not added anything to it. During discussions with participants on data in this column, it has appeared that category (a) indications are marginally more numerous than those of (b).

The single most important premise underlying every module is that sensitivity to and sustenance of sound normative values are causally dependent upon *disciplined introspective ability*. If therefore we turn our attention to the 'very good' and 'good' columns, and add the percentages of each end-result parameter, we find that 'introspective ability' (IA) does emerge with the highest score—almost 84 per cent. This score appears to justify the contents and processes employed in the modules. Also, IA has scored the highest (60 per cent) in the 'good' column, and second highest (23.6 per cent) in the 'very good' column.

When we turn to 'ethical sensitivity' (ES), it is seen to score the fourth highest (78 per cent). But what is even more significant is that ES has secured the highest percentage for 'very good'. Since we have already argued that to speak of values in organizations by excluding the ethico-moral dimension is fruitless, our data for IA and ES taken together present a truly encouraging phenomenon.

'Coping with frustration' (CF) has secured the third highest (78.9 per cent) for 'very good' and 'good' put together. Since it is widely believed that the present era is one of 'revolution of rising expectations', it follows that it should also generate, at the very least, an 'evolution of growing frustrations'—like a dark shadow chasing a bright light. This unrecognized fact of our *dwandwic* existence is quite important for the strategic management of individual lives. Be that as it may, we feel that improved ability in coping with frustrations strengthens a person at the base. Armed with more internal security, he or she can then boost the probability of maintaining or increasing dignity and nobility in behaviour; and this is after all what values are about.

EFFECT OF 'VALUES SYSTEM' MODULES ON:

	Very Good (%)	Good (%)	No Change (%)	Bad (%)	Total Responses
1. Personal Health	14.3	53.3	31.6	0.8	405
2. Domestic Life	22.0	51.0	27.0	—	404
3. Boss Relationships	20.2	49.0	30.4	0.4	402
4. Colleague Relationships	22.8	57.8	19.2	0.2	403
5. Subordinate Relationships	20.9	54.5	24.4	0.2	402
6. Ethical Sensitivity	28.8	49.2	21.2	0.8	392
7. Coping with Frustration	21.8	57.1	20.6	0.5	403
8. Introspective Ability	23.6	60.0	16.2	0.2	402
9. Work for Work's Sake	19.0	48.8	31.2	1.0	400
10. Creativity	16.8	50.7	32.5	—	404
11. Encouragement from Boss	8.4	51.8	39.0	0.8	392

Thus, taking IA, ES and CF scores together we feel that the modules are moving in the right direction for values-based organizational effectiveness, of which these three parameters are the crucial building blocks.

Numerically, the second highest combined score for 'very good' and 'good' belongs to 'colleague relationships' (CR)—80·6 per cent. This should augur well for strengthened team-work in the Indian milieu. The contributions of heightened IA, ES and CF should be quite pertinent for improved CR.

We wish 'work for work's sake' (WWS) had fared better than it has (67.8 per cent); there is a strong inter-dependence between ES and CF on the one hand, and WWS on the other. Unless, in the long run, WWS reaches nearer the scores for ES and CF, high levels of IA alone may not be able to sustain improved ES and CF.

Although none of the eleven end-result parameters has scored less than 60 per cent for 'very good' and 'good' combined, yet the lowest in the league (60·2 per cent) is for 'encouragement from boss' (about the ideas and processes of the modules). Read with the score for 'boss relationships' (BR), 69·2 per cent, which also is relatively low, it appears that the true, humane aspect of hierarchism is yet to blossom in this sample.

Questions 12, 13 and 14 intended to explore the extent of *individual* follow-up—through reading, mind-stilling exercises, etc. Here, however, the scores are very low. Thus, less than 10 per cent did some reading, once or twice daily to reinforce the concepts and principles. Similarly, less than 30 per cent practised the mind-stilling exercise at home on a daily basis. Attempting the latter in the office was again restricted to less than 10 per cent of the respondents.

Whenever this paradox of high scores for the first eleven items versus the low scores on the individual follow-up efforts was presented to various groups of participants, they tended to explain it by saying that the latter data did not negate the former. For, in a subtle and deep way these ideas and principles continued to seep into their inner world and influence their thinking and approach in the workplace. The modules were helping to rekindle and revivify what for most had gone underground in their awareness, though not altogether obliterated. It is for our readers to judge the merit of this interpretation. On our part, we perceive that the key problem in regard to items 12, 13 and 14 is that for too long the majority of us have escaped the rigours of a well-regulated pattern of daily living which allows for a fixed slot or two for quietening and silencing our surface mind in order to experience the mind of light and insight.

IV. CONCLUSION: TOWARDS INSTITUTIONALIZATION

Values-inspired culture-building within organizations demands both a clear, sound, coherent and trans-mundane philosophy as well as a firm dedication to details in its translation into thought and action. The trans-mundane base of values-structure is emphasized because it is only from this raised platform of viewing oneself in relation to others in the organization, society, Nature, the Universe, that one can recognize one's pettiness of means, within given ends, and feel the urge to elevate them to dignity. Dedication to detail means evolving certain common ways of thinking, speaking, responding, behaving—in bi-personal, multi-personal and total situations. Without such a scheme no trans-mundane philosophy can permeate and breathe life into an organization. It is here especially that culture-specifity as a medium cannot be brushed aside.

Now, on both these counts we feel that Indian organizations, in general, demonstrate a pathetic lack of deep intellectual grasp and of resolute will. Many fume and fret, for somewhere in their bones they sense that things cannot or should not go on as they are. Yet they also reveal a fear, a hesitancy, almost a paralyzing indecision, resembling that of a little boy at the edge of a swimming pool before taking his first plunge. Its root probably lies in the absence of personal conviction, born of experience and realization, even amongst Chairmen and Managing Directors. The stakes in a purified, coherent, elevated values-system do not seem to resonate in the hearts of most of them. Resorting to pleas of political, bureaucratic and other interferences is yet another rationalization. If the perspective is about the quality of the legacy we are going to hand over to the next generation, and if we can take a view for the next century or so, then it must be a necessary and small price that at least some groups, some CMDs, some leaders resolve now to keep to values even if it brings them no apparent success or gain. For, the unseen, unpraised, unrewarded endeavours of such purity shall cumulatively foster a powerful wave which will eventually work more explicitly and widely in the following decades.

Against this overall backdrop, we are happy to mention examples of two kinds of efforts in the direction of institutionalization which have already emerged in a couple of enterprises:

(a) The construction of a sound-proof 'mind-stilling room'.

(b) The adoption of a teacher's role by the superior who has attended the modules.

A 'mind-stilling room' has so far been built at two places—one in the corporate office of a private sector industrial house and the other in one of the plant premises of a public enterprise. The reader may recall that an *operational precondition* for values-sensitivity and sustenance is a quiet, calm and interiorized mind. We therefore urge all senior or top management to provide for a 'mind-stilling room', which is a more fundamental need than the provision of clubs and swimming pools. The latter usually lead to a lot of useless exteriorization and to very little genuine relaxation. Usually the consciousness is lowered and vulgarized through such socialization. The 'mind-stilling room' should provide managers with an alternative facility to sit in during working hours and calm down ruffled tempers, restore nervous equilibrium, allow the mind to render authentic feedback, and even to pray if so inclined. Apart from emergencies, a regular procedure of each manager spending five minutes deep breathing and re-composing himself when entering the work-place or leaving it may also be thought of. There could be many more ways for creative use of such a facility. It could become, in course of time, a symbolic emblem of the trans-mundane in the midst of the mundane. Great care should be taken to preserve its sanctity and serenity.

The other suggestion made in the modules is that managers who participate in them should try, in their turn, to act as teachers in a real sense of their own subordinates, colleagues. The outside facilitator cannot be the true, long-term answer to the goal of values-system throughout an organization. The Deputy General Manager–Operations of a large public enterprise has enthusiastically seized on this idea, and here are the relevant portions of a letter we recently got from him about his personal experiences as a peer in a group and as a teacher of subordinates:

The personal results of the ideas and practices in modules I and II for myself have been very good. Module I has been more impact-producing compared to module II. I have felt that module II is more oriented towards giving to others in the light of *sarve bhavantu sukhina* which is a very high potential cause. Keeping the ordinary mentality in view, the average person tends to keep all good things to himself and subconsciously resents sharing. Only the broadening of vision through practice can help a person to assimilate all that is in module II. By and large I used to follow the principle of *nishkamkarma* earlier also. But modules I and II have strengthened my conviction in it. Not looking at it from an ethereal plane, this concept, when practised in real-life situations, is useful because it eliminates tensions caused by desires and enables one to be at peace within.

The results amongst group members who have attended the modules with me have also been good when I make the assessment from our team-performance point of view. Had these exposures not been given, I must say that the 'common purpose' approach would have taken a long time to adopt. Individually for each many changes may not be obvious, but the inspiration, the ideas are moulding them.

The result in respect of my own subordinate team-members, to some of whom you had also spoken briefly last time, seems to be a greater acceptance by them of myself as a team-leader. This is because they see in me one who practices what he preaches. Though I have not yet been able to cover all of them, I have nonetheless been discussing these ideas and principles in informal small groups. Yet, initially a brief talk by you to the remainder would be of help in fulfilling my role.

In a nutshell I would say that it is the SELF within which has to become radiant for others to be drawn towards It. Your modules are good guides towards realizing this SELF.

APPENDIX I
NIRVANSHATAKAM OR ATMASHATAKAM*
(SONG OF THE SELF)

I am neither the mind nor the intellect nor the ego nor the mind-stuff;
I am neither the body nor the changes of the body;
I am neither the senses of hearing, taste, smell, or sight,
Nor am I the ether, the earth, the fire, the air;
I am Existence Absolute, Knowledge Absolute, Bliss Absolute—
I am He, I am He (Shivoham, Shivoham).

I am neither the prana nor the five vital airs;
I am neither the materials of the body nor the five sheaths;
Neither am I the organs of action nor the object of the senses;
I am Existence Absolute, Knowledge Absolute, Bliss Absolute—
I am He, I am He (Shivoham, Shivoham).

I have neither aversion nor attachment, neither greed nor delusion;
Neither egotism nor envy, neither *dharma* nor *moksha*;
I am neither desire nor the objects of desire;
I am Existence Absolute, Knowledge Absolute, Bliss Absolute—
I am He, I am He (Shivoham, Shivoham).

I am neither sin nor virtue, neither pleasure nor pain,
Nor temple nor worship nor pilgrimage nor scriptures,
Neither the act of enjoying, the enjoyable, nor the enjoyer;
I am Existence Absolute, Knowledge Absolute, Bliss Absolute—
I am He, I am He (Shivoham, Shivoham).

I have neither death nor fear of death nor caste;
Nor was I ever born, nor had I parents, friends, and relations;
I have neither guru nor disciple;
I am Existence Absolute, Knowledge Absolute, Bliss Absolute—
I am He, I am He (Shivoham, Shivoham).

I am untouched by the senses; I am neither *mukti* nor knowable;
I am without form, without limit, beyond space, beyond time;
I am in everything; I am the basis of the universe; everywhere am I.
I am Existence Absolute, Knowledge Absolute, Bliss Absolute—
I am He, I am He (Shivoham, Shivoham).

* Free translation by Swami Vivekananda.

APPENDIX–II
QUESTIONNAIRE ON THE EVALUATION OF VALUES-SYSTEM MODULES

DATE:

Organization:

PLEASE CROSS (X) ONLY ONE BOX FOR EACH QUESTION:

1. Effect on personal health (eg. stress, sleep, digestion, breathlessness, headaches, etc.

   Very Good ☐

   Good ☐

   No Change ☐

   Bad ☐

2. Effect on relationships in domestic life (eg. wife, children, parents, brothers, etc.)

   Very Good ☐

   Good ☐

   No Change ☐

   Bad ☐

3. Effect on relationships with boss (eg. trust, frankness, poise, confidence).

   Very Good ☐

   Good ☐

   No Change ☐

   Bad ☐

4. Effect on relationships with colleagues (eg. friendliness, co-operation, trust, straightforwardness).

   Very Good ☐

   Good ☐

No Change

Bad

5. Effect on relationships with subordinates (eg. their work commitment, discipline, acceptance or generation of new ideas, affection).

Very Good

Good

No Change

Bad

6. Effect on sensitivity to ethical issues (eg. bribes, data manipulation, backbiting, hiding facts, hypocrisy)

Very Good

Good

No Change

Bad

7. Effect on the ability to cope with frustrations, denials, postponement of expectations.

Very Good

Good

No Change

Bad

8. Effect on the ability to introspect. (eg. impatience, arrogance, pride jealousy, selfishness).

Very Good

Good

No Change

Bad

9. Effect on the ability to work for its own sake with non-attachment to its results.

Very Good ☐

Good ☐

No Change ☐

Bad ☐

10. Effect on the ability for creative thinking for problem-solving.

Very Good ☐

Good ☐

No Change ☐

Bad ☐

11. Support and encouragement re. the ideas and processes of the Values-System programmes from the team-leader (eg. informal inquiries, periodic informal group meetings).

Very Good ☐

Good ☐

No Change ☐

Bad ☐

12. Reading the Relevant Literature

☐ Twice a day

☐ Once a day

☐ Occasionally in a week

☐ Occasionally in 3 months

☐ None at all

13. Performance of the Exercises learnt in the programme at home

☐ Twice a day

	Once a day
	Occasionally in a week
	Occasionally in 3 months
	None at all

14. Performance of the Exercises learnt in the programme in office.

	Twice a day
	Once a day
	Occasionally in a week
	Occasionally in 3 months
	None at all

RERERENCES

1. S.K. Chakraborty, *Managerial Effectiveness and Quality of Work-Life* (Delhi: Tata McGraw Hill), 1987.
2. *Idem, Foundations of Managerial Work* (Bombay: Himalaya, 1989).
3. Ibid., Ch. 15.
4. Sri Aurobindo and the Mother, *On Self-Perfection* (Pts. I to IV), and *On Work* (Pondicherry: Sri Aurobindo Ashram, 1973).
5. *Idem, On Self-Perfection* pt IV, p. 25.   6. Ibid., pt IV, p. 15.
7. Ibid., p. 16.   8. Ibid., pt II, p. 16.
9. Ibid., p. 18.   10. Ibid., p. 18.
11. *Idem, On Work*, p. 25.   12. Ibid., pp. 26–7.
13. *Idem, On Self-Perfection*, pt II, p. 17.   14. Ibid., pt IV, p. 18.

APPENDIX–III

A letter from the Head of the Management Development Division of a very large private enterprise:

About my ownself, as a result of attending the two modules, I have this to report:

1. I seem to feel energetic, much happier than before, look forward to my daily prayers and daily walk (I do deep breathing while walking but not at prayer time).
2. Domestic life is quite satisfactory. So is work life. I don't get angry so easily. When I get angry I realize it much more quickly and try to calm down.
3. Relationship with my superiors is as good as before. I don't put up a show.
4. With respect to colleague relationship, it is as good as before. I still have difficulties with a few even though I try to accept most of what they want.
5. Subordinate relationship is reasonable. I never allow ego to affect a decision. Accept viewpoints of subordinates even though they are contrary to mine. I try not to impose my authority over them. I am much more understanding, at least that is what I think. But, I find leadership messy. Sometime I do give the feeling that I am consulting a subordinate but as a matter of fact, I have already made up my mind. I tend to judge people and don't seem to be able to change this.
6. When I get frustrated, I think about 'Higher Self', 'Pure Mind'. And remember your hymn:

    I have a body, but I am not the body,
    I have the senses, but I am not the senses,
    I have a mind, but I am not the mind,
    I have the intellect, but I am not the intellect.

    It brings me bliss and my frustration lessens.
7. I like introspection now.
8. I have always enjoyed my work. In fact, I am now trying to balance work life with family life. I do believe I have overworked and have not been as close to my family as I should.
9. About creative thinking, I don't really know the change. But, I do think of 'Mind Stilling'.
10. My immediate boss has always been a source of inspiration. Perhaps, now I am more convinced about the importance of values in work as a result of your programme. My boss had always given this importance.

    Overall your programme has certainly made a lasting impact on my mind. I feel guilty that I cannot live upto it all.

5

SOCIO-CULTURAL CHANGE AND THE MANAGER'S TRAVAILS

This Chapter and the next present a non-technical, straightforward impressionistic survey of the contemporary managerial milieu in India. They reinforce considerably the need for learning and practising the ideas and processes presented in the previous chapters.

I. THE GROANING ENGINEER

In September 1988, while conducting some programmes on 'Managerial Effectiveness and Values System' at IPCL* in Baroda, we had a series of intimate breakfast-table conversations on four mornings with an American engineer. He was then touring many parts of the world on business assignments. Around fifty years of age, he happened to be a Chinese immigrant settled in New York for the last four decades or so. Here is a capsule of what he narrated with admirable candour and deep pathos about his socio-psychological state:

I have a German–American wife, three boys and my own nonagenarian mother living together. Mom won't stay with her daughters settled in other parts of the world. She will only live with her son. I have a round-the-clock, round-the-year nurse to attend to my mother. After our last boy crossed seven, my wife told me that she was henceforth going to work as a full-time professional doctor (she was qualified). So, she has now her independent timings, and obviously they don't match mine. When in town, after I return from office, I prepare the meals for all of us. On Sundays, if I am at home, I find that all have gone to keep their own engagements. There are five telephones in our home, and every ten minutes I have to pick up one or the other just to say that I don't know the whereabouts of my sons or wife. Each

* Indian Petrochemicals Corporation Ltd.

room has a television set too. Our home has also a lawn which is even bigger than the one for this guest-house. It is my duty to trim and tend to it every Sunday. Maybe on Saturday evenings we go for a social party to some friend's place, or they come to ours. We all end up by eating, drinking and stuffing ourselves like pigs. Since my business operates internationally, a phone call from India or Paris or London drags me out of my sleep in New York. This happens daily. In the States too I travel a lot—and often try to snatch some rest under a tree by the highway. I now feel at the end of my tether. What you told me today I will cling to [some preliminary guidelines for deep breathing, mind-stilling etc., were given]. This is something at last which I have got entirely for myself. How I admire and envy the closeness and warmth in Indian families when some of my Indian friends invite me to their's for long hours—maybe even for a day or two at times!

II. Is Change Being Deified?

Perhaps the title of this chapter suggests that socio-cultural changes are in process and given. All we have to do is only to try to bend to the dictates of any winds of change blowing across our social shores. It is this implicit orientation which needs to be challenged. The need for ushering in any change should, in our view, be a prior choice. Tackling or adapting to it follows. Too much attention to the latter, to the neglect of homework on the former, is quite likely to be counter-productive in the long-run. Social history proves this time and again. Thus, we find American psychiatrists admitting today that amongst the greatest source of stress is the changes in society's attitudes towards sex, including sexual permissiveness and the new social roles of the sexes.[1]

It is quite common to hear at various forums frequent pronouncements by many weighty speakers and writers to the following effect: 'exponential rates of change', 'high-velocity environment', 'increasing uncertainty', 'mounting complexity', 'information revolution', 'winds of turbulence' and so on. Often the members of the audience or readers, for the time being at least, seem to feel so scared, that as soon as there is a tea-break or lunch-break, they begin talking about the *Ramayana* serial, or something similar. Why? The fundamental truth is that man in society can never manage himself, his roles or his work, in terms of change alone. However paradoxical it might seem, successful psychological coping with external change demands a stable and enduring base line or core—primarily within the individual. Hence this runaway enthusiasm for change-in-itself is faulty on theoretical as well as practical grounds. The groaning American engineer is a telling example of what unquestioned socio-cultural change, and meek conformity to it, typically spells. We are short of honesty if we do not confess this poignant reality. Indeed, the crucial choice, conceptually, is 'complex living, low thinking', or 'simple living, high thinking'? According to R. D. Laing, a British psychiatrst:[2]

A child born today in the United Kingdom stands ten times greater chance of being admitted to a mental hospital than to a University. This can be taken as an indication that we are driving our children mad more effectively than we are genuinely educating them.

It may be useful, therefore, for us to take a fresh look today at the familiar pejorative 'resistance to change'. Could it be that this also is one of God's built-in design of factors in man to help him to constitutionally preserve his inner balance and mental harmony?

III. A Few Salient Aspects of Socio-Cultural Change in India

Let us continue this chapter in the mood of an anxious critic. Some socio-cultural changes now occurring in India, which we feel are very basic, will be highlighted below. It is of course not expected that everyone will agree with everything that is being said.

(1) *Rights-Orientation Displacing Duty-Orientation*: In 1988 a group of western pop musicians organized a 'human *rights* night' in New Delhi. This is indeed symptomatic. It covers up a great fallacy. The need of the hour, on a priority rating, is 'human *duties* day'. Only if the teacher does his 'duty', are students' rights satisfied. Only if the boss does his 'duty' of caring for his subordinates, can their rights of participation and autonomy be better taken care of. Only if the bank clerk attends to his 'duty' at 10 a.m. sharp, will the customer's right to the token to encash a cheque be met. If the manufacturer does his 'duty' to produce and sell a good quality product, the buyer's right to value for money is fulfilled. Examples are a legion. Indeed, if duty-orientation does not predominate our endeavours, ugly things will always continue to occur and come to light, as in the wake of the human rights night mentioned above, exposing the hollowness of the slogan and the show. The out-and-out duty-oriented role modelling, for example,

in the *Ramayana* and *Mahabharata* epics, is given eloquent expression by a French authoress Simone Weil:[3] 'The notion of obligations comes before that of rights, which is subordinate and relative to the former.... A man left alone in the universe would have no rights whatever, but he would have obligations.'

It is also observable that higher education, better economic status and the like, seem to incite greater rights-orientation amongst the majority of Indians. In truth, the reverse should have happened in India—higher education at the expense of a poor country should have reinforced duty- or obligation-orientation towards society. Recently one of the IITs discovered from a survey that the most important reason for its graduates migrating to the West was the attraction of 'more comfortable living'.

When we shared this information with a national conference audience on Indian ethos and values in February 1990, a professor from another IIT said that his own assessments indicated that it was not so much the 'pull' factor of the USA, but more the 'push' factor from India which made the students emigrate. All this is mere sophistry—reasons being invented (through our sharp intellects), to justify actions stemming from self-centred emotions. 'Motherland' as an emotion has no place in the intellectual territory of such bright young men and women—from IIMs, IITs, Medical Colleges, etc. alike.

In a recent survey of managerial values we discovered that a sample of 603 replies indicated an average score of 3·57 on a 5-point scale (1—highly desirable to 5—highly undesirable) regarding an item 'going abroad and settling there'. This meant that this habit was regarded as being close to 'undesirable'. Similarly, for another item: 'HRD should be primarily duty-oriented', the average score from 550 managers was 1.68, meaning 'desirable'. These are encouraging professions in a questionnaire setting, but there seems to be manifest gap between such professed intentions and the actual responses when we come to the crunch.[4]

(2) *Exteriorized Orientation Displacing Interiorized Orientation*: We in India are missing an essential insight, namely that the eastern temper is essentially introvert, compared to the western temper which is dominantly extrovert. Efficiency, sincerity, goodwill, gratitude, approval, love need not to be demonstrated by a constant flow of words and gestures. Such efforts often entail, in the eastern view, a dilution, indeed, vulgarization, of the depth of

the inner *bhavana*. From such exteriorization to a mere show or a facade is a proximate step.

Another aspect of exteriorization is its inevitable inducement towards increasing dependence on externals, missing out on the deep sense of inner self-sufficiency. Needless needs multiply. We chase after them with *greed* and *speed*, which are probably the twin arch-villains of the society we are trying to build for ourselves. In October 1988 we had a long discussion with two Norwegian management consultants touring India. At one stage one of them was painting a wondrous picture of a society living by computer-bred 'any-information-just-in-the-wink-of-an-eye'. After he had finished, we gently asked him: 'Would such a society be able to contain greed and speed'? He remained silent and changed the subject.

We do not realize that such endless exteriorization increasingly alienates us from our own inner essence or self. Marxian alienation is insignificant compared to such self-alienation. This is what Viktor Frankl diagnoses as the gravest psychological problem of the advanced nations and calls it 'existential vacuum.'[5] External variety and richness conceal internal sterility and poverty.

(3) *The Secular Orientation Displacing the Spiritual Orientation*: Much is being written and spoken daily for secularism and against spirituality in India today. Unfortunately, it appears, the meaning of neither is clear in our minds. Maurice Wilkins, a Nobel laureate in Biophysics,[6] has this to say:

I must say regrettably that the world view which is engendered by science is in many ways a very undesirable one because it does focus so much on the material aspects of life and on technical solutions to human problems. I think this is very bad for the human attitude.... They are all just living for having a bigger television or some new clothes or something idiotic.

In sharp contrast to this frank assessment of the secular–scientific attitude, Indian writings on secularism project it as the open-sesame to liberalism, humanism, charity and what not.

Bede Griffiths, an octogenerian Oxford scholar in literature, having made India his home for more than thirty years, warns us thus about secular reason:[7]

Reason can either be subject to the eternal Law, the Universal Reason, and then it becomes Wisdom, it knows the Self, or it can seek to be the master of the world, and then it becomes demonic. It is the demon of the modern world.

Griffiths then tells us how Western youth comes to India today to revive the sense of inner meaning of life now lost to the West, and laments that due to the current wave of modernization India also is in danger of losing this sense of the sacred, the holy, the spiritual in everything. In our haste to catch up with affluence we are forgetting that in man's social life both the secular and the spiritual instincts are vital needs. Responsible world opinion is therefore increasingly veering towards the conclusion that it is the vitalized spiritual instinct which should tame and tutor the secular instinct, rather than the other way round. It appears that the world of Indian mangement thought is altogether cut off from this epochal turn-around in human thought.

(4) *Skills-Orientation Displacing Values-Orientation*: In 1962 the UNESCO report on global education was entitled *Learning To Do*. Two decades later (1982) the same report was christened *Learning To Be*.[8] It is not difficult to visualize that the mistaken priority of 'learning to do', i.e. skills, is now being acknowledged as such, and rectified by admitting the priority of 'learning to be', i.e. values.

The chief hurdles working against excellence on the human side of Indian organizations do not seem to be centred around paucity of any skills. They are primarily centred in values. Cooperation, sharing, trust, dedication, humility, honesty, work-ethic are all values, not skills. They need long nurturing at the deeper level of *bhavana*. Skills and technology have no answer in this domain. For these *bhavana*s to grow and flourish, our organizational soils need fertilization with ethico-moral and spiritual nutrients. Quality of products and services is dependent not so much on quality circles, as on the quality of the mind of each member of the circle. Otherwise, how do we explain this simple daily experience of ours: ceiling fans in our homes bought thirty years ago still work noiselessly and their regulators still regulate, while all brands of their sleek modern equivalents are neither noise free nor is their speed amenable to regulation?

(5) *Quality of Domestic Life Messing Up Quality of Work-life*: In a recent book on the management of stress among organizational leaders and executives, the introduction offered the telling forecast that by the end of 1990 more than 50 per cent of American children will belong either to the single-parent, or step-parent or no-parent category. This datum is used by the author as a major

element in the construction of the emerging scenario of stress.[9] The moral is clear: the quality of domestic life transmits its inevitable impact to the quality of work-life. Besides, the quality of domestic life is not a function of cars and VCRs, or air-conditioners and packaged holiday tours. Truly, it lies in a deep and serene home atmosphere which we should build to douse the scorching flames of stress stoked by our work-life. It seems quite logical to presume that marital loyalty and fidelity being given a go by, organizational loyalty and fidelity should also be scoffed at. The latter is, indeed, the theme of the parable, narrated by Blanchard and Peale, of a marketing chief who was on the brink of being hired by another firm on the promise by the applicant that he would pass on his present employer's secrets.[10]

What is the trend in India today in this respect? Are we, like the West, bent on committing the folly in its entirety and then making, a few decades later, heroic noises about tackling the gratuitously invited problems of major socio-cultural changes which were uncalled for in the first instance? If the indications amongst the MBAs of the IIMs are worth anything, they are ominous. Increasingly both spouses are beginning to rush out of their homes at 8 a.m. and coming back at 8 p.m., bloated with stressful experiences during the 12-hour interval. Either they avoid having a child to earn more money together; or if they have one, it is left to the care of a grandma or an *ayah* or a creche. Thus, there is a reinforcing cycle of stress both at home and in the work-place. Recall the groaning American engineer!

(6) *The New Breed Displacing the Old Breed*: A few years ago two American authors on management strategy and organization had written the following:[11]

Now we have the New Breed of the seventies, and he is quite something else. This young man reflects the almost passionate concerns of youth in the 1970's—concerns that largely go unappreciated by the 'over thirty' crowd. These concerns include individuality, openness, concern for social environment, humanism and change.

This sounds so impressively charged with idealism that as an antidote let us also hear an American professor of philosophy, Alan Bloom, from his 1987 best-seller, *The Closing of The American Mind*:[12]

Modern psychology has this in common with what was always a popular opinion, fathered by Machiavelli—that selfishness is somehow good. Man is self, and the self must be selfish.... The great change is that a good man used to be the one who cares for others, as opposed to the man who cares exclusively for himself. Now the good man is the one who knows how to care for himself, as opposed to the man who does not.

The second strongly contrasting viewpoint just quoted demonstrates once more the point made earlier by us: management writers and thinkers (even teachers), more often than not, seem to be constructing flattering scenarios about the attitudinal profile of the new breed, and about contemporary socio-cultural reality as a whole. We would not like to believe that they lack depth or candour. What's wrong then?

However, not all is lost. While revising this chapter, we discovered Longenecker *et al.*'s (1989) data-based survey on the subject of generation gap and business values. Based on a thorough analysis of 2156 completed questionnaires (10,000 were mailed) from managerial and professional business employees in the USA, they offer the following concluding observations:[13]

For managers concerned with ethical performance, our survey reveals an area of concern and possible danger. For whatever reason, there appears to be a greater ethical laxity among younger managers and professionals in business. Senior managers can no longer assume that younger managers and professionals are similar in their ethical views to the cadre of middle-aged or older managers with whom they have most contact.

Turning to the state of affairs in India, we find more truth in Bloom's mature assessment. As an example, how else can we explain to ourselves the fact that numerous top executives of well-known companies speak in fairly condemnatory terms about our management graduates who tend to change three jobs in five years and much else. A few companies we know have vowed not to touch such 'guys'. We have personal experience of such 'guys' who swindle campus banks on the strength of teller accounts. Undeniably, these recruiting organizations must also as a whole share much of the blame. It is they who have made these 'guys' swollen-headed by rushing for campus interviews and swooping on them with fat salaries. Can teachers escape sharing the blame altogether? No. Constant harping on autonomy, freedom of decision-making, motivation, recognition, career growth and the like is apt to generate a one-sided, perverse disposition within the 'guys'. The climate in our renowned technical institutes is probably no better.

(7) *Self-Actualizing Orientation Displacing Self-Transcending Orientation*: For the last few years many western writings on managerial or motivational psychology are drawing our attention to some gaping holes in the reality of self-actualization. Thus, Edwin Nevis, writing recently in the *Journal of Applied Behavioural Sciences* about his Chinese experience in implanting western motivational theories, has observed that in the individualistic American milieu, self-actualization is basically plain narcissism.[14] Those of us who swear here by the self-actualization theory may plug their ears from such profanity! Other writers have also pointed out that self-actualization in practice actually converts most interpersonal relationships into instrumental transactions for self-advancement.

What is the Indian picture? In all our organizational consulting assignments over the last decade and a half, we have consistently observed that the spirit of grievances from the clerk to the Directors is identical and only the scales or items vary. We are however expected to believe that, with all the lower-order needs more than amply met, the Director would optimize self-actualization. Yet, the kite soars very high in the sky, with its eyes fixed on the carrion on the ground. On the contrary, we have seen examples in other walks of life, e.g. a musician, a teacher, an artist who demonstrate very high levels of self-actualization, without much whining or grumbling about the palpably poor satisfaction of their lower-order needs.

This brings us to the power of self-transcendence. Actualizing the lower, empirical, *varaha*-self is a largely futile game. It is only when this self begins to be transcended that real worthiness in individual behaviour starts to blossom. The aim is self-transcendence. Self-actualization will still come, but as a by-product of the march towards self-transcendence—for the *Vishnu*-SELF.

IV. CONCLUSION: WHAT COULD BE DONE?

In conclusion let us hint at a few ideas for honest and sincere consideration and implementation:

(1) If any wave of socio-cultural change has the potential for accelerating cultural imitation (not assimilation) or psychic root-

lessness, it must immediately be challenged. The question of tackling the effects of such change should not then arise. Did not the Japanese do exactly this?

(2)   India must develop her own standards of judging what socio-cultural ideals or models to preserve and what to discard, and stop going merely by the half-baked verdicts delivered by those foreign scholars (and their eager Indian followers) who cannot but be superficial about India. Thus, if Rama is described in their writings as a veritable abdicator or a wife-baiter, an Indian should also know that from Tulsidas to Sri Ramakrishna, countless Indians have been, and are being, transported to the highest levels of bliss and self-transcendence by the mere utterance or repetition of Ram-*nam*—nor should Gandhiji be forgotten.

(3)   If modernity is entitled to question tradition at every step, there is every reason also for tradition to question modernity. Superstition and obscurantism attach equally to modernity and tradition, only the *nama* and the *rupah*—the name and the form—change. Of this Bertrand Russell says:[15]

Men in the past were often parochial in space, but the dominant men of our age are parochial in time. They feel for the past a contempt that it does not deserve, and for the present a respect that it deserves still less.

He may have said this almost six decades ago, but his warning remains entirely valid today.

(4)   Our education at all levels must found itself upon a definition of the true superordinate goal of human life. Accordingly, the definition of 'progress' must also be corrected. We should listen here to Vivekananda: the purpose of education is to reveal the *perfection* already in man and the purpose of human life is to manifest the potential *divinity* already in man.[16] As for 'progress', it must be judged not merely in terms of objective measurable indices, but in terms of what it contributes to man's inner balance, harmony and purity. Progress must be re-defined and pursued in subjective terms such as these. Guenon, the French thinker, said scathingly about 'Progress' and 'Civilization':[17]

Certainly ... these two words play one of the most important parts in the battery of formulae which those 'in control' today use to accomplish their strange task of collective suggestion without which the mentality that is characteristic of modern times would indeed be short-lived.

136/ Management by Values

(5)   In consonance with the foregoing spirit, any socio-cultural change which is potentially high-entropy, *pravritti*-dominated, i.e. which could be the cause of greater dissipation and disorderliness in the earth's non-renewable resources, should be halted, e.g. increasing number of cars being used, or use of personal computers by more and more people, or increased consumption of mass-produced, packaged fast foods and so on.[18] Instead, any low-entropy, *nivritti*-regulated change should be preferred, even if it implies a gradual return in many cases to the so-called tradition or past. This will require courage and vision of an extraordinarily different order, but posterity will be greateful to us if we can demonstrate this now.

REFERENCES

1. 'Stress! Can We Cope?', *Time*, 6 June 1983, p. 48.
2. Quoted in 'India Needs the Indian Experience in Education', *Prabuddha Bharata*, vol. 93, March 1988, pp. 84–5.
3. S. Weil, *The Need For Roots* (London: Ark Paperbacks, 1987), p. 3.
4. S.K. Chakraborty, *Value Orientation in the World of Indian Management/Administration* (Calcutta: Vivekananda Nidhi, 1990), pp. 16–17.
5. Viktor Frankl, *Man's Search For Meaning* (New York: Pocket Books, 1963), pp. 167–8.
6. M. Wilkins, quoted in *Interviews With Nobel Laureates and Other Eminent Scholars* (Bombay: The Bhaktivedanta Institute, 1986), p. 44.
7. B. Griffiths, *Return to The Centre* (London: Collins, 1987), pp. 16–17.
8. Quoted in 'India Needs the Indian Experience in Education', p. 86.
9. R.N. Jones, *Human Relations Skills: Training and Self-help* (London: Guildford & Kings Lynn, 1987), Preface.
10. K. Blanchard, and N. Peale; *The Power of Ethical Management* (New York: William Morrow & Co., 1988), pp. 11–16.
11. J.E. Ross, and M.J. Kami, *Corporate Management in Crisis* (New Jersey: Prentice Hall, 1973), p. 237.
12. A. Bloom, *The Closing of the American Mind* (New York: Simon & Schuster, 1988), p. 178.
13. J.G. Longenecker, J.A. McKinney, and C.W. Moore, 'The Generation Gap in Business Ethics', *Business Horizons*, vol.32, no.5, September–October, 1989, p. 14.

14. E. Nevis, 'Using an American Perspective in Understanding Another Culture: Towards a Hierarchy of Needs For The People's Republic of China', *The Journal of Applied Behavioural Science*, vol. 19, no. 3, 1983, p. 262.
15. B. Russell, *The Scientific Outlook* (London: George Allen & Unwin, 1931), p. 277.
16. Swami Vivekananda, *Rajyoga* (Calcutta: Advaita Ashrama, 1976), pp. 200–1.
17. R. Guenon, *East and West* (London: Luzac & Co., 1941), p. 30.
18. J.E. Rifkin and T. Howard, *Entropy—A New World-View* (New York: Bantam Books, 1981), pp. 245, 250–1.

6

SOCIAL VALUES AND INDIVIDUAL ATTITUDES
Whither Behaviour?

I. Values: VAB or BAV?

The title of this chapter suggests three cause-and-effect relationships, namely:

(a) The causal status of 'social' values, and the resultant status of 'individual' attitudes and behaviour.

(b) The causal status of 'behaviour', and the resultant status of 'attitude' followed by 'values', or the 'BAV' model in brief.

(c) The causal status of 'values', and the resultant status of 'attitudes' followed by 'behaviour', the sequence being 'value-to-attitudes-to-behaviour', or the 'VAB' model.

We propose in section II to deal mainly with (a), as it projects a vision of the dynamics between society and the individual. It implies that it is the individual who is always shaped by society. Hence, first change the social values; changes in individual attitudes and behaviour would follow. This position, however, begs the question: who change(s) the social values in the first place? Or, do the latter change autonomously? We shall return to it after considering some specific contemporary values which, by common consensus, appear to have displaced some older ones in our environment.

So far as (b) is concerned, it is only recently that managerial sociology is beginning to rediscover the significance of concrete rituals and rites in values and culture formation. At the base rituals and rites are no more than a set of disciplined behavioural movements, with the underpinning of some higher principle—from 'left-right, left-right' or 'stand-at-ease' in physical training drills, to singing the national anthem or company song in large groups when standing to attention. It is disciplined repetition of these behaviour procedures which can impress our mind with enduring and useful practical attitudes and values (*samskaras*). Thus, the BAV strategy should merit serious consideration as a practical complement to the intellectually more appealing VAB model. This chapter, however, does not deal with BAV in any detail. It concentrates rather on the VAB model and discusses some thorny issues within this frame. Those who work on organizational culture via the VAB model, particularly in India, do not seem to appreciate that the 'deep structure' of any society (more so of India because it has the longest recorded history amongst living civilizations), must be thoroughly examined and internalized before dishing out such fresh or modified values-paradigms as could yield constructive results.

II. THE SPECTRUM OF CHANGES: A DIVER'S EYEVIEW

Several organizational studies, in-house management development programmes and environmental scanning by us over the last fifteen years or so suggest the following picture of values (predominantly personal rather than organizational, for nearly all cherished organizational values have their first source in an appropriate personal values-system) in transition:

From	*To*
Contentment	Avariciousness
Selflessness	Selfishness
Duties	Rights
Giving	Grabbing
Patience	Haste
Humility	Arrogance
Understanding	Information
Self-restraint	Promiscuity
Discipline	Indulgence
Vertical	Horizontal
Centre	Circumference
Subjective	Objective

From	*To*
Metaphysical	Physical
Sacred	Secular
Holy	Profane
Emotional purity	Intellectual sharpness
Transcendent	Empirical
Spirit	Matter

Real-life examples given below illustrate some of these changes.

● *Contentment to Avariciousness*: A retired District Judge recently told a retired Joint Secretary that even many District Magistrates today are involved in the network of graft. No wonder then that even IIT and IIM graduates think nowadays of joining the IAS!

In January 1989, the Director of a major division in a large and highly profitable public enterprise was forced to meet and negotiate, across the table, with the Officers' Association new terms for enhancing the rates of medical facilities to them simply because a few weeks earlier some unfair anomalies in respect of such benefits to the staff employees had been corrected in the upward direction. The Association's grouse was that the previous differential between the average levels of remuneration of the officers and the staff had been narrowed down. A few conscientious officers privately confided to us: 'what more do we want?' However, the vast majority of them aspire ceaselessly to get rich quick at the organization's cost. The appendix to this chapter gives a full list of the benefits enjoyed by officers of this company.

Does all this not reveal the absence of idealism beyond one's self amongst the top ten per cent of this poor country? How correctly had Sri Aurobindo once remarked that generally people are altogether blind to the ugliness of their actions; that one must be very high on the scale to see that what one does is ugly.

● *Humility to Arrogance*: A few years ago L.K. Advani, recounting his experiences in the early days of Indian Parliament, narrated an episode which was to him a 'battle of courtesies' between Shyama Prasad Mookerjee and Jawaharlal Nehru, and said that the entire House was nearly thrilled to tears by their dialogue. In contrast, today we have 'battles of arrogance' in the most hallowed institutions of our democracy—Parliament and Universities and the rest. The Japanese industrial empire of

Matsushita insists upon 'humility' as one of the spiritual values among its employees, but our Indian firms can go only so far as 'openness', or 'customer orientation' or similar phrases (see chapter 1). Yet, many of these organizations complain about the arrogance of IIM graduates. A recent TV serial 'Kennedy'-showed how all the colleagues of President Kennedy used to rise from their seats whenever he entered or left the room, and addressed him as 'Sir'. In some of our prestigious academic institutions, even students frown upon and reject such norms. Do we not have a Sanskrit saying: *vidya dadati vinayam*?; or is *vinay* (humility) a feudal mentality?

- *Self-Restraint to Promiscuity*: A fine-tuned battle of wits built up a few years ago regarding the impending menace of AIDS in India. At one point a hornet's nest was stirred up by a doctor's official suggestion for monitoring cohabitation of Indian nationals with foreigners as a preventive measure against AIDS. Instantly, the entire news-media took on the garb of the knight-in-armour to save individual liberty. There could be pros and cons to both points of view but what has tended to be entirely lost sight of or obscured in this debate is the real danger of unbridled, socially harmful promiscuity in the name of individual liberty. The doctor seemed to have been sincere in offering that suggestion. Aldous Huxley once remarked: 'We [modernists] object to morality because it interferes with our sexual freedom.' God knows how many homes are being defiled by the current video craze in India!

- *Duties to Rights*: This is almost akin to considering the reaction as more important than the original action. Sociologically speaking, the need for asserting rights follows only when the corresponding duties are not discharged. If a society or culture possesses a comprehensive theory and workable scheme of duties, then insistent emphasis on and renewal thereof should be a better way of organizing social transactions than mobilizing catchy and half-baked rights movements. Thus, when as teachers we do not perform our duty of dedicated study and research, our students, by asserting their rights to learn by sit-ins or slogan-shouting, are engaged in collective dissipation of energy. It is more important to rekindle the sense of duty in us, the teachers, by reference to whatever relevant classical principles are enshrined in our culture. In another sphere, the solely rights-based trade union movement, which seems to be living beyond its time, symbolizes this damaging displacement of perspective. Moreover, duty-based cooperation at all levels is a much better prescription for mental health than rights-based competition. Modern man, however, seems bent on undermining his mental health. This latter is prevented by gradual attenuation of the lower (*varaha*) self and development of the higher (*Vishnu*) Self. Work done as duty, in turn, achieves this transformation.[1]

● *Subjective to Objective*: There are several correlates of this transition in the preceding list, e.g. metaphysical to physical, transcendent to empirical, spirit to matter, etc. Let us consider the process of annual performance appraisal of individuals. Ten years ago we were an ardent advocate of using MBO to lend greater objectivity to performance appraisal. We would condemn appraisal forms which were either entirely or predominantly based on the various dimensions of human character, e.g. honesty, integrity, fellow-feeling, patience and the like on the grounds that they are too subjective and it is impossible to rate them judiciously. We should, therefore, be happy today to see more and more organizations stripping their appraisal forms of such subjective intrusions. But alas! We are not.

The deeper theoretical argument for our back-tracking is the growing realization of the ancient Indian verity that the subjective is always the cause, the objective the effect. There is a piece of deep wisdom: 'things are thoughts'. The visible output in the form of a product or service or behaviour always stems from an inner subjective milieu soaked in values of one kind or another. Our hunch, therefore, is that since values like patience, integrity, etc. are disappearing from society, leaders in organizations (or professors in IIMs and IITs) being no exception, the moral stamina for judging others on such criteria is also vanishing. There is in consequence a vicious downward spiral. Some recent empirical studies in the USA are candid enough to admit that beneath the exterior picture of neat objectives, a host of subjective problems infest the actual process of MBO. Our own experience with MBO in India corroborates this. By pretending to eliminate the subjective from the surface, one does not eliminate it from beneath. Indeed, the bull of the subjective must be caught by its horns, and firmly managed, but our masquerade of objectivity is the true danger.

Many a manager/administrator has strongly protested against

our thesis that '*all* decisions, without exception, are subjective in the ultimate analysis; therefore the subjective of the decision-maker must be purified'. With glamorous computers and the din of the information revolution and decision-support systems constantly around, decisions are now more objective than ever before, they claim with conviction. But this is naïve and is tantamount to saying that computers take the decisions, not the manager! Besides the hard facets of timeliness and accuracy, all decisions are also expected to be *fair*—a soft, subjective aspect. What are we doing to improve the quality of our own *internal* decision-support system, the *antahkarana*, which alone can ensure *fairness*?

● *Transcendent to Empirical*: There is today great ballyhoo about empiricism—especially in the corridors of academia. The glamorous variety and clamorous noise of empiricism are so high-pitched that we miss an insight of capital importance: the empirical is merely a grosser manifestation of the subtle, the transcendent—not necessarily manifest to our muddled senses. A simple example at the mundane level may help: a huge banyan tree and the tiny seed from which it grows. The empirical is already involved in the transcendent, the gross in the subtle—this is the law, the fact.

The empirically-inspired, positivist intellectual, bravely coursing his or her way on a flat existential plane, laughs at and derides the beliefs of the common man in the transcendent with the telling epithet 'superstitious'. The former fails to understand that almost every so-called superstition of the unliberated man has been originally inspired by a humble recognition of the transcendent within his scheme of life. This value of instinctive humility before the transcendent is installed right in the midst of his daily routine through rites, rituals and symbols of great imaginative vigour— provided we have an open mind to understand them in this light. Thus, the common traditional man retains more of his instinctive inclination towards a vertical existential mode than does the modern. The intellectual man should not scoff at it. Instead, he ought to refine it and creatively adapt it for healthier organizational life. The lesson of humility should return to us via the resurrection of the transcendent in our mind's chamber. Thus, we often feel that it is a supremely arrogant superstition of modern society to consider the transcendent phoney. Bede Griffiths[2] (1976), for example, says:

This was the essential thing (in ancient cultures), *to keep contact with the Transcendent*, so that human life did not become closed on itself. But the modern world has removed every such point of contact. Everything has become profane, that is, outside the sphere of the holy ... Young people now come to India from the West, seeking to recover the sense of the sacred, the inner meaning of life, which has been lost in the West. *But India too is losing it rapidly*. [Emphasis added.]

If the Indian manager is a 'man' first, and only then a manager, does he not need to begin to consider such holistic orientations at the earliest?

• *Emotional Purity to Intellectual Sharpness*: In December 1988 the Personnel Manager of a well-known private sector firm informed us at a Workshop on Values-System held at the IIM-C Campus that, on the basis of systematic data analysis done by a specialist agency, the firm was getting clear evidence that its new trainees who had scored quite high on the intellect-related para- meters tended to score rather low on the values-related parameters. Einstein had long ago warned us that we 'should take care not to make intellect our God', and even earlier Vivekananda counselled that intellectual education alone takes no care of the heart; it only makes men ten times more selfish. He exhorted us:[3]

Through the *intellect is not the way to solve the problem of misery*, but through the heart. If all this vast amount of effort had been spent in making man purer, gentler, more forbearing, this world would have a thousand fold more happiness than it has today. *Always cultivate the heart*. [Emphasis added.]

Intellectual sharpness, without emotional purity, readily gets perverted to cunning manoeuvres for personal gain or vendetta (recall Shakuni in the *Mahabharata*). Also, an impure emotional base triggers false intuitions and inspirations—which the sharp intellect is only too ready to execute with lethal perfection, e.g. Hitler's tragic case. Introspection within organizations will reveal countless examples of such events. A Buddha or a Shankara or a Gandhiji have shown us how both emotional purity and intellec- tual brilliance can coexist, provided the right methods for self- transformation are followed.

• *Selflessness to Selfishness*: Here is a sentence from Alan Bloom, a professor of philosophy in the USA, who has produced a best-selling—and a breath-taking—survey of the contemporary American mind, condemning outright its growing and blatant selfishness:[4] 'Our desire becomes a kind of oracle we consult; it is now the last word, while in the past it was the questionable and dangerous part of us.'

This is what happens when the normative is studiously banished from the portals of education and training, and positivism is allowed to pamper our sensual propensities. Vivekananda had bluntly told us that all selfishness is contraction and all contraction is death. Empiricism in itself may not be bad, but a fetish for it certainly is and is becoming our undoing.

If the scheme of the society is based entirely on the value of selfishness (for motivation is merely sweetened jargon for selfishness), it is quite futile to talk of openness or cooperation amongst individuals. At a recent two-day meeting in Delhi, where about fifteen luminaries in the field of management education had assembled to thrash out the details of courses for specialization in 'human resource management' for the students of a university, we saw fresh evidence of the lack of sensitivity and urgency in regard to the problem of attitudes and behavioural values at the grass-roots level. In the list of about 30 to 40 items discussed, not one pertained to 'human values' *per se*. Words like 'skills', 'tools', 'techniques', 'dynamics', etc. were however used very freely. Much time was spent on a course item entitled 'Compensation and Reward Plans' which may be thought of as according full academic sanctity to the syndrome of rising collective greed and selfishness amongst the top ten per cent of India's population.

We also recall that in a recent in-company workshop on Values-System, at some point when we had occasion to refer to the Harishchandra-episode (of supreme self-sacrifice) in the *Rama-yana*, one top executive dismissed its message as purely idealistic. This when, from Gandhiji's autobiography, we learn how, as a mere Mohandas, a schoolboy, he used to be moved to tears by reading the story; and that even when he had grown up, its inspiring quality remained with him, regardless of its historicity or otherwise.[5]

- *Discipline to Indulgence*: A few years ago a senior executive of a prestigious bank in India told us that when he had joined the bank there was a strict code of conduct: no officer of the bank would accept any invitation to parties thrown by the business or industrial community, or even a cup of tea from them. Today, however, this injunction has been withdrawn on the plea that mixing with people at such parties provides officers with greater opportunities to gain practical insights into the thinking and doings of the business world! Thus, the superior wisdom of the earlier injunction to preserve the unimpeachable integrity of the bank seems to have made little sense to its later and more modern captains. A *shreya* value of the highest order, discipline, for such an institution was sacrified to the *preya* behaviour of socializing for the dubious value of picking up information in a milieu dripping with greed and self-indulgence. It is not understood that a value like discipline in large organizations must be institutionalized through explicit behavioural codes and rituals.

Some years ago, in one of the earliest refineries in the public sector, an employee was permitted to go out of the refinery gate during working hours only on three specific counts, e.g. to the hospital, under the authority of three different kinds of gate passes. If such a person returned later than the time authorized on the card, specified amounts were deducted from his or her salary for each minute of delay. This rule was adopted from a foreign oil company then operating in India. The senior executive, who gave me this information, lamented that today such fines have been withdrawn, and discipline has eroded entirely.

• *Metaphysical to Physical*: The so-called modern society is becoming more and more physical, i.e. grosser or *sthula*. The more gross it is, the more real it is—we think. It does not occur to us that the tendency to accept the gross as truly real is directly the outcome of the incapacity of our mind to grasp the reality of the subtle or *sukshma*. Compare the savage in the forest with the educated city dweller. The relative difference is clear. But the civilized urbanite is so crowding his daily existence with the gross redundancies of technological society that he is also turning into an elegantly attired savage within the concrete jungle of cities.

The clue to this predicament seems to be this: truly speaking, man has no need of the physical, except as a means to the metaphysical. Only a little serious reflection will reveal the incontrovertible truth of this statement. When I desire to have a colour TV set, it is not the physical set itself that I need; rather I am seeking the metaphysical satisfaction or pleasure of watching colour pictures. When I aspire for an automobile, once more the mainspring is metaphysical. If, therefore, it were possible for us to condition our minds to the centrality of the metaphysical in our secular existence too, then we might open up the true path for values-oriented management of our needs for the physical. For, the ultimate metaphysical argument is that, the *sukshma* source of satisfaction or happiness, or peace is, *ab initio*, entirely internal to man. 'The Kingdom of Heaven is within', as the Bible says. So, begin slowly but surely to seek it directly and be peaceful, wholesome and effective. The goal of satisfaction — which must be metaphysical — through externals alone is bound to be a process of clash and confusion. Thus, the inner *poornatwa* theory is unassailable.

In the 8–14 January 1989 issue of *The Illustrated Weekly of India*, Rajani Kothari rightly highlighted the dangerous phenomenon of accelerating divisiveness in Indian society which had been accompanying planned economic development. We are glad that this analysis echoes precisely the point we have also been emphasizing for some years. Our seers have always warned us in words something like this: 'matter divides, spirit unites'. It is the unitive core of the spirit or the metaphysical which the modern mentality is loath to consider and accept. Spirit in this context, needless to say, has nothing to do with the unholy ghost of politicized religion.

Thus, if primary value is placed on the common ground of metaphysical reality, then attitudinal and behavioural difficulties in the domain of physical or social reality could either be prevented much earlier, or could be resolved without moving nearer to disaster. The principle is that the gross can be managed much better in the light of the subtle. But this subtle is not just the intellect as it is now possessed by us. It is the pure, radiant, divinized heart.

III. Conclusion: Sorting Out the Cause and Effect Sequence

Looking back at the issues posed in the beginning, and after patient observation and personal experience of daily events over a long period, we think that, in the operational sense, the BAV model, and its implication that disciplined behaviour could and does also result in attitude and values formation, has to be given adequate consideration. For most of us, values still seem to be quite elusive, although the word is intellectually becoming more and more respectable. Values in Indian culture have their own characteristic 'deep structure', scarcely visible at the surface. Therefore, changes at the behavioural level also, which are more externalized, should be introduced—at least simultaneously—along the grain of the deep structure, accompanied by our intellectual familiarization with value concepts. Organizational culture-building efforts through symbols, rites and rituals should reflect this practical aspect. For, symbols and rituals are but concretized values, concretized philosophy, e.g. the ritual of touching the feet of elders (*pranam*) in Indian society is a behavioural expression of the attitude of 'respect' for experience and age, and of the value of 'humility' in human intercourse.

As to the question whether society is the cause and the individual the effect or vice-versa, we are inclined towards the latter. Otherwise, we cannot explain the Buddhas, Christs, Mohammeds, Nanaks, Vivekanandas, Gandhijis, or even Marxs and Maos. The idea that the climax of true individual autonomy lies in the will to remould society, and not in the sham autonomy to turn a slave to its fleeting fads, can be grasped only by recalling these visionaries. Coming to the crux, there is nothing collective about their endeavours, except at a much later stage in their lives. The first few decades of their careers have been a period of silent, solitary, intense incubation. They never waited for society's values to change first, hoping that their own attitudes and behaviour would follow suit through some automatic mechanical process. The message is clear: each one of us must begin the journey of personal responsibility for values or attitudes or behavioural transformation here and now, in order to leave behind a better social milieu for posterity. To argue that history throws up such men when society needs them is to lapse into passivity and to fail to respond to the inspired call for self-transformation that their selfless endeavours engender. As for embarking on such a self-willed voyage, a much deeper and enduring vision of 'man–society–cosmos' is required than modern scientism seems to be providing. If indeed the VAB model continues to grip our mind, then it must be founded on the 'deep structure' of Indian culture. Innovation in this field, without a clue about the nature of this 'deep structure', might cost our organizations very dearly. All the pairs of 'from-to' mentioned above constitute, in our view, the symptoms of gross deviations from our 'deep structure'—lured by the false promise of historicism (a corollary of biological evolutionism) even in matters of eternal principle, a warning Guenon had sounded long ago (1937).[6] Historicism claims, in effect, that the later the better and the earlier the worse. As managers of matters mundane, let us recall once more the words of Bede Griffiths,[7] if not of our Tagores and Aurobindos:

If mankind is to survive ... it can only be through a total change of heart, a *metanoia* which will make science subordinate to wisdom. The discursive reason which seeks to dominate the world and imprisons man in the narrow world of the conscious mind must be dethroned, and must acknowledge its dependence on the transcendent Mystery, which is beyond the rational consciousness.

Griffiths and Einsteins, Aurobindos and Vivekanandas are all passionately exhorting us to seek the source of enduring human and social values (i.e. the *shreya* instead of the *preya*, the electable instead of the delectable) in the traditional thought of the past which has immensely more to offer than we realize. Unfortunately, modern management literature has nothing basic to offer in carrying out a genuine reconstruction of values-system in our organizations. Methodologically it shows off a lot, but conceptually it is on the whole shallow and sterile. The modern mind must, therefore, rid itself of the superstition that the past is plain anachronism and may be safely buried. Values are concerned with truth, not novelty, and admit of the superiority of only the spiritual over the social and the secular.

The breath-taking upheavals of 1989 in all the East European countries, the return of the spiritual and religious freedoms, the liquidation of monopoly communist parties and so on make us recall the prophetic vision of Sri Aurobindo (1909):[8]

After all God exists and if He exists, you cannot shove him into a corner and say, 'That is your place and as for the world and life it belongs to us'. He pervades and returns. Every age of denial is only a preparation for a larger and more comprehensive affirmation.

It is the ascendancy of the blind dynamism of the expansive *rajasic* movement in human consciousness which is at the root of all the ten degrading transitions in value-orientation discussed above. Ackoff (1984), a respected name in management science, had almost entirely summed up this assessment in lamenting that 'Alienation, hopelessness, frustration, insecurity, corruption, tyranny and social unrest are only a few of the many symptoms, of deeply rooted malfunctioning of societies and their institutions'.

It is the revival of the illumined and serene dynamism of the *sattwic* movement which is now the need of the hour to restore sanity and balance in our dealings with ourselves and our environment. This shift of emphasis is to be willed and executed by the individual first, and only then will society change for the better.

APPENDIX
FACILITIES TO OFFICERS

1. *Leave*

a) Earned Leave	32 days a year.	

8 days are to be availed and 24 days can be encashed. EL can be accumulated upto 240 days. In case of resignation, retirement and premature death, the payment for the accumulated EL will be paid to the employee.

b) Sick Leave	10 days a year.	

1 day's Sick Leave at a time can be availed without production of a medical certificate. This facility can be availed to a maximum of 10 times a year

Sick Leave also can be accumulated upto 240 days. Partial encashment of the accumulated Sick Leave as per the formula is also permissible.

c) Casual Leave	10 days a year.	

This can be availed to a maximum of 6 days at a time, prefixing and suffixing off days and holidays.

d) Festival Holidays

12 days a year in accordance with the Factories Act.

e) Special Casual Leave

Duration is from 1 day to 14 days. This is granted in case of blood donation, sterilization operation, attending sports, territorial army camps, etc.

f) Special Casual Leave for 48 hrs. of work

Those who are working for 48 hrs. per week are eligible to 5 days Special Casual Leave per quarter. If this Special Casual Leave is not availed within the next quarter, then in the 3rd quarter 5 days salary is paid to him along with his salary for the month.

2. *Medical Expenses*

Medical expenses for the families are borne by the Corporation. If the parents are dependants and live under the same roof, they are also entitled to total medical treatment.

In case of outside referral for treatment by a specialist, in addition to the medical expenses, the travelling expenses are also borne by the Corporation. Whenever an escort is essential, in accordance with the advice of the company's Medical Officer, the travelling expenses of the escort are also paid.

3. *LTC* (Leave Travel Concession)

Employees are eligible to LTC twice in a block of 4 years. In one block of 2 years LTC is provided for visiting the home town and in the next block the employees are entitled to go anywhere in India.

LTC facility is also extended to dependant parents.

If the employee does not want to avail the LTC facility upto 5000 kms (to and fro) for each individual of the family it can be encashed.

However, for encashment, 5 days leave is essential (including Saturday, Sunday and weekly off).

4. *Working of extra hours on holidays*

When an employee works for 4 hours or more on holidays/off days, he is entitled to Rs 120/- per day. For working beyond the normal working day to a minimum of an additional 2 hours, an employee is entitled to Rs 60/- as out of pocket expenses.

5. *Canteen Subsidy*

Lunch and snacks are provided at a subsidized rate at the plants.

6. *Housing facility*

Although the BPE norm is 70 per cent satisfaction level, for officers at the plant locations housing is provided for 100 per cent of the officers.

House rent is deducted at the rate of 5 per cent of the basic pay. Electricity, water charges and scavenging charges are Rs 11/- per month. If a refrigerator is used an additional amount of Rs 6/- is levied as electricity charges.

7. *Conveyance Allowance*

A Gr. officers are entitled to Rs 225/- per month as scooter allowance. From B Gr. and onwards the car allowance is in the range of Rs 650/- to Rs 910/- per month. This allowance is paid when the scooter/car is purchased by the employees.

8. *Car Purchase*

The actual price of the scooter/car is given as a loan. The loan is recovered in 108 instalments with easy interest of 2½ per cent p.a.

9. *House Building Loan*

House building loan is sanctioned upto a maximum of 2.5 lakhs. 5½ per cent interest is levied on this loan amount.

10. *Furniture Loan*

Officers in Gr. D and above are entitled to furniture purchase loan ranging between Rs 1,600/- and 2,400/-. 2½ per cent interest is levied on this loan.

After 7 years of the purchase of the furniture, employees are entitled to buy the furniture at book value.

Rs 2,000/- is paid in alternate years for repair and upholstery replacement costs.

11. *Briefcase*

Officers are re-imbursed the cost of a briefcase after every 3 years. The cost varies between Rs 450/- and 700/-, depending upon the scales.

12. *Transfer Benefits*

On transfer from one location to another, the following benefits are given

  i) Transfer TA Rs 3,000/-
  ii) Settling Allowance—30 days Daily Allowance at the prevailing rate of the place of posting.

iii) Actual fare for the family and dependant parents by the entitled class (1st class/AC class/Air). TA and DA for all the members are also given for the journey.

iv) Loading and unloading charges on the truck at Rs 500/-

v) A & B Gr. officers are provided with one truck and C & above Gr. Officers are provided with 2 trucks for shifting their household materials. Insurance for the household materials is also reimbursed.

13. *School Facility*

One English medium school and one Central school are run at each plant location.

14. *PF/Gratuity/Pension*

Contributory PF at the rate of 8.33 per cent and Gratuity upto a maximum of Rs 1 lakh.

Earlier uniforms were provided, i.e. 2 pairs of summer uniforms, one winter uniform, one pair of shoes, 2 pairs of socks per year. Washing allowance of Rs 25/- per month was provided to all officers.

Now, in lieu of the uniform items, a pension scheme has been started. The cost of the uniform items is paid into the pension fund. In addition to this, a certain amount is to be contributed by each individual employee. This varies from 2½ per cent of the basic pay, depending upon length of service. The scheme has been introduced with the assistance of the LIC.

15. *Group Insurance Scheme*   A, B & C Gr. officers are provided with an insurance coverage for Rs 50000/-. They have to pay Rs 50/- per month.

For officers in Gr. D and above the insurance coverage is for Rs 1 lakh and deduction per month is Rs 100/-.

Out of the above amount, 2/3rd goes to LIC and 1/3rd goes to the personal account which is refunded with interest only at the time of retirement.

16. *Benevolent Funds*
   a) Unit Benevolent Fund   Officers and staff can enrol themselves with a membership fee of Rs 5/-. In the event of death/disablement of any employee, Rs 15/- is deducted from the members coming month's salary. The amount so collected is paid to the next of the kin within a month.

   b) Corporate Benevolent Fund   Each employee deposits Rs 10/- per month. In the event of death/disablement Rs 500/- p.m. is paid to the family members for 5 years.

17. *Tea Allowance*   Every month Rs 25/- is provided as tea allowance to each officer.

18. *Bonus*
   a) Profit-Linked Bonus   According to the formula, officers are not entitled to get this benefit. However, since last year an

	amount of Rs 3840/- is being paid to each officer as reward.
b) Productivity-Linked Bonus	Based on—
	i) Capacity utilization of the primary unit-weightage is 55 per cent
	ii) Capacity Utilization of the secondary unit-weightage is 25 per cent
	iii) Fuel consumption and loss reduction—if 10 per cent more than the targetted figure is achieved then the weight-age is 15 per cent
	iv) 10 per cent reduction of budgeted overtime is achieved then the weight-age is 5 per cent
	(for items (iii) & (iv) there is negative rating also)
19. *Long Service Award*	After 20 years of service, each employee is provided with a HMT Quartz wrist watch with day and date.
20. *Retirement Gift*	At the time of retirement a gift worth of Rs 1500/- is provided.
21. *Safety Award*	Marks are given for achieving one million accident-free man-hours. Marking is not uniform. After achieving one million man hours, it is proportionately reduced for 2, 3 or more million man-hours. On the basis of marks the amount to be distributed is decided. Instead of giving a cash award, gifts are normally purchased and distributed.

REFERENCES

1. Swami Gambhirananda, *Katha Upanishad* (Calcutta: Advaita Ashrama, 1980), verses I. ii 1–2, pp. 34–6.
2. S.K. Chakraborty, *Managerial Effectiveness and Quality of Work-life: Indian Insights* (New Delhi: Tata McGraw Hill, 1987), pp. 2–3.
3. D. Mercer, *IBM: How the World's Most Successful Corporation is Managed* (London: Kogan Page, 1987), p. 31.
4. R.T. Pascale, and A.G. Athos, *The Art of Japanese Management* (Harmondsworth: Penguin, 1982), p. 51.
5. T.J. Peters, and R.H. Waterman, jr., *In Search of Excellence* (New York: Harper and Row, 1982), p. 285.
6. C.C. Pegels, *Japan vs. The West* (Boston: Kluwer Nijhoff, 1984), p. 16.
7. Swami Vivekananda, 'Rajyoga' in *Collected Works* (Calcutta: Advaita Ashrama, 1962), vol.I, p. 293.
8. Mercer, op. cit., pp. 231–3.
9. M. Hiriyanna, 'Philosophy of Values' in *The Cultural Heritage of India* (Calcutta: Ramakrishna Mission Institute of Culture, 1983), vol.III, p. 648.
10. R. Tannenbaum, and S.A. Davis, 'Values, Man, and Organizations', in *Organizational Development*, eds. N. Margulies and A.P. Raia (New Delhi: Tata McGraw Hill, 1975), pp. 12–25.
11. J.A. Lee, 'Changes In Managerial Values', *Business Horizons*, July–August, 1988, p. 32.
12. Rabindranath Tagore, *Japanyatri* (Calcutta: Vishwabharati, 1976), in Collected Works, vol. 29, pp. 330, 340–1, 347.
13. E.C. Nevis, 'Using an American Perspective in Understanding Another Culture: Towards a Hierarchy of Need for the People's Republic of China', *The Journal of Applied Behavioural Science*, vol. 19, no. 3, 1983, pp. 250, 255.
14. Ibid., p. 256.
15. C.P. Lindsay and B.L. Dempsey, 'Ten Painfully Learned Lessons About Working in China: The Insights of Two American Behavioural Scientists', *The Journal of Applied Behavioural Science*, vol. 19, no. 3(1983), p. 266.
16. R. Guenon, *East and West* (London: Luzac & Co., 1941), p. 10
17. G. Hofstede, and M.H. Bond, 'The Confucius Connection: From Cultural Roots to Economic Growth', *Organizational Dynamics*, Spring, 1988, p. 17.
18. Ibid., p. 18.   19. Ibid., p. 20.
20. C.R. Pangborn, 'India's Need and The Ramakrishna Movement' in *A Bridge To Eternity—An Anthology* (Calcutta: Advaita Ashrama, 1986), p. 523.

7

DETACHED INVOLVEMENT
Work-Ethic and Ethics-in-Work

This chapter is a re-examination of the work-psychology of the
Gita—which is a primer of management-by-values. Of this text
there have been a number of brilliant detractors—especially Indians.
We realize that to begin life with a dose of scepticism is probably
healthy, but to culminate it on the same note cannot but be a major
tragedy. That is, scepticism as a means of reaching a faith may be
good; not otherwise. In this context an eloquent testimony to faith
by Aurobindo[1] is a salutary beginning:

Faith is a necessary means for arriving at realization, because we are ignorant
and do not yet know that which we are seeking to realize; faith is indeed ... the
gleam sent before by the yet unrisen Sun.

As a participant in diverse learning situations, frequent confirma-
tion is obtained of the principle that we tend to discover in
something which we are already predisposed to see, e.g. negative
fatalism in the 'theory of *karma*', and fail to detect the profound or
the salutary which is not already in us. 'Objective intellect' thus
seems to be a mere myth; and so too the assertion that 'facts speak
for themselves'. They do not. Thus, we recall the following sharp
public rebuke delivered to us by an HRD expert for citing the
relevance of the work-theory of the *Gita* to a conference audience
in 1988: 'Shall we in India speak of and teach the *Gita* to our
Muslim brothers?' We wish this rising star in HRD had read the
Bede Griffiths' comment on the *Gita*:[2] '[it] can become a manual
of spiritual guidance for the West. It has a universal message'; or a
letter by Azeemoddin in which he speaks of 'the *Gita*'s most
profound philosophy, cutting across the barriers of all religions,
races and civilizations of the world'.[3]

I. WORK COMMITMENT

Verse 2:47 of the *Gita* advises non-attachment to the fruits or results of actions performed for one's own selfish ends. Dedicated work has to mean 'work for the sake of work'. If we are always calculating the likely date of promotion springing from hard work, then it is not work commitment; it is promotion commitment! And since the workings of the world are not designed to respond to our calculations, this promotion may be elusive. Then what happens to our work commitment? So, the *Gita* rightly avoids turning work commitment to a contingent principle. If we are unable to measure up to its height, surely it is more honest to confess our own weakness rather than to fault the verse.

There are people who argue that being unattached to the consequences of one's action would also make one unaccountable, whereas accountability is a cornerstone of good management.[4] This is an entirely wrong construction. As a sequel to *Vishada Yoga*, chapter II in the *Gita* is in entirety nothing other than an incisive essay arousing the temporarily lost sense of accountability in Arjuna—according to his *swadharma* (law of one's being). It is indeed a 'key result area' for Arjuna, the *kshatriya*, to fight a righteous battle, not for personal aggrandizement but after having exhausted all peaceful means of reconciliation. The consequences of avoiding such a battle, both for him and society, are vividly set out before him. By no means are the broader social ramifications of Arjuna's crisis of dejection and withdrawal ignored. Besides, the theory of *karma*, of cause-and-effect, making the doer responsible for the consequences of his deeds, is frequently invoked in the *Gita*. Detachment from the avarice of primarily selfish gains by discharging one's accepted duty is advised; but by no means from the consequences of avoidance of duty or wrongful discharge of one's responsibilities.

An even more practical consequence of the *sadhana* for working with 'detached involvement' (*nishkam karma*)—for that is how we may internalize the essence of 2.47—is its signal contribution towards *psychological energy conservation*. At the same time, it is among the surest and most enduring preventive methods against stress and burn-out in the work-situation. Without realizing this, persons selfishly and greedily waiting for the fruits of work coming their way are destined to be the victims of destructive stress. One has to engage in quiet inner *sadhana* to appreciate the true merit of the verse, for it does not hold out a technique, but beckons us towards *anubhuti*, a deep inner feeling. It has been rightly said that the best means to effective work is to *become* the work itself. To attain this state *nishkam karma* is the right attitude because it prevents the ego, the mind from dissipation by speculation about gains or losses.

II. SELF-ACTUALIZATION

It is necessary for all of us to clearly appreciate the vital distinction between 'self-actualization' (SA) and 'SELF-realization'. Nearly a score of organizational studies done by us reveal beyond doubt that self-actualization, even in Maslovian terms, is a far cry amongst members. People at the highest echelons, with all their lower order needs satisfied, vent their views in the same tone and words as clerks do—only the scale is different. We believe that more often it is a poor teacher or an unsung artist who is an authentic self-actualizer, rather than a general manager or an executive director or a management institute don. In recent years many writings have appeared in standard western journals criticizing the myth of SA and cautioning about the individualistic, self-seeking and narcissistic impulses fostered by it. Our inability and reluctance to de-contextualize concepts like SA, which are born of a highly individualistic ethos, lead to grave distortions in our work-milieu. The casualties are our cherished goals of cooperation, sharing, trust, large-heartedness and the like.

Theoretically, the problem is: if it is the crude, raw, empirical, lower-order self which seeks actualization, then the ethically dubious manifestations of SA are inevitable. Some Western academics are more honest in recognizing this than others. In India of course we all prefer to stay mesmerized. We do not wish to hear that there is the trans-empirical higher Self too—which by definition is *poorna*. It is this which is the essence. It need not be actualized; it is waiting to be realized because it is self-existent, like the clear blue sky above the hanging clouds. Indeed, the lower (*varaha*) self has to be transcended, not actualized. Only then does social responsibility, humanism and the like flower spontaneously. 'Detached involvement' in work is a universally practical method to transcend the polluting haze of the lower self, and rise into the luminous brightness of the *poorna* (*Vishnu*) Self.

III. De-Egoization

We Indians are in the habit of measuring our greats in terms of those of the west, e.g. Kalidasa is the Shakespeare of India, or Bankim Chandra is India's Walter Scott. But the thought of Lord Krishna as the Peter Drucker of India wins the palm from them all[5]—a Drucker who, with due respect to him, does not seem to be aware of the important distinction between 'knowledge worker' and 'wisdom worker', while Lord Krishna expounds at length the latter (*sthitaprajna*). Yet the sun has to be shown with a candle! The Russells, Eliots, Toynbees and Einsteins have long been bemoaning the Cinderella treatment given to quiet wisdom, enticed as we are by the flamboyant cancan dance of arrogant knowledge, but management scholars have no time for them either—far less for the *Gita*.

Bede Griffiths (1983), already mentioned above, again says about the *Gita*:[6] 'It is the spirit of God speaking to the spirit of man and teaching him how to conduct life. That is why it is such a practical book. The *Gita* defines: *yoga samatwa uchyate* (see later) and Griffiths explains:

You suffer, but you do not give way to suffering. You have inner balance, a harmony of mind. This then is the first condition, not to seek the fruit of one's work ... this does not mean indifference to the work ... the work must be done with detachment.[7]

Why? For, as Griffiths says again:[8] 'It is the ego which spoils the work'; or 'If his ego goes into anything he does, it spoils his work'. Yet, and yet, one is told that unlike modern management, the *Gita* has nothing to motivate performance excellence! True enough. The *Gita* does not motivate—its purpose is to *inspire*. But we do not want to be inspired, or so it appears.

A German author, E. Deutsch (1968) explains the kernel of the *Gita*'s message for work thus:[9] 'This means to perform action with loving attention to the divine; it means to redirect the empirical self away from its ego-involvement with needs, desires, passions. When this is done, any action can be performed with skill.' And yet we are exhorted by our many good Indian brothers to cast aside the *Gita* in pursuit of excellence. One wonders who truly the 'foreigners' are.

We may now turn with profit to Tagore's (1914) sensitive portrayal of the spirit of the *Gita*'s work ethic:

- In the *Gita* we are advised to work disinterestedly, abandoning all lust for the result.... The man who aims at his own aggrandizement underrates everything else. Compared with himself the rest of the world is unreal. Thus in order to be fully conscious of the reality of all, man has to free himself from the bonds of personal desires.[10]

- This is the *Karma-yoga* of the *Gita*, the way to become one with the infinite activity by the exercise of the activity of disinterested goodness.[11]

- Therefore working for love is freedom in action. This is the meaning of the teaching of disinterested work in the *Gita*.[12]

In the first quotation we notice Tagore's accurate description of the true face of self-actualization; in the second of the continuum between infinite action and individual action; and in the third his pointing out that detached work is true freedom. It is a wide, non-selfish love which becomes the staying power of 'detached involvement', and these indeed are the insights which later western writers like Griffiths and Deutschs have also gained.

IV. DE-PERSONIFICATION

The rational–secular mind may also be invited to perceive that the entire dialogue in the *Gita* is clearly amenable to de-personification. In this conceptual light it is a counselling–communication session *par excellence* between the empathetic yet stern Cosmic or trans-empirical Intelligence and the individual empirical intelligence. That these two ought to be in communion is an imperative of Indian psycho-philosophy. Many are the ways of striving towards such communion. The muddled confusion of the secular mind is in acute need of the clear light of the transcendent or the spiritual and should attempt to shed its awe of it. The priority, the hierarchy of imperatives needs to be clear—the secular is indeed subordinate to the spiritual.

It is also important to appreciate the Cosmic–individual communication process from another meaningful point of view. The theory is that supporting the discrete discontinuities at the empirical level is the unbroken continuity of the Cosmic or trans-empirical consciousness. Individual intelligence or consciousness is a fraction of this universal, all-pervasive consciousness. Our normal awareness, intelligence, etc. only apparently function discretely. This causes a deterioration in their quality of performance. The theory further holds that this Supreme Intelligence has the intrinsic property of maintaining a linkage with each unit of individual intelligence. But as a needle smeared with mud is not attracted by a bar magnet, so the sullied individual intelligence cannot be catalysed by this pull of the Supreme Intelligence. The main process advocated in the *Gita* for restoring this link–pull dynamics rests on *bhakti* (devotion), *prapatti* (surrender), and *nirdwandwa* (equipoise). The first two constitute a sincere, intense emotional pining to rediscover the lost link. This is why sincere prayer is such an effective psychological process. The third is a strong-willed determination to keep the mind free of and above the dualistic see-saw of daily experiences. 'Detached involvement' in work is the key to this *nirdwandwic*[13] status. These preparations gradually lead to a stage where the person begins to feel the Supreme Intelligence acting as the authentic inner support, guide, and critic of the individual intelligence. This de-personified 'individual consciousness–Supreme Consciousness communication process' approach to the *Gita* might suit those temperaments better which are averse to deification, personality cult, *virat purusha* and similar means for internalizing the laws of higher life.

V. Work-Ethic v. Ethics-in-Work

The message implicit in this rather contemporary phrase 'work-ethic' seems to be one of vigour and ardour for sustained hard labour in pursuit of a given or chosen task. When Lord Krishna rebukes Arjuna sharply for his unmanliness and imbecility in recoiling from a righteous battle,[14] it is the call for work-ethic that rings in it. Poor work-ethic is a consequence of *tamo-guna* (or the veiling power) overtaking the individual's psyche. The stinging rebuke is intended to bring alive the temporarily dormant *rajo-guna* (or the projecting power) in Arjuna.

However, in chapter 16, the *Gita* offers a detailed enumeration of two kinds of psychic energy resources or endowments: *asuri sampat* or demonic resources, and *daivi sampat* or divine resources. The manifest effects of the predominance of one of these two sets of sources of driving energy— for both contribute to work-ethic in their own way—are typically described as follows:

(a) *Daivi*: 'The Blessed Lord said: fearlessness, purity ..., giving, self-control, sacrifice, ... straightforwardness ..., self-denial, calm, absence of fault-finding, ... absence of greed, gentleness, modesty, ... absence of envy and pride—these are the wealth of the man born into the Deva nature.'[15]

(b) *Asuri*: 'Thus occupied by many egoistic ideas, deluded, addicted to the gratification of desire, doing works but doing them wrongly, acting mightily but for themselves, for desire, for enjoyment, not for God in themselves and God in man, they fall into the unclean hell of their own evil.'[16]

It is clear that the work-ethic inspired by *daivi-sampat* is akin to that which *sattwa guna* stimulates, while that triggered by *asuri-sampat* is cognate with *rajo-guna* stimulation. Thus, in *sattwa-guna* work-ethic is in holy alliance with ethics-in-work. Therefore, the goal set for Arjuna is not mere work-ethic (for does not Duryodhana too demonstrate this in good measure?), but work-ethic leavened with ethics-in-work. Similarly, in the Ramayana, Ravana and his son symbolize strong work-ethic along with weak ethics-in-work in relation to the Ram–Hanuman combination which also has strong ethics-in-work.

It is in this light that the counsel *'yogah karmasu kaushalam'*[17] needs to be understood. *Kaushalam* means skill or method or technique of work. This is an indispensable component of work-ethic. What does 'yogah' mean in relation to this 'kaushalam'? What kind of skill is this *yoga* which should be the basis of work-ethic? To answer this we should know that elsewhere in the *Gita* it has been said: *samatwam yogah uchyate*,[18] i.e. unchanging equipoise of mind is called *yoga*. Therefore, as Tilak rightly says:[19]

From this it becomes clear that the special device ... for the sinless performance of actions, namely an equable mind, is what is known as *kausala* (skilful device), and that performing actions by this *kausala* or device is ... known as *yoga* ...'

Now, by making an *equable mind* the skill-foundation of actions, the *Gita* seems to have achieved in one stroke a grand unification of work-ethic with ethics-in-work. For, without the ethical process being duly protected, no mind can attain *samatwa* or equipoise. As the German proverb goes: 'A clean conscience is the best pillow.' And *sattwa guna*, being intrinsically a support for stronger ethical sensitivity and observance is, in turn, conducive to *samatwa*. Thus, both skills (work-ethic) and values (ethics-in-work) seem to reach a natural confluence.

It should also become evident that verse 2.47, which lays down the principle of reducing our attachment to personal gains from work done, with its obverse of controlling the aversion to personal losses, is the most foolproof prescription for the gradual attainment of *samatwa*. The common apprehension about practising non-attachment to the fruits of one's action is that it eliminates one's incentive for effort and work—and thus strikes at the root of the work-ethic. This is however a misunderstanding, for this advice is to be judged as relevant to man's general and overriding quest for true mental happiness. Thus, Tilak, while affirming the intention behind all work to make it sensible, explains thus the import of this verse in practical affairs:[20]

But if one goes much further than that (intentionality), and allows his mind to be afflicted by the attachment (*asakti*), ambition, pride, self-identification, or insistence of mine-ness (*mamatva*) which exists in the mind of the doer with reference to the result of the action in the shape of the feeling that: 'whatever action is performed by *me* with the intention that "I" should necessarily get a benefit from a particular act of *mine*; and if thereafter there is any obstruction in the matter of getting the desired result or benefit, the chain of misery starts.

The principle of *anasakti* in verse 2.47 is thus a basic rule for freedom (commonplace ideas about motivation being really roads to slavedom or bondage), and hence happiness.

Sri Aurobindo, however, interprets '*yogah karmasu kaushalam*' somewhat differently. He says that true skill-in-work is the ability to perform any kind of work while remaining in inner union (*yoga*) with the Supreme Intelligence. Thus, he adheres to the root *yuj* for *yoga*, and draws this natural meaning from the counsel cited above. Such capacity enables the individual intelligence of the doer to decide and act with reduced error and confusion because its path is lighted up by the error-free Supreme Intelligence. In Aurobindo's own words, work done in *yoga* is most potent and efficient, 'for it is informed by the knowledge and will of the Master of works ...'[21] We feel it is possible and necessary to reconcile Sri Aurobindo's view with Tilak's. For, without *samatwa*, supported by active *sattwa guna*, this inner *yoga* with the Supreme Intelligence cannot be felt and realized. On the other hand, once this inner *yoga* begins to be perceived even slightly, the return to *samatwa* under disturbing circumstances becomes both easier and quicker.

VI. CONSTELLATION OF FACTORS AND WORK-RESULTS

In the previous sections the theory of detachment from the selfish results of work done has been explained in terms of the need to reduce our hankering for personal successes or abhorrence of personal reverses from efforts undertaken. The intention is to minimize our vulnerability. Chapter 18 of the *Gita* provides a wider canvas for cultivating such detachment. Verses 18.13–15 explain that the final results from a course of actions depend upon:[22]

- *adhisthana*, i.e. the frame of body–life–mind as the standing ground of soul in nature;
- *karta*, i.e. the doer himself, the ego;
- *karanam*, i.e. the various senses used;
- *vividh chesta*, i.e. the various efforts made, or functions of the vital breath; and
- *daiva*, i.e. the super-personal cosmic power which governs unseen the results of human actions (*adrista*).

Now, judged in the light of this interplay of causal variables, the rational conclusion to be drawn is: (a) if the result of sincere effort is a success, the entire credit for this should not be appropriated by the doer; (b) if the result of sincere effort is a failure, then too the entire blame does not accrue to the doer. The former attitude mollifies arrogance and conceit, and minimizes soaring expectations. The latter disposition prevents excessive despondency and de-motivation. Both combine to preserve the original 'skill' of *samatwa* sought by the excellent worker. Inner *samatwa* thus gained becomes a bulwark against psychological vulnerability.

Some people argue, in the light of verse of 2.47 alone, that it is relevant only to social reformers and public men, but not to the private career of an ambitious individual.[23] This is incorrect, for, in that case it has to be assumed that such individuals have already gone beyond personal greed and ambitions for a great cause. This is clearly untenable. In the wider arena of *lokasamgraha* or general welfare, it is detachment cultivated on the basis of verses 18.13–15 which becomes relevant. For the rest like us, both 2.47 and 18.13–15 need to be assimilated in combination.

VII. The Law of Sacrifice and Service Through Work

One of the profoundest insights for human beings is that the supreme law of all existence—cosmic or human—is sacrifice. A tree, without the intrusion of reflective consciousness, conforms instinctively to this law quite comprehensively. Other examples in sub-human Nature abound. But the human being, with his or her additional endowment of reflective consciousness, tends often to flout this law, causing perversities and imbalances in the social order. The *Gita* theory holds that since all creation is the effect of sacrifice by the Cosmic or Supreme Being, the cycle of creation is broken if human beings do not return all they have got to the One Source.[24] Human energy and talent, power and strength are all variegated reflections or embodiments of the grand act of sacrifice and manifestation by the One. To work without being aware of this pervasive cyclical process of exchange is a violation of the supreme principle, preparing the ground for weakened ethics-in-work. While explaining this superordinate orientation towards work-life, Aurobindo conveys the sense of the relevant verses:[25] 'as expressive of a practical fact of psychology and general law of Nature and so apply them to the modern conceptions of inter-change between life and life and of ethical sacrifice and self-giving ...'

This theory is the quintessence of the 'giving model of motivation' which we have discussed earlier.[26] It coincides with the conception of man-in-society growing under a five-fold debt system (*deva, rishi, pitri, nri* and *bhuta rin*) right from the moment of birth. His or her life in society can, therefore, end on a satisfactory ethical note if all the actions are inspired (not motivated) by the humble feeling of an obligation to liquidate these debts.[26] The question of rights and claims is only secondary and derivative. Griffiths has also expressed this conception beautifully:[27] 'I am not my own possession; I am a gift—my being is a gift from God. I have got to return that gift. Sacrifice is this return. Its purpose is to make a thing sacred, to return it to God.'

Now, there is another complementary dimension of work-psychology to be touched upon. If the Indian view of the final *adhyatmika* goal of life (release or liberation or *moksha*) is acceptable, then all work done by the empirical self or *vyavaharika vyaktitwa* has to be viewed as a gradual process of wearing out of *karma* (*karma-kshaya*) and *samskaras* attaching to it because of its past—proximate and remote. The *paramarthika vyaktitwa* or higher or trans-empirical SELF is by definition free from the *guna–*

karma–samskara cycle because it is beyond *prakriti. Moksha* is only a constant awareness of this SELF—even though living in this body–mind frame (*videha-mukti*). If then work can slowly begin to be done with this inner resolve in the mind's hinterland that all this is being done simply to exhaust the momentum of past *karma*s and *samskara*s, then fewer fresh grooves and sticky nodes will spring in the psychic soil. This will gradually ease the mind, freeing it of burning cravings or *trishna*. In all this effort the only *trishna* which is permitted is that of permanent contact with SELF which is Bliss.

It is in this light that the *Gita*'s distinction between *yajnartha karma* and *purushartha karma*, and interpreted by Tilak, assumes significance.[27] The former, performed in the spirit of sacrifice (discussed earlier), is a practical way of preventing our work from throwing ever-newer chains of bondage around us. But the latter, performed for the benefit of the doer, reinforces the binding effect of *karma* or work.

There is another process of achieving such *karma-kshaya*, if the conceptual re-orientation demanded by the idea of sacrifice does not suit or proves too difficult. This process is that of *bhakti-yoga*, i.e. to try to will to act all the time with the inner awareness of offering it all as a loving service (*sevabuddhi*) to the Supreme or the Lord or the *Ishta*. It is a sweet, gentle and emotionally enriching process. If *karma-yoga* (verse 2.47) can thus be blended with *bhakti-yoga*, we might as well be working towards what could be termed *sevayoga*—with the urge of *samarpan* and *nivedan* at its base. In our own time Vivekananda and Gandhiji have given us working demonstrations of *seva-yoga*. Not through sacrifice (apparently) but through service to the Supreme we burn up the seeds of *samskara*s, leaving the mind-screen clean to *see* the SELF. Dobson employs a picturesque phrase, 'countercheating the genes', to communicate this very process of *karma-kshaya*:[29]

Now in Bhakti Yoga what we do is to countercheat the genes. If you like to pick flowers, you don't pick them for corsages. You offer them in the worship. If you like to cook, you offer it in the worship. All of the things you do, you offer in the worship. You see, that is countercheating the genes.... The actions you do in the worship couldn't possibly bear fruit.

Clearly *seva* or service and *bhakti* or worship convey the same meaning in this context.

So, how do we sacrifice or promote a service work-ethic and ethics-in-work simultaneously and organically?:

(a) 'work-ethic' through the constant powerful drive to experience SELF, the ultimate goal, sooner than later;

(b) 'ethics-in-work' through feeling of humble obligation to return a debt, or through the tender emotion of serving one's beloved.

It is evident that all this is about transformational psychology in work-life.

VIII. 'KARMA-VADA, KARMA-YOGA', ETHICS-IN-WORK AND WORK-ETHIC

It is frequently observed that people tend to mix up *karma-vada*, or the 'theory of cause-and-effect via *karma*', and *karma-yoga* or the 'the yogic science of doing work with *samatwa*'. Not that they are entirely unrelated. Yet it is helpful to clearly understand that *karma-vada* is an ethico-moral law of causation for regulating *karma*, which includes thoughts (*manasa*), words (*vacha*) and actions (*karmana*). Thus, even a thought wave of envy or hatred is a *karma*, a cause, which will produce its inevitable consequence in one way or another at some later point in time. If someone knowingly cheats his organization for personal benefit, this too is a *karma*, a causal force, with its corresponding backlash. On the other hand, the integrity of promises made, for example, is a causal force which will not die before producing its wholesome consequence—whether we have the sensitivity to perceive this linkage or not. This essence of *karma-vada* in human affairs corresponds to the Cosmic Law or *ritam* which orders and governs the Universe. Its internalization helps an individual to become mature, introspective, and muster the courage and strength to hold himself or herself accountable for everything that happens to him—especially the adverse and the bad. This principle is very clearly expressed by Aurobindo:[30]

... in the mental and moral world as in the physical world there is no Chaos, fortuitous rule of chance or mere probability, but an ordered Energy at work which assures its will by law and fixed relation and steady succession and the links of ascertainable cause and effectuality.

But then, it reflects such determinism only in relation to past *karma* and its present or future effect(s). The arrow has been shot from the bow, it cannot be recalled. Yet, the free will aspect inheres in *karma-vada* in terms of the will-to-change now for the future. One may choose not to shoot the next arrow. If the present has been an effect moulded by the past, it goes without saying that this very present can be the beginning of a new lease of causes for an altered future.

While *karma-vada* thus provides a firm psychological basis for 'ethics-in-work', *karma-yoga* supplies the psychological basis for 'work-ethic' through *samatwa* yoga. This prevents burn-out in work—*Yudhasya vigata jwara* (fight without mental fever, as the Lord exhorts in the *Gita*). Now, cultivation of non-attachment to the fruits of work is advocated as the process of achieving *samatwa* or the *vigata jwara* state. Non-attachment leads to the gradual emancipation of the inner self from the vagaries of external stimulations, both favourable and adverse. We then begin to work with true independence and freedom in the intrinsic and internal sense. Vivekananda hurls the deflating epithet 'beggars' at all of us because we work with a trader's mentality—even in love. This brings misery and contempt on ourselves. Here is an inspired rendering by him of the essential strength of non-attachment in work:[31]

We get caught. How? Not by what we give, but by what we expect.... The great secret of true success, of true happiness then is this: the man who asks for no return ... Ask nothing, want nothing in return. Give what you have to give; it will come back to you—but do not think of that now...

In the Indian arena of work today, should not this then be the perspective underlying all managerial roles undertaken by people among the fortunate top ten per cent of this poor country?

Besides, of course, only when non-attachment is assimilated in the light of what has just been stated, do we truly approach the goal of *yoga* with *karma* (i.e. *karma-yoga*), and not *yoga* with selfish acquisitiveness as is now the case. Once this begins to be cultivated, it is easy to see that ethics-in-work will be reinforced from another positive angle, and not rest only on *karma-vada*. In other words, non-attachment is the key to both inner poise as well as ethical choice.

IX. CONCLUSION: 'GITA' AS TRANQUILLIZER OR ENERGIZER?

Sivaraman is right when he says that the *Gita* is meant for the management of one's life as a whole.[32] Surely a manager's life is but an aspect of human existence, and hence subject to the same common basic principles for humanity as a whole. Its verses peddle neither two-minute noodles, nor one-minute panaceas. Even if we use Doraiswamy's phrase 'energy pill', how can independent India glibly forget so soon the hundreds of young men and women from certain States of India who went to the gallows or bore bullets on their chest for a free India—all with the *Gita* to inspire them? How is it then that the *Gita* is dubbed a mere tranquillizer?[33]

Unfortunately, the modern rational–secular mind often runs aground in the quagmire of sensationalist irrationality. Speed and greed are its twin drives—and its undoing. Such a mind is apt to discover many apparent contradictions in a profound yet concise work like the *Gita*. Patience and humility are required to resolve them. One should pause and question one's understanding, rather than criticize the work itself. If these contradictions are only 'apparent', then a rash conclusion that its verses are merely an excellent tranquillizer is unwarranted. If Radhakrishnan can be challenged for importing his 'modernity' of thought to interpret the *Gita*,[34] then what prevents someone else from challenging even more strongly the queer misinterpretations of the *Gita* by importing neo-moderns like Maslow and Drucker, respectable though they are in their own spheres?

Finally, we have read about many lives and also witnessed a few, which have erected their edifice of existence on the basis of the *Gita*. How have they gone about it? Each day they have systematically memorized a few verses from it, and then meditated deeply on their meaning. Thus have the verses slowly come alive and revealed to them their true message, as it were. When we assault a work like the *Gita* with our intellect alone, it tends to withdraw itself into its shell like a tortoise. So, an initial disposition of respect is useful. If we lack it, it is our misfortune. The *Gita* itself says: *shraddha-mayoyam purusha*, i.e. man is made up with the stuff of faith.[35] Gandhiji himself had warned young India against the tendency to reject works like the *Gita* which crystallize the experiences of so many *rishis* who were by no means superstitious.[36]

REFERENCES

1. Sri Aurobindo, *Letters on Yoga* (Pondicherry: Sri Aurobindo Ashram, 1971), Part One, p. 22.
2. B. Griffiths, The Cosmic Revelation (London: Collins, 1983), p. 92.
3. G. Azeemoddin, Letter to the Editor, *The Hindu*, 30 June 1989.
4. P.K. Doraiswamy, 'Relevance of Bhagvad Gita to Management', *The Hindu*, 10 January 1989.
5. Ibid.   6. Griffiths, op. cit., p. 91.
7. Ibid., p. 94.   8. Ibid., p. 93.
9. E. Deutsch, *The Bhagavad Gita* (New York: Holt, Rinehart & Winston, 1968), p. 168.
10. Rabindranath Tagore, *Sadhana* (New Delhi: Macmillan, 1988), p. 16.
11. Ibid., p. 48.   12. Ibid., p. 64.
13. Sri Aurobindo, *The Message of The Gita* (Pondicherry: Sri Aurobindo Ashram, 1977), verse II.45, p. 35.
14. Ibid., verses II.2–3, pp. 13–14.   15. Ibid., verses XVI.1–3, p. 224.
16. Ibid., verse XVI.16, p. 227.   17. Ibid., verse II.50, p. 37.
18. Ibid., verse II.48, p. 36.
19. B.G. Tilak, *Srimad Bhagawad Gita Rahasya* (Poona: Tilak Bros., 1935), p. 78.
20. Ibid., pp. 150–1.   21. *Idem, The Message of The Gita*, fn. 2, p. 37.
22. Ibid., pp. 246–7.
23. S. Krishnan, Letter to The Editor, *The Hindu*, 30 June 1989.
24. *The Message of The Gita*, verses III. 14–16, pp. 52–3.
25. Ibid., fn.1, pp. 52–3.
26. S.K. Chakraborty, *Managerial Effectiveness and Quality of Work-life: Indian Insights* (New Delhi: Tata McGraw Hill, 1987), Chap. 5.
27. B. Griffiths, op. cit., p. 49.   28. B.G. Tilak, op. cit., pp. 72–3.
29. J. Dobson, *Advaita Vedanta and Modern Science* (Chicago: Vivekananda Vedanta Society, 1983), p. 16.
30. Sri Aurobindo, *The Problem of Rebirth* (Pondicherry: Sri Aurobindo Ashram, 1983), p. 76.
31. Swami Vivekananda, *Work And Its Secret* (Calcutta: Advaita Ashrama, 1985), pp. 10–11.
32. S.M. Sivaraman, 'The Inner Power From The Gita', *The Hindu*, 21 March 1989.
33. P.K. Doraiswamy, op. cit.   34. Ibid.
35. *Idem, The Message of The Gita*, verse XVII.3, pp. 232–3.
36. M.K. Gandhi, *The Teaching of the Gita* (Bombay: Bharatiya Vidya Bhavan, 1962), p. 39.

8

SACRO-SECULAR* SYMBIOSIS
India's Vision of Humanism

This chapter has been prompted partly by a recent article on the role of humanities in management education.[1] It is a timely and courageous piece, bringing a whiff of fresh air into the present atmosphere in management education charged with fetid technicism (e.g. the call for the invention of team-building 'technologies'). It is well to recall that the once-great British Empire stood on the shoulders of the liberal (humanities)-educated Oxbridge alumni. Our limited purpose in this chapter is, however, to share a few reflections on a major policy issue advocated by Singh: to keep the 'sacred' literature out and to usher the 'secular' in, while drawing upon the humanities. We believe this stance to stem from an inadequate comprehension of India's 'deep structure'.

I. CULTURE-SPECIFICITY OF HUMANISM

If it is suggested that 'humanism'and the 'humanities' are to be treated at the transcultural level alone, it is unlikely to be either realistic or useful. True, in an orchestra all the musical instruments have to follow the same notes in unison. But the sitar is played in its own style, the sarod in its own, the violin, the flute and the *shehnai*

---

* We prefer to remain with that meaning of 'secular' as it is understood all over the English-speaking world, i.e. materialistic, worldly, non-spiritual. India's politically conceived special meaning of secularism, i.e. equality towards all religions, should search for or create another word. An example of this latter is the address delivered by Dr S.D. Sharma, India's Vice-President, on 'Secularism in The Indian Ethos' at Shantiniketan in April 1989. Incidentally, while it mentioned many worthy names, the pertinent case of the Indian National Army under the leadership of Subhas Chandra Bose was omitted—an outfit which was a grand confluence of nearly all the religious streams.

all have their respective distinctive styles and 'tools'. Clearly, therefore, culture-specificity has to be accorded primary recognition
within a theoretical framework which seeks organic resonance
amongst human wills in Indian organizations. Tagore had outlined
the content of this specificity in one of his lectures at Harvard
University in 1913. He told the elect audience that the city-wall
habit and training of the Western mind took pride in subduing
Nature assumed to be hostile, and led it to an artificial dissociation
between man and Universal Nature. He added:[2] 'But in India the
point of view was different; it included the world with the man as
one great truth. India put all her emphasis on the harmony that
exists between the individual and the Universal.'

What was the result of this vision of the harmony of man and
the cosmos (not mere utilitarian interdependence)? The Indian
ethos ceaselessly strove to weave this vision into man's world of
feeling and action. By meditation, service, and regulation of daily
living, India tried to help each individual to work towards a
consciousness where 'everything had a spiritual meaning'.[3] This
scheme of human development gave priority to realization and not
acquisition,[4] to the power of union and not possession.[5] The
relevance of these insights to values in work-life hardly needs
elaboration.

As recently as in 1976 Toynbee had voiced the same concern for
restoring the vanishing spiritual elixir to cure us of our social
afflictions:[6]

I agree that the sickness of modern society can be cured only by a spiritual
revolution in the hearts and minds of human beings. Social maladies cannot be
remedied by organizational changes; all attempts at such remedies are superficial.... The only effective cures are spiritual.

While Toynbee has placed his finger on the right pulse—at least in
our view—Tagore has given us the deeper and unique Indian
rationale for bringing the sacred into the heart of the secular.
Similarly, Bede Griffiths, moved profoundly by the sacred simplicity of true India, lamented, also in 1976, that the modern age had
turned everything (secular) 'profane' and 'meaningless' by ban-
ishing the 'holy', the God, the transcendent Reality from the
world.[7]

II. THE SACRO-SECULAR ROLE MODEL

From the days of India's Heroic Age till today, the archetypal leader–managers have been Janaka, Krishna, Buddha, Ashoka, Harshavardhana, Akbar, Shankara, Gobind Singh, Tilak, Tagore, Vivekananda, Gandhiji and so on. The common thread binding them all is clearly of managing the secular in the light of the sacred or spiritual. How true it is that the Indian mind has always revered much more the memory of the Dharmashoka—the serene builder of the sacred empire of the mind—than that of Chandashoka, the violent builder of the secular empire of matter. It is of fundamental importance to grasp this culture-specificity of India. The secular and the spiritual have never been compartmentalized by her true leader–managers—even in our own times. The effort has always been to sacralize, i.e. to spiritualize the secular. Whenever they have been artificially separated, the country seems to have grievously suffered due to a lack of a systems approach.

Singh's article refers at length to Gandhiji. What was the unseen foundation of his role for both idealizing and actualizing? Undoubtedly spiritual practices or *sadhana* in the pure, classical sense of the term—*japam, prarthana, mouna, upavasa,* etc. He was, in essence, a product of the *Gita* and the Upanishads. So, Gandhiji as a psycho-physical entity will perhaps not be repeated. But the spirituo-secular symbiotic model he re-lived has been India's genius throughout her history. If authentic Indian culture continues or is allowed to live, at least amongst those few who strive to 'realize' it as their life-goal, such archetypal models will continue to reappear on the Indian scene. When Gandhiji said '... introduce the religious element in politics, you revolutionize the whole of your political outlook',[8] he was obviously contradicting Singh in anticipation. Earlier in California, in 1900, Vivekananda had offered a lucid interpretation of the principle underlying Gandhiji's assertion.[9]

... if you want to speak of politics in India, you must speak through the language of religion. You will have to tell them something like this: 'The man who cleans his house every morning will acquire such and such amount of merit, he will go to heaven, or he will come to God.' Unless you put it that way, they won't listen to you. It is a question of language. The thing done is the same. But with every race you will have to speak their language to reach their hearts. And that is quite just. We need not fret about that.

Yet today we always hear the opposite slogan. Why? Because the modern Indian does not understand Gandhiji's basic strength: the synthesis of the spiritual or sacred (intrinsic religion) with the secular. We merely talk volumes about what Gandhiji did, but ignore or overlook the rigorous nitty-gritty of the 'how' of his self-mastery underlying the 'what' he did. As he himself said: 'What I want to achieve ... is self-realization, to see God face-to-face, to attain *Moksha*. I live and move and have my being in pursuit of this goal. All that I do by way of speaking and writing, and all my ventures in the political field, are directed to this same end.'

Both Gandhiji and Subhas Chandra Bose—proceeding on different premises and with different methods—had in common demonstrated supreme courage and self-sacrifice in winning the nation's independence. Each respected the other's greatness. The legendary INA (Indian National Army or Azad Hind Fauj) phenomenon, to which thousands of people belonging to all segments of Indian society had rallied, sprung from the spell-binding inspirational quality of Bose's leadership, similar to Gandhiji's. 'Jai Hind', as a mode of social address quite common even today, is symbolic of the spirit of struggle of the humble against the mighty.

The moot point here is this: the stupendous self-sacrificing motivation attained by a Gandhiji or a Bose or a Vivekananda is a sacred, not a secular, process, and indeed they were all richly spiritual personalities. Unless we are prepared to go beyond the secular symbols, institutions, writings, and rituals of our Ram Mohun Roys, Bal Gangadhar Tilaks, Sister Niveditas, Radhakrishnans, and Vinoba Bhaves and try to reach for their underlying *tapasya, titiksha, brahmacharya, tyaga, prapatti* and so on, we may gain precious little from their work and lives for our self-transformation. Learned papers and Ph.D. theses are all the harvest they will yield. To manage our wills—and that is the prime individual responsibility—in wholesome directions for attaining *prajna*, the 'sacred', is indispensable for managing the 'secular'. The 'authority' of these 'neo-classical' Indian giants is indeed, if we may say so, 'sacro-secular'. This is the continuation of a hoary, unbroken tradition peculiar to India. As they did for us, do we not similarly owe it to our posterity to nourish this lifeline of India?

The Bodhisattwa model in Mahayana Buddhism is based on six *paramita*s (perfections): *dana* (charity), *shila* (self-controlled conduct), *kshanti* (forbearance), *virya* (heroic strength), *dhyana* (meditation), and *prajna* (wisdom). When *prajna* is attained it becomes identical to *karuna* (compassion). This fusion blossoms into *upaya-kaushalya*, i.e. skilfulness of means. When Bodhisattwa, equipped with such a profound and sacred value foundation for his skills, turns his eyes and mind towards the secular problems of humanity, he becomes a true benefactor, enlightener.[11] Tagores, Gandhijis, Vivekanandas, Ramanas and the like are all our contemporary Bodhisattwas. The Bodhisattwa model is perhaps the ultimate symbol of sacro-secular symbiosis.

III. A Few Modern Experiments for Sacro-Secular Education by Indians

In the field of education in India, the creative experiments of Vivekananda Tagore, and Aurobindo are luminous landmarks. They had built national institutions which have been attracting worldwide talent and have acquired international recognition. Their structures, systems, symbols, values, rites, rituals, etc. need to be studied to know how minds, steeped equally well in Eastern and Western wisdom, had thought and worked directly for man-making education in India. Thus, in 1910 Sri Aurobindo, while elaborating on a principle of education, had said:[12] 'The task is to find it [something divine in each], develop it and use it. The chief aim of education should be to help the growing soul to draw out that in itself which is best and make it perfect for a noble use.'

In 1920–1 Tagore-the-drop-out had spoken at length to the Americans about his 'Vishvabharati' in Shantiniketan. On the object of education he said:[13]

... to give man the unity of truth. Formerly when life was simple all the different elements of man were in complete harmony. But when there came the separation of the intellect from the spiritual and the physical, the school education put entire emphasis on the intellect and the physical side of man. We devote our sole attention to giving children information, not knowing that by this emphasis we are accentuating a break between the intellectual, physical and the spiritual life.

One of the major underpinnings of the educational institutions of the Ramakrishna Mission consists of the following declaration by Vivekananda:[14]

The present system of education is all wrong. The Mind is crammed with facts before it knows how to think. Control of the mind should be taught first. If I had my education over again and had any voice in the matter, I would learn to master my mind first, and then gather facts if I wanted them.

Gandhiji too, in his role as a teacher at the Tolstoy Farm, had given top priority to the culture of the heart, the building of character—which meant developing the spirit to know God.[15]

As already stated, humanism, in the Indian parlance, is incomplete without accommodating the spiritual/sacred dimension in an individual's daily existence. It is our consistent observation that whereas some of the best amongst the physicists and other scientists (Max Planck, Einstein, Schroedinger, Roger Sperry, John Eccles, Eugene Wigner, Eddington, Jeans, Capra, David Bohm, Heisenberg and many others) have been clearly speaking of the urgent need to expand and enrich the vision of man by accepting his spiritual/metaphysical/ 'fifth' dimension as well, most of the well-known social scientists shy away from such an enlargement of their paradigm. This is a puzzle we have not yet been able to solve, especially because physics and other material sciences are supposed to deal with matter, and social sciences with the human. The Indian view clearly is that an individual is not fully human until his or her spiritual core gradually becomes fully alive, no matter whether he or she is a manager or a mendicant. This has been the foundation of the three institutions mentioned above. If modern western thought wishes to confine itself to 'secular humanism', then clearly the Indian ethos has always espoused 'spiritual humanism'.

We think it is essential that the essays, short stories, letters, biographies and autobiographies of great personalities should also be considered to be a more compact and direct sources of inspiration. Thus, Tagore's Hibbert Lectures at Oxford (*The Religion of Man*), or his lectures at Andhra University (*Man*) are more germane to students than his novel *The Home and The World*. He is also regarded as the father of the modern short story movement in India. Moreover, our own Kalidasa, Bankim Chandra, Premchand, Sarat Chandra, Subrahmanya Bharati and the like should also have equal place in the list of authors within the scheme of humanistic orientation which Singh rightly espouses. No Indian student should possibly miss Vivekananda's *Lectures From Colombo to Almora*, containing the most inspiring calls to values and ideals for nation-building. Equally indispensable are Aurobindo's *The Foundations of Indian Culture*, and Gandhiji's *An Autobiography*. We do not believe that an Indian student, by first acquiring a firm mooring in his or her own culture, will later be blind to what is good and worthwhile in the humanistic thoughts of other cultures. In fact, with this sequence he or she has a much better opportunity of assimilating the right and relevant things from the latter, instead of aping their superficial banalities. Besides, the opposite sequence frequently breeds a destructive contempt for his own foundations. John Dewey, the American philosopher, had once clearly drawn our attention to the dangers of a particular type of openness which pervades many a great intellectual figure in India:[16] 'The open mind is a nuisance if it is merely passively open to allow anything to find its way into a vacuous mind behind the opening.' Thus, the other day a well-known economist, during a discussion on values, was very happily quoting an Alfred Marshall dictum: 'Instead of emphasizing the nobler aspects, one should emphasize the stronger aspects of a man.'

IV. Need for 'Sadhana'

Emphasis on the 'management of will' is entirely correct. Yet, unfortunately, most of us do not realize that a large proportion of 'sacred' literature, especially in India, is aimed at helping us to strengthen and elevate our will—sometimes by direct processes like deep breathing or concentration, and at other times through stories and parables. If and when secular literature echoes the glory of wholesome human will, is it not almost always traceable to some kind of a spiritual mooring—beyond one's selfish ego? Mere intellectual stirring does not reform human will. Some sustained inner *sadhana* at the experiential level is necessary. Of course, initially we need to have some yearning for personal experience of such processes and practices. Then the links between these two complementary domains begin to be gradually perceived.

A few years ago an M. Phil. student produced an outline for his thesis entitled: 'Effective Management Styles for Indian Industry.' He had shown this outline to a renowned economist and a former Deputy Governor of the Reserve Bank of India for comment. His written comments were to this effect:

(a) Self-confidence in the Indian heritage is admirable, but what is the relevance of that heritage to large-scale management—professional or familial?

(b) You have given spiritual answers to materialist questions. My contention is that Indian heritage is integrated, i.e. it is also materialist.

It appears that the learned commentator, in his first observation, has missed the profound contribution of the essential strands of Indian heritage towards constructive self-transformation by the individual through *sadhana*. After all, management, large-scale or small-scale, familial or professional, is the work of the 'man' in the man-ager. Similarly, in the second comment, although the integral character of the Indian heritage is admitted, the commentator is unable to perceive that materialist pursuits and problems can be better handled *through* the medium of cultivated spiritual orientation. This indeed is the significance of our integral culture. However, these two observations from an eminent person do indicate that intellectual cobwebs continue to infest contemporary élite minds. Hence *sadhana* for the secular man appears to be anathema to them.

V. COUNTERWAVE TO TECHNICISM

The secular inexorably concerns itself with multiplicity, diversity, and the immediate. This causes a dense mist to shroud our consciousness. Truly speaking, materialist secularism is not even half as liberating or enlightening as it is made out to be. Our actions and inactions, decisions and indecisions suffer this contamination. No over-arching, integrating, unifying principle comes to our rescue. It is the awakening of the inner spirit which can furnish us with this systemic balance. Our externalized, objective existence by itself will remain cacophonic. The symphonic balance must necessarily grow from the internal being, and this being is not amenable to technicism. It is to be sought experientially. The analytical intellect has a necessary but minor role in this endeavour. Earlier we had pointed out the need for managers to open their minds to the 'spirituo-technical'[17] and 'spirituo-synthetic'[18] systems' views beyond the 'socio-technical' approach. We now reinforce and extend our argument further by urging managers to embrace the 'sacro-secular' systems orientation for, as Tagore puts it so well:[19] 'This search for system is really a search for unity, for synthesis; it is our attempt to harmonise the heterogeneous complexity of outward materials by an inner adjustment.'

The secular-cum-technical alone cannot yield this inner unity. Consequently, value-based effectiveness cannot be reached by this route. The sacred symbolizes the centripetalizing, *nivritti* aspect of the human psyche; the secular its centrifugalizing, *pravritti* aspect. In the short run neither is a substitute for the other. In the long run the former is superior to the latter. The four end-state values embodied in the '*dharma–artha–kama–moksha*'* system, as well as the four-phase *ashrama* system of '*brahmacharya–grhasthya–vana-prastha–sannyasa*'†—are both social schemes based on the sacro-secular ordering of relationships. To explain, the householder phase of a man's existence is also conferred the title of *ashrama*. Why plant an *ashrama* in the heart of the secular domain? This is because the root meaning of *ashrama* is a place to labour (*shram*) for the fulfilment of a *vrata* (a vow). The very word *ashram* is permeated with a spiritual flavour, so the intent of calling the householder phase an *ashram* is self-evident: sacro-secular symbiosis. Values-as-means to the attainment of any of the end-state-values— be it sacred or secular—must also be sacred. That is the essence of quality of worklife in organizations.

VI. Sacro-Secular, Low-Entropy Society

As we approach the close of the twentieth century a few tremulous voices are heard to murmur about de-industrialization, low-key technology and so on. This is because it is beginning to dawn on us that unbridled secularism, that is unalloyed objective materialism, breeds a high entropy culture and civilization. Irreversible disorder and dissipation occur when matter is converted into energy, e.g. when coal is burnt to obtain thermal power, only a fraction of the total energy is usefully harnessed and the rest goes waste. Waste-recycling is itself a costly process requiring further expenditure of energy. Since the earth on which we live is a closed system, nearly all its material resources are non-renewable. Material progress, therefore, inevitably hastens the denudation of our planet of these resources. Now, the high-need, i.e. the high-standard-of-living ethos, spells progressively more energy throughput in the total production–distribution system. This approach may yield more now, but is going to leave behind less and less for posterity. This is the irresponsibility of technology-driven secular humanism.

The sacred, the simple, the spiritual mood, on the other hand,

* Righteous conduct, economic aims, desires, liberation—respectively.
† All-round continence, householdership, withdrawal from active mundane life, total renunciation—respectively.

breeds a low-need and therefore a low-entropy culture. The rate of entropy for material resources can therefore be reduced by cultivating this mood and values-system. This will be the nature of responsible, spiritual humanism. Besides, if spirit can also be considered as a kind of stored-up energy then it is the one which, unlike matter-energy, is *not* subject to increasing entropy. Thus, more spiritual and less secular energy seems now to be our need. Hence the case for sacro-secular symbiosis.

VII. Physicists: What Have They Got To Say?

It is possible that some readers have begun raising their eyebrows, suspecting that religious ideas and kindred 'unscientific' shibboleths are being smuggled into these pages. It might therefore be instructive to examine what some of the significant figures in the realm of new physics have to say on this momentous area of concern for human beings.

(a) *Arthur Eddington*: In his passionate defence of mysticism Eddington asserted that the stage when it was 'almost necessary to ask the permission of physics to call one's soul one's own' was past, and that it was nonsense of physics to deny an 'outlook beyond physics'.[20] It is not possible, proceeding from ether, electrons and machinery to fathom the reality of human consciousness, for here we are concerned with 'ought' which takes us outside the realm of physical sciences.[21] According to him, religion is the one field of inquiry in which the question of the reality of existence has to be treated with all seriousness.[22] He argues that it is in mystical religion where 'feelings, purpose, values', which make up our consciousness, are dealt with elaborately and with conviction.[23] Admitting that the picture of experience drawn by physics 'omits so much' of vital importance, and recognizing 'that Man is not merely a scientific measuring machine',[24] Eddington declares:[25] 'I assert that the nature of *all reality is spiritual*, not material nor a dualism of matter and spirit' (emphasis added).

(b) *Max Planck*: We have encountered from time to time heated questions from some participants (including academics) in our programmes on values system to the following effect: 'Are we being asked to take such ideas (of mystical psychology) on faith? In this age of science?' We may turn to the father of quantum physics on this question of faith. In response to a question from Murphy whether science could be a substitute for the believing spirit needed in religion, Planck answered that any serious scientist realizes that on the entrance to the temple of science are inscribed the words: '*Ye must have faith*', which is the same as the believing spirit. He added further that 'imaginative vision and faith in the ultimate success are indispensable. The pure rationalist has no place here.'[26] His concluding words in this dialogue are eloquent:[27]

It [the knowledge of external reality] is a direct perception and, therefore, in its nature is akin to what we call Faith. It is a *metaphysical belief*. Now that is something which the sceptic questions in regard to religion, but it is the *same in regard to science*. [Emphasis added.]

(c) *Albert Einstein*: Here is yet another father figure of modern physics. He too wholeheartedly acknowledges the role of religion when we wish to cross the shores of 'is' into the expanse of 'should'. Objective knowledge of what 'is' cannot answer questions about the ultimate *goal* of human aspirations. 'The purely rational conception of our existence' cannot guide us towards this goal and its corresponding values.[28] Einstein says disarmingly:[29]

To make clear these fundamental *ends and valuations*, and to set them fast in the *emotional life* of the individual, seems to me precisely the most *important function which religion has to perform* in the social life of man [emphasis added].

(d) *Erwin Schroedinger*: He is the one amongst the modern physicists who had acquainted himself with Upanishadic thought with unmatched empathy and flourish. His observations on science, in the context of values and normative choices, are trenchantly forthright:[30]

The scientific picture of the real world around me is *very deficient*. It gives a lot of factual information, puts all our experience in a magnificently consistent order, but it is *ghastly silent about all and sundry that is really near to our heart*, that really matters to us. It cannot tell us a word about red and blue, bitter and sweet, physical pain and physical delight; it *knows nothing of beautiful and ugly, good or bad, God and eternity*. Science sometimes pretends to answer questions in these domains, but the answers are very often so silly that we are not inclined to take them seriously. [Emphasis added.]

It is easy to see that physicists like Schroedinger have had the insight and courage to visualize the limits of physical science based on our senses alone. They never could deny therefore the real world of emotions and feelings and normative evaluations as the very basis of human existence. Tagore too had warned the modern progressive of this folly of science by likening him to a 'general grown intoxicated with his power, usurping the throne of his king.'[31]

(e) *Werner Heisenberg*: Amongst all the physicists presented here, it is Heisenberg who seems to have grappled with the subject of ethics, values and spirituality most directly and elaborately. Like Einstein he too challenges the ability of science and technology to determine valid goals for humankind because their vision is not on the whole man and his reality but is confined to a segment only. He coins the phrase 'spiritual pattern', and says that it is an appreciation of this *pattern in a community* which alone promises to uncover the whole, the wider network of interrelations, and therefore 'it is here that the question about values is *first* decided'.[32] It is this 'spiritual pattern' that he calls the 'religion of the community'.[33] Confessing that technical advances have created new ethical problems, he asserts that the 'all too rational arguments' from science can do little to resolve these problems.[34] No, not this way. For him 'the source of ethical principles [is] in that basic human attitude which is expressed in the language of religion'.[35] Warning us therefore about the domination of technical expediency, he outlines the following prescription for us:[36]

A rationalistic play with words and concepts is of little assistance here; the most important preconditions are *honesty and directness*. But since ethics is the basis for the communal life of men, and ethics can only be derived from that fundamental human attitude which I have called the spiritual pattern of the community, we must bend all our efforts to reuniting ourselves, along with the younger generation, in a common human outlook. [Emphasis added.]

At the beginning of this section we had quoted Eddington's assertion in 1929 that all reality is spiritual, and that the matter–spirit duality is inadmissible. This is a perfect echo of the Vedantic message, and the West was sounded on it at the close of the nineteenth century by Vivekananda:[37]

Just as a physicist, when he pushes his knowledge to its limits, finds it melting away into meta-physics, so a metaphysician will find that what he calls mind and matter are but apparent distinctions, the Reality being One.

Such then is the theoretical foundation of the sacro-secular symbiosis outlined in this chapter.

VII. Conclusion: Why Lose the Paradise?

Let all of us who care for India's good with a sense of responsibility to posterity, clea. 'v understand that India's genius has always accorded priority to *subjective purification* and not to *objective quantification*. The latter must derive from the former, and not overrule it. World thinking is now realizing the crisis the secular-ist–technocentric craze has been brewing for us. Thus, Lessem, a British management writer, admits:[38]

... it is no accident of history that spiritual and material values have been split apart in the West. Indeed, it has served to advance the cause of individualism. It is only that now we are beginning to realize the costs. Secularly based individualism detracts from the making of shared meaning.

It is this very secularism, feeding on intellect and puffed by technology, which provokes Ferrell, a scientist, to ask eloquently:[39] 'Must not faith resist the technological society's preoccupation with technique and its tendency to advocate more technique where technique fails?'[39]

How beautifully too the philosopher–professor Skolimowski puts the problem in perspective:[40] 'It seems that there is a law that governs technological change: the more sophisticated technology becomes the more it disengages us from life.'

How true! e.g. my new automatic quartz watch has robbed me of one source of self-discipline—winding my spring-coil watch every morning at 7 a.m.

A well-known German project management consultant confessed to his Indian counterparts in 1987:[41] 'Science and technology have influenced contemporary values, resulting in thinking patterns that are counterproductive to designing appropriate project management approaches.'

Eccles, the Nobel laureate in neuroscience, at his candid best avers:[42] 'Man has lost his way in this age. It is what has been called the predicament of man. I think that science has gone too far in breaking down man's belief in spiritual greatness.'

Again, Peters and Waterman in the field of management have also spoken critically about the 'secular–rationalist mythology', about the 'denigration of the importance of values' by the rational model, and so on.[43]

As usual, throughout this book, we have had to reproduce for Indian readers these words from western writers and thinkers in response to the common malady of a race subject to long spells of foreign tutelage—their own savants mean little to them, or at least to the bulk of intellectuals who want to modernize and liberate India. Yet we must in the end go back to the words from the Sage of Pondicherry (1910), which neatly sum up the *raison d'être* for the sacro-secular symbiosis highlighted in this chapter:[44] 'The divorce of intellect and spirit, strength and purity may help a European revolution, but by a European strength we shall not conquer.'

REFERENCES

1. S. Singh, 'Role of Humanities in Management Education' *Vikalpa*, April–June, 1988.
2. R. Tagore, *Sadhana* (New Delhi: Macmillan, 1988), p. 5.
3. Ibid., p. 6.   4. Ibid., p. 4.   5. Ibid., p. 8.
6. A. Toynbee, and D. Ikeda, *Choose Life* (Delhi: Oxford University Press, 1987), p. 129.
7. Bede Griffiths, *Return To The Centre* (London: Collins, Fount Paperbacks, 1987), p. 12.
8. D.G. Tendulkar, *Mahatma* (Bombay: Times of India Press, 1951), vol.I, p. 299.
9. Swami Vivekananda, *Complete Works* (Advaita Ashrama, Calcutta, 1959), vol. VIII, p. 77.
10. M.K. Gandhi, *An Autobiography* (Ahmedabad: Navajivan Trust, 1972), p. x.
11. Swami Atmarupananda, 'The Six Flames of Bodhisattva's Cosmic Sacrifice', *Prabuddha Bharata*, May 1989, pp. 219, 224.
12. Sri Aurobindo, *A System of National Education* (Pondicherry: Sri Aurobindo Ashram, 1970), pp. 2–3.
13. R. Tagore, *Personality* (New Delhi: Macmillan, 1985), p. 126.
14. Swami Vivekananda, *Complete Works* (Calcutta: Advaita Ashrama, 1959), vol. VIII, p. 280.
15. M.K. Gandhi, op. cit., pp. 251, 255.

16. J. Dewey, *A Dictionary of Education*, ed. R.B. Winn (New York: Philosophical Library, 1959), p. 94.
17. S.K. Chakraborty, *Human Response in Organizations* (Calcutta: Vivekananda Nidhi, 1985), pp. 176–9.
18. *Idem, Managerial Effectiveness and Quality of Work-life* (Delhi: Tata-McGraw Hill, 1987), pp. 217, 223, 227.
19. R. Tagore, *Sadhana*, op. cit., p. 21.
20. Quoted in *Quantum Questions*, edited by Ken Wilber (Boston: New Science Library, 1985), p. 201.
21. Ibid., p. 202.   22. Ibid., p. 196.   23. Ibid., p. 194.
24. Ibid., p. 174.   25. Ibid., p. 180.   26. Ibid., p. 152.
27. Ibid., p. 154.   28. Ibid., pp. 105–6.
29. Ibid., p. 106.   30. Ibid., p. 80.
31. R. Tagore, *Personality* (Delhi: Macmillan, 1985), p. 52.
32. *Quantum Questions*, op. cit., p. 41.
33. Ibid., p. 41.   34. Ibid., p. 43.
35. Ibid., p. 43.   36. Ibid., p. 44.
37. Swami Vivekananda, *Raja-Yoga* (Calcutta: Advaita Ashrama, 1982), p. 13.
38. R. Lessem, *Global Principles of Management* (London: Prentice Hall, 1989), p. 475.
39. D.R. Ferrell, in *The Search For Absolute Values: Harmony Among The Sciences* (New York: The International Cultural Foundation Press, 1977), vol. I, p. 254.
40. H. Skolimowski, 'Information—Yes, But Where Has All Our Wisdom Gone', *The Ecologist*, vol. 14, no. 5–6, 1984.
41. L.E. Kech, 'Projects: Gap Between Theory and Practice', *Economic Times*, 31 Dec. 1987.
42. J. Eccles, *The Search For Absolute Values*, op. cit., p. 634.
43. T.J. Peters, and R.N. Waterman, *In Search of Excellence* (New York: Harper & Row, 1982), pp. 33, 51.
44. Sri Aurobindo, *The Ideal of The Karmayogin* (Pondicherry: Sri Aurobindo Ashram, 1974), p. 17.

9

HIERARCHISM
AS AN ORGANIZATIONAL VALUE

I. THE ISSUE

It is common rhetoric amongst several serious academics that hierarchy in organizations is a factor inhibiting creative, flexible and effective performance. Many social scientists tend to associate hierarchism with feudalism. Tall hierarchies are supposed to foster tight supervision with narrow spans of command. They are also alleged to clog and contaminate the communication channels. Padding up the overhead expenditure bill is another major problem of hierarchy. Hierarchy and infructuous bureaucracy seem to have become convergent. Equality, egalitarianism, autonomy, self-esteem and other cognate values also appear to have considerably stimulated the challenge to the legitimacy of hierarchism.

During our studies in Indian organizations, however, we have noticed a good deal of ambivalence with regard to hierarchy. Some of the ills of hierarchy just cited are quite evident. On the other hand, there is also widespread disappointment at the non-fulfilment of several expected forms of behaviour or functions by people holding positions at higher levels, e.g. the spirit of self-sacrifice or visiting an employee in hospital during illness. Whenever, rare though it has been, such expectations are fairly met, we have sensed a highly positive view of hierarchy among employees. These expectations seem to be quite culture-specific. The main issue then becomes: should hierarchy as such be denigrated and displaced; or should it be enriched and vitalized with the missing ingredients?

II. HIERARCHY AND CULTURE-SPECIFICITY

We think that the purely structuralist view of hierarchy ignores the more subtle aspects of interpersonal relationships. Given proper orientation, consonant with the cultural milieu, hierarchism should be able to more than offset its genuine or alleged encumbrances. While American society, whose traditions were shaped and took root in the course of only the last four centuries or so, may often perceive no great role for hierarchism in its institutions and organizations, this example is unlikely to be of relevance to the Indian scene. Unfortunately, no work has yet come to our notice which thoroughly performs this crucial task in organizational theory-building for India. So, in order to induce a mood of re-appraisal regarding hierarchy—both in the Indian manager's and academic's mind—we have to refer to some recent work done by Western researchers for other Eastern countries.

Marsland and Beer attribute the success of large Japanese firms to the application of management ideas (many of which are American) in a manner which suits the Japanese temper. Of this temper, hierarchy-based human relationships is a dominant characteristic:[1]

Japanese see all inter-relationships in terms of hierarchy—each individual is superior to, subordinate to, or (rarely) equal to another.... The concept of hierarchy pervades every aspect of the culture ... Hierarchy promotes social stability and harmony. It provides a frame of reference for relating to any other person, and it is the measure of status. It *provides pressure to adhere to common values and goals* which is what makes participative management possible without anarchy. [Emphasis added.]

Clearly then, most large Japanese firms seem to have done a good and useful job of transplanting the pervasive social and family value of hierarchism into the heartland of organizational relationships. The eastern family spirit and the western industrial ethos were made mutually compatible by a consciously willed synthesis.

In another study Lincoln, Hanada and Olson concede the undisputed truth that Japanese employees have a distinctive set of cultural expectations in their work environment.[2] What about Indian employees? Reviewing the earlier studies, Lincoln *et al.* highlight a significant morphological feature of Japanese organizational structures: low degree of horizontal (i.e. role) differentiation coupled with a high degree of vertical (i.e. hierarchical) differentiation.[3]

This, they note, occurs to facilitate maximum structural resonance with the members' cultural expectations clustering around paternalism and dependency. From their own empirical investigation the authors discovered that 'Contrary to previous accounts of the effects of bureaucratic properties on individuals ..., we found that *personal integration increased with rising organization size and vertical differentiation*' (emphasis added). They finally concluded[5] that 'As cultural theories asserting the "vertical orientation" of the Japanese anticipated, *hierarchical differentiation was observed to increase the Japanese workers' personal ties and satisfaction*. Such results conflict with dominant "universalist" theories of how workers respond to tall hierarchies.' [Emphasis added.]

The predominantly seniority-based promotion policy in large Japanese firms ensures that the essential spirit of mentorship by the elders of the youngsters is nourished within the organizations' structure. The total benefit of this policy evidently offsets the cost of not offering fast track promotions for a few brilliant high-flyers. We know of many Indian firms which are insensitive to this subtlety. Thus, in the Eastern cultural medium, proper application of familial hierarchism creates a bonding effect across people through many levels in the organization. In India this lesson seems to be missed, and hierarchism is often deemed as a recipe for separateness, authoritarianism, status-consciousness (in the pejorative sense), and the like.

Similarly, Hofstede and Bond highlight the first Confucian principle which percolates and informs the organizational milieus in the rapidly developing far-eastern economies (the Five Dragons —Hong Kong, Taiwan, Japan, Singapore and South Korea):[6]

The stability of society is based on unequal relationships between people. The 'wu lun', or five basic relationships are ruler/subject, father/son, older brother /younger brother, husband/wife, and older friend/younger friend. These relationships are based on mutual, complementary obligations: the junior partner owes the senior respect and obedience; the senior owes the junior partner protection and consideration. [Emphasis added.]

Although this list of five relationships omits one major equation, at least from the Indian viewpoint—namely, teacher/student—, the essence of these being *mutual obligations* has been identified correctly. If the respect–protection flow, or the obedience–consideration flow tends to get caught in the whirlpool of sycophancy and nepotism, this phenomenon must be traced to the loss of character amongst members of the organization. It will not do to disown our individual accountability for this degeneration, and to be quixotic about the windmill of villainous hierarchy.

Some of India's prestigious centres of management education provide sad examples of the curious effects of implanting western relationship patterns for no other reason than that they were established with initial collaboration from a few first-rate American business schools. The well-intentioned Americans came and did away with the customary Indian patterns of teacher–student relationships—both inside and outside the class. Thus, smoking by students in the classroom was allowed. Students were not required to stand when the teachers entered or left the classroom. Attendance and roll-call were not institutionalized. Teachers could be addressed by their first names. Indian faculty members, steeped in western thought, never questioned the relevance and consequences of this dangerous dismantling process. The assumption was that such a free, equal, non-hierarchical atmosphere would foster deeper learning and development.

It is time, after thirty years or so, to ask whether this brave assumption has been fulfilled. Did the students of earlier generations in Indian universities learn and develop less because a reverential distance, but not aloofness, was preserved between the teacher and the taught? One of the common experiences of this modern normative vacuum is that even as the teacher is working out an equation on the blackboard, a student-friend darts into the classroom to fetch a key or a book from a hostel-mate! When they leave campus and join organizations, the disruptive consequences stemming from such a background are easily imaginable. The same symptom is visible amongst the teaching staff as well. Thus, the 'Head of the Department' role is non-existent. Even the newest or juniormost colleague could become, by turn, a 'group coordinator', or something similar, to handle group or area matters along with his colleagues. The result most frequently is that the group or department has no unified aim or focus. Each member tends to be a law unto himself. Scores of faculty members all report directly to the Principal or Director of the institution. The consequences can be readily anticipated. The pattern of rotating heads of departments is now also prevalent in most Indian universities. Gone are the days when this role was adorned by towering luminaries who could create a niche for the department in the world of scholarship by providing long and sustained unity of direction and purpose.

Leaving Japan aside for a moment, let us look at Alston's description of *inhwa* as the key principle underlying Korean business behaviour:[7]

... *inhwa* stresses harmony between unequals. ... This term requires that subordinates be loyal to their superiors and that superiors be concerned with the well-being of subordinates. ... In the modern world *inhwa* demands that an individual offer loyalty to hierarchical rankings. ... When Koreans state that all members of a company form a 'family', the implication is that the leaders are to be obeyed as if they were family elders.

Evidently, the eastern ethos does not perceive unequal status as hostile soil for harmony and cooperation to grow. Unlike the western temper which tries to deny the reality of inequality in human relationships (this need not be confused with discrimination and misappropriated privilege), the eastern mind accepts it openly, and designs its own operational values to guide harmonious and fruitful conduct within this medium.

This kind of mutual reciprocity amongst members at higher and lower organizational levels is as much an Indian value as Japanese or Korean, as the following principle enunciated by the *Manusmriti* shows:[8] 'As a father supports his sons, so let the eldest brother his younger brothers, and let them also in accordance with the law behave towards their eldest brother as sons behave towards their father.'

Clearly, priority is given by Manu to an elder brother's *duty* towards his younger siblings. The quality and ambit of this duty, in the absence of the father, is elevated to the status of that of the father's own. Now, such an ethos is perhaps entirely foreign to the western mind, where both old parents and little babies are left to fend for themselves. Yet, in India even today this author has encountered instances of an eldest brother playing such a role, year after year, for all his younger brothers and sisters and their widowed mother. The selfless dedication and fortitude seen in each case are exemplary. It is only against this backdrop that the decision-making authority, the role of a disciplinarian and other aspects of the elder brother's position have to be appreciated. It is frequently a deeply-felt moral-cum-emotional accountability which inspires such elder brothers. They often deem it a privilege bestowed on them by God; and high degrees of self-denial by them are frequently evident. Does such a hierarchical ethos have no relevance to Indian organizations today? Hierarchy in Indian culture is certainly duty-not rights-oriented. Let the implications of this be grasped well and worked out soon. The artificial boundary of severance between family ethos and organizational ethos is doing a lot of damage to us in India. Thus, instead of taking the clue from insights such as those cited above from Japan and elsewhere, not to speak of our own, even practising top executives, perhaps inspired by certain Indian academics, can comment:[9]

Simultaneously ... the person holding an authority must also examine his boundaries for exercising his authority and consequently clarify to himself about his role boundaries. In the sphere of the management of pesonnel, one should therefore make distinctions between the work-relationship and the assumed role of a superior personality both within and outside the workplace.... We have examples of managers who assume the role of moral guardians often breaking their boundaries of work-relationship.

Now, if the eastern ethos is at home with the 'older brother–younger brother' model of hierarchical nexus, with its evident bonding and ordering effects, how can the moral dimension be left out? Or, is it that we tend unwittingly to project our own moral laxity by invoking the logic of role boundary? Since managers may often lack the courage to make their own moral reappraisal and reconstruction, it is only natural that the intellectual argument of drawing boundaries comes in quite handy. Besides, what about the frequently discussed topic of 'mentor–protégé' relationship for developing managers—even in the west? Can this theme ignore the moral aspect? Is not hierarchism implicit and in-built in this model?

We may also get a measure of the depth of the *sempai-kohai* model, as the Japanese call the elder brother–younger brother relationship, in Indian culture by making some references to our Epics. Thus, the Rama–Bharat and Lakshman–Rama relationships in the *Ramayana* merit close examination. Bharat was an unrelenting crusader against his own mother's evil design which led to Rama's long exile, even though she had done so to ensure Bharat's own ascension to the throne. Ultimately, when all his entreaties failed to persuade Rama to reverse his decision, Bharat took his wooden sandals, placed them on the throne, and ruled Ayodhya on his behalf. Similarly, throughout the period of exile and the battle with Ravana, Lakshmana acted as Rama's alter ego. How were such sacrifices on the part of the younger brothers possible? Did all this stem from the repressive or sadistic or power-hungry authoritarianism of the eldest brother Rama? Or, was it a deeper moral law, that of Ram's own supreme sacrifice for love of truth, which had unlocked the fountains of self-sacrifice and utmost fidelity in the hearts of the two younger brothers?

Similarly, at one place in the *Mahabharata*, in a brief encounter between Krishna and his elder brother Balaram, the former had asked the latter, 'Dau, why is it that you always call me "anuj"?' Balaram replied, 'Simply because it feels so good to call you "anuj".' Now, *anuj* is a simple homely word for 'younger brother', the elder being termed *agraj*. The gentle affection associated with 'anuj' is entirely a culture-specific phenomenon. Again, during the first phase of exile of the Pandavas, the five brothers and their mother Kunti had perforce to halt for a night under a tree in a dense forest, and it was to be decided who would keep vigil. Bhim, the second and strongest of them, did so first. Half-way through the night Kunti woke up and asked Bhim to rest, and said someone else would keep watch. 'Who would do that?', asked Bhim. 'Why', Kunti replied, 'Sahadev'. Bhim rejected the suggestion on the ground that it was impossible for him to wake up the youngest of the brothers; it would be too cruel. 'Then', Kunti said, 'Yudhisthir should do so.' But Bhim rejected her plea once again by saying: 'It would be sacrilegious on my part to wake up our eldest brother who is worthy of our utmost respect.' Thus Bhim stayed awake throughout the night. This small episode is an epitome of the subtle refinement which hierarchism in Indian culture stands for.

It is in this context that one feels sad when some renowned Indian scholars like Romila Thapar tend to discover only 'miraculous solutions to problems', or merely the 'fantasies of a particular section of society' being projected and imposed on others as the stuff of these Epics.[10] As to the superficiality of such intellectual assessments, we may adduce only one piece of evidence. Each year since 1987 we have been participating as a faculty in the annual Advanced Management Programme conducted by the All-India Management Association. We have observed on every occasion that the nearly forty-strong group of participants have insisted that the programme Director get the Sunday Ramayana or Mahabharata serials video-recorded by the Hotel authorities. Without fail the entire group of top managers from around the country avidly watch them played full length after returning to the hotel from the Sunday outing. And none—Muslim or Sikh, Parsi or Christian— miss this replay! As a contrast to the intellectual reaction cited above, let us therefore offer Tagore's perception of our Epic characters:[11]

In the history of idea, as distinguished from the history of fact, a hero often comes to mean, for his race, the *ideal*; and ceases to be an individual. In Aryan history, Janaka and Viswamitra as well as Rama have become historical symbols. They are composite pictures of numerous personalities having a common purpose.

What a contrast between scholastic analysis, however objective, and deep meditative synthesis!

It is also worthwhile noting that even in the West streaks of hierarchism are flashing back again. Thus, in a recent despatch from the USA to an Indian daily, Howe muses on the unnerving experience of Americans when they now hear youngsters say 'Sir' to their elders. From Howe's analysis this return to the pre-1950 era appears to have been induced in a major way because America had passed its material peak and entered into the trough of declining living standards.[12] Thus, arrogance bred by material affluence and technological success might offer a deeper clue to the bashing that hierarchy often receives in all societies, including ours. Nonetheless, even the TV serial on John F. Kennedy, shown in India in 1989, did depict how all his colleagues rose to their feet whenever he entered or left a formal meeting, and addressed him invariably as 'Sir'!

Let us depart slightly from our central theme of culture-specificity, as related to hierarchism in particular, to understand this theme in the wider context of the French bureaucratic phenomenon. Based on his intensive study of two organizations, Crozier informs us that authority in them is converted, as far as practicable, into impersonal rules. Why? Because the French abhor personalized relationships, which seem to them to border on dependence on others. Since personalized relationships can imply conformity, compromise and conflict, they are detested by the French ethos. Interpersonal harmony is prized and ensured because detailed impersonal rules exist to take care of potential conflict as well as compromise. This kind of organizational culture makes French employees feel independent and at ease. The assumed worth of open, free, informal culture in terms of creativity, motivation and so on does not seem to weigh more in the French mind than the advantages of a clearly understood bureaucratic system which functions without the intrusion of personal caprice. Does such a value-orientation prevent progress? Crozier's categorical answer is: No. He identifies successes in French affairs to be most conspicuous at the two ends of the scale—pioneering individual creative work, and highly effective group functioning in times of crisis.[13] Does this not seem to closely reflect the Indian temperament too?

Clearly, thus, even in the West the cultural mosaic is not quite as homogeneous as we commonly tend to believe. In terms of American management thinking, the French Phenomenon will perhaps be treated as a drag, as antediluvian. Yet, the French seem to have stuck to their ethos, and still do not lag far behind the USA or their European neighbours in terms of material and technological advancement. Here then is another instance of being successfully authentic to one's own cultural grain, one's 'deep structure'—a lesson which Indian thinking needs to learn immediately.

We were a witness some time ago to the following episode which shows how deep can be the disorientation of the modern Indian from his 'deep structure'. After we had explained the spirit of hierarchism in Japanese firms, a manager in his forties, participating in an in-house programme on managerial excellence, told the group how greatly embarrassed and belittled his father had made him feel a few months earlier. As he was boarding the train from his home town, after his annual holidays, his old father also got into the compartment. Then presently, with folded hands, he began to request the many passengers in the coach to help or take care of his son who was travelling alone on a long journey! This the manager found intolerable and described the episode to the group with disdain, and with shame writ large on his face. We, and quite a few others, felt sad that this manager had failed to attach any value to the expression of supreme affection in his father's behaviour. The generally cold, aloof independence running through the parent–offspring relationships of the West were obviously more sensible to him than such near-divine warmth of hierarchical relations in the Indian setting. The West is beginning to pine for the treasure it has lost and we in India are bent upon throwing away the treasure we have.

III. Theoretical Basis of Hierarchism

Having ended the previous section with a French author, let us continue with two more of them to begin this section. Fifty years ago Guenon did not mince words when writing:

(a) The chimerical prejudice of 'equality' goes against all the best established facts, in the intellectual order as well as in the physical order; *it is the negation of all natural hierarchy*, and it is the debasement of all knowledge to the level of the limited understanding of the mass. People will no longer admit anything which passes common comprehension.[14]

(b) Natural relations are turned upside down ..., all hierarchy is done away with in the name of that hallucination, equality; and as equality is after all impossible in actual fact, *false hierarchies are created*[15] [emphasis added].

Before we interpret Guenon, let us also listen to a French authoress, Simone Weil:

(a) [Hierarchism] is composed of a certain veneration, a certain devotion towards superiors, considered not as individuals, nor in relation to the powers they exercise, but as symbols.... *A veritable hierarchy pre-supposes a consciousness on the part of the superiors of this symbolic function*, and a realization that it forms the only legitimate object of devotion among their subordinates.[16] [Emphasis added.]

Then after distinguishing between 'stable inequality' caused by custom and tradition, and 'mobile inequality' spurred by the money motive, she says further:

(b) A mobile, fluid inequality produces a desire to better oneself. It is no nearer to equality than is stable inequality, and is every bit as unwholesome. The revolution of 1789, in putting forward equality, only succeeded in reality in sanctioning the substitution of one form of inequality for another.[17]

We may also hear what Huston Smith points out with great lucidity and force. According to him modern science also has a hierarchical outlook in its approach, but it is confined only to the quantitative, ontological plane of material reality. But the paradigm of hierarchy in tradition is qualitative, and embraces an altogether higher ontological plane of being. He summarizes the difference thus:[18] 'For the present we note that the view of reality as consisting of *graded levels of being* dominated man's outlook until the rise of modern science [emphasis added].

Radhakrishnan brings out this principle of qualitative hierarchy

198/ *Management by Values*

in human life through the language of mysticism:[19] 'The way to redemption is rise to the spirit above reason ... There is a reality that is deeper than the structure of reason. It is at the core of man's being and it enables him to transcend the natural.'

Taking the clue from Guenon, Weil, Smith and Radhakrishnan we may now derive the following major theoretical insights:

1) As soon as human beings lose or ignore the inner touch with their cosmic, universal, natural background, and commence the task of social and organizational engineering, they tend to commit serious conceptual errors.

2) The web of this projected universe—both physical and psychological—is necessarily spun from the warp and weft of the vertical and the lateral. Ascent or descent is as much a dimension of reality as is lateral expansion or contraction.

3) Human architecture, e.g. the steeple of a Church, the dome of a Gurdwara, the minaret of a Mosque, the spire of a Temple—all symbolize the aspiration for mute communion with the lofty infinite.

4) The superior or the elder in the family or the organization stands as the symbol of this loftiness, this ascent towards the infinite. He has to earn and protect this height through character and morality. Obedience then follows from lower levels.

5) Hierarchy, because it is symbolic, is also qualitative and not quantitative. The hierarchy, for example, of 'free', 'communist' and 'third' world countries is truly one based on money and military might. The hierarchy of income tax or wealth tax brackets is again a money-related hierarchy. Similarly, the international league tables of per capita GNP and many other variables are all examples of false and divisive hierarchies of the quantitative kind.

6) If the chief mark of man's scientific–technological progress is his hard-won victory against natural gravitation, man's inner progress must correspondingly admit of his laboured inner ascent against the natural downward gravitation of his aptitudes and impulses.

7) Equality must mean raising those numerous minds which now linger in the lower rungs, and not debasing the fewer minds which can stay in the higher states to lower ones.

8) Hierarchy implies a blend of role excellence earned as a result of effort, with the effort to live up to the excellence already symbolic of a given role. In fact, each role in society is always such a blend.

9) Hierarchism is usually an effective brake against wanton ego-centricity in interpersonal relationships—especially among the younger but more qualified personnel.

10) Hierarchism imposes a psychic covenant on superiors to strive for very high standards of conduct. Forgiveness or tolerance of mistakes by juniors is an important clause in this covenant. It also makes an occasionally needed rebuke or reprimand more accept-able and legitimate.

11) Hierarchism is functional for conflict-resolution. It is a daily scene in Indian homes where either parent can be seen, when two young children happen to be quarrelling vehemently about some-thing, admonishing the elder: 'Come on! Aren't you the elder? Can't you be generous? Don't be small-minded, my dear'; or the youngster: 'You naughty chap! Talking so rudely like that to your elder brother? When will you be a decent, civilized person. Go and say sorry.' In organizations too, when conflicts seem insoluble through logic and data, hierarchism of this nature can become a vital response.

12) Hierarchism-by-age can moderate the bristling effects of hierarchism-by-organizational status. A younger individual can become the boss of an older one through competence and allied factors. Yet, if such a boss can consciously bear in mind that a status-wise lower, but age-wise higher level person reports to him, all his manners and words towards him should be sincerely and subtly more courteous compared to those towards his own equals or those who are younger. Such processes are of course always a two-way traffic. So, the older person too has to preserve the spirit of congratulation for the younger, much in the same way as the elder brother does when a younger brother surpasses him.

13) Hierarchism can ensure patience and discipline in organiza-tions. The arrogance of assumed competence or higher degrees can be tamed if a junior-by-age is able to internalize the norm of patience when, for instance, the occasion for a promotion arises. Similarly, the senior-in-age should be chivalrous in letting a junior

rise above him in status when occasionally such a move becomes imperative in the organizational interest. Also, the restraint on abusive speech, rough tempers, unpunctuality and so on—which seniority-by-age can induce—is a useful means of ensuring a disciplined environment. Hierarchism-by-age and-by-status are both systemically integral to the effective functioning of social and organizational life in India. If it is cut asunder we reap all-round normlessness and indiscipline.

Indian social structure and Indian psychological theory both work out this root principle of hierarchy. Thus, in the *Mahabharata* we should treat the obedience of the younger brothers towards Yudhisthira, even during the obviously suicidal and immoral game of dice, as entirely symbolic. It demonstrates the observance of a principle which is beyond all contingencies of the social reality in flux. Similarly, in Yudhisthira's replies to the first two questions of the Guardian Spirit (*Yaksha*) of the pond as: (i) the mother is heavier than the earth, and (ii) the father is loftier than the sky, it is again the inviolate and non-contingent principle of hierarchy in human society for humane living which has been adumbrated. Our literal minds are a real obstacle to a proper understanding of the Epics. It is also important to note how hierarchism is put in its place by the ancient law-givers like Manu who prescribe progressively higher punishment for the same offence by individuals of higher castes. Thus the *Manusmriti* lays down:[20]

[1] Where another common man would be fined one Karshapana, the King shall be fined one thousand; that is the settled rule.

[2] In [a case of] theft the guilt of a Sudra shall be eightfold, that of a Vaishya sixteenfold, that of a Kshatriya two-and-thirtyfold.

[3] That of a Brahmana sixty-four fold, or quite a hundredfold, or [even] twice four-and-sixtyfold; [each of them] knowing the nature of the offence.

Indeed, the original theory of caste hierarchy is based on ever-stricter laws of restraint and self-denial, and not privilege, for the higher castes. These restraining codes are designed as a negative prelude to positive inner ascent. Otherwise, they would not have maintained their compelling power which is still evident in many orthodox lives. Vivekananda was never tired of asserting that the ideal must not be dragged down to the level of the practical and pedestrian, for then we eliminate this fixed pole-star for guiding our journey.[21]

Take again *sankhya* psychology which postulates three *guna*s (substance-attributes) to constitute all empirical phenomena, including human personality. These three *guna*s are: *sattwa, rajas* and *tamas*. Now, they are interrelated in a hierarchical order, where *sattwa* is relatively the highest or best, *rajas* the middle, and *tamas* the lowest or worst. That is also why Aurobindo says that *sattwa guna* is the first mediator between man's lower nature and higher.[22] Similarly, Guenon also says that *sattwa* represents the ascending thrust, *rajas* the lateral expanding pressure, and *tamas* the descending pull in man's character. While discussing their relation to the theory of five primordial elements he comments:[23] '... the horizontal aspect, as function of 'rajas', will correspond ... to heat, and the vertical aspect, as function of *sattwa*, to light ...'

Similarly, in 'tantra' psychology the progressive ascension of consciousness is figuratively explained in terms of seven *chakra*s or planes within the central channel of the spinal column, *sushumna*. The lowest *chakra* is *muladhara* at the sacral base, the middle or fourth one is *anahata* in the region of the cardiac heart, and *sahasrara* the highest in the head. So long as consciousness continues to play in the lower three *chakra*s, man's degenerative tendencies predominate. Only when it begins to reside by degrees at the *anahata* levels does he achieve genuine improvement. Once it penetrates the *sahasrara, samadh*ic ecstasy results. When there is a return look at the empirical from this transcendent level of consciousness, there is a total transformation in outlook. Mysticism and everyday life lose their boundaries in perfect harmony, as Stark points out to be the case with Sri Ramakrishna.[24] It is of course possible to visualize the complementarity of the *guna* and *chakra* theories.

In other words, once transcendent Reality is accommodated alongside empirical reality within our basic intellectual framework, hierarchism will naturally assume its irreplaceable position. No longer then can it appear as an anachronism to be got rid of. One wonders whether, if the ascending thrust of *sattwa* had held the balance against the expanding pressure of *rajas* in human history, the world might have witnessed the horrors of colonialism, world wars and worse. In this light, we find it easy to agree with Wilber when he draws our attention to the inability of psychoanalysis to make us understand our higher modes of being, and adds:[25]

> Reducing the higher to the lower,
> it saw everywhere the beast.

Yet, it is an intriguing minor puzzle why Wilber entitled one of his books *The Spectrum of Consciousness*,[26] which invokes a lateral image, and not 'Hierarchy of Consciousness'. Griffiths has seized the core of Hinduism when he sees in it a whole hierarchy from the Supreme Being, the Cosmic Lord, through the human body and sense to this world—a deep sense of 'hierarchy of being'. This is still a living current in Hinduism but, according to him, the West has lost it.[27]

Sri Aurobindo, the greatest of modern Indian philosophers by the criteria of originality and realization, should appropriately have the last word in expressing the essentiality of hierarchism as a backdrop for human affairs:[28]

Every state of existence has some force in it which drives it to transcend itself. Matter moves towards becoming life. Life travails towards becoming mind. Mind aspires towards becoming ideal truth. Truth rises towards becoming divine and infinite Spirit.

IV. REFURBISHED HIERARCHISM FOR INDIA

The vital, but unperceived distinction between the idealism of vertical hierarchism and the ideology of flat equalization has been expressed very well in the following Sanskrit verse (whose source now eludes us):

> 'Bhāva-advaitam sadā kuryāt,
> Kriyā-advaitam na karhichit,
> Advaitam trishu-lokeshu,
> Nā-advaitam guruna-saha'.

The verse says: 'One must try always to cultivate the mental attitude of equality or non-duality towards all, but refrain from showing this mental frame in external dealings irrespective of time, place and circumstance. Towards all and everything in the three worlds the practice of the feeling of equality is permissible, but never towards one's guru.' The immense practical wisdom of this lies in the fact that it embraces a true principle of human conduct: the real mental intent is always more important than the external act. We often notice in our organizations that visible efforts towards behavioural equality border on pseudo-equalization; a sham because it consists mostly of external postures. They are easy to adopt. Recasting the mental frame needs more sincere *sadhana*. If mental tuning is correctly done this way then although the person will *see* the same truth or being in both the dishonest and the honest, yet he can adjust his external dealings with them according to merit. This is how the transcendent can help the management of the empirical, the vertical of the horizontal.

If in various Indian organizations and institutions this idealism in hierarchy—both cosmic and social—is missing today, that by itself gives us little cause to reject the principle. As already pointed out, the vaster cosmic dimension of hierarchism apart, its role—in eastern cultures at least—has been to release and sustain the flow of the spirit, the feeling of total responsibility towards juniors by seniors, reciprocated by total trust of the former by the latter. In fact, in two recent encounters in management seminars with a Lt.-General and a Major-General we found them strongly contesting the common view that the army culture is brutally authoritarian. Rather, the *mai-baap* (parental) relationship between senior and junior officers is full of genuine ownership, even love, amongst them. Since there is no hope, nor is it perhaps desirable, of achieving significantly widespread automation in a densely populated country like India, our organizations must remain employee-intensive. To make such systems spring back to virility the fugitive flavour of true hierarchism must be recaptured.

In a recent article Lawler III has explored a number of substitutes for hierarchy, to yield the same results as hierarchy is supposed to do but without its accelerated overhead burden in the USA. Two of the suggested substitutes are 'vision/values' and 'emergent leadership'. Reading through the brief explanations he offers for them, we wonder how they both can avoid their intrinsic 'vertical' thrust. Vision/values have to be conceptualized and transmitted from some point in the organization. Emergent leaders in work groups must also be qualitatively 'higher' than the rest. If that be so, then how much and how long can organization structures escape reflecting these realities in terms of hierarchical levels which, we should recall, are symbolic in essence![29]

In other words, there are two principal forces in favour of retaining hierarchism in organizations:

(a) The trans-cultural, cosmic, universal aspect of hierarchism which cannot be wished away;
(b) The culture-specific social and interpersonal implications of hierarchism through tradition.

Thus, while both (a) and (b) lend validity to hierarchism as an organizational value in India, in a country like the USA too the force of (a) is valid anyway. For, congenital human egotism would be bound to create cruder ways of hierarchism if classical hierarchism-by-age were to be forcefully banished. Of course, we do not mean by hierarchism to have tier after tier in the structure for creating so-called career paths for employees. Indeed, in one of our recent consulting assignments on organization structure we categorically recommended the reduction of the existing 12 or 13 levels to 6 or 7 at most. This, however, has nothing to do with the familial, age-based spirit of hierarchism. The strong note of anti-hierarchism in transactional analysis could be culture-specific to the USA, but it tends to violate an eternal principle of creation and existence.[30] If hierarchism can, as it ought to, be lived by organizational members to keep alive generosity, affection, forgiveness and sacrifice on the part of those lower down, we do not see how it can negate freedom, empathy, balance and individuality. We feel that one major source of continual subtle pressure on the elder, the superior, the boss to enshrine and symbolize the foregoing human values will be cut off if hierarchism is derided as a mere feudal relic. Indeed, excellence, development, effectiveness and so on have a definite vertical orientation. Hierarchism is only a reflection of this logic. Lessem has reviewed networking and other organizational innovations as responses to the need for reconciling freedom with order.[31] We believe that hierarchism of eastern cultures should perform precisely this function—if its innate spirit is revived and reinforced as a major element of organizational culture building. Unlike Lessem, Lawler and others, hierarchism need not then be considered as a malignant sore for excision. Let there be innovations in the design of organizations, if that is the way it is to be, yet there is little reason to make a virtue of a necessity which is the creation of our perpetual restlessness leading to the apotheosis of change, flatteringly called 'progress'. The true spirit of hierarchism, if diligently cultivated, could greatly serve all our organizations.

In his bold futuristic book on post-industrial society management of 2001, Davis too, like Lessem, speaks eloquently of 'network' as the key to organizational design in the coming decades.[32] Networking is showered with many sterling qualities like adaptive, conscious, cooperative, self-generating, and is claimed to treat each member as the centre of the network. It is also holistic, because with the aid of electronics information systems human frailties will no longer impede information flows amongst all centres in the network. But do we realize that with humane hierarchism, as is specific to authentic Indian culture, affective lubricants like forgiveness, patience, care, support, humility, loyalty and so on make for the same movements as Davis ascribes to networking? Does holism deny holistic individual development in the organizational setting? If not, how can we support information technology to make up for human frailties? We fail to see how hierarchism, as outlined above, is competitive, non-conscious, rigid and de-individualized? Indeed, we perceive hierarchism to be the antidote to the cold, calculative and mercenary impersonality within our organizations. In India at least there is a real danger of falling into the trap of upgraded information technology, wrongly assuming this to be a substitute for the weakening fabric of human values in organizations. Its strengthening must be pursued in its own right. Revitalized hierarchism must be one line of effort in this direction. Let not the dazzle of the untested new blind us to the worth of the tested old.

Conclusion: Humane Hierarchism for Ever

The crux of hierarchism for the Indian scene is then not structural power, but filial and fraternal affection. Hierarchism in Eastern cultures has ideally been a socio-psychological lubricant ensuring less friction-prone, more adjustment-inclined interpersonal relationships. When Rosabeth Kanter states that in 'post-entrepreneurial' organizations, where subordinates are encouraged to think for themselves, where there is far greater speed and flexibility in communication, where there is more delegation and the like, managers must learn to operate without 'the crutch of hierarchism', it seems that her thought is confined only to structural hierarchy.[33] She rightly contemplates the need for greater trust, empathy, shared value-creation, learning. We wonder, however, if she is right when she suggests that they can be achieved simply by replacing hierarchy with lateral and network relationships. We nurse the same doubt about Davis' observations on this issue which are similar to hers. Our experience rather is that, besides the need for lateral relationships, it is the existence of authentic and warm hierarchical relationships which make for more genuine trust, empathy and so on. No matter how flat the structure is, filial/fraternal hierarchism will always remain indispensable. Let us see what Pascale and Athos have to say about this in the Japanese context:[34]

In Japan the *sempai* (senior) expects the *kohai* (junior) to understand *him*. If the *sempai* doesn't always perform well, the *kohai* is expected to compensate for him and not to judge him except as a total human being. The *sempai* in turn is expected to display a wider breadth of understanding than normally exists in Western enterprises. These expectations lead to more humane and nurturing hierarchical relationships.

It is perhaps a bit of an anticlimax when Kanter also suggests that today's manager must bargain and negotiate to sell ideas like any other politician. We feel that the politician is a poor model when we are speaking normatively of trust, shared value-creation, and so on. In the Indian milieu hierarchism in social relationships has in principle been a percolation of the cosmic sense of hierarchy—all the way down, as Griffiths puts it, 'from the Supreme Being, Cosmic Lord ... through all the devas, the powers of nature, to man and his intelligence and his senses, and finally to the world which is below him'.[35] The new-found anti-hierarchy enthusiasm in management writing, therefore, smacks of—if we may say so—faddish immaturity.

REFERENCES

1. S. Marsland and M. Beer, 'The Evolution of Japanese Management: Lessons For US Managers', *Organizational Dynamics*, Winter, 1983, p. 54.
2. J.R. Lincoln, M. Hanada, and J. Olson, 'Cultural Orientations and Individual Reactions to Organisations: A Study of Employees of Japanese-Owned Firms', *Administrative Science Quarterly*, March 1981, vol. 26, p. 94.
3. Ibid., p. 95–6.   4. Ibid., p. 106.   5. Ibid., p. 113.
6. G. Hofstede and M.H. Bond, 'The Confucian Connection: From Cultural Roots to Economic Growth', *Organizational Dynamics*, Spring, 1988, p. 8.

7. J.P. Alston, 'Wa, Guanxi and Inhwa: Managerial Principles in Japan, China, and Korea', *Business Horizons*, March–April, 1989, p. 29.
8. G. Buhler, *The Laws of Manu* (in *Sacred Books of The East*, ed. M. Müller), (Oxford: Clarendon Press, 1986), vol. XXXV, ix, 108.
9. S.J. De, 'The Management of Human Resources—Some Thoughts', paper presented at the 24th Annual Conference of the National Institute of Personnel Management, Calcutta Branch, July 1989, pp. 3–4.
10. Romila Thapar, 'The Ramayana Syndrome', *Seminar*, no. 353, Jan. 1989, p. 75.
11. R. Tagore, *A Vision of India's History* (Calcutta: Visva-Bharati, 1988), p. 10.
12. R.W. Howe, 'How Vietnam Changed America', *The Statesman*, 6 May 1989.
13. M. Crozier, *The Bureaucratic Phenomenon* (London: Tavistock, 1964), pp. 222–7.
14. R. Guenon, *East and West* (London: Luzac & Co, 1940), p. 66.
15. Ibid., p. 165.
16. S. Weil, *The Need For Roots* (London: Ark Paperbacks, 1987), p. 18.
17. Ibid., p. 17.
18. H. Smith, *Forgotten Truth* (New York: Harper Colophon, 1976), p. 3.
19. S. Radhakrishnan, *Recovery of Faith* (New Delhi: Orient Paperbacks, 1967), p. 94.
20. G. Buhler, *The Laws of Manu*, p. 313.
21. For example, 'Discipleship' in *Collected Works* (Calcutta: Advaita Ashrama, 1959), vol. VIII, p. 120.
22. Sri Aurobindo, *The Message of The Gita* (Pondicherry: Sri Aurobindo Ashram, 1977), p. 222.
23. R. Guenon, *Studies in Hinduism* (New Delhi: Navrang, 1985), p. 41.
24. C.A. Stark, *God of All* (Massachusetts: Claude Stark Inc., 1974), p. 106.
25. K. Wilber, *The Atman Project* (Wheaton: The Theosophical Publishing House, 1985), p. 23.
26. *Idem, The Spectrum of Consciousness* (Wheaton: The Theosophical Publishing House, 1982).
27. B. Griffiths, *The Cosmic Revelation* (London: Collins, 1983), p. 35.
28. Sri Aurobindo, *The Hour of God* (Pondicherry: Sri Aurobindo Ashram, 1982), pp. 34–5.
29. E.E. Lawler, III; 'Substitutes For Hierarchy', *Organizational Dynamics*, Summer 1988, pp. 11–12.
30. S.K. Chakraborty, *Foundations of Managerial Work* (Bombay: Himalaya, 1989), Ch. 8.
31. R. Lessem, *Global Management Principles* (London: Prentice Hall, 1989), pp. 386–95.
32. S.M. Davis, *2001 Management* (London: Simon & Schuster, 1989), pp. 77–89.

33. R.M. Kanter, 'The New Managerial Work', *Harvard Business Review*, Nov.–Dec. 1989, pp. 85–92.
34. R.T. Pascale and A.G. Athos, *The Art of Japanese Management* (London: Penguin, 1982), p. 138.
35. Bede Griffiths, *Cosmic Revelation* (London: Collins, 1983), p. 35.

10

REDISCOVERING INDIAN PSYCHOLOGY FOR MAN-AGERS*

This chapter has been motivated by some recent comments, heard and read from a few Indian academics, to the effect that there is no segment of Indian thought which could be called 'psychology'. Thus, they say, the *shada darshan*s (six systems of philosophy) nowhere speak of psychology. An erudite scholar among them has just edited a three-volume collection of writings entitled *Psychology in India*.[1] It may imply that there possibly exists no room for a volume called *Indian Psychology*. Our own rediscoveries in the soil of Indian thought, however, point precisely in the opposite direction.

We feel that since for India today nothing surpasses in importance the task of transformation of that segment of her citizens which constitutes the island of money power and organized employment, it will be a folly not to grasp and implement what Indian thought means for human psychology. Of course, while the focus here is on India, the major principles of human psychology stored up in Indian thought might also be universally valid because of its profound metaphysical moorings. We shall however try below to avoid being merely academic. To the best of our ability, we shall provide a practical orientation to enable a beginning to be made.

I. The Crux of the Confusion

An important cause for the non-recognition of Indian Psychology is probably the translation of *darshana*s into 'philosophy'. *Darshan* means to see—in the sense of pure vision. This differs radically from philo-sophy which means fondness or love for an intellectual

* This chapter is the revised version of a paper 'Does Indian Psychology Exist?' presented at a National Conference organized by Shankara Vidya Kendra, Delhi, in November, 1989.

system. So, if the goal of Indian *darshan* is to lead an aspirant to 'seeing' (not in the physical or gross sensual way), then it must also deal with practical methods and steps to achieve this goal. 'Seeing' in Indian *darshan* implies a progressive ascension of the individual's consciousness. Such ascension comes not by intellectual combat alone, but by quietening our noisy and tangled reflective consciousness. It arrives through an undulating gradient, and settles, as a deep subjective realization in the centre of one's being. As one travels towards this centre (only another way of metaphorically putting across the process of ascension), the perceptions, attitudes, values, and behaviour of the individual progressively improve qualitatively. It is this which our homes and organizations need most. Thus, Indian *darshana*s (especially *Vedanta* and *Yoga*, and also Buddhist thought) are not mere academic or speculative thought systems. They have set for themselves the supreme practical objective of taking the individual by the hand, as it were, and leading him or her up the steps to the wide, stable roof of true perspective and understanding. How can they then avoid being steeped in psychology too?

Yet another stumbling block in the minds of most educated Indians is the notion that Indian thought is either entirely abstract and irrelevant to daily life, or that it is merely exoteric religion including a mass of superstition and coercive ritual. On both counts therefore it is a wasteland to plough in the present times. What is missing in such an assessment is that all esoteric religion is nothing other than transformational psychology. Fundamentalist inter-religious strife is only an exoteric affair. Merely for this no thinking person should abandon his or her birthright to esoteric religious psychology. The task of religion is truly to bring man in touch with his Real, Infinite essence,[2] or to enable him to experience and express the potential Divinity he already is.[3] Let it be understood that academic philosophy taught in the Universities today attempts nothing of this sort. It is thus incapable of triggering integral psychological transformation. It is 'religious psychology' which is squarely concerned with this task. The *shada darshana*s, the *purana*s, the *mahakavya*s and all that in India constitute an integral synthesis of philosophy, psychology and religion. It is not in India's grain to insulate secular (*sthula*) psychology from spiritual (*sukshma*) psychology. The gross or *sthula* reality of the secular has to be subordinated to and managed in the higher light of the subtle or the *sukshma*. The sooner we grasp this ingrained holistic character of Indian thought the better it will be.

Thus, if one can sweep away the cobwebs enveloping the Indian mind, it should then be possible to grasp more concretely and usefully what Indian psychology means for us.

II. INDIAN PSYCHOLOGY OF BLISS (*Ānanda*)

The keynote of Indian psychology is permanent BLISS for every individual. This constitutes the terminal experiential and transformational goal of human existence. In our view the primary elements of the theory behind this supreme aim of BLISS is:

(1) BLISS is not happiness or pleasure. The latter are only the complementary opposites of sorrow or pain. *Ānanda* is the state where *samatwa* or equi-vision towards these pairs of opposites (*dwandwa*s) is experienced.

(2) The pursuit of pleasure or happiness at the sensual, empirical level, if made the primary basis of life, must necessarily attract their intrinsic opposites.

(3) The external, empirical, *sthula* reality is by nature an un-ending play of opposites.

(4) The empirical aspect of human personality (*vyavaharika vyaktitwa* or *varaha* self) is constitutionally prone to remain engrossed in the fluctuating tussle of *dwandwa*s, and thus always caught up in an anxious, fearful and precarious psychological existence.

(5) The trans-empirical aspect of human personality (*paramarthika vyaktitwa* or *Vishnu* SELF) is always, by definition, a state of permanent fulfilment (*poornatwa*). It is not actualized, but realized.

(6) The empirical personality is deficit-driven (due to *vasana*s), externally-directed and objectively dependent.

(7) The trans-empirical personality in man is surplus-inspired *poorna*, internally-seated and subjectively independent.

(8) The true alienation of man consists of the divorce between his empirical and trans-empirical personalities or selves.

(9) The empirical personality, trying by itself to wend its way through life and society, gets caught up in pettiness, selfishness, greed, jealousy, sycophancy, power-hunger, licentiousness, deceit, falsehood, etc.

(10) The task of true psychology is to restore to the blind empirical personality the unfailing light and perspective of the trans-empirical personality. The path to ĀNANDA lies in this. Organizations and society automatically benefit from such progress in the individual.

(11) Reaching the goal of Bliss requires restraint, control and refinement of the lower-order empirical self even while it is engaged in its multiple roles and tasks.

(12) This path awaits the footsteps not merely of the monk, but of each one of us. The definition of ignorance (*avidya*) is unawareness of this path–goal system.

If such be the theory of BLISS psychology, some leads are necessary into the sources of Indian thought which have helped us to shape this outline.

(A) *The Rigveda*:

Sri Aurobindo narrates his experiential Odyssey through this Veda with marvellous authenticity. He reveals its profound psychological import concealed under the cover of an external, nature-bound symbolic framework of ritualism:[4]

[i] '... the general object of the sacrifice, of the work, of the journey, of the increase of the light and the abundance of the waters [is] the attainment of the Truth-Consciousness, *rtam*, [and] the resultant Bliss ...'

[ii] '... the powers of Truth entering into the outpourings of the *Ānanda* in man ...'

[iii] 'For the Vedic Rishi Truth is the passage and the antechamber, the Bliss of the divine existence is the goal; or else Truth is the foundation, Bliss the supreme result.'

Thus, while Truth is an ultimate value, its august technicality and elusiveness really clothes the highest of emotional experiences—Bliss or *ānanda*.

(B) *Mundaka Upanishad*:[5]

'*Ānanda rupah amritam, yad vibhāti*' the Self (*paramarthika* or trans-empirical) that shines surpassingly as Blissfulness and immortality.

(C) *Taittiriya Upanishad*:[6]

[i] '*Anyo-antar atman-anandamayo-teneishwa poorna*', i.e. internal to the knowledge/intelligence sheath,* completely constituted of Bliss.

---

* In this Upanishad the human entity is conceived of in terms of five successive

[ii] '*Ko hyevanyatkah pranyat, yadesh ākasha anando na syāt*', i.e. who, indeed, will inhale and who will exhale, if this Bliss be not there in the supreme space within the heart.

[iii]   '*Ānando brahmeti vyajanāt,*
        Ānandadhayeva khallwimāni bhutāni jāyante,
        Ānandena jātāni jivanti,
        Ānandam prayantwabhisam-vishantiti',

i.e. he knew Bliss as Brahman; for from Bliss all beings originate, Bliss sustains them, and towards Bliss again they move and merge.

(D) *Chhandyogya Upanishad:*[7]

'*Yo vai bhuman tat sukham. Nā-alpe*
sukhamasti—bhumaiva sukham',

i.e. that which is Infinite is alone happiness (in the sense of Bliss); the finite and the trivial do not impart Bliss, the Infinite alone does.

(E) *Brihadāranyak Upanishad:*[8]

[i] '*Vijnan ānandam brahman*',
    i.e. Brahman* is Absolute Intelligence and Bliss.

[ii] '*Esha asya param ānanda*',
    i.e. the Infinite alone does.

(F) *Bhagavadgita:*[9]

'*Nāsti buddhir-yuktasya, na cha yuktasya bhāvana,*
Na cha abhāvayetah shānti, ashāntasya kutah sukham',

i.e. for one who is not in *yoga* (with Brahman or *paramarthika vyaktitwa*) there is no intelligence, no concentration; for one without concentration there is no peace; and for the unpeaceful or agitated how can there be happiness (in the sense of Bliss or spiritual delight).

(G) *Brahmasutras:*[10]

'*Ānandamayo—abhyasat*',

i.e. the Self consisting of Bliss is attainable by repetition (of the idea, mentally).

---

sheaths (*kosas*): the outmost is body or *annamaya*, beneath it is the vital or *pranmaya*, below it is mental or *manomaya*, followed by intelligence or *vijnanmaya*, and finally by the Bliss or *ānandamaya kosa*. In fact, this entire Upanishad is a marvellous composition on Bliss or *ānanda*.

* The *Brahmasutras* (1.1.2) define Brahman as that which is the cause of the origin, sustenance and dissolution of the world. Thus, the holistic essence of the entire system of existence is the same as individual Bliss.

(H) *Ādhyātma Rāmayan*:[11]

(i) *'Ānanda-sandra—amalam'*,
   i.e. a condensation of Bliss and Pure Consciousness (Rama).
(ii) *'Tasmāt-parā-ānandamaye'*,
   i.e. [Rama] of the nature of Pure Bliss-Consciousness
(iii) *'Ānandam nirmalam'* (Rama),
   i.e. of the nature of pure Bliss.
(iv) *'Ānanda-murtir-achalam'* (Rama),
   i.e. immutable Bliss-form.
(v) *'Ānandarupo, buddhi-adi-sakshi, laya vivarjita'*,
   i.e. the Ātman* (or the *paramarthika vyaktitwa*) is of the nature of Bliss,
   which does not undergo dissolution, and is the witness of the changes in
   intelligence and other elements of the *vyavaharika vyaktitwa*.

(I) *Yogavāsishtha*:[12]

(i) *'Chetasah, tyājato rupam, ānando hasitam bhavet'*,
   i.e. (one who) has acquired discrimination and thus disengaged from an
   exclusively empirical existence, can smile with Bliss.
(ii) *'Ātmānam anugachhāmi paramānanda sādhanam'*, i.e. (Janaka) shall
   pursue the Ātman or the *paramarthika* SELF for the sake of supreme Bliss.
(iii) *'Sattā sāmanya rupatmān, babhuvā anāndasāgarah'*, (Uddalaka) by recognizing his *paramarthika* SELF as one with Pure Existence, became an ocean
   of Bliss.
(iv) *'Tadabhyasāt avapantah ānanda-spanda-uttaman'*, i.e. (Uddalaka) by
   practising yoga, obtained in himself the supreme throb of Bliss as an
   effect.

(J) *Vivekachudāmani* (Shankaracharya):[13]

This work is literally strewn with dazzling compositions conveying the
message of *ānanda* in a myriad ways, e.g.:

* *'Nitya-ānanda-rasa-swarupine'* (essence of Eternal Bliss)
* *'Nitya-ānanda-swarup-aham'* (same as above)
* *'Swa ānandam anubhunjanah'* (enjoying the Bliss of the Self)
* *'Satya jnana ānanta anandarupam'* (of the nature of truth, knowledge and
  infinite *ānanda*)
* *'Para-ānanda rasānubhuti'* (the experience of Supreme Bliss)
* *'Yatra advaya ānandasukhena mirantaram'* (constant enjoyment of Bliss
  Absolute)

---

* It should be evident that Rama is only a symbol, a personification of the Blissful
*Atm*ic core within each individual body-frame.

- '*Poorna advaya ānandamayatmana sadā*' (living in the Reality, one without a second, a sage enjoys Infinite Bliss)
- '*Akhanda ānandā piyush purne*' (full of the nectar of indivisible Bliss), etc.

(K) *Avadhuta Gita* (Dattatreya):[14]

 (i) '*Ānanda vartate nityam*', i.e. (an Avadhuta) always dwells in Bliss.
 (ii) '*Dattatreya-avadhutena nirmita-ānandarupina*', i.e. Dattatreya-the-*avadhuta* is of the stuff of Bliss.

(L) *Ātmabodha* (Shankaracharya):[15]

 (i) '*Swabhāvah satchidānanda nityanirmala ātmanah*', i.e. the nature of *Atman* or the *paramarthika* SELF is that of eternal purity, reality, consciousness and Bliss.
 (ii) '*Nitya Shuddha, vimuktaika, akhanda ānanda advayam*', i.e. the nature of SELF is truly eternal, pure, free, indivisible, One-without-a-second-Bliss.
 (iii) '*Paripoorna chidānanda swarupena avatisthate*', i.e. (the SELF) exists as the embodiment of Infinite Consciousness and Bliss.

(M) *Majjhima Nikaya*:*

 (i) 'In this very life he is allayed, become cool, he abides in the experience of Bliss with a self† which has become Brahma [*brahmabhuta*]'[16]
 (ii) '... this body he [a *sadhak*] soaks, saturates, fills and penetrates with the joy and Bliss that are born of concentration ...'[17]

These gleanings from a fairly wide range of Indian thought reveal that Bliss is the terminal goal held out for man. It is an indescribably positive experience. Even ordinary human love often begs verbal expression, we may recall. It is *felt*. How much more should this then be true of Bliss: Expressions like 'identification with Brahman', 'attainment of *nirvana*', 'pursuit of *moksha*', 'knowledge of Ultimate Reality' and so on should be understood in terms of achieving the intense awareness of indestructible Bliss. If this 'achievement-motivation' is not psychological, what else is?

Let us therefore term this science of sciences *anand*ology.

III. The Means, Process and Culmination of 'Anandology'

In India the major *darshana*s are nearly always supported by clear,

---

* Buddhist canonical text in Pali.
† *vyavaharika vyaktitwa.*

step-by-step practical methods of self-culture and self-transformation, i.e. *sādhana*. Absent is the artificial segregation we see in the contemporary academic paradigm, between philosophy and psychology, religion and humanism, secularism and spirituality and so on. Let us now turn briefly to the aspect of *sādhana* (dedicated effort).

• To grasp the basic lesson that self-transformation (along the theory outlined in section II) involves the will to combine hearing, reflection and concentration or meditation (*shravanā, mananā* and *nididhyāsanā*).[18]

• *Shravanā* and *mananā* have to converge on the *tattwa* or vital idea, i.e. what is the true Self in me? The best expression of this is to be found in the refrain of Shankaracharya's *Nirvanshatakam*, '*chidananda rupah shivoham*'.

Silent hearing and reflection within on the *tattwa*: 'I am Existence–Knowledge–Bliss [like the symbolic Shiva]' helps to prepare the consciousness for a gradual rise from the *vyavaharika* moorings to the *paramarthika* platform. This can be done in airports, bus queues, bank counters, bureaucratic corridors, morning walks, by keeping to oneself and avoiding wasteful socialization or gossip.

• True absorption and transformation, however, must necessarily depend on the third process, i.e. meditation or concentration. In this stage the mind-stuff is soaked, as it were, in a symbol which represents best to the empirical, sensual mind, the state of Bliss, e.g. a Christ or Buddha, Nanak or Chaitanya, Shiva or Krishna. This is actual practice of what in psychology is known as 'the law of association'. Of course, here it is 'disciplined' and not 'free' association. The principle behind the process of *nididhyāsanā* on such a symbol is stated thus by Aurobindo:[19]

This [mastery over mind and senses] cannot be done by the act of the intelligence itself, by a merely mental self-discipline; it can only be done by Yoga with something *which is higher than itself* and in which *calm and self-mastery are inherent* [emphasis added].

• Since, however, the *vyavaharika* self (with its nine doors)[20] is constitutionally prone to the 'inside–out' syndrome, its links with the internal environment are established through the nerve channels which connect the *manas* (a component of *antahkarana*) with the outer-directed sense organs. As a result these nerve channels often become choked, as it were, with a highly mixed lot of such external stimuli or past memories. Then arises the practical need to cleanse them of such obstructive and distorting accretions so that the refined and autonomous inner perceptions can awaken. Deep, rhythmic breathing, in a comfortably seated, stable but straight posture, is a universally usable process to clear the nerve channels. This process is called *nadishuddhi* or the purification of nerve-channels.[21]

• The cleansing and purification of one's nerve channels, by a sort of high-pressure air-flushing process, has to precede *nididhya-sana* or meditation. It brings about the threefold effects of, (i) calling back the externalized mind or awareness to the inner centre; (ii) soothing the excited, tangled nervous system; and (iii) helping the mind to immerse itself in the *tattwa* of SELF embodied in the chosen personified symbol (called *Ishtam*) which has already been discussed.

• Regular practice of such concentration increases the power of unerring perception or understanding of all varieties of external stimuli. This happens because when the individual begins to identify his self with the Supreme or Absolute SELF embodied in his chosen *Ishtam*, he automatically also gains access (by degrees) to Truth and Knowledge. These cohere with Bliss, the terminal experiential state of the *paramarthika* or Absolute SELF.

• Normally, concentration on the chosen symbol (it could be an unflickering flame, the crimson-rising sun, or the golden full-moon, although lacking certainly in the true transformational potential beyond mere concentration), is done in the 'psychic heart centre', i.e. the space within corresponding to the small external cavity on one's chest. This spot is ideal for most because it represents, in physical space within the body, the transitional plane from the *vyavaharika* self towards that of the *paramarthika* SELF. However, once a certain symbol has been carefully selected, it should continue to be the object of *nididhyasana* for years to come.

• While meditating on the personified symbol of the *tattwa*, its various qualities, such as calmness, purity, compassion, truthfulness, selflessness, rectitude, and above all its untramelled Bliss, should be vividly imagined.

• Further meditation on, as and when the relevant occasion arises, friendly sharing in the happiness of someone else (*maitribhavana*), or compassionate sharing of the sorrow of an unhappy person (*karuna bhavana*) may also be undertaken. Patanjali declares that such practice produces undisturbed calmness of mind, which is the basis of *ānanda*[22].

• Over time the last two steps will lead to, as is repeatedly emphasized in Indian thought, mind-purification or *chittashuddhi*. This implies the purification of emotions and feelings. On the one hand, without *chittashuddhi*, sharp intellect tends to cause the *vyavaharika* self to wreak havoc. On the other, without the soil of a pure mind, the delicate and fine plant of the *paramarthika* Self will not sprout, and the tree of Bliss will not stand.

• Another meditational exercise which might be regularly practised is to imagine in the heart centre that through one ear the subject is hearing beautiful words of praise, welcome, affection, etc. while simultaneously through the other are pouring in scorching words of abuse, insult, hatred in the midst of which the subject is unmoved, serene, imperturbable—neither accepting the first set nor abhorring the second. This exercise leads to the development of *samatwa* or *nirdwandwa* in the midst of inevitable dualities at the *vyavaharika* or empirical level, and *samatwa*, as we know, is only the other face of Bliss. (Obviously *chittashuddhi* and *samatwa* go together.)

• One more *manana*-cum-*nididhyasana* exercise could be used: contemplate in the heart centre that a stormy sea of endless waves is roaring, but supporting it from deep beneath is the absolutely calm sea-bed. The *vyavaharika* self is the storm-tossed surface of the sea, but the serene *paramarthika* Self is the base deep down—for ever. This will lead to the effective interior handling of stress experienced by the exteriorized empirical self, although deep breathing and concentration on the chosen symbol of harmony in the main exercise should already have ameliorated stress quite considerably).

An allied and moving imagery for cultivating stress-free *samatwa* and Bliss is that of the infinite, undifferentiated blue sky. Thus, in the *Avadhuta Gita*, we find the grand refrain '*jnanāmritam, samarasam, gaganopaham*' repeated forty times over! The *tattwa* of Selfhood, it asks one to assert, is: 'I am the nectar of knowledge, homogeneous existence—like the sky.'[23]

• Since mind-purification or *chittashuddhi* is indispensable for the rediscovery of the Blissful SELF, the deep-breathing process itself can be enriched by a little more conscious effort. We know that while the *rajasic* (essentially kinetic and tangled) and the *tamasic* (essentially static and darkening) *guna*s tend to pin the *vyavaharika* self down to lower levels of consciousness, polluting our thoughts and behaviour, the *sattwic* (essentially illuminating and coherent) *guna* pushes consciousness towards higher levels. As Aurobindo says: 'The sattwic quality is the first mediator between the higher and the lower nature.'[24] Therefore, while inhaling deeply and slowly, one could imagine that an aspect of *sattwa guna* like 'patience' is entering with the air and flushing the whole system within. Similarly, while exhaling, even more slowly, it may be visualized that a satellite of *rajo guna* like 'anger' is being expelled from within. One must, however, continue with just these two elements (only given as examples here) for at least three months or so to feel some real transformation.

• Yet another exercise, beyond the basic process, is regarding the essential unity of the *paramarthika* Self amongst all individuals—irrespective of differentiation at the *vyavaharika* level. Imagine a hundred pots filled with air. They are lying separate, perhaps one tumbling over the other, causing noise and friction. Yet the next moment they are all broken. The apparently distinct pot-shaped air, in a hundred separate pots, is now really all one single, original undifferentiated mass of air. Our body–mind–intellect–senses quartets are the differentiated pots, our SELF is the undifferentiated unity—a fundamental idea or *tattwa* towards Bliss.

• Finally, mention may be made of *pratipakshabhavanam*, i.e. the process of raising contrary thoughts by deliberate inner effort. This too is an effective psychological method for *chittashuddhi*. Thus, if on receiving a coveted award or recognition we become vain or egotistic, it pollutes our mind. This may be a natural tendency, but it is not optimal. To reduce this mental pollution we have to wilfully awaken within the mind the contrary thought of humility or modesty. It is man's existential dilemma that no effort is needed to feel vain, but struggle he must to stay humble. To let weeds grow in the garden no labour is called for, but to foster a rose bush one needs to sweat.

There is of course an endless variety—nothing short of the

range of consumer goods in the largest department stores—of such practices to choose from. The essential *principles* of psychological growth reflected in them are:

1) The Blissful, infinite, core of man is within himself. 'The Kingdom of Heaven is within', or *'nābh kamal men hai Kasturi'* (the musk lies in the navel of the deer).

2) But the design of man, mysteriously, is such that all his tendencies are outgoing, through the nine doors of his body-mansion: the two ears, the two eyes, the two nostrils, the mouth, and the two lower apertures.

3) If these doors (rather the *indriya*s behind them) could be trained and disciplined to stay bolted at planned intervals for certain durations, and help localize the mind in the centre of one's being, then awareness of the *bhumaiva sukham*, of the smokeless, luminous *atman*[25] could grow.

4) Thus, all the psychological practices are *individual*, even if done in a group-setting. To lift the level of individual consciousness is their aim.

5) The cause of the external objective world lies in the subjective world—be it at the cosmic or at the individual level. Increased harmony in the human environment can be projected only from growing harmony inside man.

6) It is constructive to interpret the inherently outgoing tendencies of the human mind as hurdles wilfully placed by cosmic design for man to meet the challenge, beat them, and grasp the Blissful core which is the most inalienable of human rights—needing no declaration by the UNO or protection by Amnesty International.

7) The will has to be strengthened, and the emotions have to be purified. Intellect must not be made our God.[26] It is needed as much as a street-cleaner or a policeman is.[27] Without *chittashuddhi* it cannot perform its discriminating role correctly. It then becomes the breeding ground of all kinds of pettiness—the petty satellites of the death instinct.[28] It is the pure mind which can will nobly, or be inspired to do so, never the intellect. It is the pure heart or the pure mind alone which can see God, as the Bible says. This God is only another name for Bliss.

8) The *pravritti* of man—his outgoing, evolving, differentiating tendencies—has to be reined in by a continuous striving for *nivritti*—the inward, involving, integrating tendencies.

9) The *artha* and *kāma* goals or *purushārtha*s of men are legitimate

in his *pravritti* aspect—but have to be regulated by the *dharma* and *moksha* goals grounded in his *nivritti* aspect, supported by *sattwa guna*.

10) Intellect used in the service of *pravritti*, and its correlates *artha* and *kama*, throws the individual into the sticky and polluted net of his *vyavaharika* self, fuelled by *rajo guna*. The disciplined mind will counteract this degrading movement by inspiring the will towards purifying *nivritti*, and its correlates *dharma* and *moksha*, thus reviving his *paramarthika* Self.

11) The Cosmic Mind or Universal Intelligence or Supreme Consciousness and the human mind, intelligence and consciousness are intrinsically identical. Through the intense aspiration of a pure mind a double movement of descent of the former and of ascent of the latter can be initiated.

12) The ordinary human mind and intelligence can understand creation, but not the Creator (or the Creative Principle). They remain enthralled with the magic show, and forget to get to know the Magician himself, but without knowing the Creator, the Magician, there is no Bliss. The discursive intellect, the reflective consciousness must be stilled for this aim.

The consummation of the theory, principles and practices of *anand*ology outlined above is presented to us in Indian thought via two archetypal human models: the *sthitaprajna* and the *jivanmukta*.

(A) *Sthitaprajna*

To wipe out the despondent confusion in Arjuna's mind and brace him up for the selfless, righteous battle to protect the foundations of society, Krishna describes the *sthitaprajna* (a man of settled wisdom or intuitive insight) through verses II. 55–72. The psychological disposition of such an individual is probably best captured in verses II. 56–7.:[29]

a)   '*Dukheshu anudvignamanah, sukheshu vigatasprihah;*
       Vitaraga-bhaya-krodhah, sthitadhi munir-uchayte',

i.e. whose mind is undisturbed in the midst of sorrows and has little craving for pleasures, and from whom attraction, fear and anger have departed—such a one is called a sage of settled wisdom;

b)   '*Yah sarvatra nabhi-sneha-statta prapya, subha-ashubham;*
       Na abhinandati, na dwesti, tasya prajna pratisthita',

i.e. the person who in everything is without clinging although experiencing this good or that evil, and neither rejoices nor hates, his intuitive insight or wisdom is well-settled.

To acquire such a disposition *Yoga* (with the *Ishtam* for example) is a practical necessity. Why? Verse II.66 tells us:[30]

c) '*Nasti buddhir-yuktasya, na cha yuktasya bhavana;*
    Na cha bhavayatah shanti, ashantasya kutah sukham?',

i.e for one who is not in *Yoga* there is neither intelligence nor concentration, for one without concentration there is no tranquillity; and for the excited how can there be Bliss? Shankaracharya too evaluates the *sthitaprajna* model by the test of *sadānandamshnute*, i.e. eternal Bliss.[31]

(B) *Jivanmukta*

This model is almost identical with that of *sthitaprajna*. A *jivan-mukta* is one who lives fully liberated even within this body. Obviously, this liberation is purely psychological—a constant feeling of the *paramarthika* Self of Bliss within the framework of the *vyavaharika* self. The white coconut kernel contained inside the hard outer shell is good suggestive imagery. They are comple-mentary, but the order of preference and priority is clear. Shankar-acharya devotes thirteen verses to delineate the behavioural and emotional attributes of a *jivanmukta*. Let us take a sample of two from this list:[32]

(a) '*Ateetan-anusandhanam, bhavishyad-avicharanam:*
    Audasinyam-api praptam, jivanmuktasyam lakshanam',

i.e. not dwelling on the enjoyments of the past, not worrying for the future and looking with indifference upon the present are the characteristics of the one liberated in life.

(b) '*Ishta-anishtartha sampraptau, samadarshitaya-atmani;*
    Ubhaytra-avikaritwam, jivanmuktasya lakshanam',

i.e. when events pleasant or unpleasant arrive, to remain unruffled in mind in both cases through a uniformity of attitude is a char-acteristic of the one liberated in life.

Similarly, there are several verses on the *jivanmukta* in the *Yogavasishtha* too. Let us take two verses:[33]

(a) '*Raga-dwesha-bhaya-adinam anurupam charannapi,*
    Yo-antah vyomvad-tyachha, sa jivanmukta uchyate',

i.e. though behaving in a manner resembling (the presence of) passion, hatred, fear and the like, yet one who is extremely pure within like the sky, is said to be liberated while living.

(b) *'Harsha-amarsha-bhaya-krodha-kama-karpanya drishtibhi,*
    Na paramrishyate yontah, sa jivanmukta uchyate',
i.e. he who is not assailed or polluted within by consideration or
feeling of exultation, jealousy, fear, anger, desire and pettiness, is
said to be liberated while living.

Clearly, *sthitaprajna* and *jivanmukta* are identical ideal states of
*anandasthiti**—if we may so term it. The *sthitaprajna* / *jivanmukta*
model can therefore serve as the pole-star to guide human development. To serve this role unfailingly and inspiringly for all, this
guiding-star model must remain at a distant, transcendent point.
Although we are familiar with the trinity of ultimate values—*Satyam,
Shivam, Sundaram*, i.e. Truth, Goodness and Beauty—yet we may
now visualize them too to converge and consummate, like three
huge rivers, into the terminal ocean of Bliss or *Ānanda*. This indeed
is likely to throb more deeply and holistically in our mind than the
triple classification. Sri Aurobindo describes the aim of *jivanmukti*
in his integral *yoga* in here-and-now terms:[34] 'But the aim of our
Yoga is *Jivanmukti* in the universe; not because we need to be
freed or for any other reason, but because that is God's will in us
we have to live released in the world, not released out of the world.'

IV. 'ANANDOLOGY': ITS RELEVANCE TO HUMAN-RESPONSE DEVELOPMENT

Before enumerating some of the obvious and direct consequences
likely to flow from the practice of *anand*ology in human affairs in
general, and in organizational affairs in particular, a major doubt
amongst readers may be anticipated: how can it be of any practical
merit, conceived as it is by unworldly hermits? The best answer to
this doubt would seem to be the following observations of
Vivekananda—a person who was very much 'in' the world but not
'of' it, and was a leader and institution-builder *par excellence*:[35]

... one peculiar feature we find is that many of these thoughts have been the
outcome, not of retirement into forests, but have emanated from persons
whom we expect to lead the busiest lives—from ruling monarchs.... the very
best parts of it were thought out and expressed by brains which were busiest
in the everyday affairs of life. We cannot conceive of any man busier than an
absolute monarch, a man who is ruling over millions of people, and yet some
of these rulers were profound thinkers.

---

* The *Gita*'s *Brahmi-sthiti* (II.72) appears identical to *Ānandasthiti*.

Everything goes to show that this philosophy must be very practical ...

Armed then with adequate confidence in the practicality of Indian philosophy and psychology, the reader may now study and reflect on the following highlights germane to our work-life:

(1) Cultivation of the feeling (*anubhuti*) that the true source of abiding happiness is within should minimize the tendency to a competitive scramble for the external means to happiness.

(2) Internalization of the *bhāvanā* (e.g. via the pot-imagery) that intrinsically the SELF of all is identical, should reduce our beggar-my-neighbour selfish thoughts and actions.

(3) The first two points taken together should constitute the only theoretically sound blueprint for enhancing trust, cooperation and sharing in organizations.

(4) The feedback offered by a mind which works and goes deep into itself by a daily discipline is a more effective diagnostic and remedial process for self-correction than feedback from others. All great men have proved this.

(5) Organizational members, especially the leaders, must develop an integrated personality. The hallmark of such a personality is its spontaneous charisma. This, in turn, is dependent upon the integration of emotion and thought around a theme which is pure and exalted. The ability to pursue and achieve this integration with conviction and faith or *shraddha* is termed 'will'. Thus we hear Akhilananda say:[36]

Our emotions, urges and instincts are inseparably connected with our volition. We wish to express each one of our emotions. When the mind becomes active in its totality, we call it 'will'. Without this will we cannot translate our ideas or emotions into action or a dynamic state.... when there is conflict and confusion in the subconscious mind the will is not completed.

(6) Resolute and reflective mental repetition of affirmations like *chidananda rupah shivoham*, or *jnanamritam samarasam gaganopaham* slowly creates a new positive conditioning of the consciousness and the will—from pettiness and ugliness to dignity and beauty.

(7) Similarly, progressively deeper concentration on the *Ishtam* is a sure means of gathering our emotions to a unified, exalted focus and thus strengthening the will in a constructive way. Benoit has expressed this integration of the psyche around the *Ishtam* very well:[37]

The image organises around it, little by little, the inner world in a positive way by a process of convergence or concentration.... This process of crystallization is accomplished more completely as the image centre becomes more vast and as it is able to tie more elements in this [inner] world together.

The *Ishtam*, the sacred chosen ideal, is a symbolic figure of one's psychic being which normally remains cornered and obscured by one's physical, vital and mental beings. This psychic being is our calm, true, enlightened, changeless essence.[38] To identify with one's *Ishtam* is to identify with one's psychic being.

(8) In the *Gita* it has been advised to the secular leader (i.e. Arjuna)[39]:

> *Yat karoshi, yadashnashi, dadasi yat;*
> *Yat tapasyasi kaunteya, tat kurushwu madarpanam,*

i.e. O son of Kunti (representing individual consciousness), offer unto Me (representing Supreme/Universal consciousness) whatever you do, you enjoy, you give and you perform as askesis. This indeed is a highly practical methodology for unifying the endless diversity of our daily *vyavaharika* existence into a stable inner *paramarthika* centre. This *bhavana* may be visualized well in the picture of a group of village maidens carrying buckets of water on their heads, and yet walking together gossiping and laughing all the way. They have an intensely unified will to prevent the buckets from falling down, even though appearing to go about with casual merriment. *Bhavana* practice of this verse from the *Gita* can provide us with a central organizing principle in our daily activities.

(9) Sensitivity to and sustenance of higher order values (i.e. the *shreyah* or electable, instead of the *preyah* or delectable) implies the will to sacrifice, if need be, the lower order ambitions of the *vyavaharika vyaktitwa*, e.g. power, money, fame, etc. The 'Will-to-Bliss' outlined earlier can offer us, the leaders especially, the vital inspiration for this substitution—or rather, sacrifice. The taste for the deep existential satisfaction flowing from this process has to be cultivated with willed effort.

(10) In our penchant for the analytical approach to problem-solving, decision-making or attitude-change we ignore the reality that every event coming our way, be it small or big, is holistic in nature. Yet today we all are, at our mental level, disorganized and chaotic. Applying analysis with a chaotic *vyavaharika* mind frequently leads us from one folly to another, but we do not admit it. It is therefore crucial that we restore to ourselves the holistic

faculty through systematic daily discipline. Except meditation—concentration (*dhyana* or *nididhyasana*), there is no other planned approach to the realm of the holistic—*nanya pantha vidyate ayanayah*. We know from personal experience how forgotten imperatives, conflicting priorities, nagging value-laden dilemmas, crooked face-saving stratagems and so on are spontaneously sorted or dissolved when the mind reaches a state of calm and concentrated ease and stability. This is the state that has to be arrived at on the way to *Ānanda*.

Recently a thriving private sector industrial house paid a hefty sum for a two-day Workshop run by a foreign expert on attitude change. Sixteen top-flight people, including the Chairman, attended it. Pretty soon it was also decided to implement the process down the line. The package consisted of about eighty 'projects' grouped into several 'units'. Examples, note-spaces, check-lists and other related aspects were galore in the folder for the participants. Lecturing was minimal, but the participants had to go on reading, scoring and talking amongst themselves through every single 'project'.

This is a good example of the purely left-brained strategy of learning at the level of intellectual understanding. Gordon Allport had long ago characterized western psychology as 'excited psychology'. No wonder then that this Workshop too was an exciting experience for the participants. It so happened that the head of HRD of the firm had attended a month ago our five-day programme at the Indian Institute of Management, Calcutta on Values-System. After experiencing both programmes he met us one day to ask whether we could Indianize some of the case studies included in the 'imported' Workshop folder mentioned above. It gradually became clear that the deeper, right-lobed, brain-stilling, mind-silencing processes—all supported by sound theory—learnt at the IIM-C Workshop had not made much of an impression on him. After all, it was claimed by the foreign expert that his package had been so far usefully attended by four million people! We could not, of course, agree to his proposal.

Senior Indian managers have still, by and large, a long way to go to grasp that:

(a) *ānanda* and mind-silencing/brain-stilling go together;
(b) 'truth' (about any situation or person or problem) can be

fathomed more and more accurately as the surface-level turbulence
of the ordinary mind and intellect subsides; and

(c) wholesome attitudes cannot be effectively *internalized* without
going inside one's being and concentrating, meditating there on
integral symbols of such attitudes.

Meanwhile, the tides of high-cost 'innovative' packages of management development from the affluent, developed countries will
continue to swamp us. After all, what can the thought systems of a
materially poor country contain worth understanding and practising
anew? Why should we close our minds to thought-currents from
all over the world? True enough! Yet is it all right to close one's
mind to one's own thought systems, or at the most to give them a
patronizing glance and then forget all about it? One does run the
risk of being called a fanatic just because one has the sincerity and
courage to own and live up to the best elements of one's own
culture.

Gandhiji's (1921) readiness to keep all the windows open, but
emphatic refusal to be blown off his feet by ideas from other
cultures[40] is a psychological imperative which seems to have been
completely ignored in post-independence India. Tagore (1924) too
declared the national movement to be 'revolutionary', not a
reactionary process for it symbolized the 'courage to deny and to
oppose all pride in mere borrowings'.[41]

(11) It should be useful to admit that, except for those arising
from misunderstanding, all other conflicts are rooted in selfish
egotism—be it interpersonal, inter-group or international. So long
as the parties involved in such conflicts continue to operate from
the suffocating chambers of their petty, deficit-driven *vyavaharika*
egos, very little can be achieved in resolving them. The true, if a
little long-term, remedy lies in uplifting and expanding the
consciousness of the concerned parties, so that they can begin to
detect and detest their own littleness and ugliness. For some
months in 1989 we implemented such a process relating to the
Director–Finance and Director–Personnel of a large company. The
situation had deteriorated to such a degree that even the managers
of the two departments were locked in a kind of vicious cold war.
A number of single and joint sittings were conducted by us. Scant
attention was paid to the huge pile of notes, circulars and inter-
office memos traded between them. Instead, through deep-breathing,

mind-silencing, and brain-stilling exercises, supported by conceptual inputs and carefully selected reading extracts from Sri Aurobindo, we aimed at freeing their stifled and caged-in consciousness into a relatively generous and pure state. Practice of the exercises at home was also recommended. Below is a sample of one extract on the 'psychology of silence' given to them:[42]

In this calm, right knowledge comes.... True perception is marred and clouded by false perception, true judgement lamed by false judgement ... The activity of the mind must cease, the *chitta* be purified, so a silence falls upon the restlessness of Prakriti; then *in that calm ... illumination comes upon the mind, error begins to fall away* ... [Emphasis added.]

Our subsequent dialogues with the Chairman–Managing Director indicated the beginning of a positive breakthrough in their unhappy interpersonal relationships.

(12) To strive for a harmonious work-climate in our organizations is entirely legitimate. However, both intra-group and inter-group harmony are merely the external projection of internal harmony amongst and across the team members. This law must be clearly understood to avoid getting trapped unduly by the lure of analytically formulated, long check-lists available from several sources for improved team-work. The attainment of inner harmony by each individual, although degrees of it are bound to vary, is a holistic process. Harmony can neither be 'techniqued' nor 'tooled'. Therefore, deep concentration of the mind in one's *Ishtam*, e.g. the meditating, celestial Buddha or Nanak, which is quintessential harmony, needs to be practised. Besides, meditation on *maitri* and *karuna bhavana*s, as suggested by both Patanjali and Buddhist psychology, are indispensable methods for achieving inner harmony and Bliss. Thus Patanjali[43] speaks:

Maitri-karuna-mudito-upekashanam, sukh-dukha-punyapunya vishayanam bhavanat chittaprasadanam;

and Radhakrishnan conveys this principle admirably:[44] 'Conflicts in the world are conflicts in the human soul enlarged. If men were at peace within themselves, the outer conflicts between nations would inevitably cease ...', and adds thereafter the imperative that our leaders ought to be 'normal'. What is globally true, is also organizationally valid. *Pravritti* must be balanced by *nivritti* in our mind to achieve this inner 'normalcy'. Outer harmony should then be a natural corrolary.

(13) Indian organizations suffer a lot because of a false condition-ing amongst the majority of employees that obedience, discipline and hierarchy are contradictory to freedom, autonomy and self-respect. Truly, this is a problem of the *tamas-* or *rajas*-dominated egos which interpret freedom to reside outside themselves. Unless such a tendency is tamed by discipline and obedience, future growth of true leaders will be stunted. There is a lot of inner growth lying ahead of an individual through consciously cultivated discipline via *sattwa guna*. With a base of *sattwic ānanda* inside, the task of balancing obedience with self-respect tends to become a smooth, holistic work-style. Respect for hierarchy in eastern cultures has a deeper symbolic significance. It accommodates the trans-empirical or the transcendent in our daily social and work relationships. Of course, the superior or the senior must also comprehensively live up to this symbolism.[45] Moreover, hierarchy in the human order is an extension of this principle in the natural cosmic order. It cannot be wished away without eventual debase-ment.[46]

(14) Another recurring problem in our milieu is to blame the other side when anything goes wrong—be it interpersonal, inter-group, inter-departmental or inter-organizational. It is, however, worth recalling the vital law of physical health: unless there is a pre-disposition within the body to let an illness in, no flood of external bacteria or microbes can do it any harm. In other words, for the onset of illness only half of the cause lies outside, the other half comes from inside.[47] This principle is equally relevant to organ-izational relationships. If one decides resolutely to pursue *ānanda* as the ultimate life-goal, then let-downs or rebuffs or denials will begin to be handled more from an inside-out perspective than the outside-in one. This will lead to a gradual turning of adversity to positive uses. The very fact that one acquires a genuine inner disposition which acknowledges one's own contribution to the adverse situation, tends to create a subtle ambience inducing acceptance also by the 'other side' of its share in the cause for the trouble. One has to pick up the courage to experiment and prove the truth of this deeper law. Thus should come alive the saying: *aap bhala to jagat bhala* (if I am good, then the whole world is good). Mental conditioning such as this grows through the pursuit of *anand*ology.

(15) As managers, we not only need to make intelligent decisions,

but even more vitally we ought to take wise decisions. The latter require the capacity to see things, events and persons *as they are*. But our discursive, surface-level consciousness does not possess this ability. Objects and processes are not as they appear to the ordinary mind and senses. The true reality of empirical phenomena can be penetrated with greater assurance by a person who systematically trains his consciousness to a purer, calmer and deeply introspective state. The various practices outlined in section-III help in the gradual attainment of this state.

V. A POLEMICAL DETOUR

The cue to this chapter came from the title of a paper by Dr Eugene Taylor, presented to Harvard University in 1985: 'Swami Vivekananda and William James: Asian Psychology at Harvard in the 1890's.' Lamenting the neglect of William James in the teaching of psychology in America, because he is now considered as irrelevant to 'the basis of scientific psychology in a modern, laboratory-oriented and statistical sense', Taylor highlighted the Indian definition of psychology by Vivekananda at Harvard in 1896:[48]

By it he meant the spiritual evolution of consciousness, not simply the description of sense-data and its analysis by the mind. The very impetus for our perceptions, he said, was not stimulation from external source followed by an organism's response, but rather the active spiritual principle* in each of us which uses the mind to reach out and grasp objects in the external world ...

However, our conscious decision to write this chapter on Indian psychology, from the management viewpoint grew from the more recent reading of a pamphlet by Aurobindo which contains some of his writings on an educational system for India as early as 1910. While analysing the mind or *antahkarana* as the instrument of the educationist, he expressly uses the phrase 'Indian Psychology', and advises us to 'revert to our old Indian system in some of its principles'—especially those addressed to the goal of *chittashuddhi* or purification of mental and moral habits. Without a movement towards this goal, the intellect remains imperfect and corrupt, vitiating judgment and decision-making.[49] He draws a valid distinction between the 'heart' and the 'mind' (this is used for 'intellect'),

---

* This is variously called *Ātman, sat-chit-ānanda*, pure Consciousness, *Chaitanya, Brahman* and so on.

and says that 'education of the intellect divorced from the perfection of the moral and emotional nature is injurious to human
progress'.[50] Besides, in his work on the *Rigveda*, mentioned earlier,
Aurobindo had also laboured the point emphatically that:[51] '... the
mantras of the Vedas illuminated with a clear and exact light
psychological experiences of my own for which I had found no
sufficient explanation either in European psychology or in the
teachings of Yoga or of Vedanta ...'

In a valuable recent book Riencourt (a French writer) has carefully presented many crucial differences between the world-views
of the East and West, the chief of them being the former's superordinate engagement with the Supreme Subject, while that of the
latter with the Supreme Object. Hence:[52]

As a result of these divergent aims, whereas Western philosophies are mental
disciplines of strict intellectual *information*, Eastern philosophies are methods
of total *transformation*. To the Easterner, religion ... is psychology and method
rather than theology and dogma.... the Easterner advances from one subjective
condition to another.... the Easterner changes ceaselessly his states of consciousness (*cittavritti*).... To sum up, the Westerner aims at clear *thought*, the
Easterner at pure *consciousness* ...

What is the progressive outcome of such a pursuit of transformation
of consciousness? Says Riencourt:[53] 'Long before the goal* is in
sight, however, the striving Easterner reaches a point of spiritual
self-sufficiency† and self-possession that generates an atmosphere
of superior calm, equanimity and serenity...' Does this assessment
then not echo the psychological state of a *sthitaprajna*, a *jivanmukta*—the state which vibrates with *ānanda*-in-action, and action-
in-*ānanda*?

Preceding Riencourt by four decades, in a pulverizing assault on
modern Western thought as compared to the Eastern, Guenon had
repeatedly questioned the motives of progress, change, action,
movement and agitation—all stemming from lack of principle—
underlying the former. At one point he trenchantly observes:

What Westerners call progress is for Orientals nothing but change and
instability; and the need for change, so characteristic of modern times, is in
their eyes a mark of manifest inferiority: he that has reached a state of
equilibrium no longer feels this need, just as he that has found no longer seeks.

---

* This goal is that of complete merging of the individual ego or *vyavaharika* self with
the *paramarthika*, Self, i.e., *samadhi*.
† This is the *poornatwa* within mentioned earlier.

Thus, like Riencourt, Guenon (also a French thinker) too had detected the keynote of human development in Indian psychology: the inherent, though masked, *poornatwa* or *ānanda* in man— independent of externalities. This also is the import of freedom in Indian thought.

In his psychology of Integral Yoga Aurobindo has offered both a comprehensive rationale and a method of approach to unify or link the individual will with the Supreme or Cosmic Will. Felicity and beatitude apart, the rationale for this effort lies in the traditional principle that the individual will is inalienably grounded in and is of the same stuff as its source—the Cosmic Will. If we cut loose from this source, then our will and decision-making abilities flounder. To re-introduce the rectitude of wholesome values in our thought, behaviour and choices, this snapped link has to be consciously restored through self-discipline, prayer and surrender. The Cosmic Will or Intelligence then responds to the individual will or intelligence and Truth reveals itself. Thus Aurobindo delared:[55]

To see the Truth does not depend on a big intellect or a small intellect. It depends on being in contact with the Truth and the mind silent and quiet to receive it. The biggest intellect can make errors of the worst kind and confuse Truth and Falsehood, if they have not the contact with Truth or the direct experience.

Laura Glenn (an American) seems to have assimilated this principle and process unerringly as long ago as 1918:[56]

... only as we link our will with the Supreme Will, shall we share in the power of the one Cosmic Force which impels all things. ... Apart from the Eternal Will, the individual will has no motive power.... Man's will will not be annihilated through surrender; it will merely take its proper place in the scheme of things and share in the power of the whole.

Recently the same conviction has been shared by a famed American astronomer, Gustav Stromberg:[57]

The Universe is a manifestation of the Cosmic Will. We have been endowed with some of the elements of this Cosmic Will, and also with a certain degree of freedom in using Cosmic Energy. The potential power of the human will is very great because it is a part of the Cosmic Will and redramatizes its capacity for the creation of good.

Such prayerful *yoga* ushers in *ānanda*—much in the same way as the Ganga courses her way through the heart of India with *ānanda* and bounty because of her perennial union or *yoga* with the Gomukhi in the Himalaya.

It should have been clear already that *ānanda* and inner freedom are but two sides of the same coin. Dependence on externals for *ānanda* is a non-starter, is slavery. This principle of Indian psychology had been grasped very well by Keyserling, a German (1938):[58]

No oriental, or Eastern Asiatic, unless he belongs to a despised or a persecuted caste, is ever lacking in dignity and self-control; this is because living inwardly rather than outwardly, they all know what it is that makes man.... The democratized Western man, ..., has lost his form: he is no longer determined from within and so far no longer a free man.

The latter direction is sadly the way the beguiled contemporary Indian too is going—abandoning his unique strength. Bede Griffiths, who has lived in India for more than thirty years, narrates, nearly forty years after Keyserling, how the taste of *ānanda* from the utter simplicity of the Indian way of life captivated his consciousness, and then reflects:[59] 'What a challenge this presents to a world which takes pleasure in continually increasing human needs and so makes itself more and more dependent on the material world! Such a statement is of course blasphemy in the climate of consumerist modernization pervading the upper echelons of Indian society. This section is suffering acutely from a psychology of petty, imitative greed, which the materially advanced economies are only too willing to exploit to the hilt in the name of progress, globalization and the like.

A Japanese agro-scientist, Fukuoka, has recently written a wonderful book challenging chemicals-based modern farming, and demonstrating that do-nothing, natural farming is more humane and truly productive. Amongst his many wise statements, the ones relevant to the present context are extracted below:[60]

Extravagance of desire is the fundamental cause which has led the world into its present predicament.

Fast rather than slow, more rather than less—this flashy 'development' is linked directly to society's impending collapse. It has only served to separate man from nature. Humanity must stop indulging in the desire for material possessions and personal gain and move instead toward spiritual awareness.

Does not this call to reduce our slavery to desires (*vasana*s), for the sake of freedom, reaffirm the keynote of all that is fundamental to Indian thought?

The reader may know that a prominent and powerful set of western writers on India, with sociological leanings, have lamented the carefree, simple living style of the Indian masses as nothing more than 'pathetic contentment'. The fragile sentiment of the Indian intellectual has largely and readily been tickled by such words of condescension. We hope it may inspire them to rethink by learning from the Keyserlings, Griffiths and Fukuokas that the psychology of dignity and *ānanda* stands its own ground on inner affluence, which is rarely associated with the outer scramble for needless needs. It is time that the world as a whole seriously reflects on the following words of Vivekananda uttered nearly a hundred years ago?[61]

In the West, they are trying to solve the problem how much a man can possess, and we are trying here to solve the problem on how little a man can live.... But if history has any truth in it ... it must be those who train themselves to live on the least and control themselves well, will in the end gain the battle ...

After all, the much-maligned 'Hindu rate of growth', if adopted by others, should then be a boon for humanity as a whole!

It is also relevant here to bring to the reader's attention the direction and content of what are known as 'humanistic psychology' (third force) and 'transpersonal psychology' (fourth force). While humanistic psychology intended to go up to creativity, need-gratification, self-actualization, psychological health; transpersonal psychology attempts to deal with ultimate values, self-transcendence, unitive consciousness, cosmic awareness, spirit, etc.* Sutich, the first editor of the *Journal of Transpersonal Psychology*, while paying rich tributes to Maslow, nevertheless makes a significant observation:[62] 'A special problem was my growing realization that the concept of self-actualization was no longer comprehensive enough.'

A little later he makes another statement of equal importance—especially from the viewpoint of this chapter:[63]

I was familiar with the literature of both Western and Eastern mysticism, but I was attracted almost exclusively to the latter. I began to see that I was actually interested in the psychology of mysticism, modified by humanistic consider-ations and the Western attitude of empiricism.*

---

* Frankly speaking, of late it seems that the contents of papers published in the two journals related to these schools have substantially overlapped.

While Sutich dared to doubt the comprehensiveness of S-A theory as early as in 1976, since then many stronger and explicit theoretical challenges have been coming its way. One of the latest examples is from Daniels. After stating that Maslow's purely biological inter- pretation of selfhood offers a restricted view of human expression and interaction, and that as a signpost for personal development it reinforces Machiavellian individualism, he points to the seriously misleading consequence of S-A theory because:[64] 'In this view, the moral and spiritual life is believed to be "an aspect ... of human biology ... on the same continuum with the lower animal life ... It is a part of the Real Self".'

Daniels has paraphrased here that vital distinction which lies at the core of Indian psychology. It is clear from the above extracts, and from the previous pages, that so long as the S-A theory of motivation is centred on the biological root, it cannot answer to the goal of *ānanda*. The *vyavaharika* self, which is the same as the biological– empirical self, is in essence deficit-driven. It is the *paramarthika* or spiritual SELF to which one must ascend. Self-transcendence actually means transcendence of the biological self which is mutable, inconstant, dependent and hence miserable. No meta-motivation for this self can bring that *ānanda* or Bliss Absolute from which no regress is possible. Yet, having reached this state, Janakas and Buddhas, Christs and Vivekanandas, Nanaks and Ramanas have worked as *jivanmuktas* or *sthitaprajnas* for the love of empirical man trapped in the *vyavaharika* world. They have all had the undying unitive experience. It is wrong to assume, as Hiriyanna correctly argues, that this is a selfish, hedonistic pursuit.[65] The fact is that the consequences of attaining *jivanmukti* are the opposite of those of selfishness and hedonism.

Having said so much, it remains to add, on the basis of conver- sations and writings and course outlines in Indian Universities and management schools, that our academic brothers are either unaware of these theoretical developments, or even if aware, choose to ignore them. Probably, as Guenon had pointed out as early as

---

* We are not sure if Sutich added this modifying clause as a matter of formal decorum, for it is not clear what kind of western empiricism makes sense in the realm of mystic experience—except in the secondary or derived sense of measuring pulse beats or blood pressure or EEG for persons trying such processes.

1935, when it comes to assessing the value of classical theories of human development in the Orient, 'a uniquely "sociological" point of view proves insufficient to get to the depths of things'.[66] Forty years later Griffiths re-affirms the same view:[67] 'The social sciences are of no help: they also only study the external phenomena, they never reach the root of human personality, they never answer the question, what is man?' Earlier we ourselves had, without having read these authors, argued that sociological writing on India has on the whole been quite confusing if not altogether harmful for the Indian mind.[68]

Recently Elbert Russel has made a serious effort to demonstrate the lack of concern about the 'unconscious' in Indian psychology (rather Eastern thought). For example, he mentions not only the less intricate analysis, but almost no analysis, of the unconscious in Patanjali, and also the misunderstanding in his aphorisms of how the unconscious really operates. However, clearly the source of authority for the paper, from which these conclusions derive, is not the best or most reliable (Radhakrishnan and Moore 1957). We think that the most authentic exposition of Patanjali's aphorisms is by Vivekananda—a person who went through each step of Rajyoga himself, and had the culminating experience of the *ānanda* of *samadhi* several times in his life. Long ago—in the 1890s—he had explained all these aphorisms in full before the American intelligentsia. The technical word for unconscious impressions in Rajyoga is *samskara*, and Vivekananda explained it thus:[69]

The roots, the causes, the Samskaras being there, they manifest and form effects. The cause dying down becomes the effect; the effect getting subtler becomes the cause of the next effect.... All our works now are the effects of past samskaras; again these works becoming samskaras will be the causes of future actions, and thus we go on.

In fact Vivekananda's *Rajyoga* discusses the unconscious or *samskara*s at many places, from several points of view.[70] In a much later book, while explaining the therapeutic value of Indian psychology, Akhilananda makes the following observations:

[1] Indian psychologists also give great emphasis to the purification and harmonization of the unconscious.... the unconscious is not necessarily the storehouse of the dark side of life, nor of the conflict of the id and superego, nor again of the pleasure principle and death wish. It contains all the accumulated tendencies from individual past thoughts and actions, cultural background, and

hereditary impressions and environmental conditions. Herein lies its therapeutic value and utility.[71]

[2] When a person practices concentration for a little while, his hidden unconscious tendencies (or *samskaras*) become clear to him.... his unconscious urges are gradually and spontaneously eliminated in and through the practice of concentration.[72]

[3] Hindu psychologists recognize that, although the present condition of mind is created by past thoughts and actions, the present changed mode of living and thinking effectively transforms the mind.[73]

[4] The contents of the subconscious mind created by his own past thoughts and actions, as well as by the influence of others, can be changed or transformed by the creation of new *samskaras* or impressions.[74]

And why this emphasis on transformational psychology? To attain ultimately the Bliss of the Superconscious, or the SELF, or the Transcendent. Since the incessant bubbles and gyrations arising from the unconscious depth agitate the conscious mind, the latter fails to reflect the image of the Superconscious light which is *ānanda* and *prajna*. This is why the unconscious is regarded as a hurdle to be crossed to reach a higher pasture, and why Aurobindo had clarified that the teaching of passivity of the mind in Yoga is intended to help the will to act unhampered by the *samskaras* or old associations.[75] Instead of too much direct meddling with the unconscious, the common, normal individual is advised by Indian psychology to go for positive processes like concentrating on the luminous, harmonious form of the *Ishtam* or the silent repetition of a holy name to cleanse the unconscious of its dross. These methods support the conscious in its aspiration for Superconscious *ānanda* and enlightenment.

In his lectures on psychology in the USA in the early years of this century, Abhedananda—a brother-monk of Vivekananda—used the expression 'True Psychology'. By this he meant:[76]

True psychology will not only inform us of the psychological conditions of the brain, nerves and nerve centres of individuals, but also the true nature of the mind, our psychic existence, its scope, its relation and its continuity. It is neither metaphysics nor mental philosophy, but is the science of the *psyche* or soul. Its foundation is truth.

Vivekananda himself called this kind of true psychology the 'science of all sciences' from the most down-to-earth viewpoint:[77] 'The mind uncontrolled and unguided will drag us down, down for ever—rend us, kill us; and the mind controlled and guided will save us, free us. So it must be controlled, and psychology teaches us how to do it.'

This is brass-tacks Indian psychology for the given *vyavaharika* self. It is the foundation of *ananda*, the *paramarthika* SELF—the goal.

While conceiving this chapter we read a piece by P.T. Raju, a well-known scholar of Indian thought. He points out that the whole burden of Indian philosophy and psychology is to help man to experience the *atman* which is the same as *ananda*. This he calls the 'psychology of Indian philosophical systems' which must be remembered. It is he who has given a name to Indian psychology: 'Atman Psychology.'[78] This can well be abridged to 'Atmology'— an expression cognate to 'Anandology' suggested here. However, following Raju, it is equally valid to say that there is a 'philosophy of Indian psychology' too. In this sense, we feel that our earlier compound expression, Indian 'psycho-philosophy', is entirely tenable—although many have frowned on it.[79]

Writing in the context of Buddhist psycho-philosophy, Conze—a British authority—says that man is constantly seeking after absolute Permanence, Ease or Bliss, and Freedom, Such a psychological pursuit seems to be almost the definition of man. Like Vivekananda, he too however discovers from Buddhist psychology that, short of complete self-control (of the *vyavaharika* self or *anatta* in Buddhist terminology), such *ananda*, etc. will be elusive. Let us hasten to add however that this is too trenchant a version, true only in the ultimate sense. We, in our own present state, must necessarily look forward to gradual transformation with a long-term orientation. Slides and slips on the way should not deter us from the predestined goal of *ananda*, and during this Odyssey, it may be well to draw strength from the chastening words of Hans Jacobs, a German thinker who lived and studied in India, addressed to modern man:

In short, the order of values has become reversed. Mental laziness and lack of interest in anything of no immediate concern, strengthened by a deplorable standard of education and a pathetic lack of spiritual leadership make for a fertile soil of gullibility and superficiality on which modern man thrives and has his being. The needs of the body are satisfied but the mind is empty.

Before we terminate this polemical journey, let us refer to three more recent contributions from the West to demonstrate how classical Indian psychology is indeed being assimilated at the base level into the realm of advanced Western psychology—although often under new labels.

(1) *G. Zukav*: After contemplating the possibility that even physics curricula might include meditation exercises in the twenty-first century, he remarks:[81]

The most profound thinkers of the Indian civilization discovered that words and concepts could take them only so far. Beyond that point came the actual doing of a practice, the experience of which was ineffable. This did not prevent them from progressively refining the practice into an extremely effective and sophisticated set of techniques....

Thus, we see, through Zukav's eyes, that Indian psychology is practical *anand*ology. The one small, yet great missing factor for most of us is the will to practise. Even for the proximate utilitarian aim of penetrating insight into management problems, as those in physics, a lot could be achieved by the practice of meditational psychology.

(2) *Frances Vaughn*: After differentiating elaborately between the super-ego and the transpersonal self (TPS), she avers:[82]

The TPS is both an organizing principle and an embodiment of values; and descriptions of the TPS always reflect values that transcend egocentric concerns, and affirm participation in the large whole.

This TPS means the same as our *paramarthika* SELF, which is whole and *poorna* and, therefore, *ānandamaya*. However, we prefer the expression 'transempirical SELF' or 'trans-phenomenal SELF' to 'transpersonal SELF', for it is very much a *personal* experience or awareness, although trans-empirical or trans-phenomenal in nature.

(3) *K. Wilber*: Although wrongly attributing the theory of disidentification* (from the *vyavaharika* self) to Assagioli, when this *jnan-yoga* therapeutic concept and method was in fact introduced by Vivekananda to the USA in the 1890s[83] and elaborated at length a little later by Aurobindo,[84] Wilber rightly urges a truly integrative

* In fact the quintessential message of *jnanyoga* psychology is contained in a classic song composed by Shankara. It is called '*nirvanshatakam*' or '*atmashatakam*', meaning 'The Song of the Self'. In six stanzas we get a full view of the 'disidentification' process relating to the empirical self, complemented by the 're-identification' theme of the transempirical SELF. See Appendix I, Chapter 4.

'perennial psychology' by blending both the Eastern and Western approaches. The essential task here is described by him as follows:[85]

If we are to know Reality in its fullness and wholeness, if we have to stop eluding and escaping ourselves in the very act of trying to find ourselves ... then we have to relinquish the dualistic–symbolic mode of knowing that rends the fabric of Reality in the very attempt to grasp it.

Evidently, Wilber is impressed most by the psychology of *advaitic* monism—one's absorption in the awareness of *nirakara, nirguna Brahman*. This is however the hardest of all the ways for gaining non-dual *ānanda*—the *jnanyoga* path. The vast majority of us must begin our long march towards non-dual Bliss through the *dvaitic* process of *bhaktimarga*. The psychology of the Bible or the Koran or the Granth Sahib is also essentially this. We must be practical, although, to be sure, theoretically Wilber takes the correct position. That Reality here is coterminous with Bliss, i.e. *sat* with *ānanda*, is worth reiterating.

VI. Conclusion: The Will to *Ānanda*

Ramana Maharshi, the profound advaitist of our times, said:[86] 'The desire for happiness is a proof of the ever-existent happiness of the Self. ... Primal bliss is obscured by the non-Self, which is non-bliss or misery. ... Happiness mixed with misery is only misery.' If this is not a crystalline expression of the highest practical goal of psychological unfoldment, what else could be? It is the soundest psychological theory when we are told that any pleasure or happiness derived from external, hence objective, reality is inevitably mutable, mixed, diverse and transient. The substratum is the Real because of its unity and immutability, and it is subjective. It is beyond the mind and senses no doubt; yet these very instruments have to be trained in purity for the self-existent Bliss to reveal Itself.

Intelligent managers are today becoming quite alive to the need for physical fitness. They go jogging, perform *hatha* yoga exercises, undertake diet control, go for long walks ... All this 'objective' exercise is fine, but the wisdom is yet to dawn on the majority of them that mental fitness or mental health also needs systematic 'subjective' exercise and self-culture. The approach underlying such efforts must, in theory, be founded on *anand*ology. Nothing else is foolproof because, without a perfectly clear grasp of the ultimate metaphysical goal of Bliss, we cannot manage our journey through the physical in a way that can reinforce our mental health.

Sometime ago this author had written about Will-to-Yoga.[87] Reference was then made to Freud's will-to-pleasure, Adler's will-to-power, and Frankl's will-to-meaning. It was suggested that the will-to-meaning needs a still deeper foundation in the Will-to-Yoga. The *Gita* tells us about *yogakshema*—our striving to get something, and then struggling to retain it after possession. It all depends then on what direction this *yogakshema*, i.e. will-to-*yoga*, takes. If it is focused solely towards the commonplace objects of human existence, conveyed through the deceptive word 'ambition', then man remains engaged in a perennial fight against himself, against his constitutionally true existential goal, i.e. will-to-*Yoga* with the Supreme Subjective. At this point in time we are a little clearer about the true experiential resultant of such Will-to-*Yoga*, namely, *ānanda*, so we now suggest the expression 'Will-to-Bliss' as the mainspring of *anand*ology. This then is our estimate of Indian Psychology. The hard-nosed realist and positivist, objectivist and pragmatist may yet ask: what do you *really* gain from such a brand of psychology? Dasgupta, an outstanding exponent of Indian philosophy to the world-at-large, had anticipated this query from his Northwestern University (USA) audience way back in 1926 and responded thus:[88]

... I shall frankly confess that one certainly gains nothing that will show itself in one's bank account. But with all my appreciation and admiration of the great achievements of the West in science, politics and wealth, the Upanishadic spirit in me may whisper from within: What have you gained if you have not gained yourself, the immortal, the infinite. What have you gained if you have never tasted in your life the deep longing for deliverance and supreme emancipation.

As and when the man in the man-ager hearkens to this call, then it is Indian psychology which is ready with practical systems to lead him forward. Neither in European nor in Greek, nor even in the earlier Hellenic civilizations have we anything resembling the elaborate practices of Indian psychology, as Jacobs (1961) points out.[89] Later Roger Walsh (1976), a neurophysiologist and psychiatrist, offered us a touchingly candid account of his own transformation to a positive and humbly receptive view of oriental psychology through experience:[90]

In any event, there was a deepening appreciation of the extraordinary wisdom contained in some of the Eastern psychologies. Much against my will, and with no lack of resistance, I was forced to acknowledge that these traditions and their founders and advanced practitioners knew much more about the workings and depths of mind than I had ever imagined.

We trust and hope that testaments such as these will inspire Indian managers to begin to experience and express the truths which are already theirs in the first place.

REFERENCES

1. *Psychology in India: The State of the Art*, ed. J. Pandey (New Delhi: Sage Publications, 1988). In this 3–volume anthology exceeding 1000 pages, not one title of a paper seems to indicate an acknowledgement of 'Indian Psychology'.
2. Swami Akhilananda, *Hindu Psychology—Its Meaning For The West* (London: George Routledge, 1948), p. 202.
3. Swami Vivekananda, in *Rajyoga*. See *Collected Works* (Calcutta: Advaita Ashrama, 1962), vol.I, p. 257.
4. Sri Aurobindo, *The Secret of The Veda* (Pondicherry: Sri Aurobindo Ashram, 1971), pp. 84, 92, 43.
5. Swami Gambhirananda, *Mundaka Upanishad* (Calcutta: Advaita Ashrama, 1978); verse II.ii.7, p. 60.
6. *Idem, Taittiriya Upanishad* (Calcutta: Advaita Ashrama, 1980), II.v.1, p. 102.; II.vii.1, p. 126; III.vi.1, pp. 166–7.
7. Swami Swahananda, *The Chhandyogya Upanishad* (Madras: Sri Ramakrishna Math, 1980), 7.23.1, p. 534.
8. *The Brihadaranyaka Upanishad* (Madras: Sri Ramakrishna Math, 1979), 3.9.26–8, p. 284; 4.3.32, pp. 341–2.
9. Sri Aurobindo, *The Message of The Gita* (Pondicherry, Sri Aurobindo Ashram, 1977), II.66, p. 43.
10. Swami Vireswarananda, *Brahma-Sutras* (Calcutta: Advaita Ashrama, 1978), 1.1.12, p. 37.
11. Swami Tapasyananda, *Adhyatma Ramayana* (Madras: Sri Ramakrishna Math, 1985), I–2, p. 1; I–24, p. 5; I–33, p. 6; I–43, p. 7; VII–106, p. 99.
12. Jnanananda Bharati (tr. Samvid), *The Essence of Yogavaasishtha* (Madras: Samata Books, 1985), 6.36–7, p. 59; 11.23–4, p. 115; 15.40, p. 156; 15.51, p. 158.
13. Swami Madhavananda, *Vivekachudamani of Shri Shankaracharya* (Calcutta: Advaita Ashrama, 1974), verses 486, 488, 514, 522, 524, 526, 557, 584.
14. Swami Ashokananda, *Avadhuta Gita of Dattatreya* (Madras: Sri Ramakrishna Math, 1981), VIII.6, p. 165; VIII.10, p. 167.
15. Swami Nikhilananda, *Atmabodha* (Madras: Sri Ramakrishna Math, 1983), 23, p. 150; 36, pp. 161–2; 40, p. 165.

16. S. Radhakrishnan, *The Dhammapada* (Madras: Oxford University Press, 1974), Introduction, p. 46.
17. Oskar Schloss, *The Majjhima Nikaya* (Munchen, 1924), p. 244.
18. *The Brihadaranyaka Upanishad*, 2:4.5;4:5.6.
19. *The Message of the Gita*, p. 42, fn.1.
20. Swami Gambhirananda, *Svetaswatara Upanishad* (Calcutta: Advaita Ashrama, 1986), 3.18, p. 137—two ears, two eyes, two nostrils, the mouth, and two lower apertures, all opening outwards.
21. Sri Aurobindo, *A System of National Education* (Pondicherry: Sri Aurobindo Ashram, 1970), p. 17.
22. Swami Vivekananda, *Complete Works*, vol.I, I.33, p. 222.
23. *Avadhuta Gita*, III. 3–42.
24. *The Message of the Gita*, p. 222.
25. Swami Gambhirananda, *Katha Upanishad* (Calcutta: Advaita Ashrama, 1980), II.i.12–13, pp. 92–3; II.iii.17, p. 130.
26. Albert Einstein, *Out of My Later Years* (London: Thames & Hudson, 1950), p. 260.
27. Swami Vivekananda, 'Practical Vedanta' in *Collected Works*, vol.II, p. 306.
28. Dag Hammarskjöld, *Markings* (London: Faber & Faber, 1964), p. 99.
29. *The Message of The Gita*, pp. 39–45.
30. Ibid., p. 43.
31. *Vivekchudamani*, 426, p. 161.
32. Ibid., pp. 163, 432, 434, p. 164.
33. *Yogavaasistha*, III.27, p. 28; XI.44, p. 119.
34. Sri Aurobindo, *The Hour of God* (Pondicherry: Sri Aurobindo Ashram, 1982), p. 30.
35. *Collected Works*, vol.2, pp. 291, 292.
36. *Hindu Psychology—Its Meaning For The West*, p. 78.
37. H. Benoit, *Let Go* (London: George Allen & Unwin, 1962). pp. 256–7.
38. Sri Aurobindo, *Letters on Yoga*, quoted in *Living Within*, ed. A.S. Dalal (Pondicherry: Sri Aurobindo Ashram, 1989), pp. 25–6.
39. *The Message of the Gita*, 9.27, p. 145.
40. M.K. Gandhi, *India of My Dreams* (Ahmedabad: Navajivan Publishing House, 1959), p. 175.
41. R. Tagore, *The Religion of an Artist* (Calcutta: Visvabharati, 1988), p. 9.
42. Sri Aurobindo, *The Ideal of the Karmayogin* (Pondicherry:Sri Aurobindo Ashram, 1974), p. 40.
43. *Rajyoga*.
44. S. Radhakrishnan, 'General Preface' to the Buddha's 2500th Parinirvana anniversary publication of Pali texts by the Bihar Government (1958–60), p. ii.
45. S. Weil, *The Need For Roots* (London: Ark Paperbacks, 1987), p. 18.
46. R. Guenon, *East and West* (London: Luzac & Co., 1941), p. 66.

47. Swami Vivekananda, 'Work and its Secret', *Collected Works*, vol.II, pp. 7–9.
48. E. Taylor, the quoted article in *Prabuddha Bharata*, Sept. 1986, p. 374.
49. *A System of National Education*, p. 20.
50. Ibid., p. 7.
51. *The Secret of The Veda*, p. 37.
52. A.D. Riencourt, *The Eye of Shiva* (London: Souvenir Press, 1980), pp. 69–70.
53. Ibid., p. 72.   54. *East and West*, pp. 44–5.
55. Sri Aurobindo, *Truth* (Pondicherry: Sri Aurobindo Society, 1973), p. 22.
56. Laura Glenn, *Development of The Will* (Boston: The Vedanta Centre, 1918), p. 11.
57. G. Stromberg, *Man, Mind and the Universe* (Los Angeles: Science of Mind Publications, 1977), p. 16.
58. C.H. Keyserling, *From Suffering to Fulfilment* (London: Selwyn Blount, 1938), pp. 202–3.
59. B. Griffiths, *Return to The Centre* (London: Collins' Fount Paperbacks, 1976), p. 11.
60. M. Fukuoka, *The One-Straw Revolution* (Friends Rural Central: Hoshangabad, 1988),p. 110.
61. *Collected Works*, vol.III, p. 181.
62. A.J. Sutich, 'The Emergence of the Transpersonal Orientation: A Personal Account', *The Journal of Transpersonal Psychology*, vol.8, no.1, 1976, p. 7.
63. Ibid., p. 8.
64. M. Daniels, 'The Myth of Self-Actualization', *Journal of Humanistic Psychology*, vol.28, no.1, 1988, pp. 27, 32–3.
65. M. Hiriyanna, 'Philosophy of Values' in *The Cultural Heritage of India* (Calcutta: The Ramakrishna Mission Institute of Culture, 1983), vol.III, p. 652.
66. R. Guenon, *Studies in Hinduism* (Delhi: Navrang, 1985), p. 57.
67. B. Griffiths, op. cit., p. 68.
68. S.K. Chakraborty, *Human Response in Organizations* (Calcutta: Vivekananda Nidhi, 1985), pp. 69–72.
69. *Rajyoga* in *Collected Works*, vol.I, p. 245.
70. Ibid., pp. 207, 208, 219–20, 237–8, 240–3, 245, 247.
71. Swami Akhilananda, *Mental Health and Hindu Psychology* (London: George Allen & Unwin, 1952), p. 12.
72. Ibid., p. 22.   73. Ibid., p. 85.
74. *Hindu Psychology—Its Meaning For the West*, p. 76.
75. Sri Aurobindo, *The Ideal of The Karmayogin*, p. 87.
76. Swami Abhedananda, *True Psychology* (Calcutta: Ramakrishna Vedanta Math. 1979), p. 36.

77. Swami Vivekananda, 'The Importance of Psychology' in *Collected Works*, vol.VI, p. 30.
78. P.T. Raju, 'Indian Psychology', in *The Cultural Heritage of India*, vol.III, pp. 582, 584.
79. S.K. Chakraborty, *Managerial Effectiveness and Quality of Work-life* (New Delhi: Tata McGraw Hill, 1987), p. 7, pp. 28–9.
80. H. Jacobs, *Western Psychotherapy and Hindu Sadhana* (London: George Allen & Unwin, 1961), p. 33.
81. G. Zukav, *The Dancing Wu Li Masters* (London: Fontana, 1982), pp. 327, 330.
82. F. Vaughn, *The Inward Arc* (Boston: New Science Library, 1986), pp. 43, 45.
83. Swami Vivekananda, *Collected Works*, vol.VII, p. 46—the word *dis-identify* is directly employed here on p. 435, vol.VIII, pp. 6, 26, etc.
84. Sri Aurobindo, *Living Within*, pp. 23–6.
85. K. Wilber, *The Spectrum of Consciousness* (Illinois: The Theosophical Publishing House, 1982), p. 46.
86. *Reflections on Talks with Sri Ramana Maharshi*, ed. S.S. Cohen (Tiruvannamalai: Sri Ramanasramam, 1979), p. 11.
87. S.K. Chakraborty, *Foundations of Managerial Work-Contributions From Indian Thought* (Bombay: Himalaya, 1989), pp. 79–81.
88. S.N. Dasgupta, *Hindu Mysticism* (New Delhi: Motilal Banarasidass, 1976), p. 168.
89. H. Jacobs, op. cit., p. 90.
90. R. Walsh, 'Things Are Not as They Seemed' in *Awakening The Heart*, ed. J. Welwood (Boston: New Science Library, 1985), p. 115.

11

METAPHYSICAL EMPIRICISM IN LEADERSHIP AND INSTITUTION-BUILDING
The Role-Model of Swami Vivekananda

It was a revelation to read the following striking words in a recent book on management by two American authors (1988):[1]

America's boardrooms need *heroes* more than Hollywood's box offices need them. *Heroism is a leadership component* that is all but forgotten by modern management. Since the 1920's, the corporate world has been powered by managers who are rationalists.... But we are not talking about good 'scientific' managers... Managers run institutions; *heroes create them*. [Emphasis added.]

This crown of 'the hero' was exactly what Rolland had conferred in 1931 upon Vivekananda, while concluding the chapter on 'The Ramakrishna Mission' in a profound biography.[2] The same American authors also refer to the key role of *values* in the shaping of corporate culture, and assert that 'In creating values that will work, managers are *forced to live life* as they say they would... *Whatever the circumstances*'[3] (emphasis added). This again is precisely what V.K.R.V. Rao (1979)—an eminent Indian economist and educator—concluded after referring to a fiery letter written by Vivekananda from America to a disciple in India:[4]

These forceful words only indicate the importance he attached to *values* and how they should dominate every walk of life, ..., and values also included a deliberate attempt to *practise them in one's personal life* [emphasis added].

We have, therefore, tried here to inform primarily our contemporary organization builders, managers and administrators that a careful study of the leadership–institution building aspect of Vivekananda's multi-dimensional personality should be enormously rewarding. It would indeed be quite a folly to brush aside this contribution of his under the false stereotype that after all he has been only a world-shunning monk who had created a spiritual outfit for otherworldly pursuits! Nothing can be farther from the truth. Let us see how he married the metaphysical with empirical, the spiritual with the social, the sacred with the secular.

I. THE METAPHYSICAL KEYNOTE: THE FIRST PRINCIPLE

The double-winged Ramakrishna Math and Mission (RKMM), as it evolved during the period 1886-97, is an institutional embodiment of Sri Ramakrishna's words to Narendranath (later Swami Vivekananda): 'serve *shiva* in *jeeva*'.⁵ The inherent *Shiva* is sacred, the apparent *jeeva* secular (i.e. material, mundane). Out of this seed grew the stem: '*atmano mokshartha, jagat hitaya cha*'. This was Vivekananda's re-articulation of the mission for the missionaries of the sacro-secular adventure. In this chapter an attempt is being made to glean a range of ideas and principles, implanted by Vivekananda in this sacro-secular institution, for consideration by our modern secular organizations. It may be worthwhile to remember that when the RKMM was constituted and its foundations laid, no formal management literature on leadership, organization development, institution-building and the like existed. Yet, today the RKMM is an international institution, with 125 centres, garnering a rich harvest of trust, gratitude and credibility about its sacro-secular contributions to humanity.

As mentioned earlier in chapter 8, the pursuit of sacro-secular symbiosis is the very first lesson modern institution-builders—at least in India—may want to learn from Vivekananda's conceptual framework. The sacred, the pure, the enduring is always rooted in the trans-empirical, the trans-mundane, the metaphysical. This helicopter-flight, as it were, to a higher altitude helps the mind to gather true perspective and wide vision. If then it descends on the empirical terrain, it is more likely that our mind can tackle and negotiate the ground-level problems with greater maturity, balance and hence effectiveness. The secular is then better manageable in the clear inner light of the sacred.

Social scientists on the whole appear to make a major mistake in trying to understand Indian culture and ethos by either denying it altogether or denigrating its over-arching metaphysical backdrop. Indian society and tradition constitute a unique and thorough translation of the ultimate metaphysical goal–means system into a ceaseless song of daily life. Without recognizing this 'deep-structure', the examination of India's surface structure can and does lead to ineffectual conclusions about sense of time, authority, hierarchy, change, discipline, women's role and a host of other things. An example of this is an innovative volume published from Holland in 1989, trying to interpret Indian culture and Indian management as a couple.[6] It is quite a useful and sincere study based on fieldwork in India, but it skims only the surface structure of Indian culture— the references throughout the book produce this impression. Yet, in our view, no work which wishes to assess Indian culture and relate it to secular affairs, including management, can afford to bypass the Tagores, Vivekanandas and Aurobindos. Even Gandhiji's deeper foundations have not drawn the researchers' attention. Yet, all these archetypal Indians, to suggest a phrase, are 'metaphysically empirical'—the Indian keynote.

Thus, one of the chief mistakes of the contemporary managerial mind is to consider the secular and the sacred as contradictory forces. It is caught in an 'either–or' trap. By contrast, in authentic tune with the Indian genius, Vivekananda (1897) asked us to be seized and conscious of the gentle dew-drop-like 'fascination' of the 'practical spirituality' of India.[7] To prevent the secular from turning profane, the use of the purifying re-agent of the sacred or the spiritual is essential. The drama of *Chandashoka* being transformed into *Dharmashoka* is amongst the most cherished Indian symbols of this sacro-secular symbiosis. The Indian Empire of the Mind attained its highest apogee and expansion as a *consequence* of this transmutation. Similarly, in the *Ramayana* we have the significant symbolic transformation of the secular criminal, Ratnakar, into the immortal spiritual bard, Valmiki. King Janaka and Emperor Akbar have also echoed this keynote in their own times.

Let us examine therefore in some detail how this first principle has found amplification in Vivekananda's epochal endeavour. Today some people even in the USA, where he offered the first public articulation of this principle, regard these expositions as Vivekananda's 'unopened gift' to America.[8]

II. VIVEKANANDA'S INSIGHTS INTO A LEADER'S QUALITIES

To begin, we reproduce here a set of ideas, enunciated with intuitive spontaneity by Vivekananda, which may help us to develop the outlines of a theory of leadership:

[1] 'I am persuaded that a leader is *not made in one life*. He *has to be born* for it. For the difficulty is not in organization, and making plans; the test, the real test of a leader, lies in holding *widely different people together*, along the line of their common sympathies. And this can only be done *unconsciously*, never by trying.'[9]

[2] 'It is selfishness that we must seek to eliminate! I find that whenever I have made a mistake in my life, it has always been because *self* entered into the calculation. Where *self has not been involved*, my judgment has gone straight to the mark.'[10]

[3] 'More and more the true greatness seems to me that of the worm, *doing its duty silently*, steadily, from moment to moment, and hour to hour.'[11]

[4] '... it is a very difficult task to take on the role of a leader. One must be *dasasya dasah*—a servant of servants, and must accommodate a thousand minds. There must not be a shade of jealousy or selfishness, then you are a leader.'[12]

[5] 'Know partiality to be the chief cause of all evil.'[13]

[6] 'It is absolutely necessary to the work that I should have the enthusiastic love of as many as possible, while I myself remain *entirely impersonal*. Otherwise jealousy and quarrels will break up everything. A leader must be impersonal ...'[14]

[7] 'Do not try to lead your brothers, but *serve them*. The brutal mania for leading has sunk many a great ship in the waters of life.'[15]

[8] 'Be the servant of all, and do not try in the least to govern others. ... Nobody will come to help you if you put yourself forward as a leader. ... *Kill self first* if you want to succeed.'[16]

Let us explore the implications of excerpts (1) and (6) in particular. When Vivekananda says that 'a leader is not made in one life' he, in effect, is affirming the theory of repeated births—and strivings—towards a great goal or mission. One physical life-span is probably inadequate to scale the peak of excellence in leadership or other attainments. So, when in an individual's present existence, working itself out before our eyes, we notice an awesome and inexplicable burst of superlative qualities of head and heart, instead of calling it a freak of Nature, we should adopt the more rational view that there can be no *effect* without a preceding *cause*. Thus, when the likes of Shankaracharyas or Vivekanandas stamp their feet upon the human stage, we should be able to visualize the unswerving toil of prior bodily existences which must have been the underlying 'investment' for the 'return' of leadership excellence now reaped from them by the society in which they are born. To be a 'born leader' one has indeed to work very very hard—adopting a very long-term view of the *ātman's* journey through many bodily lives.

The second point about the first excerpt is that a 'born leader' possesses the transcendent, trans-empirical, intuitive sure-touch quality of inspiring a whole set of people working with him. The 'past' labours of the present leader have made the process of unifying diverse minds, for a cause, look effortlessly spontaneous. In other words, achievement of effortlessness in the present leadership role may indeed be founded on efforts exerted in existences outside the pale of the leader's own and our view.

In excerpt (6) Vivekananda stresses the 'impersonal' orientation of a leader. The expectations of organizational members regarding fairness, objectivity, integrity, consistency and the like in the course of hundreds of daily decision-making issues—often trivial, at times momentous—can be ensured only by *impersonality* in the leader's mental domain. This does not mean disinterested apathy or indifference. It means that, like Buddha, if necessary, even the leader's own son Rahula can be publicly chastized and debarred from functioning in the organization if found falling short of the norms and standards laid down for all.[17] Do the offices of leadership at the highest levels in India have a lesson to learn from his principle and example?

Besides, it is impersonality of this nature which alone can impart wisdom, and freedom from narrow bias or petty prejudice. Tagore (1926) has aptly intuited: 'Limitation of the unlimited is personality.'[18] So, the cultivation of impersonality means a journey towards the freedom of the wide and unlimited perspective—a critical need for ensuring a leader's credibility with team-members. Ferris (1988) very rightly underscores the need for love in the leader for inspiring people.[19] To sustain this inspiring quality of love it must, however, firmly hold on the impersonal, the unlimited.

References to the 'killing of self first' (excerpt 8), and to the elimination of even a 'shade of selfishness' (excerpt 4) match perfectly with the impersonality principle cited above. Thus, it is often the case that the father's or mother's personal love, i.e. 'self-ish' love, rather *moha*, about one's offspring which causes erosion of credibility and trust amongst others. Leaders in organizations also have their 'offspring'. The little, insecure self of the leader gravitates around them, partiality is born, and dedicated excellence dies.

It is a remarkable psychological principle which Vivekananda transmits to us through his confession in excerpt (2): his judgments and decisions had been unerring whenever his self had not inter-posed itself as a filter or screen between the situation on the one side and the decision on the other. The selfish, impure, unripe empirical self—of which we are so often mistakenly conceited—congenitally distorts our perspective. Hence objective decision-making remains a chimera. So, via *jnan marga* one may try to eliminate altogether this lower self, or *vyavaharika vyaktitwa*. That only Vivekanandas can do. What can lesser leaders do?

This is where excerpts (3) and (7) make more practical sense to the ordinary mortal. The imagery of the little worm doing its duty minute by minute, silently, is indeed powerful. This may be con-trasted with the current popular cry for 'dynamic' leadership which quite often is just flamboyant talk with very little real and durable substance. The principle is: the greatest acts are performed in the deepest silence. Thus, beginning to treat the silent but intense performance of any duty falling to one's lot as a sacred privilege to serve the *shiva* in *jeeva* is a mellower and more feasible route to follow than the scorching path of direct dismissal of the lower self.

Silence has just been mentioned. There is undoubtedly an intimate association between silence and sacredness, but silence and power too are strongly correlated. Hence a key to the understanding of leadership and institution-building by the Vivekanandas, Tagores Gandhijis and Aurobindos is their capacity for disciplined intro-version. It is from the depth of inner silence that they derived their power and vision to lead and build. Aurobindo (1918) delineates the principle arrestingly:[20] 'The activity of the mind must cease, the *chitta* be purified, a silence falls upon the restlessness of *prakriti*. Then in that calm, in that voiceless stillness illumination comes upon the mind, error begins to fall away ...'

Rolland too has, in his study of Vivekananda, asserted that in principle interiorization and silence never mean diminution of action. He rejects inferences about the social passivity of India as springing from her mystic, introvert bent. Instead, he declares:[21]

'... her interiorization, where the fires of her threatened life have taken refuge, is the principle of her national resurrection'.

III. VIVEKANANDA'S INSIGHTS INTO INSTITUTION-BUILDING

We glean from Romain Rolland the following assessment about the genesis of the RKMM:[22]

A *real leader* of men does not omit the smallest detail. Vivekananda *knew* that if he was to lead the peoples to the conquest of an ideal, it was not enough to inflame their ardour; he had to enrol them in a *spiritual militia*. The chosen few must be present to the people as types of the *new man*; for their very existence was the pledge of the Order that was to be.' [Emphasis added.]

We think that in that sizzling phrase *spiritual militia* (also later called apostolic militia)[23] Rolland once more captures for us the *sacro-secular* keynote on which this chapter began. The ideological mainspring of the RKMM is coiled up in this sacro-secular, spiritual, apostolic militia.

The sacred or spiritual wing of this militia was really born during 1986-7 at the Cossipore Garden House where Sri Ramakrishna had spent the last few months of his life, under the ardent care of his young disciples and householder devotees. This banding together for an altruistic cause came to be institutionalized later as the Ramakrishna Math. The secular or activist wing of the Order was called the Ramakrishna Mission (Association, at inception), launched by Vivekananda on 1 May 1897.[24]

The innovative elements in this two-winged organization structure were:

(a) The *brahmachari*s and monks were (and are) automatically the members of both the *Math* and the Mission—the spiritual and the secular limbs respectively.

(b) The Mission's membership was thrown open to the lay public and householders.

(c) The top management of the *Math* was to be called the Board of Trustees, whereas that of the Mission the Board of Governors.

(d) The members of the Trustee and Governing bodies were to be identical (and still are).

(e) Most of the branch centres in India combine both *Math* and Mission activities; only a few are purely *Math* centres.

(f) Branch centres abroad exist as *Math* centres—for spiritual activities only.

(g) Trustees/Governors are elected from amongst monk members by vote. Only those members who have had a tenure of 20 years or more in the Order can cast their votes in favour of one or more names from a list initially prepared by the existing Trustees. For decision-making three-fourths majority is prescribed. Both monks and *brahmacharis* are included in this process.

(h) Each centre is financially on its own—although it can borrow sums from the Headquarters under specific conditions.

(i) Each centre strictly follows the principle that sums of money belonging to one account or activity-head will never be used, even for very short periods, to meet deficits under other activity-heads.

Thus, on-going coordination and synthesis between the sacred and the secular, between *atma-moksha* and *jagat-hitam*, had been built into the organization, on democratic principles, right at birth.

So far as the R.K. Mission is concerned, its superordinate goals and guidelines are:[25]

(a) to strive for the temporal, mental and spiritual advancement of humanity,

(b) to pursue the establishment of fellowship among the followers of different religions,

(c) to train men to be competent teachers of such knowledge or sciences as are conducive to the material and spiritual welfare of the masses,

(d) to provide and encourage arts and industries,

(e) to introduce and spread among the people in general Vedantic and other religious ideas,

(f) to have no connection with politics.

It seems clear that, if one tries to subdue or eliminate the little self, as Vivekananda has been quoted earlier to have advised, then all work and duty automatically begins to be transformed into spiritual performance on the part of the doer. Thus, the Mission ruled out the conventional assumption that secular duty and spiritual progress were mutual enemies. Although the setting for managers, administrators, businessmen and others is qualitatively different, the lesson to ponder appears to be: *if the missionaries are expected to move from the spiritual to the secular, the managers are equally expected to move (psychologically) from the secular to the spiritual.* It is not a glib external shift of pastures, but a determined inner odyssey.

Besides the Master's ignition of the initial spark of 'service of God in man' within Vivekananda's soul, there are a few other allied factors which seem to have prompted him to found the R.K. Mission in the style that it emerged. Thus, we learn that while in America he told a lady that he had met the greatest temptation of his life in America! The lady, stunned, asked: 'Who is she Swami?'. The Swami had a hearty laugh and replied: 'Oh! dear, it is not a lady. It is organization.'[26] This instinctive recognition by him of the need for organization for serving the people of India has been inter- preted at a deeper level by Nivedita. According to her, this meant that the traditional love in monks for the remote and highest spiritual ideals had to be transmuted into an abiding and selfless enthusiasm to work collectively with discipline for the city and the state. The highest and most *disinterested* individuals could do this best.[27]

Coming to economic and industrial organizations. While the literature is today beginning to talk of ideas like 'organizational culture', 'superordinate goals', 'spiritual values',[28] the foundation of *disinterestedness* (i.e. selflessness) beneath all this is hardly recog- nized. If at all it is mentioned by a few, most others reject it outright as negative, unmotivating. Clearly, the immense strength- giving and purifying properties of disinterested work are not understood by us. Not only this; so narrow seems to have become the notion of self-interest in present-day Indian organizations that discipline in the work-place has become the worst victim. Yet Vivekananda, the great institution-builder that he was, once gladly confessed that the greatest achievement of the English was 'that they had known how to combine obedience with self-respect'.[29] Management thinkers and writers in India should do well to assimi- late the meaning of this practical wisdom.

A unique element was introduced to protect the institution (RKMM) from sundering apart in the times ahead: the Order was to represent for centuries to come the 'physical body of Rama- krishna'.[30] Thus, a form, a structure was invested with pulsating life, unflagging inspiration and exalted emotion. Each member who joined (and joins) the Order was (is) indoctrinated in the spirit that all work that might come his way should to be treated as Sri Ramakrishna's work. Anyone doing work with egoistic motives, or causing harm to the Order's reputation would be committing sacrilege towards the Master himself. Afterwards Vivekananda and the Holy Mother have been added to this process of mental bonding amongst the members of the Order. Obviously the leaders, the founders have to demonstrate very high degrees of selflessness and purity to become, in course of time, the psychological rallying points for succeeding generations of members. Like Mount Kailash of the Himalaya they must strive to become and remain unpolluted summits. Can and should modern secular organizations, aspiring to be institutions, utilize this convergent, trans-mundane myth as the basis for their culture-building strategies? Or do they assume that merely the mundane aims can serve as enduring materials for healthy culture formation? Jimmy Carter, a former US President has spoken very aptly about this classical basis of leadership, although not exactly in the vein of the sacred:[31]

High moral and ethical standards are essential ... Honesty, truthfulness, integrity and unselfishness—these are always there. And whenever a leader violates these basic principles, through arrogance or ignorance, there is a derogation of duty.

Yet another pillar of the RKMM institution, grounded and enshrined in its constitution and rules prepared by Vivekananda, was (and is): 'keep politics at arms length'. In his assessment, each country could achieve true excellence only along the distinctive grain of its own ethos. Lasting greatness and strength could not be achieved by a vain attempt to erase or ignore this grain. For India this grain was identified by him to be the constant aim of spiritualizing our entire existence, and not politics or social conflict.[32] The RKMM thus had to (and continues to) work exclusively at this base level. No contamination from other lines of pursuit, even though perhaps legitimate in themselves, would be (or is) permitted. Rolland had opined that this cautiousness of Vivekananda was wiser than Gandhiji's attempt to blend religion and politics.[33] This fundamental insight into institution-building has proved its beneficence beyond doubt—for the RKMM has succeeded in maintaining and enhancing its credibility with all segments of society and all shades of government during the past decades. It is easy to see that this achievement has sprung from the superordinate goal for the RKMM as visualized by Vivekananda's warm heart:[34] 'I must see my machine in strong working order, and then knowing for certain that I have put in a lever for the good of humanity, in India at least, which no power can drive back, I will sleep without caring what will be next.'

One of the fundamental aspects of institution-building is to invest it with a distinctive character of its own. This subtle character almost oozes out, as it were, through the pores and tissues of the institutional body. Very recently writings on organizational culture formation (e.g. Beyer and Trice, 1987)[35] in the West are recognizing the importance of rituals, symbols, collective rites, corporate folklore and the like to hold the psyche of a large number of persons, beyond a critical size, at a unified, synchronous wavelength. It is the combination of these carefully chosen elements which, through a period of sustained indoctrination and practice, crystallizes into a distinctive institutional character—'the way things are done here'. All petty and mundane irritation—an ever-present scourge in all organizations—tend to dissolve in the medium of such a culture carefully nursed with myths and symbols. Rationality and intellect alone are unable to act as the anodyne. Here are, therefore, certain examples of how Vivekananda had foreseen this strategic management variable almost a century ago, and built them into the life-style of the RKMM—both in its internal and external existence.[36]

(1) Whenever any activity is to be performed collectively by all the members of a centre it has to be preceded by ringing a bell.

(2) No visitor can spend a night at the *Math* without permission from its Abbot.

(3) Visitors will be entertained in the guest parlour only.

(4) All inmates have to wake up early, wash and clean their own clothes and surroundings.

(5) Everybody should perform some physical exercise.

(6) The Abbot should ensure that the inmates engage in spiritual practices in the early hours of the morning.

(7) As far as is practicable, everybody should take their meals at one time and place.

(8) Afternoons will be used for small group, individual and full assembly readings and discussions.

(9) After sunset again individual spiritual practices will have to be performed.

(10) All work and communication will be done quietly and peacefully.

(11) Members going out for work to places away from the particular

centre have to send every week a detailed letter about their
activities to the Abbot. The latter has to maintain custody and
copies of such letters.

Besides, during our own visits to many centres of the RKMM all
over India, we have observed a few additional features which are
now typical of this institution:

(1) Every morning, before sunrise, in all centres where a marble
image of Sri Ramakrishna exists, a brief and quiet *mangalarati* is
performed. Householder guests staying at the centre can also
participate in the serene beauty of this ritual.

(2) Before lunch and dinner a *sloka* from the *Gita* is recited
collectively (basically informing the whole process with a revival of
the awareness of *Brahman*). In many centres, after finishing these
meals, the glory of the Trinity of The Order—Sri Ramakrishna, the
Holy Mother and Swami Vivekananda—is also recited in chorus.

(3) Wherever a marble image of Sri Ramakrishna has been installed,
the entire 24-hour routine of the centre revolves around Him—as if
He were physically present.

(4) Whenever any member of the centre goes out for work, he
visits the *sanctum sanctorum* and begs Sri Ramakrishna's permission and blessings, and on his return he again goes there and offers
his work at His feet. If the Abbot leaves the centre for some days,
all the other members collect by his side at the moment of departure
and recite the glory of the Trinity of the Order.

(5) The evening vesper service in all centres has a set of three
prayers sung in chorus by devotees—lay and other. Of these two
had been composed by Vivekananda himself—and both on Sri
Ramakrishna without naming him.

(6) The symbol or monogram of the Order was yet another creative
contribution of Vivekananda's to institution building. The symbol
represents man's efforts, through the four *Yoga*s, to cross the
ocean of life into Eternal Bliss.

(7) Seniority of age is always honoured. Thus, even the Abbot or
the hierarchical head of a centre, before leaving the place for some
days on official duty or otherwise, touches the feet of all senior
monks present to seek their blessings.

(8) All key decision-making in each centre is mostly centralized in
the Abbot, e.g. whether a lay devotee can stay as a guest for a few
days. Even if this means delay in many instances, yet this seems to

be more than compensated by better coordination, consistency and integrity of decision-making.

(9) Except on Sundays, every evening after dinner a reading-cum-discussion session is held. Usually a young *brahmachari* reads a few pages from a biography of one great spiritual personality or another. All are welcome. Informal discussions also take place.

The transcendent or metaphysical uplift obtainable from the myth of the RKMM as the embodiment of the Master himself may remain unfathomable to the ruling management theorists. The primary meaning of myth is not something baseless and fictitious; it is the story about some great and inspiring act or event or process in the past of a family, a society, a community or an organization. Any standard dictionary will show this. Its function is to shatter, from time to time, the cocoon of sterile individualism and liberate the mind, in one great stroke, from its constricted grooves into a wider vision. Thus, the myth of the bandit Ratnakar doing *tapasya* for 60,000 years to transform himself into the poet–sage Valmiki must not be taken literally. All it conveys is a feel for the stupendous dedication and self-discipline called upon by the goal of self-transformation. It lifts our imagination with a wrench from the finite to the infinite, inspiring us thereby to a great commitment. Thus Owen very aptly says:[37]

Myths are the stories of a group's culture which describe its beginning, continuance and ultimate goals. These stories are so much part of that fabric as to define that fabric and institution.... I view ritual as the dramatic re-enactment of a myth.... The role of myths and rituals in organization transformation is critical, for they shape and form the culture, which in turn provides the power, purpose and values of the organization.

Enough has been cited above to show that those management writers or practitioners who are sceptical about the 'prescriptive' nature of such rules, rites and rituals are probably unable to think hard in practical terms. No evidence probably exists anywhere in the world to prove that enduring institutions have ever been built and sustained without resolute devotion to one set of 'prescriptions' or the other to nurture a structure of lofty emotions and feelings.

IV. Vivekananda's Own Leadership Modelling

Like all great leaders of humanity, Vivekananda was most spontaneous. A pure transparent mind, combined with burning love for all (*samadarshita*), was the bedrock of his leadership role. In contrast, many modern ideas on techniques and skills of leadership, or on technologies for team-building appear to be superficial by comparison. With selfishness being completely burnt out of his mind, he could transmit the conviction into his brother monks and other members of the Order that, during the initial years of the RKMM, the democratic principles of decision-making had to be held in abeyance. Such principles could be followed later when, with better spread of education, members would be more capable of abandoning *self-interest* and *personal prejudices* for public good. Until such time the organization had to be run by a 'dictator' whose authority everybody must obey.[38] Yet he himself took no official post in the newly-formed RKMM. He had even handed over all his savings in America to a brother monk, and later begged a few coins from the latter for a trip to Calcutta!

A great irony of modern India, however, is that the more educated we are becoming, the greater is our penchant for rights and claims, for selfish aims and ambitions. Higher education is clearly not making us less selfish, as Vivekananda had hoped. The organized sector of India is an epitome of rights-*sans*-duty orientation. Yet, our opinion-building élites espouse greater participation, democracy etc. This is a serious dilemma for India. It is rooted in the fact that most leaders in Indian organizations tend themselves to be morally and ethically vulnerable and cannot therefore muster the courage of a Vivekananda to declare that democratic principles should be kept frozen for some time. Hence, they tend to put up an empty façade of democracy. With their own credentials suspect, their followers and subordinates also function in a moral vacuum, for nothing is a stronger proof of such vacuum than the clamour of rights alone at the cost of duties. Duty-orientation in organizations alone can sustain a values-led, moral culture, and only then can organizations become truly democratic institutions. How else can we understand the functioning of grass-roots democracy when monarchs like Janaka or Ashoka used to manage India? True, all leaders cannot become Vivekanandas. That does not, however, undermine the relevance of his model—ever reminding them of the gap they have to bridge. Otherwise, gimmick-oriented, technique-inspired superficiality may continue to masquerade as professionalism.

Effacement of the lower self or the 'unripe ego' was another major characteristic of Vivekananda's leadership style. Thus, although his Master had uttered all kinds of picturesque super-latives about Vivekananda,[39] yet on one occasion he was almost on the verge of washing the feet of a distinguished Buddhist missionary who had come to visit the Belur Math.[40] Latu Maharaj* or Swami Adbhutananda was one of Vivekananda's *gurubhai*s. In later life he recounted two incidents which had occurred at Belur *Math* when the latter had begun to gradually implement the details of daily procedures to regulate *Math* life. Vivekananda had just introduced the rule of ringing daily a morning bell to awaken the inmates for meditation etc. Latu Maharaj was unwilling to fall in line, so the next morning he was about to leave for Calcutta. Vivekananda asked him why and was told bluntly that his meditational ability was not cut to respond to a made-to-order, sound of the bell stimulus so he would prefer to be on his own. Vivekananda under-stood, and relaxed the rule for him. Some days later another *gurubhai*, Swami Premananda (Baburam Maharaj) could not wake up to the sound of the bell. Vivekananda later admonished him that if the seniors, who had formulated these rules, themselves failed to observe them, how could the rest be expected to comply? Premananda quite readily agreed. In a few moments he also suggested that this rule should henceforth include a proviso that those who failed to wake up on time should undergo some punishment. Vivekananda listened very calmly, then suddenly tears began to roll from his eyes and he spoke in sobs: 'How could you ever imagine, Baburam, that I could punish you': Soon Baburam too began to weep. Presently, Swami Brahmananda came in and was amazed to see the two *gurubhai*s weeping silently. Having heard them both, he then announced: 'The punishment for this infraction would henceforth be that the guilty would arrange for his food that day by *madhukari* (i.e. by begging not more than a handful of grains from each householder).' Hearing this Premananda was very happy, and gladly bore the punishment![41]

Conventional reasoning or logic can scarcely comprehend this sort of blend of 'autocracy–democracy', expressing itself in the form of 'love'? Yet, it is probably this very trans-rational process which Konosuke Matsushita also seems to be attempting for his

---

* He was the only absolutely illiterate disciple of the Master, and was at first a mere domestic servant of one of the Master's householder devotees.

organization for, he says about the true goal of his role:[42] 'To model love. I am the soul of this Company. It is through me that our organization's values pass.'

Ferris too is boldly correct when he says:[43] 'Organizational love is concerned with all aspects of health: physical, emotional, mental and spiritual.... It is a feeling of compassion and of deep interest in another's welfare.'

However, to saturate an organization with love of this nature the role models of Vivekananda or Matsushita are indispensable, and this love must be impersonal to be limitless and credible. To acquire this spiritual *sadhana*, along with secular management, is the answer.

With respect to the taming and annihilation of the ego of his own *guru*-ship we hear from Shuddhananda—an initiated disciple of Vivekananda—the following declaration by his guru:[44] 'I want each one of my children to be hundred times greater than I could ever be. Everyone of you *must* be a giant—must, that is my word.' About Vivekananda's own humble attitude towards Sri Rama-krishna, Vimalananda—another disciple of Vivekananda—com-municates his own impression:[45]

These words were really startling to us for more than one reason. Here was a man who was being idolized, nay actually worshipped by so many, and this man in their very presence confessing his inability to represent his guru!* 'What an unpretentious man is before us' said we to ourselves.

Yet another dimension of Vivekananda's role-modelling has prime significance for the Indian manager: his practical and authentic reconciliation between *jnana* and *karma*. By this achieve-ment he, at one stroke, had demonstrated the relevance of the trans-empirical summit of Indian thought to the gruelling demands of the work-situation at the empirical level. Let us listen again to Rolland's estimate of this singular synthesis:[45]

His whole edifice bears this double impress: the basement is a nursery of apostles of truth and social service who mix in the life of the people and the movement of the time. But the summit is the *Ara Maxima*, the lantern of the dome, the spire of the Cathedral, the Ashrama of all Ashramas, the Advaita built on the Himalayas, where the two hemispheres, the West and the East, meet at the confluence of all mankind in absolute Unity.

---

* This related to Vivekananda's frequent criticism in America of the greed for money and wealth pervading that society. He later felt deep remorse for such criticisms because his guru had never spoken a single derogatory word about any culture or society.

Again, at a less philosophical and imagery-laden level, he had commented thus somewhat earlier in his book:[47]

Sanskrit, Oriental and Western philosophy, manual work and meditation alike were taught there [the *Math*]. He himself set the example. After his lessons on metaphysics he tilled the garden, dug a well, and kneaded bread. He was a living hymn of Work.

All this could be crystallized for the manager/administrator into the following: to gain insight and true perspective into knotty management problems, systematic de-cerebration, *pratyahara* and mind-stilling are essential. Without going *inside* no *insight* is possible. Regular practice of such a process can slowly enhance one's capacity for deeper understanding from a higher level, as it were. Armed with this ability one can tackle problems with greater confidence and positive value-orientation.

We learn another important lesson in leadership from the way Vivekananda performed it. Management literature talks about 'formal' and 'informal' leaders, and also about the 'acceptance' theory of leadership. Almost immediately following the formal registration of the RK Mission, he had resigned from its President-ship. In fact, the first President of the Order is always understood to be Brahmananda. But Marie Burke writes,[48] 'Yet, *leadership was implicit* in Swamiji's very being. Whatever his legal position in the Ramakrishna Math and Mission was to be during the last year or so of his life, he *remained the leader*; it could not have been otherwise.'

This symbolic act of relinquishing the Presidentship is signi-ficant in the light of the current espousal by many management pundits of the view that leaders need to be motivated through hope of greater power, name, fame, etc. But if selfless service has to be the true basis of leadership values—*dasasya dasah*—then obviously something needs to be done to correct the mercenary orientation in the world of management and government. The sooner contem-porary leaders realize that loyalty and obedience have to be commanded on the basis of unimpeachable integrity, rather than demanded on the basis of crafty short-term bargains of convenience, the better for the future of the country. This is exactly why, despite his frequent fits of anger, and the impatient bulldozing of his ideas and plans, none of Vivekananda's *gurubhai*s could ever dream of whittling down their love and support for him. His style seems to have been an epitome of *vajradapi kathorani, mriduni kusumadapai—*

tougher than the thunderbolt, yet more delicate than a flower. We therefore find it difficult to accept Satswarupananda's comments on Vivekananda's leadership, e.g. 'Such a high-strung character is not meant for constructive work ... such a quick and capacious brain ... is too great a stumbling block for any kind of teamwork'.[49] In managerial parlance, 'entrepreneurs' always have an element of the capricious, unpredictable, yet trail-blazing genius in them. They create. 'Managers' maintain and impart steadiness to what an 'entrepreneur' creates. The 'entrepreneur–manager' is a good model to interpret the relationship between Vivekananda and his *gurubhai*s. Thorough purity and instinctive goodness, and not two-minute skills, alone constitute the well-spring of such a style. Since Vivekananda was purity incarnate, Jitatmananda aptly refers to the former's own vision of the basic purpose of the RKMM of emerging as a gigantic *'purity-drilling machine'*.[50] Satprakashananda too has pointed out Vivekananda's repeated and unerring diagnosis that the basic deficiency of the world is not economic, cultural or political, but the goodness of man, and has rightly argued that:[51] 'the efficient working of an organization, vast or small, does not depend primarily on its constitutional laws and agreements but on the sincerity, the self-sacrifice, and the enthusiasm of its individual members'. The Indian psyche responds instantly to leaders who are selfless—this is the lesson from Vivekananda-the-institution-builder (also demonstrated later by Tagore, Gandhiji and Subhas Bose).

Recently the theme of charismatic leadership appears to be gaining renewed attention. Thus Hater and Bass have differentiated between 'transformational' and 'transactional leadership'.[52] The former inspires response levels higher than those expected in a calculus of give-and-take, while the latter struggles for contingent *quid pro quo*s of performance against rewards. The first basis of 'transformational' leadership is therefore stated by them to be 'charisma', whereby the leader instils pride, faith, a sense of mission and the like. Simply stated, all this means that the team-member is always kept alive to a vision which transcends his small self. Vivekananda was able achieve this effect on his *gurubhai*s and disciples in the highest degree. What was the underpinning of such charisma? Hater and Bass do not furnish any clues to this fundamental question. Clearly, for Vivekananda, it was absolute unselfishness, combined with an all-embracing, divinized love which could, nonetheless, permit sensitive personalized consideration without causing mistrust in others (e.g. Latu Maharaj's case).

This has a vital lesson: professionalized careerism and charismatic-transformational leadership are utterly incompatible. Professional, competitive careerism, with the lower self or *vyavaharika vyaktitwa* as the primary fuelling agent, may grab or usurp leadership positions in various organizations, but it cannot inspire 'performance surplus' in any field. However, if constructive, selfless charisma—by cultivation or instinct—brings forth a formal leadership role to a person, then both the leader and the led are twice-blessed. To our mind the role model of Sri Krishna in the *Mahabharata*, stripped of the few miracles which have been interpolated into his actions, is the epitome of charismatic transformational leadership. Careerism constricts the mind because of mercenariness, and mental constriction is anathema to constructive charisma.

The RKMM has demonstrated a radical transformation of the only pattern of monkhood accepted in India since time immemorial—cutting loose from the world and realizing oneness with God—to the new model of searching for God in man within society by serving him and it in the spirit of '*shiva* in *jeeva*'. Vivekananda's metaphysically-rooted charisma was the secret. To us it appears that this story of transformation wrought by the RKMM has a great moral for our economic organizations: their leaders too should seek their own metaphysical roots and charisma and introduce the opposite movement of informing all secular endeavour with the purity of the transcendent, the beyond, the spiritual. With the example of Vivekananda's transformational leadership, and in the light of what Hater and Bass have to say, it is difficult to accept Fiedler (an authority on leadership research) and Garcia's view that environment is more important than personality in accounting for leadership behaviour.[53] If the leader adapts to and follows the environment, enabling predictability of behaviour, is he then a leader at all? Could he ever be a transformational leader in the context of concern for ethics, values and culture?

V. CONCLUSION: TOWARDS CLASSICAL LOVE AND DISCIPLINE

In sum, the hood of the mythological snake-god Vasuki which appears to uphold the world of the RKMM is made up of *love blended with discipline*. The early decades of the Buddhist monastic organizations were also informed with these very supreme ingredients. As for love, Saradananda speaks thus about their days spent at Cossipore during the last phase of the Master's physical existence[54]:

The pure, selfless love of the Master on the one hand and the wonderful spirit of friendship of Narendra [Vivekananda] and his noble company on the other, united together *to bind them in such a sweet and tender*, yet hard and unbreakable bond...[emphasis added].

Should members and leaders of commercial enterprises and bureaucracies try to replicate such a milieu? Perhaps not. Yet, any manager must be capable of verifying that even a fraction of such love evinced by him in his work-situation can almost always win a positive response from others. Sincere and quiet determination along with consistency—and not loud, tactical show—are imperative. Yet, these features are so very scarce. At the same time, the very fact that an economic enterprise almost stinks with the air of *kanchana* (money) necessitates (and not denies, as is commonly held) deliberate cultivation of the metaphysical ideal of *detached involvement* as a deodorant.

Regarding discipline. As already mentioned, Vivekananda had told Nivedita that what had impressed him most about the English was their remarkable ability to reconcile self-respect with obedience (a major facet of discipline). Once again, management literature and teaching miss out on this basic prerequisite for institution-building. Thus, in March 1990 a few professors of a post-graduate residential institution proposed that henceforth unauthorized overnight absence of any student from the campus should attract a fine of Rs 10 per night. To this another colleague remarked immediately that this would amount to asking students to be absent by paying a mere Rs 10! What about the fine of Rs 250 for unjustified pulling of the chain in a running train then? Does this mean an invitation to pull chains and pay Rs 250? Similarly, what about a library charging fines for late return of borrowed books? Extending such a view, the whole of the legal apparatus should be dispensable. Is this a conceivable reality? Another professor also commented jeeringly that this might end up by the locking-in of students in their hostels. It is perhaps not realized by such well-meaning advocates of liberty that generally automatic self-discipline can only follow long spells of imposed or induced discipline from a higher level or agency which has the welfare of the members concerned in mind. This is practical common sense in human affairs. One must be able to think clearly about three levels of freedom—the students' freedom of unauthorized absence, the teacher's freedom to expect full class attendance and the institution's freedom to sustain a minimum level of disciplined conduct—and prioritize them.

Vivekananda had cried himself hoarse about the biggest malady of Indians—jealousy.[55] It is apparent from his writings that he had realized that excessive jealousy and poor discipline went together. Hence he was never tired of warning the members of the RKMM about this great evil. Once when Nivedita had imputed jealousy to his own character, he had thundered back:[56] 'Your letter indicates that I am jealous of your new friends. You must know once for all I am born without jealousy, without avarice, without desire to rule—whatever other vices I am born with.'

Nowadays some reputed Indians (e.g., Mulk Raj Anand) use the columns of important national newspapers in English to exhort us to work towards and create 'new values' for a 'new' India. Heritage has no answers.[57] Unfortunately, they do not formulate clearly what these 'new values' ought to be. Nor do they seem to understand the essence of the Indian heritage, and so urge 'new experiments' to create 'new values'. The real task is not to try new experiments, but to re-learn, re-internalize the old values and truths. The RKMM itself is a model experiment of this type. How correctly does A.N. Marlow, while writing on 'Vivekananda in Europe', express the fundamental principle for institution, indeed, nation-building, in a vein contrary to Anand's:[58] '... what mankind needs for its help and salvation is not novelty but truth'. The Indian intelligentsia (in journalism and academia especially) seems to be mesmerized by the novelty-parading modern civilization, and often it seems not to know the import of what it is writing or thinking on India's present predicaments. Thus, Anand, in the same piece mentioned above, argues for escaping the clutches of 'karmic fatalism'. Yet, Arnold Toynbee, the great historian, interprets '*karma*', or actions as constituting an '*ethical* banking-account' for man, *karma* as the determinant of ethical levels, and *karma* again—not scientific or technological progress—as the producer of happiness or misery.[59] All this deeper import of the *karma* theory eludes Anand. Basic truths are not at all easy to cultivate and sustain. Compassion, love, discipline, honesty, self-sacrifice, etc. are deceptively simple truths, yet they require a life-time of vigilant labour, *sadhana*, to live by in each generation.

Nobody expects that economic enterprises or bureaucratic establishments should or could ever turn sacral in the full sense. Yet, if they have to work well for and by the Indians, the RKMM is an institutional model worthy of serious and urgent attention from them even though it may belong dominantly to the sacral end of the spectrum. This is because it is an institution into which its leader had breathed a vitality unique in its creative synthesis of the *believing* mind and the *critical* mind;[60] the assimilating, trusting mind and the excluding, rejecting mind; the Eastern mind and the Western mind, the spiritual mind and the secular mind, the loving mind and the disciplined mind.

REFERENCES

1. D. Terrence and A. Kennedy, *Corporate Cultures* (London: Penguin 1988), p. 37.
2. R. Rolland, *The Life of Vivekananda and The Universal Gospel* (Advaita Ashrama, 1965), p. 146.
3. *Corporate Cultures*, p. 33.
4. V.K.R.V. Rao, *Swami Vivekananda* (Government of India, Publications Division, 1979), p. 219.
5. Swami Gambhirananda, *History of the Ramakrishna Math and Mission* (Calcutta: Advaita Ashrama, 1983), pp. 18, 27.
6. *India, Culture and Management* (Rotterdam School of Management, 1989).
7. Swami Vivekananda, *Collected Works* (Calcutta: Advaita Ashrama, 1989), vol.3, p. 110.
8. E. Stark, *The Gift Unopened: A New American Revolution*, 1988, reviewed by E. Nelson in *Prabuddha Bharata*, Oct. 1989, pp. 432–9.
9. Sister Nivedita, *The Master As I Saw Him* (Calcutta: Udbodhan, 1977), pp. 96–7.
10. Ibid., p. 150.   11. Ibid., p. 165.
12. Swami Vivekananda, *Complete Works* (Calcutta: Advaita Ashrama, 1959), vol. VI, p. 322.
13. Ibid., p. 324.   14. *Complete Works*, vol. VIII, p. 429.
15. *Letters of Swami Vivekananda* (Calcutta: Advaita Ashrama, 1976), pp. 108.
16. Ibid., pp. 228–9.
17. P. Carus, *The Gospel of Buddha* (Madras: Samata Books, 1987), pp. 143–5.

18. R. Tagore, *The Religion of an Artist* (Calcutta: Visva-Bharati, 1988), p. 22.
19. R. Ferris, 'How Organizational Love Can Improve Leadership', *Organizational Dynamics*, Spring 1988, p. 45.
20. Sri Aurobindo, *The Ideal of The Karmayogin* (Pondicherry: Aurobindo Ashram, 1974), p. 40.
21. Rolland, op. cit., p. 345.
22. Ibid., p. 116.   23. Ibid., p. 128.
24. *History of the Ramakrishna Math and Mission*, p. 24.
25. Ibid., p. 95.
26. *Reminiscences of Swami Vivekananda* (Calcutta: Advaita Ashrama, n.d.), p. 144.
27. *The Master As I Saw Him*, p. 52.
28. R.T. Pascale, and A.G. Athos, *The Art of Japanese Management*, (Harmondsworth: Penguin, 1982), pp. 51–6, 81.
29. *The Master As I Saw Him*, p. 53.
30. Rolland, op. cit., p. 283; and *Rules of the Sri Ramakrishna Math* (in Bengali), pt.II, items 4, 10, 12, 13.
31. A.M. Webber, 'Jimmy Carter: The Statesman as CEO', *Harvard Business Review*, March–April 1988, p. 63.
32. Rolland, op. cit., p. 168.   33. Ibid., p. 114.   34. Ibid., p. 134.
35. J.M. Beyer and H.M. Trice, 'How an Organization's Rites Reveal Its Culture', *Organizational Dynamics*, Spring 1987, pp. 5–23.
36. *Rules of The Sri Ramakrishna Math* (in Bengali), last section, items 22, 21, 20, 10–19.
37. H. Owen, quoted by R. Lessem in *Global Management Principles* (London: Prentice Hall, 1989), p. 688.
38. Swami Nikhilananda, *Vivekananda: A Biography* (Calcutta: Advaita Ashrama, 1987), p. 241.
39. Swami Nikhilananda (trans.), *The Gospel of Sri Ramakrishna* (Madras: Sri Ramakrishna Math, 1974), pp. 793–4.
40. *Eastern and Western Disciples, Life of Swami Vivekananda* (Calcutta: Advaita Ashrama, 1974), p. 547.
41. C.S. Chattopadhyay, *Sri Latu Maharajer Smritikatha*, Bengali (Calcutta: Udbodhan, 1976), pp. 280–1.
42. K. Blanchard and N.V. Peale, *The Power of Ethical Management* (New York: William Morrow, 1988), p. 87.
43. Ferris, op. cit., p. 44.
44. Swami Abjajananda, *Swamijir Pada Prantey* (Bengali—Belur Math: Ramakrishna Mission Sarada Peeth, 1972), p. 14.
45. Ibid., p. 109–10.   46. Rolland, op. cit., p. 314.   47. Ibid., p. 145.
48. L. Marie Burke, *Swami Vivekananda: His Second Visit To The West* (Calcutta: Advaita Ashrama, 1973), p. 734.
49. Swami Satswarupananda, 'Ramakrishna Mission' in *A Bridge To Eternity* (Calcutta: Advaita Ashrama, 1986), p. 442.

50. Swami Jitatmananda, *Swami Vivekananda: Prophet and Pathfinder* (Madras: Sri RK Math, 1985), p. 169.

51. Swami Satprakashananda, *Swami Vivekananda's Contribution To The Present Age* (St. Louis: The Vedanta Society, 1978), pp. 14–15, 16.

52. J.J. Hater and B.M. Bass, 'Superior's Evaluations and Subordinate's Preceptions of Transformational and Transactional Leadership', *Journal of Applied Psychology*, vol.73, no.4, 1988, pp. 695–6.

53. F.E. Fiedler, and J.E. Garcia, *New Approaches to Effective Leadership* (New York: John Wiley, 1987), p. 51.

54. Swami Saradananda, *Sri Ramakrishna The Great Master* (trans. by Swami Jagadananda), (Madras: Sri Ramakrishna Math, 1984), vol. II, p. 1018.

55. Swami Vivekananda, *Complete Works* (Calcutta: Advaita Ashrama, 1959), vol. vi, pp. 252, 256, 278, 306; vol. viii, pp. 298, 300.

56. M.L. Burke, op. cit., p. 713.

57. For example, Mulk Raj Anand, 'Inherit or Create?', *The Statesman*, Calcutta, 29 June 1988.

58. A.N. Marlow, 'Vivekananda in Europe' in *Swami Vivekananda in East and West*, eds. Swami Ghanananda and Geoffrey Parrinder (London: The Ramakrishna Vedanta Centre, 1968), p. 109.

59. A. Toynbee, and D. Ikeda, *Choose Life* (Delhi: Oxford University Press, 1987), pp. 317–19, p. 325.

60. C.R. Pangborn, 'India's Need and the Ramakrishna Movement' in *A Bridge To Eternity* (Calcutta: Advaita Ashrama, 1986), pp. 523–4.

12

MENTAL HEALTH
Rise From the 'Yayati-Syndrome' to
'Ātmic Poornatwa'

The previous chapters have a close bearing on the mental health of a manager. Here we offer a kind of consolidated picture about this end-state, i.e. sound mental health. It is this subjective, meta-physical state whose attainment ought to be and is the sole *raison d'être* of every objective pursuit. Empirical blindness to this real aim of the managerial role can only be at our peril. We may here define sound mental health as that state of *the mind which can maintain a calm positive poise, or regain it when unsettled, for progressively longer durations or quickly, in the midst of all the external vagaries of work-life and social existence.* For a healthy stress-free mind, internal constancy and peace must be the only valid response to external vagary and turmoil.

I. THE IMPEDIENTS TO SOUND MENTAL HEALTH

(A) The circular relationship between physical health and mental health apart, we shall list below some of the major causes of impaired mental health from causes 'internal' to the individual manager. At the same time, it is these which are most relevant also to the realm of values. We must acknowledge this picture of our inner world, and also recognize that sound values and mental health go together. Positivist denial of normative issues seems to have exacerbated mental tensions and afflictions in contemporary times. Auguste Comte's 'logical positivism' and Pitrim Sorokin's 'sensate society' seem to have been intimate companions, bearing heightened mental illness as an unfortunate offspring.

- Greed — for money, power, recognition, etc.
- Jealousy — regarding one's own information base, resources, etc.
- Envy — regarding someone else's achievement, rewards, talent, etc.
- Egotism/Vanity — regarding one's own accomplishment
- Impatience — springing from the above four.
- Suspiciousness — springing from the first four
- Anger — springing from the above six
- Frustration — springing from the first five

Every single in-depth organizational study conducted by us shows that its members are badly trapped in the quagmire of these debilities. Considering such thorns in the human mind to be only 'natural', intellectual learning bypasses them. When the fabric of work-life is then rolled on the carpet of such thorns, bleeding is only to be expected—'naturally'! Two major outcomes of the preceding combination of unhealthy emotions within the organizational setting are:

- Competition   • Ambition

Both these motive forces essentially weaken most role players by making them dependent and vulnerable. This happens because the 'ambition–competition' drive is commonly grounded in a fantasy world of rewards, promotions and much else in the manager's mind. This dream is, however, nearly always shattered for the majority. Is this vast cost worth paying for just a few sparks which may fly off the grinding wheel of competition? Are there no alternative routes to improvement and excellence than the competition–ambition drive which is prone to degeneration—particularly at the interpersonal level? A supreme failing in each of us, at the interpersonal level, is our penchant for suffering and anguish through comparison with the few individuals who are better off in any respect. As much as ninety per cent of our mental health problems could be traced to this single deficiency in our make-up. Hardly any of us, however, has the natural bent for happiness and peace by comparison with the numerous individuals who are worse off. In the national perspective of a poor country like India, the manager (and the IIM-professor too) would profit by realizing that for every single person who is better off than him there are at least a hundred, or even more, who are worse off.

We know the question of fairness v. unfairness will inevitably arise to rationalize anger, jealousy, frustration, etc. Here again we should acknowledge yet another persistent reality of organizational life: when the outcome matches favourably with our own hope the decision is always fair; when it does not, it is always unfair. Each one of us thinks, feels like that. Can any external system on earth resolve this problem?

A personal fall-out of the ambition–competition thrust is often the silent erosion of one's ethico-moral fibre. The value of a chosen success-symbol, i.e. the end-state value, overrides the values-as-means in acquiring that symbol, e.g. tax evasion, undercutting prices for market share, spreading canards against a business rival, cultivating illicit relationships with one's secretary, and the like. Once again, we are insensitive to the deeper reality that such transgressions do eat into our mental poise and harmony. We cannot sleep well at night because we have, by such means, denied ourselves a good conscience which, as the German proverb goes, is the best pillow. Of course, due to *maya*, the 'objective' gain of money saved, or extra market share, or physical enjoyment secured looms much larger in our mind than the 'subjective' loss of sound sleep—at least for the time-being.

The 'technology–greed' comradeship also operates as a pervasive backstage force contributing to our accelerated mental ill-health. Technology goes on blindfold in an endless race of not only meeting some of our true 'needs', but also of creating more and new 'greeds'. Put in another way, unbridled greed finds in technology a faithful ally, mocking at Gandhiji's profound utterance: 'there is enough for everybody's need, but not for everybody's greed'. Our daily existence is, therefore, becoming increasingly exteriorized and dependent. Without realizing it, we are willingly falling prey to mounting inner vacuum. Through TVs, VCRs, PCs and what not, every moment of our quiet inner life is being snatched away. The other day the Chairman of an industrial house in Delhi showed us at his home his school-going grandson lying on his chest on a big mattress and reading a comic while taking his afternoon tiffin. He expressed deep concern that this boy was always complaining of boredom, was constantly at something, and could hardly spend even a few minutes silently, doing nothing. The garden did not interest him at all. The mother was most anxious to train the boy to be a well-rounded individual. To this end everything was on the agenda: horse riding, swimming, canoeing, skating and so on. Besides, he must also secure the first rank in his class! A month later we met an English-speaking Polish tourist at Vrindavan. He had migrated to Sweden and had been working there for nearly fifteen years. Currently he was teaching in a school. For several years before he had been working as a computer programmer, with a good salary and in a sophisticated work-environment. Why did he leave such a dream job then?—we asked. He gave a startling reply: 'I had to quit that job because I began to suffer from "burnout"—you know what I mean. During the last year or so of that work I felt as if each day a fraction of my brain was being plucked out by the computer.' This pathetic confession reminded us of Shakespeare's lament, 'Life is a tale told by an idiot, full of sound and fury, signifying nothing'! Again, in our own day William Faulkner has despaired about 'life's mad steeplechase to nowhere'. All the much-touted successive modern 'revolutions' are thus relentlessly and ultimately exteriorizing man's being and awareness, leading to drift and anomie.

We may also touch upon 'suspiciousness', listed at the beginning of this section as a significant cause of mental health. One of the most tragic characters portrayed in English literature is that of Shakespeare's Othello. Othello-the-Moor succumbed to his suspicions about the fidelity of that purest of heroines, Desdemona and crying: 'It is the cause, it is the cause my soul;' strangled her to death. On the other hand, in Tagore's Bengali novel *Ghare Baire* (*The Home and the World*), the hero Nikhilesh allowed his charming and accomplished wife Vimala to associate herself intimately with the activities of the firebrand pseudo-revolutionary, Sandip. Nikhilesh knew about her growing infatuation for Sandip, yet kept his cool and dignity. Finally, a repentant Vimala realized her error and returned her full loyalty to Nikhilesh. Panicky, jealousy-fed suspicion was the undoing of the Othello–Desdemona poem; serene, idealism-fed trust had resurrected the Nikhilesh–Vimala song. These characters, therefore, have an important lesson for organizational members in the sphere of mental health. It is quite possible that we gratuitously invite mental illness through the compulsions of creeping suspicion. The greedier, more egotistic, and selfish a person is, the more likely he is to suffer from suspiciousness.

(B) A little attention should now be paid to some causes of mental ill-health which are 'external' to the individual. These causes are often called 'stressors' and include skill obsolescence, job change, work-pressure, transfers, stock market crisis, unemployment, weak empathy from boss, militant unionism, student agitation, problems with neighbours, uncertainties of demand or supply or both, and so on. Now, when 'constant change' is the only constant in modernity, these consequences are unavoidable. So long as we all behave as passive individual recipients of these impacts of change (progress?) in the externals, apart from organizational palliatives like re-training, transfer allowances, forecasting etc. applied to some of the stressors we have no redemption. The only effective response seems to lie *within* the individual. To this we shall turn in detail in the next section.

A more universal and true response to the change-for-the-sake-of-change motive itself, and to its consequences of stress-burnout, also needs to be sought at the level of principle. Indian sages and thinkers of profundity, down to our present times, have never compromised on two principles: (a) that needs cannot be quenched by satisfying more needs, just as fire cannot be quenched by pouring more fat into it; (b) that change presupposes stability, so before embarking upon or accepting any change the hidden anchor of stability must be clearly grasped. In the modern West too there have been thinkers of great sensitivity, although outside the domain of management thought, who have challenged the exaltation of change and progress. The French thinker Guenon (1941) had sharply castigated this trend:[1]

Nothing that relies merely, as their [European] civilization does, on the material order of things can hope for more than transitory success; change, which is law in this *essentially unstable domain*, may have the *worst consequences* in every respect, and these consequences will come with all the more *lightning rapidity* as the speed of change grows greater and greater.

... a civilization which never ceases to move, which has *neither tradition nor deep-rooted principle*, obviously cannot have a real influence on those which possess just those things that it lacks itself. [Emphasis added.]

Dewey, the American philosopher remarked about 'progress':[2] 'The more we do and the more we accomplish the more the end is *vanity* and *vexation*. The more striving, the more attainments perhaps, but also assuredly the *more needs and the more disappointments*'. (Emphasis added.) A British thinker, Joad, also voiced his grim forebodings when he said:[3] 'Man's true enemy is within himself; it lies in the strength of his own *uncontrolled passions and appetites* ... new-won power over nature has not tamed these; on the contrary, it has rendered them *more violent* because it has given them *greater opportunity for gratification*' (emphasis added).

All these warnings from profound minds have so long been swept aside, especially since the seventeenth century. We are all beginning to model ourselves, unconsciously, after the tragic king Yayati in the *Mahabharata* who, in order to revel and enjoy endlessly the pleasures of the flesh, bartered his old age with the youth of his obliging youngest son for a mythical thousand years, and finally returned lost and penitent to the son, pleading that he take back his youth. Let us call this universal phenomenon the '*yayati*-syndrome'.

Tagore (1913) gives us a classic word-picture of the *yayati*-syndrome:[4]

In sin we lust after pleasures, not because they are truly desirable, but because the *red light of our passion* makes them appear desirable; we long for things not because they are great in themselves, but because our greed exaggerates them and makes them appear great. These exaggerations, these falsifications of the perspective of things, break the harmony of our life at every step; we lose the true standard of values and are distracted by the false claims of varied interests of life contending with one another. [Emphasis added.]

Each successive dazzling scientific–technological application leads only to a deeper penetration of the *yayati*–syndrome into the mind of man. As a result he continues to sink into a deeper mental morass.

The *yayati*-syndrome constitutes the underlying generic nature of all externally-directed achievement, acquisitive or response motivations, characterized by inner conflicts amongst *reason, emotion, will* and *conscience*. For example, an employee's conscience might tell him to do an honest day's work, yet the emotion may prompt him to relax, and the will is weak enough not to subdue this emotion in favour of conscience. Again, someone's emotion urges him to hate his detractor, but reason says hatred is bad, and once more the will lets the emotion overcome reason. In yet another instance, there is a natural calamity, emotion prompts someone to donate a large sum in aid of the sufferers, reason wants to use this act to further some self-interest and this time the will fails again—but against the purity of the original emotion. We always get caught in such tangles which cost us our mental health. Analytical recipes will not dissolve them. Holistic orientations are needed to harmonize and integrate them. We will illustrate this through a recent counselling session we did.

A young manager in his late thirties came to discuss with us a new job offer which had just come his way. We knew that for the previous two years he had been having a harrowing time, including supersession, loss of job, etc. largely because of an inexplicably vindictive attitude adopted by the new expatriate head of the organization. Personal interviews sought by him were unproductive The new job was 'General Manager–Finance' in another multinational company, much smaller than the first. Talking of the many pros and cons, the manager said that one never knew, things might turn out better in the present firm, and that there was not much headroom in the flatter structure of the organization which had offered him the new job. To this we responded firmly: 'Look, you must clearly ask and tell yourself whether you are a whole man first, or a mere executive. Havn't you had enough of the rat race and competition? Do you want to lie in this mental whirlpool through your career. Isn't there likely to be a saner milieu in the new organization with only two or three GMs and just one tier above that before the Board level. Financially too you will on the whole be better off now. Wouldn't you prefer to lead a steady and peaceful inner life from now onwards?' This barrage brought him back to a better sense of perspective.

II. Counselling for Illness to Health—In the Mind

Let us first list below a few vital guidelines whose practice could restore our personal command over mental health, and then discuss them one at a time:

(1) To cultivate a sound philosophy of life,
(2) to identify with an inner core of self-sufficiency,
(3) to nourish a *nirdwandwic* mental orientation,
(4) to strive for excellence through 'work is worship',
(5) to build a stable and exalted inner reference point for the integration of contrary impulses, emotions, etc.,
(6) to pursue ethico-moral rectitude,

(7) to cultivate the *sattwa guna*,
(8) to practise self-discipline through deep breathing,
(9) to develop the habit of radiating goodwill and harmony from the centre of one's being,
(10) to practise contact with the Supreme/Universal Consciousness through the spirit of surrender.

Unless a counsellor himself or herself is internally fortified, or is genuinely inclined to be so, with some experiential certitude along these lines, he or she can do precious little to lead the counselee to mental health.

• *A Sound Philosophy of Life*

A merely empirical, mundane, secular philosophy of life—no matter whether capitalist or communist—cannot be a sound one. The current pace of existential disenchantment within both the free world and iron-curtain countries is strong evidence of this. The transcendent, trans-empirical, spiritual dimension is essential for mental health. This is symbolized by Mikhail Gorbachov's momentous meeting with the Pope in the Vatican in November 1989, and his assurance to him on the freedom of spiritual pursuits by all in Russia. Akhilananda had expressed this viewpoint to the West in clear terms nearly four decades ago:[5]

We must have a sound philosophy of life.... This life, this finite existence, cannot satisfy the infinite nature of man. Basically the infinite is within us. 'Lo, I am with you always.' Consequently, there will be dissatisfaction with anything short of that divine presence. The wealthiest man is dissatisfied with his wealth. We have seen time and again that people of wealth, power and position are disturbed because their inner nature is not satisfied.

In principle there is nothing dubious about transcendent Reality. It is only the infatuation of the contemporary mind with the sensual gross which recoils blindly from the supra-sensual subtle. Achievement motivation for the Infinite is, in the long run, more efficacious for mental health and sound values than the modern idea of achievement motivation at the secular–mundane level.

Once the supra-sensual yet serene subtle is admitted within our scheme of life, then we are compelled towards the achievement of inner calm, peace and purity. This attainment itself then becomes one's superordinate ambition in life. Were not the Buddhas, the

Christs, the Shankaras, the Vivekanandas, the Nanaks, the Kabirs the Ramanas ambitious personalities? Consequent on such a redefinition of ambition, therefore, greed, envy, jealousy—all centring on empirical pursuits—begin to loosen their stifling hold on the mind. The more this occurs, by slow degrees, the more one grows in mental health.

A Tagore or a Gandhiji—both intense workers in their chosen spheres of work—was each a worthy exemplar of mental health. The principal reason for this achievement was that they had both risen above the congenital selfishness of the ordinary empirical self. They both could visualize themselves as fulfilling the following destiny, to borrow words from Aurobindo:[6] 'Let us lead forward God's movement, play out His play, work out His formula, execute His harmony, express Him through ourselves in His system.

'This is our joy and our self-fulfilment; to this end we who transcend and exceed the universe, have entered into universe-existence.' In other words, to become a faithful instrument of the Divine for the betterment of this world becomes the goal of such a supra-mundane philosophy of life within a given situational context. Instead of negating life, this pursuit then enables an individual to use all the natural *vrittis* or faculties in a just and elevating way. This striving to position our psyche as an instrument of the Divine Master or the Supreme Intelligence is the key strategy in managing a sound philosophy of work life.

A question often asked is: 'We are managers, and not philosophers. How is all this of any use to us in our managerial roles?' The answer is: 'Each manager is indeed a philosopher anyway—be it of selfish hedonism, or of competitive gladiatorialism, or of other variants of the same genre.' Nobody can perform without a philosophy, howsoever implicit it may be. Hence, to acquire an explicit and theoretically sound philosophy is always preferable. It is a pity that management thought still avoids, by and large, seeking relevant nourishment from the wider expanses and higher reaches of human thought and experience. It tends to erect boundaries around itself too sharply and artificially—picking up the fence-posts only from utilitarian economics, statistical sociology, rodent psychology and the like. Thus, long after Tagore (1913) had urged mankind to reconstruct his life on earth by grasping the eternal law that it is that Infinite which is always seeking expression and fulfilment through the finites (and the empirical man is such a finite),[7] we hear Bede Griffiths (1982) tirelessly urging the Western mind to discard its merely rationalistic and schizophrenic philosophy of splitting the material from the ideal, the body from the Spirit, the immanent from the transcendent—while considering the former to be the only reality worth focusing on. It is the unitive philosophy of an organic whole of man, nature and cosmos which is the great strength of Vedanta and Buddhism, as Griffiths affirms.[8] This characteristic was also noticed and clearly brought out by Hans Jacob (1962) when he stated that the individual Being and Universal existence must be realized as intrinsically linked up.[9] Since man-agement is by and for man, there is no reason why managerial thought should not show the courage to take a dip into this pool of holistic vision. A recent book by Lessem from the UK has demonstrated this courage by speaking of 'metaphysical management'.[10] This is an encouraging sign. Unless each individual manager makes some conscious and sustained effort towards experiencing such holism within and through his work, there may be little hope for mental health in the increasingly turbulent times we are bent on creating for ourselves. Drucker's (1986) interesting speculations on 'managing in turbulent times'[11] will be of little avail unless man first begins to pay attention to his growing inner turbulence.

- *Inner Core of Self-Sufficiency*

The age-old counsel of wisdom, 'simple living, high thinking' has been jettisoned in favour of 'complex living, low thinking'. Yet the old adage remains the true road to *real* freedom and independence, and is based on the theory of autonomous self-sufficiency built into the design of man. For instance, when someone experiences deep sleep, and after waking up expresses to his spouse a sense of profound happiness and fulfilment, what is it due to? In that state his or her mind, senses, intellect had all ceased to function as usual. He or she had no desires, no grabbing, no acquisitions, no struggles. It was veritable dispossession. How then could this most profoundly positive feeling of well-being be explained? It can only lie in the fact that wholesome sufficiency, fulness is already intrinsic in us. The most widely used term for this intrinsic core of self-sufficiency (*poornatwa*) is *ātman**. In chapter 2 of the *Gita*, Arjuna

---

* The terms *paramarthika vyaktitwa*, higher SELF, trans-empirical SELF, etc. mean the same thing as *atman*.

is offered the following 'physical' characterization of the *atman*: 'weapons cannot cleave it, nor the fire burn, nor do the waters drench it, not the wind dry; it is uncleavable, it is incombustible, it can neither be drenched nor dried, eternally stable, immobile, all-pervading, it is for ever and ever'.[12] In chapter 3.17 again the following experiential account is given by Krishna-the-mentor to Arjuna-the-protégé:[13] 'But the man whose delight is in the Self and who is satisfied with the enjoyment of the Self and in the Self he is content, for him there exists no work that needs to be done.' (The last portion means: no work is needed for selfish ends.)

Two major difficulties in correctly appreciating our *atmic poornatwa* can be anticipated: (a) how do we continue to experience inner *poornatwa* in the waking state and the work-life?; (b) what will happen to progress, ambition, development and the like if we live by *atmic poornatwa*? To take the second issue first, once the logic of *atmic poornatwa* is clearly grasped, then we shall automatically redefine progress, development, etc. Progress will then be judged by the degree to which one is able to preserve conscious awareness of one's *poornatwa* about which one is now unconscious. Ambition will begin to imply the tireless striving to stay established in the feel of *atmic poornatwa*, even as one is involved in one's work. Krishna in the Mahabharata war is a perfect working model of this ambition. '*Yudhyasya vigata jwara*', i.e. 'fight without mental fever' was, therefore, the counsel Krishna offered Arjuna.[14] For a manager who begins to follow this line of progress, decision-making, planning, leading and the like will undergo positive transformation—since they all spring from a progressively healthier mind. The subjective is the cause, the objective is the effect; or, the unmanifest is the cause, the manifest is the effect—as we have said earlier.

As to the first problem, sustained *sadhana* can be the only answer. Since our conditioned self is so completely oblivious of the intrinsic *poornatwa*, we have to undergo gradual de-conditioning, followed by re-conditioning by pursuing a regular discipline in daily life. Some ideas about such processes have been shared in the previous chapter. The basic theme of this deconditioning–reconditioning process is inspiringly captured in Shankaracharya's *Atmashatakam* (or *Nirvanshatakam*) included in appendix I of chapter 4.

Will not the feeling of *atmic poornatwa* exacerbate our arrogance and isolation? Not at all. Were the Buddhas or Mahaviras or Ramanas or Vivekanandas arrogant and haughty? They were flowing rivers of compassion for all humanity. This happens because, with a growing feel of *atmic poornatwa*, the sorrows and miseries, the falls and sins of all beings affect their hearts so deeply, instantly and universally that they are ever ready to lay down even their lives for their succour. The individual consciousness of such personalities unites with the Universal Consciousness—which then forms the base for all-embracing goodwill and empathy. This is a worthy ideal for the manager.

It is worth recalling here the point made earlier in chapter 3 that the cultivation of *poornatwa* has to be seen as a counter-weight to the pettinesses flowing from our deficit-driven empirical self. The uglinesses and frustrations of the 'hungry self' are manifestations of mental ill-health. Hence too, the apprehension about heightened conceit arising out of *atmic poornatwa* is, in principle, a misplaced one. In fact, arrogance and pettiness go together only in our lower self. A healthy mind, aglow with *atmic poornatwa* is in no need of arrogance or conceit to prop it up. With *atmic poornatwa* gradually subduing the *yayati*-syndrome, dignity begins to be restored in all our transactions. Sinetar, a sensitive American authoress, has recently reflected this awareness by writing about our 'most sacred interior self which is complete and lacks nothing'.[15]

● *'Nirdwandwic' Mental Culture*

For this clue to mental health we may turn once more to the *Gita*. In chapter 2 we hear Krishna repeatedly counselling Arjuna to cultivate the disposition of either: (a) equality towards, or (b) transcendence above the dual experiences of many varieties. Thus:

[a] *Sukh-dukhe same kritwa, labh-alabhau, jay-ajayau;*
    Tato yuddhaya yujyaswa, naivam papam vapyasyasi.[16]

[b] *Traigunyavishaya veda nistraigunya bhavarjuna,*
    Nirdwandwo nitya satwastho niryogakshema atmavan.[17]

The significance of these counsels lies in their articulation of the great truth that the texture of our empirical existence is made up of *dwandwic* experiences—like the warp and weft of a fabric. This is the root of energy dissipation through stress. Imagine the plight of Arjuna in 'Vishad Yoga' (chapter 1 of the *Gita*). There he stands bemused, indecisive and paralysed at the most crucial juncture. He is under overwhelming stress due to the two opposite sets of emotions raging in his mind: the scorching hatred and burning anger at the cruel deeds of the Kaurava cousins, and the awful sorrow and fear at the prospect of fighting against the most venerable Bhisma, Drona and others like them. Arjuna's crisis is a supreme symbol of *dwandwic* stress. We always live feverishly, caught in the swings of contrary or polar events like success and failure, praise and criticism, gain and loss, and so on. The gospel 'seek pleasure, avoid pain' is entirely false. It is contrary to the very essence of empirical fact. This is that the more avidly an individual seeks pleasure, the more inexorably does pain also chase him or her. The more an individual enjoys praise, the more he or she detests criticism. This swinging characteristic of the mental pendulum is a major source of stress, burnout and the like. Laura Glenn (Sister Devmata), an American lady, made this point very pithily: 'How can we eliminate this joy-killing trait [vanity]...? Cease to feed it. Cease to run away from rebuke and criticism. Cease to reach out for recognition and commendation.'[18] Hence, either an individual teaches himself resolutely to treat both praise and criticism as *equally* deserving or undeserving, or transcends them both and stays firm in his true *atmic poornatwa*. This is why Krishna counsels Arjuna to achieve the *nirdwandwic* status—the state of 'transcendent equilibrium', if we may say so. He imparts this instruction only *after* informing His protégé of his *atmic poornatwa*. This conviction and feel is a good ground for the culture of *nirdwandwic* equanimity.

Aurobindo elucidates the state of *nirdwandwic samata* as follows:[19]

Whatever the unpleasantness of circumstances, however disagreeable the conduct of others, you must learn to receive them with a perfect calm ...

Equality means a quiet and unmoved mind and vital, it means not to be touched or disturbed by things that happen or things said or done to you ... it means self-mastery over the vital movements—anger and sensitiveness and pride as well as desire and the rest,—not to let them get hold of the emotional being and disturb the inner peace, not to speak and act in the rush and impulsion of these things, always to act and speak out of a calm inner poise of the spirit.

Clearly, therefore, *dwandwa* and *nirdwandwa* have nothing to do with *dwanda* of thesis and antithesis in dialectical materialism.

Apart from the intellectual assimilation of such ideas, meditational effort also is essential. Two imageries are very useful for meditation in this spirit: (a) the turbulent and roaring surface of the sea, with the eternally calm and serene depth below; and (b) the thundering, dark and rolling clouds overhead, with the ever-present deep and vast blue sky also above. After meditating for some time on such imagery, and before rising from one's seat, one could silently will and resolve, and instruct the subconscious, so to say, that no matter what turbulent or dualistic experiences might come one's way during the day, deep down within the psyche the calm sea-bed or the serene blue sky is going to stay, is going to stay ...

- *Excellence Through 'Work-is-Worship'*

Today we often hear speeches or see banners with the dictum 'Work is Worship'. This is only a sterile slogan. When the motive force behind excellence is competitive egotism, it is bound to affect mental health adversely. For humans in humane systems we have to seek and practise an alternative basis for excellence. The gospel 'survival of the fittest' should be banished to the jungles. 'Work is worship' and 'survival of the fittest' are incompatible gospels.

Let us begin very simply. When a devotee goes to a temple, or sits before the deity in his own home, he takes some offering with him. Within his means, even the poorest devotee is careful that whatever little he has to offer—a flower, a fruit, a sweet and the like—is pure, fresh, nicely peeled, neatly arranged, and so on. In other words, he brings forth a more 'excellent state of mind' than is customary otherwise, while presenting his little gift to the Lord. This is worship in the conventional, literal sense.

Thus, objective excellence in work necessarily implies subjective excellence within the worker. Therefore, the practical imperative for an individual is to extend the same spirit as that of the devotee-in-the-temple to the situation of the worker-in-the-factory/office. A secretary typing a letter, a project officer preparing a report, a scientist working on an R & D project, a sales manager attending to a customer, a maintenance engineer tending a machine, a professor writing a book and so on—are all apt examples showing the scope for investing the work process with the spirit of worship of the Lord. Excellence then has a transcendent motive. It ceases to ignite the scorching flame of competitive rivalry. Every act can be managed, with some effort, through this inspiration. Worship is no longer then confined only to occasional formal rituals in the temple or other similar place. This is how the secular and the sacred can mingle to produce sound mental health, with excellence in work flowing as a natural corollary.

There is a deeper cosmic principle too which ought to make it imperative for us to work in the spirit of worship or sacrifice. The *Gita* adumbrates in verse 3.9 the concept of *yajnartha karma* (work as sacrifice) as a means of freedom from the bondage of *dwandwic* success and failure of the lower self. Aurobindo (1938) dives deeper than this personal goal to uncover for us the universal import of this art of excellence in work:[20]

All life, all world-existence is the sacrifice offered by Nature to the Purusha, the one and secret soul in Nature, in whom all her workings take place, but its real sense is obscured in us by ego, by desire, by our limited, active, multiple personality; [and]
Sacrifice is the law of the world and nothing can be gained without it, neither mastery here, nor the possession of heavens beyond, nor the supreme possession of all.

Later we hear Griffiths (1983) stating emphatically that since everything is received from above, everything must be returned as well. Therefore, all work in the spirit of sacrifice or worship is this return to God, making our acts sacred.[21]

The atheist or agnostic might demur from all this. There is no Lord or God for his rational mind. Mystic intuition means nothing for him. He cannot comprehend the perfect fusion of rationality and intuition in Aurobindo and his ilk. Yet, and yet, we are told, he too has a prayer: 'O! God, if there be a God, save my soul, if I have a soul!'

- *Integration Centring on a Constant Inner Focus*

While the goal of attaining the *nirdwandwic* or *dwandwatita* status is basically a *jnan marga* one, i.e. the path of discrimination, and may appeal to the rational bent, yet it is perhaps the most difficult route to mental health. It is given only to a few to be able to tread solely that path. For the majority the devotional mood is more easily accessible, and hence the path of devotion or *bhakti marga* is more generally applicable. Even that towering *advaita janani*, Shankara, was brimful with *bhakti* as his numerous devotional compositions show.

The pilgrim of the *bhakti marga* accepts the *dvaitic* approach to the Supreme through a personified God, and ardently cultivates an emotional relationship with his chosen God-symbol as a Father or Mother or Friend or Beloved. Whatever dualistic or *dwandwic* experiences he undergoes are then felt by him to be His dispensations. He thus receives both gain and loss, praise and criticism as flowing from the beneficent Lord. Even when pummelled by adversity, or puffed up by success, after the initial tremor is over, he recoups inner equilibrium by saying something to this effect to himself: 'O, Lord, this praise or success is really your due, for it is you who paved the way for it to reach me'; or alternatively, 'O, Lord this criticism or denial is only your way to teach me to grow in fortitude.' How truly did Christ exclaim: 'Thy will be done, not mine.' By this process of sublimation, especially for the so-called negative experiences, the individual can effectively control his hard feelings and retaliatory motives against the apparent source of the blow. This is the way to prove the truth of the adage: 'Sweet are the uses of adversity.' As for the positive experiences, this method is an antidote to egotism and vanity. Thus, by regular practice of this process, our conflict-ridden emotions and feelings can be slowly integrated at one transcendent internal reference point. Then the book of life slowly begins to reveal fresh meaning.

Organizational studies done by us have proved time and again that it is only this kind of inner orientation which can usher in better mental health amongst the members, and hence also improved organizational health. Systems, procedures, structures are at worst only cosmetic or, at best mere palliatives. These attempts are often like trying to tackle chronic rheumatism (to use a Vivekanada-metaphor)[22]—the pain simply gets pushed around from one point to another in the body.

Practical spiritual psychology in India has lent concreteness to the process outlined above by developing the method of concentrating on one's *Ishtam* in the 'cave of one's heart' (the *garbha grihas* of our temples, i.e. the *sanctum sanctora* are only symbolic of this heart's cave). The *Ishtam*, as we know, is an emotionally congruent, luminous human form of the transcendent, trans-empirical, ultimate Reality—of which God is the simplest and most widely accepted term. The *Ishtam* thus personifies one's own SELF or Reality—the *atman*. In meditation one tries to identify with the eternal purity and serenity of one's *Ishtam*. By the law of association, the mind-stuff begins to get purer and more illumined through such dipping or soaking process, as it were. While this goes on, the individual also consciously strives to relate all his external activities to *Ishtam* with whom he is beginning to identify—he eats to Him, he sleeps in His lap, he builds the home to Him, he transfers a reward or recognition to His feet, he sublimates his anger by being angry at having lost his temper with someone while his *Ishtam* withdrew inner support for the moment, and so on. As the day rolls on he 'steps back', freezes himself, as it were, by holding his breath for a few moments—as often as he can remember—and plunges inside the heart to take a look at the radiant and beaming *Ishtam*. All this is practical integration of personality around a wholesome central core within an individual. The practice of this inward movement to such a fixed point is what Aurobindo calls 'the way to liberation' because thereby all[23] '... knowledge, works and the heart's longing becomes one in a supreme unification, a merging of all their divergences, an intertwining of all their threads, a high fusion, a wide iaentifying movement.' It is indeed time that managers, and all the rest, try to understand and sit down to practise mental health in this sense. Here intellectual wrestling or theorizing will be of little avail.

Ronald Nixon (Krishna Prem) is correct in assailing the abstract symbolism of modern science, and in espousing the 'infinitely richer feeling–content' in the concrete ones.[24] This is exactly what the *Ishtam* can do for us, and it is this process of constant offering in Bhakti Yoga which Dobson calls 'countercheating the genes'.[25]

- *Ethico-Moral Rectitude*

A large proportion of stress, anguish and other symptoms of poor mental health is caused by our ethico-moral infringements—wilfully or otherwise. We ought, therefore, to start by discarding the mechanical view of the universe for the moral one. Vivekananda had indeed characterized the world as a *moral gymnasium*[26] for human development. Its implication is that to attain mental health ethico-moral exercises are essential, and the world presents us all with a constant supply of situations to practise and test our ethico-moral vigour. Just as an athlete tries to transcend and not buckle before the hurdle or the height put up by the trainer, so do we need to view all incitements and temptations coming our way as hurdles placed before us by the Supreme Trainer to be crossed over. This is one secret of mental health.

A major plank of Indian thought, through all its schools, is the ethico-moral law of cause-and-effect, called the theory of *karma*. A proper grasp and internalization of the *karma* theory is a great support for the world-as-a-moral-gymnasium paradigm. Instead of nurturing fatalism, a common superstition about *karma*, it places full accountability for every happening—good or bad—on the individual himself or herself. No God or fate needs to be invoked. If at all fate is admitted, it is once more the individual's own creation. We have examined this theory exhaustively in an earlier work (1987).[27] It will suffice to reproduce here a few lines on *karma* from Vivekananda:[28]

This is the law of *karma*. Each one of us is a maker of his own fate. This law knocks on the head at once all doctrines of predestination and fate and gives us the only means of reconciliation between God and man. We, we, and none else are responsible for what we suffer. We are the effects and we are the causes. We are free therefore. If I am unhappy, it has been of my own making, and that very thing shows that I can be happy if I will. ... The human will stands beyond all circumstance.

What does this imply for human conduct and mental health? The message is: if a wrong *karma* is unleashed now, it *will* return to the doer as a damaging effect later even though his memory, notoriously short and selective as it is, may not be able to trace the cause–effect link. Of course collective *karma* is a valid extension of individual *karma*, and can be used to interpret human and national histories over centuries. Wilber appears to be hasty when he excludes collective *karma*, family *karma* and social *karma* from the matrix of individual *karma*.[29] The truth of the matter is that, once again, an individual finds himself or herself in a certain wider frame of *karma*–like being born in a given culture, or existing in a certain period of history, or working in a particular milieu due to his or her own *karma*. As the *Gita* amply and emphatically declares, if a person starts his journey on the path of righteousness but cannot consummate this in one life, he is born again, and perhaps again in more congenial surroundings to commence his unfinished labour from the point where he had left it.[30] This indeed is an inspiring assurance. Wilber is also wrong in principle to bring in chance while talking of *karma*.[31] It is only will that is admitted in *karma* theory. This deterrent thought process is a salutary need within each one of us. It is no use being pretentious about our ability for rectitude. At the same time, it is also a powerful incentive to stay on the right track—for a wholesome, good, honest, truthful cause now must bring forth a corresponding effect later. This two-way conviction is founded, not on mere speculation, but on the ineluctable law of cosmic order, *ritam*. It needs no great imagination to realize that the more ethico-morally sound a person is, the more mental peace he will have—even if he faces material deprivations. It also helps him develop greater internal strength, for he then ceases blaming everyone else for any adversity visiting him. This attitude of blaming others indicates weak mental health.

Toynbee offers an insightful interpretation of ethics and *karma* in the context of human society as a whole:[32]

The ethical level of a society ... depends on the state of the karma-account of each of the participants in the society ... Thus the ethical level of a society, unlike its scientific and technological level, is fluctuating and precarious. Karma, not scientific and technological progress, is the factor in human life that produces welfare and happiness or, alternatively, misery and sorrow.

In effect, Toynbee is tracing the genesis of society's health through the law of *karma*. Clearly too, individual mental health is treated by him as the cause of societal health and not the other way around.

One doubt which often rankles in the minds of many is: if being ethico-morally right is a good cause, why do we find such people suffer and fall behind? Where is the incentive mentioned above? Aurobindo also asks this question and responds to it:

Must the ethical power always turn perfectly into some term of kindred hedonistic result? Not entirely; for love is a joy in itself, but also love suffers ...; but in the end we may say that love, because it is born of universal Delight, triumphs in its own nature ..."

and cautions that '... this mechanical rebound is not the whole principle of karma'.[34]
In other words, for the far too limited, warped and stereotyped vision of the common man it would be dangerous to brush aside the truth that the *karm*ic web spun by him will unerringly bring about its burden of conflict and suffering if the *karma* is perverse (or its benediction, if it is exalted)—as Ronald Nixon also has

observed.[35] After all, as we see it, it is not at all difficult to detect daily instances of *karm*ic backlash all around us, although it may be relatively more problematic to decipher examples of *karm*ic benediction—due to our profuse jealousies and misanthropism.

Another important point. The deterrent function of the *karma* theory gradually becomes dispensable as one grows in the feel of *atmic poornatwa*, for ethico-moral transgressions occur due to the insecurity and fears of the deficit-driven lower self. *Atmic poornatwa*, as it begins to be realized, leads to spontaneous reduction of ethical deviations.

• *Cultivating* Sattwa Guna

As we know from Patanjali's *Yogasutras*, the *Gita* and other sources, *sattwa guna* is the most superior ingredient in the constitution of our empirical personality or *vyavaharika vyaktitwa*. Its colour-symbol is pure white, and its function is to give an upward push to human consciousness and illumine it. *Rajas*, red being its colour-symbol, imparts dynamism and expansiveness to our character; it also contributes to greed and anger and other concomitant negatives. Finally, *tamas*, black being its colour-symbol, drags the consciousness down and is the veiling power of *prakriti*.[36] It is also declared that the result of work done with *sattw*ic poise is *nirmalam*, that with *rajas*ic unrest is *dukkham*, and that with *tamas*ic delusion is *ajnanam*.[37] These few ideas should suffice to show that enhanced *sattwa guna* will contribute positively to mental health. Clearly, this will be complementary to the nurturing of the inner core of self-sufficiency, of a stable inner reference point, and of a *nirdwandw*ic psychic positioning described earlier. If the stakes in *sattwa guna* are so wide and deep, what can we do for its enhancement?

For one thing, the very effort of meditating on one's *Ishtam* is so holistic that it automatically kindles more and more *sattwa* in us. Besides, the practice of silent repetition of a holy name is a time-honoured method for achieving *sattw*ic *shuddhi* (purity). Gandhiji has been the best-known exemplar of this psychological technique in our time. He declared to the youth in 1926:[38] 'In my humble opinion, effort is necessary for one's own growth. It has to be irrespective of results. *Ramanama* or some equivalent is necessary, not for the sake of repetition, but for the sake of purification, as an aid to effort, for direct guidance from above.' Of course, most modern managers may like to pretend that they do not understand what this 'direct guidance from above' is all about! Yet, undaunted Gandhiji reiterated his conviction two decades later:[39] 'There is no doubt that Ramanama is the surest aid. If recited from the heart, it charms away every evil thought; and evil thought gone, no corresponding action is possible.'

This process is called *japam*. It is a mental discipline of multiple merits. Thus, by developing this habit we can prevent random distractions of the wayward mind. Furthermore, to a problem from transactional analysis— 'unstructered time', e.g. indefinite delays in Indian airports—*japam* provides a concrete and constructive response. Solitary morning walks can also be used for *japam*. Again, if one has a chosen *Ishtam*, then in times of outside meditation, *japam* should be done with the holy name of the *Ishtam* itself. Such then is the holistic nature of mental health techniques held out by our tradition. *Japam* is, of course common to all branches of the Indian tradition: Hinduism, Islam, Sikhism, Christianity, Buddhism, etc.

It has been mentioned earlier that all work should be done in the spirit of a sacred sacrifice, a humble offering. Now, this too will inevitably stimulate *sattwa*. Silent, self-effacing charity is another means of improving *sattwa guna*. As the Koran says: 'Even the left hand should not know what the right is giving.' Below another means of increasing this *guna* will be highlighted.

• Disciplined Breathing

Here is a strikingly powerful parable.[40] Once a king was wrongfully angry with a faithful minister and ordered him to be locked up in a solitary cell atop a high tower. At nightfall the loving wife of the minister, with a veil over her face, softly walked up to the base of the tower, and asked in a hushed voice what she could do to help him escape wrongful imprisonment. The minister asked his wife to collect the following things: a beetle, a little honey, and packs of silken thread, pack thread, stout twine and rope. When she returned with all the items, the minister asked her to tie the end of the silken thread to one of the hind legs of the beetle, to smear a drop of honey on its thorns, and then to place the beetle along the wall of the tower with its mouth upwards. She did his bidding. The beetle crawled up chasing the honey, and ultimately it reached within the grasp of the minister, who got hold of the silken thread tied to it, and let it go. Then he asked his wife to tie one end of the pack thread to the bottom end of the silken thread. Thus he pulled up the pack thread. Similarly, through the pack thread he got hold of the stout twine and finally the long thick rope. Using the long rope he recovered his freedom.

Now, this symbolic story conveys the following fundamental psychological process:

Silken thread = Breathing motion
Pack thread = Nerve currents
Stout twine = Thoughts
Rope = *Prana* (vital, primal energy).

What needs no telling, yet what we fail to truly grasp, is that breathing constitutes *the most basic existential process* for all living entities. While non-human species cannot perform any voluntary management of this basic existential activity, humans can do so. Therefore, 'breath management' is the first step for all development and health, and most certainly for mental health and development. Breath is the silken thread of our existential fabric.

The most simple breathing exercise we always take our Values-System programme participants through is that of deep, slow, uniform, noiseless breathing—in through one nostril and out through the other; and repeat the cycle the next time by inhaling through the second nostril and exhaling through the first. The eyes are closed throughout. The thumb and forefinger are used to operate the nostrils. About fifteen cycles in each sitting is good enough—but needs to be done on a more or less empty stomach. Exhaling ought to be consciously done at a slower pace than inhaling. The breath should not be held in or out—except that after each exhalation a pause for a few seconds is needed before commencing the next cycle. This exercise produces high levels of satisfaction from all participants without exception—as is borne out by the written notes (see chapter 4) obtained from the, e.g. feeling of tranquillity, cool brain, great ease of mind, as if the external world vanishes, most refreshing, greater feeling of self-control and so on.

The other cherished psychological advantage to be gained from disciplined breathing is much better control of our own thoughts.

By controlling and managing breathing well we can control and manage our thoughts better. Surely this is a basic input for effective performance.

As regard improvement of *sattwa guna*, while inhaling one is required to imagine and feel that a particular element of it, say patience, is entering into oneself with air and spreading through the being. Again, while exhaling, a selected aspect of *rajas guna*, say anger, will be consciously expelled from within. Persistence for a few months with the same elements is necessary.

Frederick Herzberg had wisely pleaded a few years ago, in his keynote address to the American Management Association, that the contemporary computer-centred manager must do some emotional unwinding and bring back passion and feeling to work on a daily basis[41] (recall our conversation with the Polish programmer cited above). In his speech there was, however, no hint about any practical method for unwinding. It is of course impossible to tell whether he was aware of simple breathing exercises or not. Here in our programmes we carry our participants through two further steps: to breathe normally but continue to *feel* the synchronization of the gentle breath with the controlled mind, as it were, and thereafter to try to *feel* that the space inside the top of the head is slowly getting emptied of all thoughts–problems–information–images, and a kind of *serene void* is emerging there. This is de-cerebration in practice. This *feeling* of void and ease inside the brain-space ripens over a few months, and the individual then tends to get sort of 'addicted' to it—a compelling urge to wind up a hard day with cerebral unwinding. Cerebral health and mental health can thus go together.

• Radiating Goodwill and Harmony

There are just too many knots in our hearts. We are careless about the eruptions of hard feelings within us. They occur too quickly and frequently. It may be for this very reason that we choose to ignore them—or rather submit to them. They however eat into our mental health, and create grave psychic burns.

Patanjali's *yoga* psychology has offered us the following principle to revive mental health from the clutches of hard feelings:[42]*Maitri-karuna-mudita-upekshanam, sukh-dukha, punya-apunya, Vishayanam bhavavnat chitta prasadanam*. This counsel means that one should, for mental poise or peace or ease or calm, practise the *bhavana*s, i.e. inner mood or disposition of:

- friendliness towards the happy
- compassion for the unhappy
- gladness towards the virtuous
- indifference towards the wicked.*

It is however the opposites like hatred, callousness, jealousy, mean delight which infest our mind, turning it impure and unhealthy. Buddhist psychology too deals with the very same prescription,[43] and the Advaitic text *Yoga Vaashishtha* also refers to this recipe.[44]

The technique for cultivating healthy mental attitudes or *bhavana*s is also provided by Patanjali: *pratipakshabhavanam*,[45] or the deliberate raising of contrary or opposite thoughts. Thus, friendliness is the *pratipakshabhavana* of envy or hatred, compassion that of callousness or insensitivity, and gladness that of berating or slighting. Like alkali, the first of each pair neutralizes the acidic counterpart, as it were.

Since these healthy *bhavana*s are usually limited and ephemeral, the process of gradually universalizing and stabilizing them in our work-place has to be pursued through the meditative technique. Leggett, after our ancient and modern forerunners in this field, has presented the case for the meditative process very well:[46]

Until the reactions in ordinary life have begun to modify themselves along the lines of the meditations, the cultivation of intensity has only begun; [and]

... until there is considerable power of meditation, it is often found that the acts do not have the expected results.

There are four (may be others also) ways of meditating on these *bhavana*s:

(a) To meditate in the heart on one's *Ishtam*, e.g. the luminous form of the Buddha, seated in serene contemplation, who is amongst the highest human manifestations of compassion, etc. Such meditation has a slow yet sure osmotic effect upon the individual's consciousness.

(b) To meditate in the heart on individual(s) who happen to be the object of hatred, envy and similar hard feelings, and to bathe

* This does not mean indifference to the wickedness of those for whom one is responsible. It is meant to guard us against idle gossip. Conze translates *upeksha* as 'impartiality' which is acceptable. See reference 40.

his (their) vivid forms with the feeling of love, compassion and the like. Initial attempts may be mechanical, but sincere application definitely pays off after a few days. Thus, one works on the knot and dissolves it internally prior to entering into transactions with people in relation to whom the hard feelings are strong or have festered over a long period. Once the internal breakthrough is achieved a comforting feeling of inner expansion and serenity is experienced. This is mental health.

(c) Whenever hard feelings of one kind or another stray into our mind from sundry sources—other than these of the particularly strong and specific kind mentioned in (b)—one should be able to activate consciously from the heart centre the power to radiate thoughts of goodwill, welfare, happiness, peace towards them. This can be done, for instance, while commuting back home from office, and reflecting about some of the people who might have incited hard feelings. One can also do this in the morning while travelling to the work-place—bathing and soaking the mind in consciously raised healthy *bhavana*s as a preventive measure against the day's likely onslaughts. Group meetings may, as a rule, be preceded and ended by collective meditation which will include the three steps mentioned under the previous theme, and include a fourth step where each person will consciously try to radiate from the heart's luminous core peace and harmony and goodwill towards *all* in the group without exception, unconditionally. In some organizations engaged in values-system programmes with us, this process is getting institutionalized. The results are quite promising. Teamwork and individual mental health should be the simultaneous beneficiaries.

(d) To develop the ability to visualize one's own *Ishtam* to be seated in the heart of all persons one might encounter during the day. After sufficiently long persistence one develops by this method the power to perceive a fundamental identity with others—although there may be differences or clashes with many at the outward, surface-level. This, in turn, gradually prevents the entry into the mind of hard feelings from outside, as it were, in the first place. An in-built repellant to ward them off seems to grow.

Why should such subjective, inner processes work at all? What is the proof? Where are the data? Just as we can *know* whether an apple is sweet or sour only by taking the trouble of biting it, so is basically the case with these processes. Managers in our programmes have been 'tasting' some of this 'doing'. The preceding chapter has already offered some notes from them as evidence. However, let us at least get across the theory behind the *expected positive outcome on others* of one's own conscious effort to build a subjective centre of radiation of goodwill and harmony, which becomes day by day more authentic, open and all-embracing. We can do no better than to go to Vivekananda (1900) for a correct explanation of this theory:[47]

... the man who has control over his own mind assuredly will have control over every other mind.... a pure, moral man has control of himself. *And all minds are the same, different parts of one Mind.* He who knows and controls his own mind knows the secret of every mind and has power over every mind.

[Emphasis added.]

Decades later the physicist Arthur Eddington echoed the central point in Vivekananda's assertion by declaring that the 'stuff of the world is mind-stuff'.[48]

• *Supreme/Universal Consciousness* and Surrender*

What Vivekananda had termed Mind (see above) is the same as Supreme or Universal Consciousness, or the Infinite, or *Brahman*. That this Supreme Subjective is the ground and stuff of all phenomena, subjective, is now acknowledged widely amongst the more imaginative and sensitive scientists. To quote Sperry, a Nobel scientist (1983):[49]

Current concepts of the mind–brain relation involves a direct break with the long-established materialist and behaviourist doctrine that has dominated neuroscience for many decades. Instead of renouncing or ignoring consciousness, the new interpretation gives *full recognition to the primacy of inner conscious awareness as a causal reality*. [Emphasis added.]

That this 'inner conscious awareness' is identical with the Universal Consciousness was also pinpointed by Vivekananda when he said that 'the microcosm must bear testimony to the macrocosm, and the macrocosm to the microcosm', and that the essential parts of

---

* It should be understood that consciousness is not the same as consciousness in the context of modern psychology. While the former is the irreducible base and ground of all existence, the latter only means ordinary awareness.

psychology accord perfectly with the essential parts of physical knowledge.[50]

Using the word 'Intelligence' to convey the same meaning as Mind or Consciousness, Aurobindo had decades ago enunciated this revolutionary yet perennial principle:[51]

Intelligence possesses us, not we intelligence; intelligence uses us, not we intelligence.

Surely for modern material science such recognition is 'new', but not so for the mystic science of the East and West. It is Intelligence or Consciousness or Mind which descends, so to say, into endless varieties of forms to work out Its empirical manifestation as an integral part of Its inscrutable play or *leela* and then ascends again. Shankaracharya's refrain *'chidananda rupah, shivoham'* proclaims this primacy of Consciousness. The key task for human intelligence is to seek reintegration with the Supreme Intelligence, and not engage in a vain attempt to achieve total severance. We are therefore in agreement with the physicist David Bohm in calling the new field of 'artificial intelligence' to be really one of 'artificial intellect'.[52]

The cultivation of this reversed understanding about our substratum or ground has great practical relevance for mental health and effective decision-making. First, it leads to a gradual emancipation from our falsifying ego-ruled consciousness. This state of our psyche creates confusion, distortion and non-receptivity of signals as they are. The pure, universal Consciousness that had been barred from the psychic arena through our wrong conditioning, begins to assume its rightful place. As a result, the manager's feelings, reason and the like—the instruments used in daily work—begin to move from a lower, limited comprehension to a higher, wider one. Therefore we hear the following counsel in the *Gita*:[53]

> '*tasmaat sarveshu kaleshu*
> *mamanusmarah yuddha cha*'; that is
>
> 'therefore under all circumstances remember
> Me and then fight'

This 'Me' is both the all-enveloping Supreme Consciousness and the individual's pure consciousness or *atman* within. Why is such an integration between the two being suggested as a categorical imperative? It is because the individual intelligence is error-prone, while the Supreme Intelligence is error-free.

Second, this process leads simultaneously to a deeply restful mental state because an ineffably reassuring and unfailing source of inner guidance grows up within. It is this kind of mental health which has been the mainstay throughout the momentous lives of Tagores, Gandhijis and others of their type, here and elsewhere. This state is to be experienced, not merely intellectualized.

Now, *how* does one proceed to gain this experience, having first been convinced of the rationality of the argument just advanced? This is where the attitude of surrender or *prapatti* becomes crucial. Arrogant, egotistic, wrestling minds always snap this essential nexus. The humble receptivity of a quiet mind is indispensable for letting in, as it were, the all-pervading Supreme Intelligence or Consciousness. A steady and firm, patient and willing opening up towards the Supreme is needed. Authentic prayers—not in the spirit of any bargaining whatsoever—with a yearning for this access for its own sake are very useful. All truly great human beings have always prayed. The Supreme then responds to their call. Why? The answer is the same: the mind and Mind, intelligence and Intelligence, consciousness and Consciousness are parts of the same integral whole. Thus when a pure, aspiring mind persists in sending up its appeal with fervour, the Mind is only too eager to reciprocate. That is why our mystics often say: 'If you move even one step towards Him, He advances ten steps towards you.' This is Grace reciprocating surrender. They also advise us to know and realize that it is the constitutional prerogative of the human to assert his or her claim to this most authentic and enduring of all relationships—much beyond and behind the unreliable and con- tractual empirical relationships—that with his or her own ground, the Supreme Consciousness or God. Mental certitude and health then both arrive with gentle but sure footsteps. Gandhiji speaks thus from his own realization:[54] 'I verily believe that one who literally follows the prescription of the Eternal Mother need never grow old in mind. Such a one's body will wither in due course like leaves of a healthy tree, leaving the mind as young and as fresh as ever.'

Gandhiji's words may be supplemented by these from Auro- bindo:[55]

All can be done by the Divine,—the heart and nature purified, the inner consciousness awakened, the veils removed,—if one gives oneself to the Divine with trust and confidence, and even if one cannot do so fully at once, yet the more one does so, the more the inner help and guidance come ...

III. Conclusion: The Subjective, Not the Objective

The concluding observation above might scandalize readers. Yet, in search of mental peace, satisfaction, happiness—and health—we all suffer the fate of king Yayati by ceaselessly pursuing objective things. We re-enact the scene of the camel in the desert which chews thorny bushes at every turn, even as its mouth turns into a bleeding mess. Psychotherapy, shorn of such metaphysical depth, is not of much assistance in the task of restoring lost mental health or improving it. Alan Watts has called professional psychotherapy 'psychohydraulics'.[56] In the words of Tagore, we must polish up our 'sensibility for simple aspects of existence' which has been dulled by constant external diversions.[57] The preceding pages are an invitation to get on with this job of combating the *yayati-syndrome* through *atmic poornatwa*. We have tried here to show that it is possible—indeed, essential—that from time to time we ought to try to pursue the Supreme Subjective in its own right, without habitually getting trapped and tripped in the labyrinth of the objective which is only a means, and that too apparently, to the end of subjective fulfilment. Rather, the individual should apply himself to appreciating that, while the Supreme Subjective is the Reality, the supreme objective is just a pure mirage. Mental health will grow when this distinction begins to convince him, and in a healthy mind healthy values should naturally flourish.

There will still remain a common doubt amongst the majority that, after all, whatever has been said above is only religion and spirituality, and whether it is at all possible to glimpse or achieve anything in this life! It may therefore be emphasized again that the human being is indeed a spiritual entity—both at the base and the apex. Whatever contrary notions we may now have, it is a fact that spiritual religion is the ultimate source of healthy values. Not long ago the World Health Organization accepted spiritual health as the fourth dimension in the total health of man—physical, mental and social being the other three. As to when something may be attained we have the solemn and authentic assurance:[58] '*swalpamapyasya*

dharmasya trayate mahato bhayat'; that is, not a bit of *sadhana* can
go waste; even a little well-directed effort will deliver us from the
grand fear. However, even this divine pledge may not inspire faith
in those who choose to stand aloof as rational sceptics, often
perhaps to avoid the task of self-transformation.

Finally, probably the best method of reinvigorating mental
health is to cut loose, at least once a year for about ten days, from
all kinds of work and everybody and repair to some quiet place far
from the madding crowd. Nature and one's own mind should be
one's only companions, and perhaps a few books of the kind
mentioned frequently in these pages. Lofty thoughts for lifting the
consciousness, sinking deep into the calm of silence, and talking to
ones mind should be ones only activities. Verbal silence for three
or four days in this span is a powerful restorative. The calm mind
can then, like a witness, begin to observe its own self-deceptions
and compulsive failings. Crucial resolutions could be made for
essential self-transformation. All this enables the mind to rise
above the whirl of commonplace emotions, and provides a serene,
wide and integral perspective on life spanning both the past and
the coming years. Clearly, the usual executive holidays do not serve
the purpose.

This is so because organization-sponsored annual jaunts usually
turn out to be an extension of the same *yayati*-syndrome which
infects the entire existential ethos of the growing breed of professional managers. Banks and similar institutions are now heavily
publicizing their new 'Consumer Product Services' activity which
tends to tempt us all into greedy indiscretions. When we tried once
to make this point to the Vice-President of an international bank,
we were made to look foolish by the volley of professional arguments in support of such business which was all for the welfare of
the citizen!

A recent survey by the National Consumer Council of Britain
has disclosed that in pursuit of affluent living styles the British are
sinking increasingly into debt (via credit cards, mortgages etc.).
They owed in 1990 on average twice as much as they did in 1980,
despite an eight per cent rise in per capita disposable income.[59]
How can minds burdened with the thought of debt stay healthy?
'Cut your coat according to the cloth' is indeed a sage counsel for
mental health. Since Britain is an industrial society, a bulk of the
sample surveyed by the Council might have consisted of managers

and industrial employees. Besides, in all probability they would also have undergone training in the motivational theories of Maslow, Herzberg, McClelland *et al.* Since, despite the sophistication claimed for them, they are all need-based motivational theories, springing from the limiting central assumption of the 'biological core' of human beings, we surmise that they have done nothing to lift motivational aspirations to abstract, lofty levels (self-actualization and all that) amongst organizational members in general. Unless therefore a paradigm shift, centring on the transcendent or spiritual or *atmic* core of human beings takes place, we do not see much hope in these popular motivational theories for mental health. The *vyavaharika vyaktitwa* (see chapter 4) alone is a fragile base for mental health. The *paramarthika vyaktitwa* has to be given a fair chance.

In the appendix to this chapter we reproduce a recent letter from an IIM-C student which shows how the Values System course undergone by him seems to have helped him to secure release from the grip of the *yayati-syndrome*, and opened the door to mental health.

APPENDIX
Letter from a student

Respected Sir,

I take this opportunity to express my gratitude to you for helping to find myself back to a state which I lost ever since I left school and joined an IIT. My mind had left me and was constantly wandering about looking for gains in the external material world ever since I left home and began residing in the hostel at Kharagpur. I lost peace of mind and could not be satisfied with anything. After clearing IIT I worked for a year in a pretty good organization called Procter & Gamble but there again the same problem continued but I could not reason out what it was that troubled me. This state of mind continued in my first year at IIM(C) as well, during my summer training at American Express too, until one fine morning when I came for the purpose of 'window-shopping' to the first Man–Ethos lecture and to my surprise discovered that herein lay the answer to my problems. The exercise, especially the first three steps, definitely seems to be having a very powerful effect in terms of providing me peace and satisfaction for the rest of the day. That feeling of restlessness seems to be curbed to a large extent. I definitely feel more relaxed while dealing with my wingmates, and enjoy my weekend trips home. I share some oᶠ my learnings in the Man-Ethos class with my parents and sister. Of late I've been reading some words of Swami Vivekananda and the book 'Religion of Man' by Tagore which are very similar to what you mention in Class. Barring the mid-term week, I've been regular with the exercise and do it at six every morning, and at times if I find I am having difficulty in concentrating on my studies I do a condensed form of the first three steps of the exercise and it definitely helps. My ability to concentrate on class lectures has improved a lot and I find time to do a lot of reading, as well as playing the Hawaiian Guitar. The feeling of paranoia about grades and jobs has definitely got reduced and I am enjoying each day of my life. In short I have been able to get away from the dyspeptic and jelly-fish existence which I formerly lived and I feel I am a much better person. Sir, Thank you so much. May you continue to inspire future IIMCians who would be lucky enough to read through the implications of this course in case they come to attend the first lecture.

Yours obediently,

REFERENCES

1. R. Guenon, *East and West* (London: Luzac & Co., 1941), pp. 106, 109.
2. J. Dewey, *Dictionary of Education*, ed. R. B. Winn (New York: Philosophical Library, 1959), p. 108.
3. C.E.M. Joad, *Guide to Modern Wickedness* (London: Faber & Faber, 1947), p. 55.
4. Rabindranath Tagore, *Sadhana* (Delhi: Macmillan, 1988), p. 32.
5. Swami Akhilananda, *Mental Health and Hindu Psychology* (London: George Allen & Unwin, 1952), p. 99.
6. Sri Aurobindo, *The Hour of God* (Pondicherry: Sri Aurobindo Ashram, 1982), p. 21.
7. *Sadhana*, pp. 34, 58.
8. B. Griffiths, *The Marriage of East and West* (London: Fount Paperbacks, 1985), p. 57.
9. H. Jacobs, *Western Psychotherapy and Hindu Sadhana* (London: George Allen & Unwin, 1961), p. 146.

10. R. Lessem, *Global Principles of Management* (London: Prentice Hall, 1989), pp. 509–96.
11. P.F. Drucker, *Managing in Turbulent Times* (London: Pan Books, 1983).
12. Sri Aurobindo, *The Message of the Gita* (Pondicherry: Sri Aurobindo Ashram, 1977), II. 23–4, p. 20.
13. Ibid., p. 53.   14. Ibid, 3.30, p. 60.
15. M. Sinetar, *Ordinary People as Monks and Mystics* (New Jersey: Paulist Press, 1986), p. 153.
16. *The Message of The Gita*, op. cit., 2.38, p. 24.   17. Ibid., 2.45, p. 35.
18. Sister Devmata, *The Habit of Happiness* (California: Ananda Ashrama, 1930), p. 54.
19. Sri Aurobindo and The Mother, *On Happiness and Peace* (Pondicherry: Sri Aurobindo Society, 1973), pp. 20, 21.
20. *The Message of The Gita*, pp. 51, 81.
21. B. Griffiths, *The Cosmic Revelation* (London: Collins, 1983), p. 49.
22. Swami Vivekananda, *Collected Works* (Calcutta: Advaita Ashrama, 1958), vol. II, pp. 171–2.
23. *The Message of The Gita*, p. 148, fn.
24. Sri Krishna Prem, *Initiation Into Yoga* (Delhi: B.I. Pub., 1976), p. 65.
25. J. Dobson *Advaita Vedanta and Modern Science* (Chicago: Vivekananda Vedanta Society, 1983), p. 16.
26. Swami Vivekananda, *Collected Works* (Advaita Ashrama, Calcutta, 1958), vol. VII, p. 69.
27. S.K. Chakraborty, *Managerial Effectiveness and Quality of Work-life: Indian Insights* (Delhi: Tata McGraw Hill, 1987), pp. 84–95.
28. Swami Vivekananda, *Collected Works* (Calcutta: Advaita Ashrama, 1989), vol. 3, p. 125.
29. K. Wilber, 'On Being A Support Person', *The Journal of Transpersonal Psychology*, vol. 20, no.2, 1988, p. 156.
30. *The Message of The Gita*, verses 6.40–5, pp. 106–7.
31. Wilber, op. cit., p. 156.
32. A.J. Toynbee and D. Ikeda, *Choose Life* (Delhi: Oxford University Press, 1987), p. 325.
33. Sri Aurobindo, *The Problem of Rebirth* (Pondicherry: Sri Aurobindo Ashram, 1983), p. 111.
34. Ibid., p. 112.   35. *Initiation Into Yoga*, p. 106.
36. *The Message of the Gita*, verse 14.18, pp. 208–9.
37. Ibid., verse 14.16, p. 207.
38. M.K. Gandhi, *Ramanama* (Ahmedabad: Navjivan, 1977), p. 10.
39. Ibid., p. 15.
40. Swami Vivekananda, *Collected Works* (Calcutta: Advaita Ashrama, 1962), vol. I, pp. 143–4.
41. Quoted in 'Highlights of AMA's 57th Annual Human Resources Conference' by H.Z. Levine, Personnel, vol.63, no.3, Sept. 1986, p. 23.

42. Swami Vivekananda, *Collected Works*, vol.I, pp. 222–3 (verse I. 33).
43. E. Conze, *Buddhist Thought in India* (London: George Allen & Unwin, 1983), pp. 80–91.
44. J. Bharati, *The Essence of Yogavaashishtha* (Madras: Samata Books, 1985), verse x.61.108.
45. Swami Vivekananda, *Collected Works*, vol.I, verse II.33, p. 261.
46. T. Leggett, *The Chapter of the Self* (London: Routledge & Kegan Paul, 1978), pp. 96, 98.
47. Swami Vivekananda, *Collected Works* (Calcutta: Advaita Ashram, 1958), vol. II, p. 17.
48. Quoted in A.D. Riencourt, *The Eye of Shiva* (London: Souvenir Press, 1980), p. 31.
49. R.S. Sperry, *Science and Moral Priority* (New York: Columbia University Press, 1983), p. 112.
50. Swami Vivekananda, *Collected Works*, vol.II, p. 432.
51. *The Hour of God*, p. 57.
52. D. Bohm, and F.D. Peat, *Science, Order and Creativity* (New York: Bantam Books, 1987), pp. 220–3.
53. *The Message of The Gita*, verse 8.7, p. 127.
54. M.K. Gandhi, *The Teaching of the Gita* (Bombay: Bharatiya Vidya Bhawan, 1962), p. 71.
55. Sri Aurobindo and The Mother, *Surrender and Grace* (Pondicherry, Sri Aurobindo Society, 1986), p. 4.
56. A. Watts, 'Psychotherapy and Eastern Religion: Metaphysical Bases of Psychiatry', *The Journal of Transpersonal Psychology*, 1974, vol.6, no.1, p. 19.
57. Rabindranath Tagore, *The Religion of An Artist* (Calcutta: Visva-Bharati, 1988), p. 25.
58. *The Message of The Gita*, verse II. 40, p. 33.

GLOSSARY

Adhyatmika   spiritual
Adrista   the unseen forces influencing our existence
Advaita   non-dual(ism), a major branch of Vedanta
Agraj   elder brother
Aham   ego or I-ness
Aham Brahmasmi   I am identical with Brahman, i.e. the Universal or
    Supreme; one of the four great Truths of Vedanta
Ahankar   vanity, egotism
Ajnanam   ignorance
Anahata   the fourth nerve centre in the spinal column in the region of the
    cardiac centre
Ananda   permanent, autonomous, inner Bliss which is man's essential
    character
Anandasthiti   settled in Bliss
Anandology   the art and science of experiencing and becoming *ananda*;
    the science of Bliss
Anasakti   non-craving
Antahkarana   the inner organ (psychologically), with four layers as it
    were
Anubhuti   deep feeling
Anuj   younger brother
Artha   the economic aspirations of secular life
Atman   the indestructible core of perfection and bliss in transitional
    individual body-frames
Asakti   craving
Ashrama   a place to labour for the consummation of a vow, especially a
    spiritual one
Atma Shatakam   a Sanskrit poem of six stanzas by Shankaracharya,
    characterizing the true, higher Self
Avidya   primal ignorance

Bhakta   devotee of God
Bhavna   a cultivated and rich mental disposition
Bhavna-shuddhi   purification of one's world of feelings and emotions
Bhumaiva Sukham   happiness only in the Infinite
Bhuta   sub-human species

Bodhisattwa the prior incarnations of the Buddha for the welfare of mankind

Brahmacharya continence of sex, speech, etc upto the age of twenty-five

Brahmisthiti staying settled in the full awareness of the Supreme, the Universal, the Infinite, the Ultimate Cause

Buddhi the analysing, discriminating layer of the inner organ (*antah-karana*)

Buddhi-vritti intellect-dominated propensities

*Chakra*s the seven nerve centres within the central channel of the spinal column

Chaturvarga the four goals of life, i.e. *dharma, artha, kama, moksha.*

Chitta the memory-base in our inner organ, also heart (in the psychological sense)

Chittashuddhi purification of the memory-base, of heart

Dandaniti the process of just chastizement

*Darshana*s the various Indian schools of philosophy based on the 'seeing of Truth' by seers

*Deva*s the supra-human forces, powers or Gods

Dharma the mode of rightful conduct in secular life

Dharma vyavastha social order based on rightful conduct

Dukkham sorrow

Dvaitic dualistic

Dwandwic the tension between dualities, opposites

*Dwandwa*s dualities, opposites

Ekatmanubhuti the deep feeling of oneness with all creation

Gita or *Bhagwad Gita* a compendium of the gist of Indian psycho-philosophy, included within the *Mahabharata*

Grahasthya the householder phase, from the age of twenty-five to fifty

*Guna*s three substance-attributes or psychological substances constituting our personality

Guru a revered exemplar and teacher, specially of spiritual idealism

Hridaya-Vritti feelings-dominated propensities

*Indriya*s external sense organs and their internal counterparts

Ishtam one's chosen deity or form of Supreme purity and perfection for meditation

Ista dhyanam meditation on the *Ishtam*

Japam silent repetition of a holy name

Jivanmukta   while living in this world, yet free and liberated within
Jnani   one who has realized the Supreme, the Real
Jnanyoga   the discipline of discrimination between the real and unreal to achieve union with the Supreme

Kama   the desires of secular life, lust
Karma   human thought, words, and deeds
Karma-Kshaya   the wearing out of *karm*ic effects
Karmasu   doing work
Karma-vada   the *karm*ic doctrine of cause and effect
Karuna   compassion
Kaushalam   the skill of working
Kohai   younger brother (in Japan)
Krodha   anger
Kshatriya   the warrior, royal community

Leela   the Divine, cosmic play at the empirical level
Lobha   greed, avarice
Lokasamgraha   selfless work for the welfare of all

Mahabharata   the world's longest epic poem, in Sanskrit, highlighting the ethico-moral battle between right and wrong
*Mahavakya*s   Great Truths
Maitri   friendliness towards the happy
Mamatwa   infatuation, narcissism
Manas   the component or layer of our inner organ which converts stimuli and signals into thoughts, feelings, etc.
Manusmriti   a classical text of social governance
Maya   the apparent, impermanent reality; the folly of taking the transient for the permanent
Moksha   emancipation from the cycles of repeated physical births and death for the permanent, full flowering of *atman*
Mouna   silence
Mudita   happiness at the virtues of others
Muladhara   the lowest nerve centre at the bottom of the central channel of the spinal column

Nadishuddhi   purification of nerve channels
Nama   name, label
Nididhyasana   meditation
Nirakara   formless
Nirdwandwic   without or above the dualistic experiences of the opposites
Nirguna   without any attributes
Nirliptata   inner detachment

Nirmalam　stainless
Nirupadhic　without adjuncts, appellations, attributes
Nirvan Shatakam　a Sanskrit poem of six stanzas by Shankaracharya
　　characterizing the true, higher Self
Nitya　the causeless Absolute
Nivedan　offering
Nivritti　the propensity of internal self-sufficiency
Niyama　external and internal purification of body and mind
Nri　mankind

Paramarthika vyaktitwa　the transempirical, higher SELF
Pauranic　that which derives from the *puranas*—a major narrative
　　branch of Indian literature which puts across the highest thoughts
　　to the commoner
Poorna　the Infinite, self-existent wholeness
Prajna　realized wisdom
Preya　apparently pleasant, though actually harmful
Prakriti　the female, active but inconscient principle
Pranam　bowing to the feet of a deity or a revered person as a mark of
　　respect
Pranayama　science of regulating the vital breath
Prapatti　surrender to the Supreme, the Universal, God
Prarthana　prayer
Pratipakshabhavanam　to think contrary thoughts
Pravritti　the outgoing propensities to hanker for something
Purusha　the conscious but inactive aspect in creation, vide Sankhya
　　theory
Purushartha karma　work done for its own sake
*Purushartha*s　the goals of human existence

Rajas　the *guna* (psychological substance) of activity, expansion, projec-
　　tion
Ramayana　the second grand epic poem of India
Rin　debt
Rishi　a seer of Truth
Ritam　the Cosmic Law of cause and effect
Rupah　form and differentiation

Sadhana　a disciplined process of inner purification and perfection
Sahasrara　the highest nerve centre in the central channel of the spinal
　　column, in the head
Samadhi　the complete mergence of the individual ego with the Supreme,
　　the Eternal
Samaj　society

Samarpan   willing surrender
Samatwa   equality, equivision
Samskaras   the accumulated residual impressions of our overt thoughts, words and deeds
Sankhya   a dualistic theory of creation, outside the pale of Vedanta
Sangha   the organized units of Buddhist monks
Sannyasa   total inner and outer renunciation after the age of seventy-five
Sattwa   the *guna* (psychological substance) of illumination, ascension, revelations
Satyam   truth
Sempai   elder brother (in Japan)
Seva-yoga   the yoga of service
Shada Darshana   the six systems of Indian philosophy
Shavasana   the corpse posture for total relaxation, from Hathayoga
Shivam   goodness
Shraddha   faith, will
Shreya   the truly wholesome, though often apparently repelling
Sthitaprajna   one who is of settled wisdom
Sthula   gross, crude
Sukshma   subtle, refined
Sundaram   beauty
Swadharma   the law of one's being
Swarupah   the undifferentiated unitive Reality underlying all name and form

Tamas   the *guna* (psychological substance) of inertia, darkness
Tapasya   askesis, intense *sadhana*
Tattwa   vital idea or theory
Titiksha   forbearance
Trishna   insatiable, burning desires or cravings
Tyaga   renunciation

Upadhis   attributes, adjuncts, appellations
Upanishad   visions of ultimate Truth contained in the concluding part of the Veda
Upavasa   fasting
Upeksha   indifference to the wickedness of others towards oneself

Vanaprastha   repairing-to-the-forest phase, at the age of fifty
Vedanta   the concluding philosophical observations of the Vedic seers, also called the Upanishads
Vidya   true learning
Vikara   degeneration
Vikshepa   stress, torment, tension

Vishad Yoga   the first chapter of the *Gita*, depicting the confused, *tamasic* state of Arjuna's mind

Virat Purusha   the causal Cosmic or Universal Being

*Vritti*s   faculties, dispositions, attitudes

Vyaktitwa   personality

Vyavaharika   the empirical, externally active aspect

Yajnartha Karma   work done as sacrifice or worship of the Supreme

Yaksha   guardian spirit

Yama   ethical disciplines like not killing, truthfulness, not stealing, etc.

Yayati   a King in the *Mahabharata* whose lust made him exchange his senility for the youth of his youngest son

Yoga   union

Yogakshema   the effort to obtain the unattained, and the struggle to retain the attained

INDEX